MAWDUDI
AND THE MAKING OF
ISLAMIC REVIVALISM

Mawlana Mawdudi

MAWDUDI
AND THE MAKING OF
ISLAMIC REVIVALISM

Seyyed Vali Reza Nasr

New York   Oxford
OXFORD UNIVERSITY PRESS
1996

Oxford University Press

Oxford   New York
Athens   Auckland   Bangkok
Calcutta   Cape Town   Dar es Salaam   Delhi
Florence   Hong Kong   Istanbul   Karachi
Kuala Lumpur   Madras   Madrid   Melbourne
Mexico City   Nairobi   Paris   Singapore
Taipei   Tokyo   Toronto

and associated companies in
Berlin   Ibadan

Copyright © 1996 by Seyyed Vali Reza Nasr

Published by Oxford University Press, Inc.

198 Madison Avenue, New York, New York 10016-4314

Oxford is a registered trademark of Oxford University Press, Inc.

Library of Congress Cataloging-in-Publication Data
Nasr, Seyyed Vali Reza, 1960-
Mawdudi and the making of Islamic revivalism / Seyyed Vali Reza Nasr.
p.   cm.
Includes bibliographical references (p.   ) and index.
ISBN 0-19-509695-9
1. Maudoodi, Syed Abul 'Ala, d1903–1979.   2. Muslims—India—
Biography.   3. Muslims—Pakistan—Biography.   4. Jamā'at-i Islāmī-yi
Pākistān—Biography.   I. Title.
BP80.M34N37   1996
297'.1977'092—dc20   95-201

3 5 7 9 8 6 4 2

Printed in the United States of America
on acid-free paper

For my father,
my first teacher

Acknowledgments

I would like to thank the American Institute of Pakistan Studies and its director, Charles H. Kennedy, the Joint Committee on South Asia of the Social Science Research Council and the American Council of Learned Societies, and the Faculty Research Grant Committee of the University of San Diego for fellowships between 1989 and 1994 to carry out the research for this book. This study has been enriched by discussions with a number of colleagues. In particular, I would like to thank Charles J. Adams, Daniel Brown, Sikandar Hayat, Karen Leonard, Barbara D. Metcalf, Francis Robinson, John O. Voll, Myron Weiner, and Stanley Wolpert. Noman ul-Haq made invaluable comments on my translation of Urdu passages and especially Mawdudi's poetry. Mumtaz Ahmad, Zafar Ishaq Ansari, John L. Esposito, and Seyyed Hossein Nasr read some or all of the chapters, corrected many misperceptions, and made useful comments for which I am most grateful. I am especially in John Esposito's and Mumtaz Ahmad's debt: John for his unrelenting support from the very beginning of this project and Mumtaz for his meticulous observations, which have improved this study immensely, and for pointing out important nuances in discussing Mawdudi's life and thought, all along guiding me to valuable sources.

In Pakistan and India, Israr Ahmad, Khurshid Ahmad, Khwaja Amanu'llah, the late Allahbakhsh K. Brohi, Javid Ahmadu'l-Ghamidi, Sayyid As'ad Gilani, Begum Abidah Gurmani, Maryam Jameelah Sahibah, Begum Mahmudah Mawdudi, Mian Tufayl Muhammad, Mawlana Sayyid Abu'l-Hasan 'Ali Nadwi, Hakim Muhammad Sa'id, and the late Ja'far Qasmi shared their recollections of Mawlana Mawdudi with me and were of great assistance in locating important sources. I am indebted to them all. Muhammad Suhayl Umar deserves a special note of thanks; this book would not have been possible without his support and advice. Various themes of this book were presented at seminars at Columbia University, Harvard University, the University of California at Los Angeles, and the University of Pennsylvania, all in 1994. I am grateful for the comments of those who attended those sessions.

Margaret Ševčenko has, as always, done a superb job of editing this book and making it more readable, and Cynthia Read and the editorial staff of Oxford University Press have done a wonderful job of producing it. Of course, none of those mentioned here are in any way responsible for the views expressed in the following pages.

Contents

Note on Transliteration and References

All Urdu, Arabic, and Persian words have been cited using a simplified transliteration system that eliminates diacritical marks other than the 'ayn and hamzah. Vowels are rendered by i, u, and a; on occasion, e or o is substituted to convey a spelling more in line with the local pronunciation of the name or source cited. The use of u instead of w and ia as opposed to iya reflects the closest approximation to the local pronunciation of the name or source in question. Well-known terms, such as jihad, nizam, purdah, and ulama, appear in anglicized form. A glossary of Arabic, Persian, and Urdu/Hindi terms is provided at the end of this book to make the reading easier.

Personal names are rendered in accordance with the transliteration rules cited here, even when they are not spelled that way by the persons in question. The only exceptions are names such as Khomeini, Bhutto, or Ayub Khan, where the particular spelling has become established in Western literature. In transliterating personal names, the collapse of vowels and the particular pronunciation of Arabic or Persian words typical of Urdu have been retained (for example, Hashmi rather than Hashimi). Whenever the transliteration of a directly quoted source differs from the one employed here, the variations have been respected. All translations from Urdu were done by this author.

A note is also in order with regard to the references. The names of all interviewees who have contributed to this study are cited both in the notes and in the bibliography. The date and place of the interviews are cited only in the bibliography, as are the translations of the titles of Arabic, Persian, and Urdu books and articles, and the names of publishers of books, journals, and periodicals. When requested by an interviewee, the name has been withheld and the term "interviews" has been substituted. Direct quotations and references, whenever possible, are drawn from official and published English translations of the original Urdu works. However, when required, reference has been made to the original Urdu source. Translations of the titles of Arabic, Urdu, and Persian works are given only in the bibliography. Finally, in all sources in order to reduce confusion, the spelling of Sayyid Abu'l-A'la Mawdudi has been made uniform, although spellings of his name vary widely in various sources. Particular spellings of his name in titles of works, however, have been retained.

MAWDUDI
AND THE MAKING OF
ISLAMIC REVIVALISM

Introduction

The development of Islamic revivalism as a social movement is closely tied to the life histories and intellectual contributions of particular individuals. It is they who advanced the formative ideas, spoke to the concerns of various social groups, shaped public debates by selecting which ideas would be included and which would not, and related individual and social experiences to lasting questions and concerns about freedom, justice, good, evil, and salvation. In short, they articulated an ideology, one that uses social impulses to make a new discourse possible. The biographies and ideas of men like Mawlana Mawdudi (1903–1979), Ayatollah Khomeini (1900–1989), and Sayyid Qutb (1906–1966) therefore are not only essential to historical investigation into contemporary Islamic thought and action but critical to understanding it. They allow us to locate the roots of Islamic revivalism in specific processes and events, sharpening the focus of the more general explanations that have revolved around the larger forces of industrialization, urbanization, imperialism, or uneven development.

Mawlana Sayyid Abu'l-A'la Mawdudi's life and thought is worthy of particular attention in this regard for a number of reasons. He was one of the first Islamic thinkers to develop a systematic political reading of Islam and a plan for social action to realize his vision. His creation of a coherent Islamic ideology, articulated in terms of the elaborate organization of an Islamic state, constitutes the essential breakthrough that led to the rise of contemporary revivalism. His writings were prolific, and the indefatigable efforts of his party, the Jama'at-i Islami (Islamic party), first in India and later in Pakistan, disseminated them far and wide. Mawdudi is without doubt the most influential of contemporary Islamic revivalist thinkers.[1] His views have influenced revivalism from Morocco to Malaysia, leaving their mark on thinkers such as Sayyid Qutb and on events such as the Iranian revolution of 1978–1979, and have influenced

3

the spread of Islamic revivalism in Central Asia, North Africa, and Southeast Asia.[2] Mawdudi's contribution to the development of Islamic revivalism and its aims, ideals, and language is so significant that it cannot be satisfactorily understood without consideration of his life and thought.

In writing this book I hope to further the understanding of the phenomenon of Islamic revivalism through a systematic study of Mawlana Mawdudi's life and ideas. His biography provides fresh insights into the origins of Islamic revivalism, his ideology explains the nature of this revivalism as an intellectual current and a political movement, and the combination shows how the structure of his arguments are related to the formative influences and key events that shaped them. The biography is the context for the ideology.

Mawdudi's life and thought also suggest that Islamic revivalism is more than just some reactionary effort born out of a cultural rejection of the West. In Mawdudi's case, at least, it is closely tied to questions of communal politics and its impact on identity formation, to questions of power in pluralistic societies, and to nationalism. Mawdudi's arguments were anti-Western, but they were motivated by Muslim and Hindu competition for power in British India. He sought an interpretation of Islam that would preclude the kind of cultural coexistence that the Indian National Congress party promised.[3] Islamic revivalism therefore entailed a process of identity formation that could compete with both traditional Muslim identity and secular nationalism. It was defined in large measure in terms of imagining a new Muslim community that was distinct from both.[4] To do this, it borrowed from the West, even as it challenged it, and used its tools to achieve its purpose, particularly the printed word in lieu of the oral tradition that had dominated Muslim life and thought until then.[5] The Jama'at disseminated texts that created an environment in which ideology could be related to social concerns and a collective movement could emerge that would lead to the founding of an Islamic nation.[6] For the Jama'at, that nation was none other than the *ummah* (holy community), the core of the promised Islamic state. This shows that religion can be a component, or even a vehicle, for expressing nationalism. The Jama'at's texts have competed with nationalist propaganda for the hearts and minds of Muslims and have performed the same sociopolitical function of presenting an ideal Muslim community that would be both a refuge and a vehicle for empowerment. Mawdudi made Islamic revivalism the ideology of choice for those who feel marginalized and declassé and fear social disorder.

Mawdudi's ideas emerged at a time of flux in the history of the Muslim community of India. His views were informed by the acute despair that gripped that community and was directed at finding solutions to its plight. At the time, Muslims lacked political consensus and a united leadership. They were divided along linguistic and ethnic lines and dominated by the traditional structures of authority. Mawdudi's aim, much like the Khilafat activists—those Indian Muslims who sought to preserve the institution of the caliphate after World War I—before him, was to arrest this decline and to reassert its claim to power. To realize this objective, he sought to underscore Muslim identity and to foster unity and accord so that the needs of the Muslims could be addressed at the national level. Once that was accomplished, the community could then establish viable political structures rooted in the cultural symbols of Islam that would be able to sustain a broadly based movement in a modern political context.[7]

The first step was to assert Indian Muslim identity in the face of a departing colonial order and the political aspirations of the Hindu majority. His vision was rooted in Indo-Muslim cultural traditions, political sensibilities, and the legacy of Muslim rule, which in India shaped the Muslim worldview and set the agenda for Muslim politics. Mawdudi was clearly driven by this vision, which "tended to stress the dichotomy between Muslims and non-Muslims, and to reject the 'dualism' obtained by subjecting Muslims to non-Muslim law."[8] Although a one-time Indian nationalist, he had succumbed to the lure of Muslim communalism in the post-Khilafat period after his encounters with the Hindu revivalism of the Shuddhi and Sangathan movements and the ever more apparent Hindu domination of the Congress party under Mahatma Gandhi. As a political activist, he understood the power of Islam as a symbol in galvanizing the Muslim community and legitimizing political action. Many of these ideas later carried a different significance, both in his works and in the writings of numerous Islamic thinkers across the Muslim world, but they were nevertheless rooted in the contest to define Muslim identity in India before the partition.

Paul Brass argued that communalism was an instrument of the Muslim elite, who deliberately used Islam to serve their political interests;[9] Francis Robinson found its origins in the directives of the Islamic faith itself.[10] At first glance, Mawdudi's case would seem to support Brass's thesis in that political interests led him to Islamic revivalism; however, Mawdudi never had a secular outlook on politics. His political choices were always—to varying degrees—informed by his faith. This is not to say that he was motivated by primordial values embedded in Islam or directives inherent to that faith. In fact, his political career is neither an example of an Islamic impulse articulating a communalist perspective nor a ploy to use Islam for political ends. Mawdudi more likely was moved by the Muslims' attachment to the legacy of Mughal rule, which could be described as the right of Muslims to rule and the undesirability of living under non-Muslim law.[11] Moreover, for Muslims community is always more important than the individual,[12] and in Mawdudi's view, man could only realize his spiritual potential if the community did so, and the community could do so only if it was purely Islamic. These considerations were more pertinent to a ruling minority anxious over the prospect of political subjugation. They arose from an instinct for self-preservation and a reaction to the uncertainty of life in a Hindu India.[13]

In articulating a revivalist interpretation of Islam, Mawdudi wove Islamic dicta and the normative values of the ambient culture of Indian Muslims into a program with a distinct agenda. As his ideas developed, his emphasis shifted from widely shared Indo-Muslim traditions to narrowly interpreted Islamic doctrines. He put forth a view of Islam with an invigorated, pristine, and uncompromising outlook that would galvanize Muslims into an ideologically uniform, and hence politically indivisible, community, one that would assert its demands and remain unyielding before the overtures of Hindus.[14] Mawdudi's aim was to scrape away centuries of Hindu cultural influence by replacing assimilation with expurgation, accommodation with reassertion, diversity with unity, and submission with defiance. By confirming the distinctive qualities, cultural identity, and social values and mores of Muslims, Mawdudi would erect around the ever more vulnerable and anxious Muslim community an impregnable communalist wall that would exclude outside influences. It was Mawdudi's objective to obviate the possibility of the kind of cultural dialogue and coexistence—assimilation and accommodation—on which the program of the Congress party and its promise of a secular Indian republic was predicated.[15] In cultural seclusion, he hoped, the dejected Muslim community would once again be emboldened. The Islamic identity of the community had to be revived before political mobilization and social action were possible. Still, because revivalism was a radical approach that could have only limited support, its importance in Muslim politics on the eve of partition was minimal. It did, however, eventually find a life of its own and evolved into an all-encompassing perspective on society and politics that has become a notable force in South Asia and has influenced life and thought across the Muslim world.

Because I am concerned here with the origins of Islamic revivalism in the life and works of Mawlana Mawdudi, I will deal primarily with those years in Mawdudi's life when his ideological perspective was formed, his aims were outlined, and his role in politics was defined. Much has already been written about his works and ideas. His teachings on a range of issues—from Islamic history to the status of women, economics, revolution, politics, and religious exegetics—have all been studied. It will serve little to reiterate what has been amply outlined elsewhere.[16] Of interest here is the essence of Mawdudi's message as distinct from the teaching and worldview of traditional Islam within the debate in which his vision took shape: to delineate the structure of the system of thought that he articulated, highlight the directives that are inherent in his corpus of ideas, and determine the pattern and nature of the Jama'at's program of action. Traditional Islam here refers to "those societal norms and institutions that [Muslims perceive] as congruent with or continuing older precedents and values, and as important if not essential to [their] identity,"[17] and which they believe that, in its totality and structure—entwining and enveloping values, practices, and institutions—embodies the truth of their faith and serves as the repository of its spirituality.[18]

The importance of determining the exact boundaries of Mawdudi's ideology lies in the fact that his views remained close enough to traditional Islam to at times make distinctions between the two nebulous. But the differences, though subtle, were fundamental. This book will go beyond a literal reading of Mawdudi's works to seek a greater understanding of the structure of his arguments and the religious and political directives of his oeuvre. Special attention will be given to the factors that controlled the extent and scope of his influence over his audience and determined the nature of his authority. This will enable us to make better sense of why Islamic revivalism developed as it did and how the interaction of ideas and their sociopolitical context shaped its ideological perspective and vision of political authority.

I

THE *MUJADDID* FROM HYDERABAD

Sardar Patel: "What would convince Sirpur that history exists?"
Jaya: "Exile."

Gita Mehta, *Raj*

Everyone who is left far from his source
Wishes back the time when he was united with it.

Jalal al-Din Rumi

1

The Formative Years

Sayyid Abu'l-A'la Mawdudi was born on September 25, 1903 (3 Rajab 1321), in Awrangabad, Deccan, the youngest of Sayyid Ahmad Hasan Mawdudi's five children and the second son from his second marriage. The Mawdudis claimed a proud heritage. They were descended from one of the most prominent branches of the Chishti Sufi order,[1] a lineage that was later an important aspect of Mawdudi's claim to authority.[2] In 1932, he wrote "I belong to one such family that has a 1,300-year history of guiding, asceticism and Sufism."[3] The Chishtis traced their origins back to a family of sayyids (descendants of the Prophet) of the *ahlu'l-bayt* (descendants of the Prophet through his daughter, Fatimah)—a mark of nobility among Muslims of the subcontinent—who in the tenth century initiated "the exalted Chishtiyah Sufi *silsilah* (lineage)" in Afghanistan.[4] Mawdudi traced his lineage directly to Khwaja Qutbu'ddin Mawdud Chishti (d. 1133), from whom the Mawdudi sayyids took their name, and whom Mawdudi described as the *shaikhu'l-shuyukh* (master of the masters) of all the Chishti orders of India.[5] Later, Chishti spiritual luminaries such as Khwajah Mu'inu'ddin Muhammad Chishti (1132–1246), buried at the shrine of Ajmer, came from the spiritual line of Qutbu'ddin Mawdud.[6] The progeny of Qutbu'ddin Mawdud, known as the Mawdudiyah, played an important role in the history of the Chishti Sufi order in India. Noteworthy among them was Abu'l-A'la Mawdudi (d. 1527), Mawdudi's namesake, who moved to India from Afghanistan in the sixteenth century.[7] Mawdudi credited this ancestor with establishing the Chishti order in the Indian subcontinent and, therefore, by implication associated himself with the very provenance of India's preeminent Sufi order, which had also been instrumental in the spread of Islam in northern India.

Little is recorded of the history of the Mawdudis following their migration to India. Mawdudi reported that in the eighteenth century they settled in Delhi, a city with which the family has continued to identify itself closely. Mawdudi, who was six generations removed from those of his ancestors who first settled there, never ceased to live according to Delhi's traditions.

Mawdudi's father, Sayyid Ahmad Hasan, was born in 1855 in Delhi to Mir Sayyid Hasan, a well-respected notable of the city, a man of learning and piety, and a Sufi *pir* (spiritual master) of modest stature.[8] Mir Sayyid was also a man of worldly influence and had been close to the courtiers of the last Mughal emperor, Bahadur Shah Zafar (d. 1862).[9] The British sack of Delhi in 1858 and the subsequent fall of the Mughals reduced the Mawdudis socially and politically. This fall from grace left an indelible mark on the family.

Because the Mawdudis were related to the renowned modernist thinker Sayyid Ahmad Khan (d. 1898) through Ahmad Hasan's mother, many of the young men of the family, including Ahmad Hasan, were recruited to attend the Anglo-Oriental College at Aligarh. In fact, Mawdudi reported that his father was among the college's very first students and boasted that he was the contemporary of Sir Muhammad Rafiq and Sir Buland Jang.[10]

The family's commitment to the Aligarh experiment, which was designed to empower Muslims by giving them an education in modern subjects just as it reformed their faith to accommodate modernity,[11] was far from firm. Because the Mawdudis were from Delhi and thus loyal to the various institutions of Mughal rule, they had suffered under the British Raj, established in 1858, and harbored anti-British sentiments. As a leading family, they had remained detached from the culture and mores of the colonial establishment. It was therefore with great reluctance, and because of the respect that the family had for Sayyid Ahmad Khan, that Ahmad Hasan's father acceded to his son's enrollment at Aligarh.

The family's suspicions about Sayyid Ahmad's experiment, characteristic of the attitude of traditional Muslims, remained unabated,[12] and Ahmad Hasan was not allowed to stay there long. His father called him home when he learned that he had played cricket, wearing *kafir* (unbeliever, English) clothes.[13] Ahmad Hasan never finished his modernist education and was sent instead to Allahabad to study law, but the imprint of Aligarh modernism remained with him for some years.

When he had completed his law degree and a brief stint as the tutor of the Rajkumar of Deogarh, Ahmad Hasan moved in 1896 to Awrangabad, where Mawlvi Muhyu'ddin Khan, a relative of the Mawdudis, was the chief justice. He took a special interest in Ahmad Hasan and helped launch his career. Under the influence of Mawlvi Muhyu'ddin, who was also a Chishti *pir*, Ahmad Hasan "abandoned his British ways, and adopted the ways of his religion and native culture."[14] In 1900 he, and possibly his wife, embraced Sufism, and took *bai'ah* (an oath of allegiance to a Sufi master)[15] with Mawlvi Muhyu'ddin, and pursued the mystical path. So much of Ahmad Hasan's time was spent in meditation and ascetic practices that his legal profession began to suffer. In 1904 he sold all his property and left Awrangabad, taking his family to Delhi, where they settled at the Arab Sara'i village near the shrine of Nizamu'ddin Auliya'.[16] For the three years Ahmad Hasan was in Delhi, he remained completely immersed in his mystical pursuits while his family fell into destitution.[17]

In 1907 Mawlvi Muhyu'ddin summoned his disciple back to Awrangabad, where he chastised Ahmad Hasan for his excesses.[18] Acting on the advice of his *pir*, Ahmad Hasan returned to his law practice but vowed never to defend a case based on deceit. He would review each case thoroughly and would agree to represent only those whom he deemed to be in the right.[19] Although this sanctimonious attitude gave him great peace of mind, it meant that his clients dwindled. He did manage to obtain a modest income from his practice and collected about 100 rupees a month from the rent of the family's buildings in Delhi.[20] He continued to practice law in Awrangabad until 1915, when he moved to Hyderabad and subsequently to Bhopal.[21] In Bhopal, he suffered a stroke that paralyzed him, and four years later, in 1920, died at the age of sixty-five.

In its social limitations, cultural confusion, and the tendency to "return to Islam"—Sufism in his case—for solace, Ahmad Hasan's life was somewhat symbolic of the fate of the Muslim gentry during colonial rule. These lessons were not lost on his son.

Mawdudi's mother's family, being of Turkish origin, also carried a mark of nobility; they had migrated to India during the reign of Awrangzeb and had served the Mughals and later the Asifiyah nizams of Hyderabad as military generals. As a result, they had risen to prominence in Delhi, and later in Hyderabad, and had become a family of nawabs (Muslim princes and nobility) and *jagirdars* (landlords). In his autobiography, Mawdudi boasted of the glorious tradition and the aristocratic heritage of his maternal family.

Mawdudi's maternal grandfather, Mirza Qurban 'Ali Baig Khan Salik, had been a poet and a writer and close to the Delhi circle around the renowned Urdu poet Mirza Asadu'llah Ghalib (1796–1869).[22] In 1862, Salar Jang 'Azam put Salik in charge of Hyderabad's educational affairs. In that capacity, and under the aegis of Nawab 'Imaddu'dawlah Bilgirami, he wrote an article entitled "Makhazin al-fawa'id" (Sources of benefits), in praise of which Mawdudi later wrote, "Although Hyderabad had, since olden times, been a center of literary activities, it [Makhazin al-fawa'id] is one of its most important accomplishments."[23] This literary heritage, of which Mawdudi was so proud, gave him a taste for scholarship and letters that was instrumental in shaping his later career. The young Abu'l-A'la, enamored as he was of his Chishti lineage and his mother's aristocratic background with its tradition of chivalry, statesmanship, and literary accomplishment, was all the more distressed at the visible decline of Muslim power, especially in Delhi and Hyderabad where Mawdudi's family had been associated with Muslim courts.[24]

Abu'l-A'la had been born to Ahmad Hasan and Ruqiyah Begum just before his father committed himself to mysticism. His birth, wrote Mawdudi in the style of hagiographers, had been augured well by a "great man" who had visited Ahmad Hasan three to four years earlier and had advised him to name his son Abu'l-A'la after his great ancestor who had brought the family to India.[25] Abu'l-'Ala, a beautiful child, was the favorite of his father and the recipient of much paternal attention.[26] Mawdudi's autobiography suggested that his father was a great influence on him, especially in his idealism, piety, and humility. In the

Khud niwisht, Mawdudi wrote of his father's interview for employment at Deogarh in such a way that there is clearly a moral lesson to be learned:

> The Maharaja of Deogarh had called two prospective tutors from Delhi in order to choose one to oversee his son's education. One of the two was my father and the other a former professor of my father. Upon arriving in Deogarh my father found out that his professor was also summoned by the Maharajah. He immediately sent a message to the Maharajah that he was not able to compete with his professor and asked permission to return to Delhi. On the other hand his professor responded to the situation by saying, "He [my father] has been my student and is but a child before me, how could he teach like me?" Having seen glimpses of the characters of the two, the Maharajah said, "We are not in need of the professor. We prefer his student."[27]

Mawdudi was impressed with his father's religiosity, and his character was shaped as much in compliance with, as in contrast to, his father's approach to religion. The hardship that it inflicted on the family augmented the sense of deprivation already present in a sharifian (noble) family of Delhi displaced by the fall of the Mughals and living a life of exile in the Deccan, where Muslim power again was on the decline.[28] Mawdudi's somewhat ambivalent attitude toward his father and his early childhood is best captured in the following passage:

> A year after I was born my father washed his hands of the world, and for three years lived like an ascetic. Later on, although he had returned to the world, it was not to his old world which he returned, but to a purely religious one. The result of this revolution in his life was that as I opened my eyes and gained my senses, I found myself in a religious setting. My father's and mother's lives had a distinct religious coloring. Their example and our upbringing imprinted my heart and mind with religious fervor.[29]

It was in Mawdudi's education, more than anywhere else, that Ahmad Hasan's influence was apparent. Despite his religious preoccupations, he took a great interest in the education of his sons and supervised them personally. Ahmad Hasan had wanted Abu'l-A'la to become a *mawlvi,* a theologian and religious scholar.[30] Mawdudi initially was educated at home. His early education began with the study of Persian and Urdu and soon included Arabic, *mantiq* (logic), *fiqh* (jurisprudence), and hadith (traditions or sayings of the Prophet). English and Western science and thought were deliberately excluded from this curriculum.[31]

Ahmad Hasan emphasized ethics and proper behavior in the education of his sons, and he took pains to inculcate in their young minds an understanding of their heritage. At nighttime Ahmad Hasan would sit at their bedside and tell them stories about the great men of Islam and the glories of Islamic history. Mawdudi wrote, "These interesting stories filled my mind with a deep feeling for religion."[32] Ahmad Hasan also read to his children from the emotional articles of *Al-Hilal,* Abu'l-Kalam Azad's (1888-1958) widely read exordium to contemporary Islamic revivalism in India.[33]

The Mawdudis viewed themselves as "Delhiites," and life in the Deccan only reinforced their devotion to the culture and mores of Delhi. Ahmad Hasan sought to implant a loyalty toward the city of his origins in his sons. Wrote Mawdudi,

"Special attention was paid to our speech and accent. I lived in the Deccan for twenty years without adopting a single local pronunciation, and continued to speak in pure Urdu."[34] To achieve this, Ahmad Hasan forbade his sons from mixing with other children, encouraging them instead to fill their hours of loneliness with reading and studying. His vigilance in this regard was such that "if he heard any of us or the bearer utter a wrong word, or pronounce a word incorrectly, he would make us stop, and would correct us."[35] Ahmad Hasan's discipline was reflected not only in Abu'l-A'la's fidelity to his cultural roots and his self-reliant and distant demeanor but also in his lucid style and powerful command of Urdu.

Although Abu'l-A'la harbored a desire to write, chances for doing so seldom presented themselves; his father encouraged him to read instead. In 1914, when Mawdudi was eleven, he was enrolled in the eighth grade at the Madrasah-i Fauqaniyaḥ of Awrangabad.[36] This school was affiliated with the 'Uthmaniyah University of Hyderabad, which taught both traditional and modern subjects. A few months later, he was compelled to take the required examinations and did well in all subjects except mathematics, which had not been included in his curriculum. In spite of that shortcoming, the principal of the school allowed him to enroll in the more advanced *mawlvi* section. It was there that Mawdudi for the first time became acquainted with the natural sciences.

Mawdudi continued his education in religious subjects as well. At the *mawlvi* section he studied the *Book of miqat* in *mantiq,* the *Book of Quduri* in *fiqh,* and the *Book of shama'il-i Tirmizi* in hadith.[37] His mastery of Arabic, which he had been studying when he was still being schooled at home, was such that, at the age of eleven, he translated Qasim Amin's *Al-Mir'ah al-jadidah* (Modern women) from Arabic into Urdu. This celebrated work of the renowned Egyptian modernist thinker criticized the treatment of women in Islam and argued for such reforms as abolishing the insistance on head covering. The translation confirmed Mawdudi's great talent. He recollected:

> During this period [1914] my brother encouraged me to translate Qasim Amin's book, *Al-Mir'ah al-jadidah,* from Arabic to Urdu. God knows where the pages of that translation are today, but I remember that the lucidity of that translation made my father very happy, and even encouraged my brother [Abu'l-Khayr] to write. This was my first work.[38]

For a child who had hitherto been raised in seclusion, attending school proved difficult.[39] His command of Urdu, his knowledge of public issues, and his ability to master difficult texts exceeded the expectations of his teachers and set him apart from his classmates. Reticent and reluctant to engage in games, Mawdudi found himself isolated from others of his age. In retrospect, he viewed this seclusion as a boon:

> Since I had originally been kept secluded, in this there existed benefits as well as drawbacks for me, such that when I became involved in society I was conscious and aware. My father in his talks and education had taught me how to distinguish between good and evil. My early education at his hand had left an indelible mark upon me such that I would not easily fall under the sway of various influences.[40]

Mawdudi's overtly intellectual orientation at such a young age had also made him phlegmatic. There existed an undercurrent of conceit and haughtiness in Mawdudi's aloofness—a feeling of superiority and distinction intrinsic to the intellectual but also lonely circumstances in which he was raised. He was known for his laconic comportment and condescending self-righteousness through- out his life, qualities that permitted him to claim the mantle of leadership and to regard himself as above others, as capable of being the veritable interpreter of their faith.

Mawdudi lived in Awrangabad until 1915, when his family moved to Hyderabad and he enrolled at the local *daru'l-'ulum* (seminary).[41] Its principal of in those days was Mawlana Hamidu'ddin Farahi (d. 1930), a graduate of Aligarh University and a close associate of Shibli Nu'mani (1857–1914), an important Islamic thinker and writer associated with Aligarh and later the Nadwatu'l-'Ulama. He was an erudite commentator on the Qur'an and a sup- porter of Muslim education whose ideas were reflected in the curriculum of the 'Uthmaniyah University of Hyderabad and the Madrasatu'l-Islah of Sara'i-i Mir in A'zamgarh, United Provinces.[42]

Mawdudi was unable to benefit fully from the education at the *daru'l-'ulum* because soon after their arrival in Hyderabad, Ahmad Hasan fell ill and moved on to Bhopal, leaving Abu'l-'Ala in the care of his mother. Six months later, Ahmad Hasan suffered his stroke, an event that forced Mawdudi to leave Hyderabad for Bhopal in order to attend to his father.[43] Ahmad Hasan's pro- longed illness and the family's worsening financial situation compelled Mawdudi to abandon his studies and "to experience some of life's bitter realities."[44] At the young age of fifteen he was forced to earn a living.

While in Bhopal, Mawdudi became acquainted with Mawlana Niyaz Fatihpuri, who encouraged him to pursue a career as a writer. The desire to write was very strong in him, but his style was still "that of a novice."[45] He con- tinued to polish it until "[b]y 1921 [he] had [his] own style, and did not copy anyone."[46] Writing became an important cornerstone of his activities, and his Urdu style become a source of power and prominence, which he utilized with prudence:

> I believe that every thought has its own vocabulary and each thought has to be expressed in the proper balance of words. Therefore, I believe it is enough to choose the right words, and there is no need for unnecessary entanglements. I was able to economize on writing and to devote most of my time to gathering information, evidence, and sources for my thoughts. Having ordered my thoughts in my mind, transferring them to the paper does not require much. I pay so little attention to playing with words that I usually do not read a written text of mine for a second time, unless some particular responsibility is involved in the content.[47]

Journalism and Turn to Politics

In 1918, Mawdudi finally decided to pursue a writing career. He moved to Bijnur in the United Provinces, where his brother, Abu'l-Khayr, was editor of the journal *Madinah*. Mawdudi's stint as a journalist at *Madinah* lasted for only two months—

possibly because the journal closed down. The two brothers then moved to Delhi.[48]

In those days Delhi was embroiled in politics. The young Abu'l-A'la was captivated by the cosmopolitan city of his origins and soon became engrossed in its politics. He immersed himself in reading and exchanging ideas, and, given his family's anticolonialist proclivities soon gravitated toward the independence movement. He was greatly impressed by the poetry of Ghalib (d. 1869), Mu'min (1801–1851), and Muhammad Iqbal (1877–1938), and he even read the works of *taraqqi-pasand* (progressive or modernist) thinkers, whom he later claimed he had always abhorred.[49] His readings on modernity and the West were thorough, and he discovered the intellectual lure as well as the challenge of modern scientific thought. His later works refer to an amazing array of Western thinkers, from Plato, Aristotle, Augustine, Liebniz, Kant, Saint Simon, Comte, Goethe, Hegel, and Nietzsche to Darwin, Fichte, Marx, Lenin, and Bernard Shaw.[50] Although he was skeptical about the premises of modernist thought and suspicious of its intent, he nevertheless made a serious effort to understand it and to resolve the philosphical differences between tradition and modernity. It was during this period that he started to learn English, which in turn made a more diverse selection of Western sources available to him.[51] Mawdudi became particularly interested in understanding the theoretical basis and practical application of modern scientific thought in the context of an Islamic worldview. In 1918, when he was only fifteen, he wrote an article entitled "Barq ya kahruba" (Electricity or electricity)[52] for *Ma'arif*, a journal published in A'zamgarh. *Barq* is a modern word for electricity; whereas *kahruba* is used in older sources. In the article he tried to explicate a scientific phenomenon associated with the West by couching it in terms that would give it cultural legitimacy.[53] In this he resembled the *nechari* (naturalist) position associated with Sayyid Ahmad Khan and the Aligarh modernists, whose works, ironically, Mawdudi had read and abhorred. Mawdudi remained keenly interested in modern scientific thought throughout his life.[54] In his later years, this took the form of concern for incorporating modern scientific ideas in the corpus of Islamic thought rather than the vague attempts at cultural revival of his earlier days.

Mawdudi's intellectual awakening in Delhi occurred in tandem with his increasing interest in politics and his participation in the independence movement. Soon after he arrived he helped form the Anjuman-i I'anat-i Nazarbandan-i Islam (Society for assistance to Muslim prisoners) to collect funds for Muslim political prisoners.[55] His political activities during this period were not based on communal or religious feelings but were directed essentially against British rule. In those years India was in the throes of great political change. The Montagu-Chelmsford Reforms, the Rowlatt Act, and the massacre at Jullianwala Bagh, all of which occurred in 1919, had further politicized the Indian masses in favor of the independence movement. Mawdudi's political sentiments followed suit; he became an Indian nationalist. In 1918 he wrote a laudatory biography of Pandit Madan Muhan Malawiyah (1861–1946), the prominent Hindu politician who served as president of the Congress party in 1909 and 1918 and as chancellor of Benares Hindu University from 1919 to 1940. In 1919 he wrote an equally laudatory biography of Gandhi—whom in later years he viewed with contempt—but it was confiscated by the police and was never published.[56]

With the onset of the Khilafat and the Swaraj (home rule) movements—the first, to preserve the caliphate, and the second, to gain independence for India—Mawdudi became even more involved in politics, placing his trust in these efforts and in their leaders.[57] In 1919 he met a patron of the Anjuman-i I'anat by the name of Taju'ddin, who edited a pro-Congress weekly newspaper by the name of *Taj* in Jubalpur in the Central Provinces.[58] Both Abu'l-Khayr and Abu'l-A'la agreed to edit Taju'ddin's newspaper and were dispatched to Jubalpur. It proved an arduous task. Not long after they took over as editors, the newspaper was closed down, and they were compelled to leave Jubalpur. They went first to Bhopal and eventually back to Delhi.

During his time with the *Taj* Mawdudi became convinced that he should pursue his education in English more seriously. In Delhi he studied English with a tutor for some five months, "after which [he] felt confident enough to continue his study of that language on [his] own."[59] For two years he read books, journals, and magazines on a variety of subjects, "using a dictionary until the correct meaning and usage of various words became known to [him], and until [he] could study history, philosophy, political science, economics, religion, natural sciences and social studies in English without difficulty."[60] These efforts also taught him about Western thought, and he remained an autodidact throughout his life.

In 1920 the two brothers, who had worked together since their stay in Bijnur, parted ways. Abu'l-Khayr left journalism and eventually became an Islamic scholar at 'Uthmaniyah University, while Abu'l-A'la became totally immersed in journalism. Taju'ddin had revived the *Taj* in Jubalpur, and Mawdudi was again invited to be its editor. Jubalpur had been at the center of Khilafat activism, and Taju'ddin was a sympathizer of the Congress party and the Khilafat movement. Through him Mawdudi became involved in political agitation, delivering many public speeches and becoming "one of the Muslims who joined hands with the Congress."[61] Of his activities in Jubalpur he wrote: "Beside the editorial work of the *Taj* I did political work also. I helped in organizing the Khilafat movement in Jubalpur and had a share in bringing the Muslims of the town into the fold of the Congress."[62] But once again his stay at Jubalpur was brief; an article published in late 1920 in which he criticized the colonial government resulted in closure of the newspaper again, and the authorities brought suit against Taju'ddin. "This was a great burden for me," wrote Mawdudi of the suit, "and I promised myself never to have others bear the responsibility for my work and always to be responsible for my pen."[63]

Living alone and becoming a political agitator changed Mawdudi's character. He gained self-confidence and acquired a sense of responsibility. The events in Jubalpur not only exposed him to politics but also put him in the limelight. He recognized his own intellectual and political abilities and developed a feeling of self-worth: "I sensed that there existed some hidden power within me which would rise and assist me in time of need. Thenceforth, I never shunned or hesitated to accept responsibility."[64] His reporting of and participation in the Khilafat movement also increased his anticolonialist sentiments. His articles during this period, both in the *Taj* and in other notable newspapers such as the *Zamindar* of Lahore, are both nationalistic and antagonistic toward British rule.[65]

Mawdudi left Jubalpur to return to Delhi, where he joined a nationalist secret society for a brief period and the Tahrik-i Hijrat (Migration Movement) to protest British rule over India.[66] The latter's name was derived from the idea that India was no longer part of *daru'l-Islam* (land of Islam) and, therefore, all Indian Muslims should emigrate to Afghanistan, where Islam continued to reign. Mawdudi soon broke with this ill-fated movement over disagreements with its leadership.

Early in 1921 Mawdudi met Mawlana Mufti Kifayatu'llah and Mawlana Ahmad Sa'id, two prominent Deobandi ulama who were, respectively, the president (*sadr*) and secretary (*nazim*) of Jam'iat-i 'Ulama-i Hind (Society of ulama of India).[67] The Jam'iat-i 'Ulama was starting a newspaper entitled *Muslim*; Mawdudi was offered the job of editor, and he filled that task until 1923, when publication was stopped.

Although editing the *Muslim* consumed most of Mawdudi's hours, he also spent time in the company of the towering religious figures of the Jam'iat-i 'Ulama-i Hind with whom he worked[68] and, due to their influence, decided to resume his studies in 1921. This time, "it was in Arabic, *tafsir* [Qur'anic commentary], *hadith*, *fiqh*, *mantiq*, and philosophy that [he] sought to gain competence."[69] Mawdudi studied Arabic and the *dars-i nizami* (a syllabus for the education of the ulama),[70] including *fiqh*, *adab* (literature), *mantiq*, and *kalam* (theology) with the eminent religious scholar, Mawlana 'Abdu'ssalam Niyazi (d. 1966).[71] Mawdudi's father had been a devotee of Niyazi, and when the family had settled in the Arab Sara'i village, Abu'l-A'la, then only a child, had been sent to the great *mawlana* to study Arabic. Mawdudi did not complete the *dars* with Niyazi,[72] however, perhaps because the *Muslim* ceased publication. In 1923 he left Delhi for Bhopal, where he spent the next year and a half at his studies.[73]

Bhopal was then under the influence of the Ahl-i Hadith, a school of Sunni Islam that developed in India in the late nineteenth century and was distinguished by its puritanical reformism and spirit of independent religious thinking. The Ahl-i Hadith's approach to Islam appealed to Mawdudi. He apparently had no direct association with its scholars, but it is difficult to imagine that he would have remained oblivious to their highly intellectual discourse because the movement had great influence in the city. Mawdudi's otherwise uneventful stay in Bhopal was most likely the time when he became acquainted with the teachings of the Ahl-i Hadith.

Mawdudi returned to Delhi again in 1924, where he met the Khilafat activist Muhammad 'Ali (1878–1931), who invited him to work on his newspaper, *Hamdard*.[74] However, Mawlana Ahmad Sa'id of the Jam'iat-i 'Ulama-i Hind, with whom Mawdudi had been acquainted since his days at the *Muslim*, was also about to launch a paper, *Al-Jam'iat* and he, too, was eager to obtain Mawdudi's services. Mawdudi chose *Al-Jam'iat*, and began there as editor in 1925.[75]

Once more in Delhi, Mawdudi resumed his study of the *dars-i nizami*, this time with two Deobandi ulama at the Fatihpuri mosque's seminary in old Delhi.[76] The mosque also housed the Nazaratu'l-Ma'arifu'l-Qur'aniyah school established by Mawlana Mahmudu'l-Hasan of the Deoband and his disciple, 'Ubaidu'llah Sindhi, to increase the influence of the ulama among Westernized Muslims.[77] At the Fatihpuri seminary Mawdudi studied hadith, *fiqh*, *adab*, and Sufism with Mawlana Ishfaqu'l-Rahman Kandihlawi, and the *Tafsir-i Baizawi*, *balaghat* (rhetoric), *'ilm-i ma'ani* (interpretive sciences), and *fiqh* with Mawlana Muhammad Sharifu'llah.[78] Mawdudi received his *ijazahs* (certificates to teach religious sciences) from the seminary in 1926 (1344 A.H.).[79] He thus became a Deobandi *'alim* and a member of the sodality associated with that school. In one *ijazah*, Kandihlawi has included Mawdudi in the chain of illustrious scholars of Islam extending back from the Deobandi ulama of the Fatihpuri seminary to Khalil Ahmad Ambahtawi (the *sarparast* [overseer] of the Deobandi Mazahiru'l-'Ulum Madrasah at Saharanpur and a great Deobandi *'alim* of the turn of the century), to Mawlana Muhammad Mazhar Nanautawi (one of the Deoband *daru'l-'ulum's* most famous teachers of hadith and former principal of the school), to Shah 'Abdu'l-'Aziz and Shah Waliu'llah of Delhi, and finally, to Imam Malik ibn Anas (716–795) (the founder of the Maliki school of Sunni law). Some may object to the idea of referring to Mawdudi as an *'alim,* but by Peter Hardy's definition of an Indian *'alim,* he qualified:

> They were certainly not a hierarchy or an order; if they were a professional body, they were without, so to speak, a registration council or a court of discipline. They were a class by their education. . . . They did not possess equal qualification or individual parity of esteem. Not much more than pretension united the product of one of the great teaching centres, say the Farangi Mahal of Lucknow. . . . As long as a man followed a traditional syllabus (here the eighteenth-century *Dars-i-Nizami* taught under the aegis of the Farangi Mahal [*sic*] had great but not exclusive prestige) and accepted the *ijma* of his learned predecessors, he would be accepted as an *'alim*.[80]

Mawdudi had had a traditional education, had studied the *dars-i nizami*, and even had an *ijazah*. By common standards he would have had no problem being accepted into the ranks of the ulama. What perhaps kept him from acting as an *'alim* was his refusal to accept the *ijma'* (consensus) of the ulama who preceded him. It is also possible that he thought that using the title *'alim* would reduce his influence among the educated classes. Shaikh reported that educated Muslims were reluctant to recognize the leadership of the ulama, whom they viewed as retrogressive. Their attitude was clearly manifested during the Khilafat movement when the ulama's prominent role as political leaders kept Iqbal and a large number of Muslim Leaguers away from the movement.[81] For a young man with political ambitions who was determined to influence the thinking of educated Muslims, the title of *'alim* was more a liability than an asset.

Although he never acknowledged it, Mawdudi absorbed many Deobandi ideas and shared many of their concerns, especially about the intrusion of colonial culture into the lives of Muslims. Like the Deobandis, Mawdudi sought to emulate "the practice of an authentic text or an idealized historical period,"[82] to exalt religious law and teach it at the popular level, to disparage popular religious rites and customs such as celebrations of Sufi festivals, and generally to create a normative order in which Muslims could live by the teachings of their faith independent of the ruling order.

Mawdudi never publicized his Deobandi training or his ties to the ulama. It was not until after his death that his *ijazahs* were discovered and references to them began to appear in the Jama'at-i Islami's literature. In his later years, Mawdudi explained that during his stay in Delhi he had concluded that the division into traditional and modern education among Muslims and the absence of any links between the two were not merely unproductive but actually dangerous.[83] He therefore had decided not to restrict himself to the regimen of either educational system, but to benefit from both:[84]

> I do not have the prerogative to belong to the class of Ulema. I am a man of the middle cadre, who has imbibed something from both the systems of education, the new and the old; and has gathered my knowledge by traversing both paths. By virtue of my inner light, I conclude that neither the old school nor the new is totally in the right."[85]

Mawdudi therefore complemented his education in *dars-i nizami* with readings in other subjects. He also started to learn German, but abandoned it after a few months when his tutor left Delhi.[86]

Again, Mawdudi was active politically at this time, and this, too, found its reflection in his writing. He contributed articles to the *Al-Jam'iat*; he defended Turkey against challenges by its European adversaries in two pamphlets, *The State of Christians in Turkey* (1922) and *Tyrannies of the Greeks in Smyrna* (1922); he translated from Arabic to Urdu a book entitled *Al-Mas'alah al-Sharqiyah* (The Eastern question) by the Egyptian nationalist, Mustafa Kamil, who was a hero of Indian Muslims of the time. In 1924 he wrote a book on Hyderabad entitled *Dawlat-i Asifiyah wa hukumat-i Britaniyah* (Asifiyah government and Britain), in which he showed that, despite his increasing interest in religion, politics and the independence movement were his main preoccupations.[87]

Impact of the Khilafat Movement

Mawdudi had been involved in the Khilafat movement through his association with Muhammad 'Ali, the Jam'iat-i 'Ulama-i Hind, and his work on *Al-Jam'iat*. He had become acquainted with the works and ideas of such Khilafat leaders as the 'Ali brothers, 'Ubaidu'llah Sindhi and Abu'l-Kalam Azad.[88] From the Khilafat activists he learned about the West and about politics; he also learned the value of social mobilization and political propaganda, as well as the utility of putting Islamic slogans and symbols to communalist and political use. Many of the ideas of the Khilafat movement, such as its anti-imperialism, its efforts to unite the various expressions of Islam in India,[89] its appeal to pan-Islamic sentiments, its use of Islamic symbols in enunciating political ends, and its belief in the viability and desirability of resuscitating the institution of the caliphate remained hallmarks of Mawdudi's political thought. But his adherence to these ideas, and especially to the political relevance of Islamic institutions such as the caliphate, was premised not on religion, but on history. He became convinced that Islam's history was relevant to the problems confronting Muslims, but he did not as yet see Islam as an all-encompassing sociopolitical model.

In 1925 Mawdudi wrote a series of articles in *Al-Jam'iat* entitled "Islam ka sarchashmih-i qudrat" (The sources of Islam's power),[90] in which he looked to the past to find solutions for problems Muslims faced in modern times. His views were clearly distinguishable from those of reform movements such as those of the Deoband or Aligarh, which—although each in a different way—emphasized a return to the strict observance of religious law and eschewed popular religious practices in their efforts to construct a homogeneous Muslim community capable of social and political action.

The Khilafat movement collapsed in October 1924 after the Turkish government abolished the caliphate. It was a bitter experience for Mawdudi, one that changed his perspective on the relevance of religion to politics. He saw the demise of the caliphate as a consequence of the machinations of Westernized Turkish nationalists on the one hand, and as the betrayal of Islam by Arab nationalists—who had rebelled against the Ottomans in collusion with Europeans—on the other.[91] As a result, he developed a deep-seated suspicion of nationalism and Westernization and became convinced that nationalism would never protect the interests of Islam because of its secular nature. His bitterness was reflected in 1924 and 1925 in his writings, in which he criticized Muslim flirtations with nationalist solutions in Turkey, Egypt, and Afghanistan and derided the ideas of Mustafa Kamil of Egypt, whose book he had translated into Urdu only a year earlier.[92]

Meanwhile, he also found cause to distrust nationalism in India. The Congress party was developing an increasingly Hindu identity under the leadership of Gandhi following the onset of the Swaraj effort in 1919. Mawdudi concluded that the democracy sought by the Indian nationalist effort would serve only the Hindu majority. In later years he recollected that he had become greatly alarmed when, in 1929, Gandhi taunted the Muslims, saying, "We will win freedom with you or without you, or in spite of you."[93] Democracy, Mawdudi said, could be a viable option for Muslims only if the majority of Indians were Muslim. Mawdudi was no longer convinced of the wisdom of Abu'l-Kalam Azad's well-known argument that Muslims should not merely participate in the struggle for independence but, rather, through revitalizing their religious heritage, should act as its leaders.[94] Mawdudi qualified Azad's dictum by stipulating that participation in the independence movement would be ill advised until the day that Muslims would be able to demonstrate a modicum of "political power, order, and will," which would enable them to confront the "arrogant attitude" of the Hindus and contest their domination in the struggle for independence.[95] As Mawdudi lost faith in the Congress party and its Muslim allies, he turned increasingly to Islam and the revival of its institutions in formulating a political strategy for safeguarding Muslim interests. He had set forth on the intellectual journey that was to take him from identification with his community to communalism and then to Islamic revivalism.

Above all else, the failure of the Khilafat movement had convinced Mawdudi that it was futile to vest hope in an institution over whose fate the Muslims of India had no control; moreover, the movement had demonstrated that there were limits to the usefulness of political agitation for preserving moribund institutions. Mawdudi, however, had not wavered in his belief in the viability of the caliphate. He merely concluded that if the caliphate was to be retained, it would have to be built anew for religious reasons and not sentimental attachment or political interests. This was not a task for a journalist, nor was a journal the proper forum for furthering this cause. Mawdudi became increasingly disenchanted with his profession, viewing it as a "mental torment,"[96] restricting and hampering the task before him. In 1928, after ten years as a journalist, he left *Al-Jam'iat*. Although Mawdudi did not refer to disagreements involved in his departure, it can be surmised from the new directions his thinking had taken that he no longer was of one mind with the pro-Congress Jam'iat-i 'Ulama-i Hind.

Reacting to Communal Violence

The Khilafat movement had ushered in an era of Muslim communal consciousness in which Mawdudi's political and scholarly activities had found expression. In the aftermath of the Khilafat imbroglio, Indian Muslims, politicized along communal lines and frustrated in the face of defeat, became increasingly aware that their community had its own particular interests. In their efforts to define their political role, Muslims encountered resistance from the colonial government as well as from secular nationalist forces. Confrontations and violence undermined the reputation of the Islamic faith among the British and the Hindus, and their denunciations in turn generated both resignation and despair among the Muslim intelligentsia.

In 1924 a number of Ahmadi missionaries in Afghanistan were brought to trial on charges of apostasy, found guilty, and executed. The Ahmadis—who follow the teachings of Mirza Ghulam Ahmad (d. 1908), a self-styled thinker who claimed to have received revelation—have always viewed themselves as Muslims.[97] The ulama, however, have rejected this claim on account of the faith's violation of the Islamic belief that Muhammad was the last of the prophets. The British criticized both the executions and the religious laws that sanctioned them. Mawdudi considered this British invective to be a condemnation of Islam as a whole, but he also realized that any Muslim response would have to be unemotional and rational.[98]

Meanwhile, the violent reaction of Muslims to the collapse of the Khilafat movement had led to communal strife across India. Hindus organized their own groups, an act that escalated the conflict. The communalist Hindu Mahasabha, and, more specifically, the Hindu revivalist party, Arya Samaj, organized the Shuddhi movement, which tried to convince both nominal Muslims who abided by Hindu norms and low-caste converts to Islam to return to Hinduism. The movement, with its stress on conversion, greatly antagonized Muslims.[99] Mawdudi viewed the Shuddhi campaign as proof of the inherent animosity of Hindus toward Islam and the beginning of the end of Islam in India, concluding that, to prevent the extinction of Islam in India, Muslims would also have to proselytize. He was also greatly disturbed by the Muslims' lackluster response to the Shuddhi campaign. He recalled in later years how humiliated he felt in 1919 when he saw the Shuddhi leader Swami Shradhanand deliver a sermon from the pulpit of the Jami' mosque of Delhi.[100]

As the Shuddhi campaign gained momentum, the Muslims grew more hostile, and acrimonious exchanges between the two communities increased. Finally, in 1925, Swami Shradhanand, who had openly slighted Muslim beliefs,[101] was assassinated, and public outrage led to a campaign against Islam in the Indian press, which criticized Muslims for this violence. Even Gandhi derided Islam "as the religion of the sword,"[102] a challenge to which Muslims were hard-pressed to respond, given the liberal political context in which the issue was debated. More often than not, the Muslim response, especially that of more Westernized Muslims, was muted and apologetic.

The anti-Islamic backlash from these two episodes, the inability of Muslim intellectual leaders to defend their religion adequately, and the climate of helplessness and resignation that prevailed among Muslims impressed on Mawdudi the need for action.

In a sermon at the Jami' mosque in 1926, the revered Muslim leader Muhammad 'Ali was believed to have echoed the sentiments of many when he said, "I wish a servant of God would stand up and provide the true Islamic position as a response [to the charges leveled against Islam]."[103] That lament was said to have inspired a "clean-shaven Mawdudi,"[104] who was present in the congregation, to rise in defense of his religion. In presenting a defense of his religion at this time, he may have been motivated by the possibility of the entire issue benefiting the Ahmadis. The Ahmadis, too, were firmly opposed to the Arya Samaj and their anti-Muslim campaigns. The Ahmadis, however, were opposed to jihad on the ground that it was incompatible with the spirit of Islam because it propagates faith through violence.[105] Since the execution of Ahmadi missionaries in Afghanistan had begun the entire debate over violence in Islam, their views no doubt were of great concern. Unless jihad was properly understood, the Ahmadi view may have been found to be more attractive to Muslims who were unhappy with both the Arya Samaj and the reaction to Shradhanand's murder. The British, too, may have concluded that the Ahmadi interpretation of Islam was more attractive. A proper articulation of the doctrine of jihad and use of violence in Islam, therefore, would contend with the perceived Ahmadi challenge.

Mawdudi set out to provide a rational exposition of the Islamic doctrine of jihad (holy war), which had come under attack as the most visible vestige of Islam's violent nature. Mawdudi's approach parted with the pedantic and syllogistic style of traditional religious texts. Conscious of the fact that in addition to reassuring Muslims of the virtue of their faith, he was to provide a response to non-Muslims, Mawdudi sought to present his arguments in a modern scholarly style. While reiterating the religious incumbency of the Islamic doctrine of jihad, the main focus of this endeavor was to prove the logic of the doctrine and to underline the juridical limitations to its use. Mawdudi's arguments were formulated in debate with Western thought, and the doctrine of jihad was discussed in the context of the laws of war and peace to which the British adhered.[106] Numerous references to Western legal sources in Mawdudi's exposition attested not only to his vast reading in English by this time but also to his conscious effort to legitimaze the practice of jihad by using the legal arguments and sensibilities of those who were "self-righteously condemning the doctrine as wanton violence."[107]

Mawdudi's research on jihad lasted for six months.[108] His treatise on the subject appeared seriatim under the title "Islam ka qanun-i jang" (Islam's law of war), in twenty-two issues of *Al-Jam'iat* beginning in February and ending in May 1927.[109] The articles were well received in Muslim intellectual and political circles. Mawdudi was lauded for his service to Islam by Muhammad Iqbal; Muhammad 'Ali; Mawlana Ahmad Sa'id of the Jam'iat-i 'Ulama-i Hind, who wrote a complimentary note about the first installment; and the eminent *'alim*, Sayyid Sulaiman Nadwi, who saw to the publication in 1930 of the articles in book form under the title *Al-Jihad fi'l-Islam* (published by Daru'l-Musannifin in A'zamgarh).[110] The accolades that followed the publication of Mawdudi's daring effort no doubt boosted his ego. Aware of his scholarly talents and the power of his pen he now became convinced that his calling lay not in journalism, but in a higher vocation.[111]

Mawdudi apparently did not find the intellectual climate of Delhi conducive to the kind of scholarly activity he now intended to pursue, for in 1928 he left for Hyderabad, where he began his intellectual transformation from journalist to scholar and later from scholar to reformer of Islam (*mujaddid*). Aside from an article in the journal *Ma'arif* of A'zamgarh on the merits of wearing only indigenous dress and rejecting Western clothes,[112] he concentrated on the historiography of Islam. Between 1928 and 1930 he produced a history of the Saljuqid dynasty—the rulers of the central lands of Islam from 1038 until 1194—and translated from Arabic into Urdu those portions of Ibn Khallikan's (d. 1282) history of Egypt that pertained to the Fatimid dynasty (909–1171).[113]

In August 1930 Mawdudi fell ill and left Hyderabad; he stopped briefly in Delhi before going on to Bhopal, where he convalesced and began gathering material for a history of the Deccan. Mawdudi continued this project in Hyderabad when he returned in July 1931. His efforts culminated in a biography of Nizamu'l-Mulk Asifjah—the prominent Hyderabadi statesman—and a brief history of the Deccan, "which sold out quickly."[114]

Until 1931, although he continued his efforts on behalf of Islam, he was still far from being truly involved in politics or advocating Islamic revivalism. He had set out to be a scholar of Islamic history and the Muslim culture of India. His interest in the Fatimids, Isma'ili Shi'is whose religious views were deemed by Sunnis to be obscurantist at best, was indicative of an interest that was historically—and not ideologically—motivated. He was eager to discover the sources for the grandeur of Islamic civilization so they could be reproduced in twentieth-century India.[115]

Mawdudi's brother, Abu'l-Khayr, was teaching at 'Uthmaniyah University and was an associate of Sayyid Manazir Ahsan Gilani at the university's renowned

Translation Institute (Daru'l-Tarjumah), where a team of distinguished scholars and linguists such as 'Abdu'l-Majid Daryabadi (1892–1977) translated into
Urdu important works mainly on British philosophy and intellectual history.
These translations introduced Western thought to India to promote debate
between modern intellectual thought and Indian culture in general, and Islam
in particular. The Translation Institute boasted a lively intellectual environment
where new ideas were presented and discussed, and many Western texts were
available in the original language as well as in the published or draft form of
their Urdu translations. The institute was most likely the source for Mawdudi's
acquaintance with many Western ideas and authors and provided him with an
intellectual environment where his own ideas could take form.

Mawdudi became an affiliate of the Translation Institute through his brother
and probably maintained that affiliation until 1937, when he left for the Punjab.
It was at the institute that he translated the segments of Ibn Khallikan's Egyptian history.[116] In 1931 he helped translate the Al-Asfar al-arba'ah (Four journeys) of Sadru'ddin Shirazi, or Mulla Sadra (1571–1641), the acclaimed Persian philosopher.[117] This voluminous Arabic work on theosophy and mysticism
is one of Islamic philosophy's most difficult and intellectually sophisticated texts.
The project involved several translators and was supervised by Manazir Ahsan
Gilani. Two of its four volumes were published in 1932; they covered the first
two safars (journeys) in 3,500 pages and took eight months to translate.
Mawdudi commented on the difficulty of the text in the Khud niwisht, but the
project provided him with an opportunity to study the Asfar (a primary text of
Islamic philosophy in India), the knowledge of which continues to this day to
be a measure of scholarly excellence and to work with Gilani, a leading Muslim
intellectual of the time.[118]

Mawdudi was influenced by Sadra's philosophy. The Sadraian notion of
man's ability to transcend the worldly realm, to realize God, and to travel with
God and in God in the world, outlined in the Asfar, provides a powerful basis
for putting forth a charismatic claim, providing the contender with moral
superiority and enabling him to reinterpret Islam.[119] More to the point, Sadra's
notions of rejuvenation of the temporal order, and the necessity of the reign of
Islamic law (the shari'ah) for the spiritual ascension of man, found an echo in
Mawdudi's works. Sadra's notion of tashkik (gradation) argued that all existence took form in movement away from God through changes in the essence of
being (harakah-i jawhariyah).[120] Therefore, by definition, worldly existence was
a privation of God. Realization of God as the object of human spirituality could
only be achieved if existence was reoriented toward God. In this endeavor the
shari'ah provided society with guidelines that could nudge the process of
becoming in the desired direction, back toward its divine origin. The shari'ah
brought about an order most conducive to man's spiritual ascension.[121] This
Sadraian formulation was reflected in Mawdudi's belief in the relevance of religion to social change.

Other echoes of Islamic theosophy, especially mysticism, can be found in
Mawdudi's thought.[122] Mawdudi was sufficiently well read in Sufism and theosophy to understand Islam's esoteric and mystical dimensions and to appropri-

ately use its metaphors, idioms, and terms. The following verse provides an example:

> In every manifestation of the idol You are reflected
> You worship Yourself O creator of the house of idols[123]

Mawdudi used the notion of reflection (*tajalli*) of God, ubiquitous in Sufi poetry, in a fashion indistinguishable from the poetry of Mir, the Urdu mystic poet:

> Rose and mirror and sun and moon—what are they?
> Wherever one looked, there was always Thy face.[124]

In Hyderabad, Mawdudi had been confronted with the unavoidable reality of the rise of Hindu power.[125] Writing on the glories of Islamic history in the last bastion of Muslim rule in India, Mawdudi was pained to see the steady erosion of the power of the nizam. In later years he lamented that when Hyderabad was ruled by Nizam 'Uthman 'Ali Pasha, all commerce was in the hands of the Hindus.[126]

Mawdudi also came to believe that the Communists, who advocated the emancipation of Hyderabad's mainly Hindu peasants, were agents in a conspiracy against Muslim rule. He held them responsible for the increasing Hindu belligerency toward the nizam's rule.[127] He no doubt misunderstood the grievances of the poor, and, enraptured as he was with the glories of Islamic history and the symbolic meaning of the nizam's state, he was unable to distinguish between protecting the political rights of Muslims and defending an unjust sociopolitical order. He was locked in a communalist outlook, where all social and political questions were subsumed under the Hindu-Muslim conflict. He became increasingly distrustful of the direction that Hindu politics was taking, and, as a result, his views on the salient issues, ideas, and movements of his time were distorted. He developed a deep-seated distrust of populist politics and socioeconomic and class-based movements. This communalist outlook limited his ability to see sociopolitical realities. As a consequence, his crusade for the preservation and propagation of Islam remained divorced from real political and social problems. He never became a populist politician or a thinker in whose works the interests and grievances of society would find expression. His political views were formed in the abstract and had little to do with the political dynamics of the society to which they were meant to refer. The intermittent confluence of aims between the Jama'at-i Islami's program in later years and the salient political issues of Pakistani society were born of conjecture rather than calculation. This apolitical approach to political thought and practice remained a mark of Mawdudi's movement and distinguished him from other revivalist leaders such as Ayatollah Khomeini, who maintained a more accommodating approach to the Left and premised his ideas on the prevailing concerns of Iranian society.[128] Mawdudi's emergence as a prominent leader whose persona and style could not be easily classified as populist or charismatic, and the continued development of the Jama'at-i Islami as a political force that has, by and large, eschewed populist politics, defy the conventional wisdom regarding the origins and development pattern of social and political movements. The case of Mawdudi and the Jama'at-i

Islami raises the possibility that political leaders and movements whose ideological perspective and program are not predicated on socioeconomic concerns, but on questions of identity and communal rights, can succeed.

Mawdudi's education in the religious sciences, mysticism, philosophy, history, and modern subjects combined with his political experiences in Delhi beginning in 1919 to push him into increasingly more uncompromising communalist lines. They gave him both the predilection to use Islam to address the problems of Muslims and the tools for doing so. From this point, Mawdudi's knowledge of Islamic history, law, theology, philosophy, and mysticism, and his reading of the Indian Muslims' political experiences in the twentieth century, led him to a revivalist position and the assumption of the authority needed to articulate it.

2

The Turn to Revivalism

Although events in Mawdudi's life up to 1930 had pointed him in the direction of Islamic revivalism, the actual turn to an Islamic ideological perspective occurred in the years from 1932 to 1937. During that time, his revivalist tendencies became manifest and his authority as a *mujaddid* took form. In 1930 he accepted an offer from Nawab Salar Jang, a leading statesman of Hyderabad, to prepare a plan for propagating Islam in that princely state. Mawdudi worked hard on the plan, but to his chagrin, the nawab took little note of it and ignored his counsel, which Mawdudi found reckless. He thought the nizam's government was both unaware of the scope of its problems and ill prepared to contend with them, and he lost faith in the nizam's state.[1] The classical institutions of Islamic history, including the Muslim princely states, could be neither easily resuscitated nor readily reproduced.[2] Mawdudi therefore began to look to Islam itself and to the revival of its values as the key to reversing the decline of Muslim power in India. The experiences of Muslim monarchies of India, their views on statecraft, and their constitutional ideals—as reflected, for instance, in mirrors of princes—were conspicuously absent from Mawdudi's teachings on the Islamic state and the Islamic constitution in later years.

In the July and August 1932 issues of *Ma'rifat*, he contributed a two-part article on the subject of *'ibadah* (worship). In the same year, at the behest of Manazir Ahsan Gilani, he wrote the *Risalah-i diniyat*, published in English under the title *Towards Understanding Islam*. Gilani, who was then Hyderabad's director of education, intended to use the book as "a required text for senior matriculation students in various colleges throughout India."[3] Mawdudi completed the book, which was to become one of his most widely read, in a mere fifteen days.[4] *Towards Understanding Islam* outlines the basic beliefs and tenets of Islam. It was meant to reinforce adherence to the faith among Muslims and plausibly to invite Hindus to consider the religion. It reflected Mawdudi's growing interest in doctrinal issues and their relevance to political questions, and it was a confirmation of Mawdudi's growing religious and academic standing. Because Gilani and the nizam's government had turned to Mawdudi to write it, great honor was conferred on him.

Although the emphatic tone of the *Risalah-i diniyat* suggests a definitive change in Mawdudi's intellectual orientation, his commitment to what he had begun to advocate publicly remained circumspect. His appeal for strict adherence to Islamic dicta and mores in his public utterances was not as yet clearly reflected in his own conduct. In 1925, when he was appointed editor of the Jam'iat-i 'Ulama-i Hind's *Al-Jam'iat*, his clean-shaven face—which was seen as a sign of less than full commitment to Islam—caused an uproar among the ulama. Only after Mawlana Ahmad Sa'id interceded on his behalf did the ulama drop the subject.[5] Ra'is Ahmad Ja'fari, the Pakistani writer and historian, recollected that when he met Mawdudi sometime around 1932, he found him to be religiously inclined but clean shaven and in Western clothes,[6] even though three years earlier Mawdudi had written in the *Ma'arif* on the virtues of adopting native attire. Even by 1937, Ra'is Ahmad described Mawdudi as "a man of middling stature, rather plump with English-cut hair, clean shaven, wearing a fez cap, Aligarh fashion trousers and Hyderabadi close-collar long coat."[7] He abandoned the fez a year or two later, but it was not until he moved to Pathankot in the Punjab that he grew a beard. So the lack of one continued to stir controversy until 1942. In that year, Mawlana Muhammad Manzur Nu'mani resigned from the Jama'at-i Islami to protest Mawdudi's unseemly conduct and the short length of his beard.[8]

All this was not hypocrisy, as some of the Jama'at's detractors have suggested, but a reflection of Mawdudi's struggle with the meaning and nature of his faith. He was working through a process and had yet to reach the conclusion that advocating the cause of religion demands strict conformity. During the very years that Mawdudi was enjoining Muslims to follow the teachings of their faith more rigorously, he himself was struggling with Islam. Notions about an intellectual transformation and an "internal conversion" appear in his biography alongside his political awakening. The Jama'at and its call to Islamic observance (*da'wah*)[9] were premised on the notion of conversion. The gradual change in the subjects about which Mawdudi wrote, from anticolonialism to the history of Islam, and finally to a revivalist formulation, show this process at work.

The years that preceded Mawdudi's adoption of a revivalist position were periods of great intellectual and religious uncertainty for him. As late as 1932, the extent and direction of his religious commitment remained open to question. His biographer, Masudul Hasan, wrote that in these years Mawdudi's faith in Islam actually wavered.[10] Mawdudi's poetry from this period reveals hitherto hidden mystical tendencies far removed from the reformist zeal he would soon display (see the appendix). Written under the pen name "Talib" (seeker—a word with strong Sufi connotations), the poems are in the style of Sufi verse but also express confusion and yearning. The poetry describes a world in which the sage (*farzanah*) is indistinguishable from the madman (*diwanah*): "The maddest of all men is in fact the wisest among them."[11] It is a world wherein "friendship is reciprocated with treachery, faithfulness with betrayal," where "the healer [*masiha*] plays with the fate of those ailing," where "poison and its antidote come in the same wine cup," where "sparks shower on the seeker along with flowers," and where "in the robes of success failures are hidden." It is an impermanent world where "a drop can cause commotions." It is not stable, but is a continuous tumult and revolt:

> O Talib! Satiation of the heart and the soul is difficult,
> But still attainable if you have manly courage [*jur'at-i rindanah*].

The poems provide a rare glimpse into Mawdudi's thinking at this juncture in his life. Although telling in their concluding counsel, the poems reflect a mystical and poetic soul in anguish and confronted with an "unjust" world wherein realities belie ideals. Yet, Mawdudi is not prepared to renounce such a world, nor is he satisfied with other worldly recompense or hermetic seclusion that are the lot of a true mystic. Instead, he seeks to change it, to re-create reality in the shape of the ideals:

> We believe in cash [*naqd*], not in credit [*tise*],
> So why narrate to us the story of paradise.

In later years, Mawdudi recalled that he began his path to faith from doubt, from *la ilah* (there is no god) to *illa'llah* (other than God).[12] The formulation described by Mawdudi resembles the Sufi teachings on contemplation and meditation (*zikr*), where the incantations emphasize the distinction between *la ilah* and *illa'llah* and carry the Sufi from the first to the second. His return to Islam was based on solid ground, however: his education at the Fatihpuri mosque seminary and reading the Qur'an. Mawdudi himself credited the Qur'an for transforming his outlook and turning him to his faith:

There was a time when I was also a believer of traditional and hereditary religion and practiced it. . . . At last I paid attention to the Holy Book and the Prophet's Sunnah. I understood Islam and renewed my faith in it voluntarily. Thereafter I tried to find out and understand the Islamic system in detail. When I was satisfied in this I began to invite others to the truth."[13]

From its inception, this reconversion was divorced from the traditional orthodoxy and from the institution of the ulama. Mawdudi downplayed his own affiliation with the Deobandi sodality and criticized the institution of the ulama openly and at times sharply. Although it is not clear from the sources when or why Mawdudi developed such a dislike for the ulama, it is apparent that he did not believe in the effectiveness of traditional Islam—including the ulama and the Sufis—in addressing the predicaments that had brought him to the study of the religion in the first place. In later years, when he became interested in organizing Muslims politically, he viewed the various ulama groups as rivals and as impediments to the realization of his objectives. Educated in modern subjects and already confident of his own scholarly, and plausibly political, promise, Mawdudi had little patience for the restrictions of the institution of the ulama:

> There was a time during my early childhood when I myself acquiesced in the tra-
> ditional orthodox religion and conventionally followed it, but when I gained direc-
> tion, this dormant practice of "we follow upon where we found our father . . ."
> (Qur'an, 2:17) struck me as completely meaningless.[14]

This castigation of the ulama was not free from the condescension that at least
in part had emanated from the esteem in which he held his own familiarity with
modern thought.

In September 1932, Mawdudi bought the journal *Tarjumanu'l-Qur'an*
(Qur'anic interpretation), published in Hyderabad by Abu Muhammad Muslih
Sahsaram.[15] Sahsaram had been an admirer of Abu'l-Kalam Azad and had named
his journal, which had first appeared in print in March 1932, after Azad's seminal translation of and commentary on the Qur'an. Mawdudi produced the
Tarjuman from his rooms in the Mu'azzam Jahi market.[16] He wrote most of the
articles himself and did all the editing but was supported by subscriptions from
the government of Hyderabad, which in 1935 stood at 300, half of the *Tarjuman's*
circulation, as well as from the city's literati.[17] Hyderabad's ulama and leaders,
such as Manazir Ahsan Gilani, 'Abdu'l-Majid Daryabadi, Abu'l-Khayr Mawdudi,
Mawlana 'Abdu'llah 'Amadi, and Mawlana Abu'l-Khayr Muhammad Khayru'llah,
wrote articles for it, which gave the journal added prestige.[18]

In its early years (1932–1936), *Tarjuman* had no particular political program, although it did have a rather preachy and pedantic tone in enjoining its
readers to return to pristine religious values.[19] Mawdudi's politics in this period
simply reiterated his earlier anticolonial sentiments, echoing the position of the
Jam'iat-i 'Ulama-i Hind at the time. After a time, the *Tarjuman* began to con-
sume all of Mawdudi's attention and to become the vehicle for his life's mission.[20] Its influence was always limited; subscriptions apparently never surpassed
the 600 mark, and half continued to be government subsidies. Of the remaining 300 copies, 200 went to Muslim institutions and libraries across India,[21]
and a number to various Muslim leaders free of charge. Fewer than 100 were
individual subscriptions. Mawdudi had expected an enthusiastic reception for
his journal and was greatly disappointed by "Muslim apathy"; he lamented this
state of affairs in his editorials in the *Tarjuman*,[22] but refused to give up. Aware
of the *Tarjuman's* financial difficulties, Manazir Ahsan Gilani and Abu'l-Khayr
Mawdudi in 1935 offered him a teaching position at the 'Uthmaniyah University,
but Mawdudi turned down the offer.[23] He remained the editor of *Tarjumanu'l-
Qur'an* until 1979. The *Tarjuman* gave Mawdudi a place to air, test, refine, and
rationalize his ideas and his vision and, despite its modest subscription list, cast
him as a leader of the Muslim community of India.

Mawdudi's religiopolitical vision was shaped by the social decline and political frustrations that the Muslims of India had been suffering since 1857. These
had become more pronounced after the Khilafat movement collapsed in 1924.
In fact, his ideas were in part the result of the failure of the Khilafat movement
to unite India's Muslims. Manzur Nu'mani, one of the Jama'at-i Islami's founders,
argued that the social and political turmoil of the years between 1924 and 1932
compelled Muslims to search for new solutions. The Shuddhi campaign, the
intensification of the Ahmadi's missionary activity, and the fall of Sharif Husain

of Mecca to the Wahhabi movement of 'Abdu'l-Aziz ibn Saud in 1924 and the subsequent upheavals in Mecca and Medina—with which Hyderabad was closely tied[24]—all helped create an atmosphere of uncertainty and impending doom among Muslims. They also compelled Mawdudi to act and attracted others to his writings.[25]

The situation confronting Hyderabad was particularly disturbing to Mawdudi. He wrote of his anxiety in the *Tarjuman*:

> This city [Hyderabad] has for some 200 years been the seat of Islamic culture and civilization. Great ulama, men of virtue, generals and courtiers are buried here. . . . What a pity that their legacy is alive in stone [monuments of the city] and dead in the people. . . . In this old Islamic settlement my eyes have searched and found neither a great man of God nor a skilled traditional craftsman. . . . Every search of mine attests to the death of that nation.[26]

He was so disturbed by what he saw in Hyderabad that he could envision no future that did not include an Islamic revival. Mawdudi's anguish at the visible decline of Hyderabad was accentuated by the bond that existed between him and this state. Not only had his forefathers worked for this order and done much to add to its glories, but he, too, had an interest in continuing the nizam's rule and maintaining ties with the state's leaders. His contacts with the Hyderabadi rulers made the plight of the state that much more immediate, tangible, and urgent.[27] Mawdudi gives 1933 as the year when his attitudes changed. Years later he wrote:

> I can divide my forty-nine years into two parts. The first thirty was spent in read-ing, listening, thinking, observing, and experiencing, and also in finding a goal in life. My thoughts are the products of reasoning of all those years of intellectual activity. Then I set my goal to strive in the path of truth, to propagate its cause, and to bring my vision into reality.[28]

He underwent a "conversion," declaring: "In reality I am a new Muslim" (*dar haqiqat mein ik naw-musalman hun*)[29] and began to consider an organization to further his cause. He wrote that the enforcement of the Islamic injunction of enjoining the good and forbidding the reprehensible (*'amr-i bi ma'ruf wa nahy 'an'l-munkar*) was tantamount to creating a party (*jama'at*) for Muslims.[30]

Mawdudi's revivalist solution and reconversion to Islam were not expressed in political terms, however, until 1937, when he traveled to Delhi. He had not been there for seven years and was startled at the changes he found. In Delhi, Hindu political ascendancy and secularization among Muslims, for which he held the Hindus responsible, were both obvious. He regarded a noticeable decline in adherence to purdah, combined with lax behavior on the part of Mus-lims, as responsible for the gains made by the Hindus.[31]

Traveling back to Hyderabad by train, Mawdudi shared a compartment with B. G. Kher, the chief minister and the leader of the Congress party in Bombay. Mawdudi, who was already apprehensive about the Congress ministries formed following the Government of India Act of 1935,[32] was so taken aback by what he understood to be Kher's high-handed treatment of Muslims that he decided then and there never to live under a Hindu government.[33] As a result of his encounter with Kher, Mawdudi began writing his vehemently anti-Congress attacks in the *Tarjuman* (they were later collected and published in 1939 as the first volume of *Musalman awr mawjudah siyasi kashmakash* (Muslims and the current political struggle in India).[34] Mawdudi's essays excoriated the Congress party, equating its claim of nationalism with a Hindu drive for supremacy in India. He doubted the sincerity of assurances the party gave to Muslims that their rights and interests would be looked after in post-independence India and questioned the wisdom of Muslims supporting the party, especially since at that time it had launched a campaign to break up Muslim communalism and mobilize support among the Muslim masses for the nationalists. When Mawdudi's brother insisted he abandon his political activities and return to scholarly endeavors, he replied:

> The crisis has come. I can foresee that the horrors ahead would wipe out the traumatic events of 1857. . . . Muslims may face yet greater misery. If a warning is not given by me, as I foresee it, the danger is imminent. I have resolved to serve the Muslim cause, to the farthest extent of my struggle.[35]

Mawdudi's writings now began to display a coherent political outlook argued rationally and systematically. His political views were now quite different from the occasional pronouncements on diverse issues found in his earlier works. His position became all-encompassing, articulate, and revivalist. He addressed himself to the Muslim supporters of the Congress party, especially those targeted by its mass contact campaign. Mawdudi had set out to repair the inroads that the party had made among the Muslims by challenging the political viability and religious wisdom of the nationalist platform and by reinforcing Muslim communal consciousness. His line of argument soon brought him into conflict with the Muslim supporters of the Congress party, most notably Mawdudi's former employers and mentors, the Jam'iat-i 'Ulama-i Hind. Its leader at the time, Mawlana Husain Ahmad Madani, who was vehemently anti-British and an ardent supporter of the nationalist platform, was actively gathering Muslim support for the party. He had detailed his views in a 1939 pamphlet entitled *Muttahidah qaumiyat awr Islam* (United Nationalism and Islam),[36] in which he supported the notion of a pluralistic Indian society and argued that Muslims could, without sacrificing their identity or interests, thrive within it. Mawdudi disagreed with this argument and opposed the very notion of a workable pluralistic society as desirable. The value of Islamic revivalism lay in good measure in making such a society impossible by hardening the Muslim position, polarizing Indian society, and limiting coexistence, social interaction, and power sharing between Muslims and Hindus.[37]

Mawdudi censured Madani openly and challenged his political and, ultimately, his religious authority, accusing him of sacrificing Islam on the altar of his anti-British sentiments.[38] Mawdudi's poignant arguments appealed to both the political sense and the religious passion of Muslims. He certainly doubted Jam'iat-i 'Ulama-i Hind's promises, and by challenging the religious basis of Madani's position, he limited the ulama's ability to use religious decrees to mobilize support for the Congress party. I. H. Qureshi reported that Mawdudi's arguments were so well formulated that Mufti Kifayatu'llah advised his colleagues against debating Mawdudi.[39] Mawdudi's challenge to Madani and the Jam'iat-i 'Ulama, widely publicized by the Muslim League, was popular with many Muslims and enhanced his prestige in his community.[40]

Mawdudi's subsequent program was not solely the politicization of his revivalist posture or a reaction to the Congress's platform, however. Mawdudi's novel perspective on religion and communal politics was, at least in part, rooted in Western sources. When Mahiru'l-Qadri met Mawdudi in Delhi in 1937 at the house of Chaudhri Muhammad 'Ali (the future prime minister of Pakistan) with whom Mawdudi was staying, Mawdudi's bed was surrounded with books—many of them in English and a number noted Communist works.[41] Mawdudi never acknowledged his debt to Western sources—nor, for that matter, to indigenous ones—but the imprint of Western ideas was significant. He used them to produce hybrid political views that best suited his own disposition and the changing reality of his society. Many of Mawdudi's views were formed in debate, rather than in conformity, with Western sources. His discourse produced an ideological orientation that was indigenous on the surface but was based on the very culture he sought to reject.[42]

Mawdudi's eclectic intellectual and ideological formulations and his own educational background fit the type that Benedict Anderson has presented as typical of Indonesian nationalist thinkers and movements. Anderson correlated the advent and development of nationalist movements in colonial settings with the emergence of a class of bilingual state functionaries whose knowledge of things Western lay at the root of their articulation of nationalist sentiments and the delineation of "an imagined community" to advocate its aspirations.[43] Although Anderson's type is best applied to the Aligarh modernists in Muslim India, if one ignores his emphasis on "state functionaries," it also tells much about the role Mawdudi was playing at the time in the Muslim community and how his background and education helped him formulate and disseminate a revivalist ideology as a parallel to and surrogate for nationalism. Although not of the Aligarh culture, Mawdudi was still a member of the "vanguard intelligentsia" who created and continued to articulate the struggle for cultural and political freedom. Certainly, Mawdudi's background resembled that of his nationalist cohorts, but his initiation into politics and political thought had come about as a result of his interactions with Hindu Congress party members.

Despite his increasingly overt use of Islamic symbols and his open call for a revival of Islam, certain aspects of Mawdudi's private life continued to cast doubt on the extent of his commitment to the cause.[44] For example, in 1937, when Mawdudi went to Delhi to find a wife, he married Mahmudah Begum, a distant cousin on his maternal side who came from a wealthy family in government service and who also owned some land.[45] The family descended from the Bukhari family of Delhi, who continue to serve as the hereditary imams of Delhi's Jami' mosque.

There is little doubt that the family's financial resources were considerable, and its effect was immediately noticeable in Mawdudi's habits. Begum Mawdudi recollected that when they moved to Pathankot to establish Daru'l-Islam (see below), there were only three houses, one of which belonged to the Mawdudis, who also owned a tonga and employed a bearer.[46] Mawdudi's comfortable accommodations there generated resentment and was one reason for Mawlana Manzur Nu'mani's opposition to Mawdudi's leadership in 1942.[47] Royalties from books or the proceeds from *Tarjumanu'l-Qur'an* would have been too meager to support his household. His marriage allowed him to forgo all outside income and devote his time to research and political action.[48] Shortly after its founding, the Jama'at was able to purchase a large area of land in the Attock District near Rawilpindi for its headquarters.

From before her marriage, Mahmudah Begum was quite liberated and modern in her ways. Early on, she rode a bicycle around Delhi and did not observe purdah.[49] Ironically, Mawdudi had complained of the absence of purdah, which he witnessed during the very trip in which he got married, as one of the reasons for dismay at Islam's future prospects. Mawdudi clearly loved his strong-willed, liberal, and independent-minded wife, however, and allowed her greater latitude than he did Muslims in general. The standards that prevailed in his household were very different from the standards he required of others, including Jama'at members.[50]

The Daru'l-Islam Project: 1937–1939

When he returned from Delhi, Mawdudi decided to expand the purview of his *da'wah* and bought land in Hyderabad to establish an Islamic institution.[51] He turned to Chaudhri Niyaz 'Ali, a retired civil servant whom Mawdudi knew wanted to establish a *waqf* (endowment) using a piece of land he owned in Pathankot (a small village in the Gurdaspur district of the Punjab) and convinced him to establish the *waqf* for his organization in Hyderabad instead.[52]

Niyaz 'Ali had also corresponded with the famous poet Muhammad Iqbal regarding his intentions.[53] Iqbal had advocated a Muslim homeland in northern India since 1930 and thought the Muslims needed a political organization. He had discussed it with a number of his friends, including Aligarh University's Zafaru'l-Hasan (d. 1951), a Kantian philosopher of renown who had been a proponent of the two-nation theory and had proposed a Muslim political organization to be named Shabbanu'l-Muslimin (Muslim youth).[54]

Iqbal was not organizationally minded and regarded education as the most effective means of bringing about a Muslim reawakening. He favored establishing a model *daru'l-'ulum*[55] in Punjab to lay the foundation for a new Islamic worldview, which would in turn facilitate the creation of a Muslim national homeland.[56] Iqbal's aim was evident in his letter to the rector of al-Azhar in Cairo, Shaikh Mustafa al-Maraghi, requesting a director for the intended *daru'l-'ulum;* Iqbal asked the Egyptian *'alim* for a man who was not only well versed in the religious sciences, but also in English, the natural sciences, economics, and politics.[57] Al-Maraghi answered that he had no suitable candidate. Iqbal was disappointed and handed the task of selecting a suitable overseer to Niyaz 'Ali, but he remained firm about establishing the *daru'l-'ulum*.[58]

Niyaz 'Ali, meanwhile, searched for a suitable administrator for his *waqf*. He turned first to the famous Deobandi *'alim*, Ashraf 'Ali Thanwi (d. 1943), but Thanwi rejected the offer. Niyaz 'Ali then tried to encourage Mawdudi to move to Punjab,[59] though he made him no firm offer and the two disagreed about the aim of the project. Niyaz 'Ali insisted Mawdudi consult with Thanwi, with whom Mawdudi was at loggerheads, along with the rest of the the Deobandi Jam'iat-i 'Ulama-i Hind.[60] Disagreements, however, were soon overshadowed by mutual need.

The situation in Hyderabad was fragile, and Mawdudi had come to the conclusion that it was not the best possible place for launching an Islamic revival.[61] This made him more interested in Niyaz 'Ali's project, and he solicited the job of administering the *waqf*.[62] Unable to find any other suitable candidates, Niyaz 'Ali was inclined to agree, but the final decision had to await a response from al-Maraghi. Niyaz 'Ali asked Iqbal to write to Mawdudi and invite him to settle in the Punjab. Iqbal arranged for him to come to Lahore and serve as the imam of the Badshahi (royal) mosque at a salary of 100 rupees per month and to partake in Iqbal's plans for the revival of Islam, *'umraniat-i Islami ki tashkil-i jadid* (reconstruction of the social aspects of Islam). Mawdudi turned down Iqbal's offer on the grounds that he did not want a paying job that would restrict his freedom.[63] Niyaz 'Ali then suggested Mawdudi as overseer of the *waqf* and secured Iqbal's agreement to this appointment.

In October 1937, Mawdudi went to Jullundar in Punjab to meet with Niyaz 'Ali. He reiterated his interests in creating a *da'wah* movement as an alternative for the Muslims to both the Congress party and the Muslim League.[64] He also asked for complete freedom of action in administering the *waqf*. Although Mawdudi's plans were not at all what Iqbal had in mind for a *daru'l-'ulum*, they did not openly disagree. Eager to secure Iqbal's blessings and to get the project under way, and possibly to use Iqbal to deal with Mawdudi, Niyaz 'Ali took Mawdudi to Lahore to meet him.

At the meeting, Mawdudi's appointment was confirmed, but Iqbal did insist that he establish at Pathankot some form of educational institution with a clearly defined curriculum.[65] Mawdudi accepted Iqbal's scheme and agreed to use the *waqf* to train a number of capable Muslim students and young leaders in Islamic law as well as modern subjects.[66] Although the project was essentially educational, the imprint of Mawdudi's politics was evident in its name, Daru'l-Islam (Land of Islam).[67] On Iqbal's suggestion, Mawdudi contacted Zafaru'l-Hasan in Aligarh to inform him of the Pathankot project.

All this cooperation was uncharacteristic of the independently minded and self-righteous Mawdudi, especially since it was clear that by no means had he abandoned his political objectives.[68] Accepting the position was, therefore, partly out of respect for the celebrated poet and the appeal of being a close associate. By then there was no reason to stay in Hyderabad, where the Muslim community was increasingly marginal to the political mainstream. The future of Indian Muslims was to be determined in the northern provinces, especially the northwestern ones, so that was where Mawdudi had to be.[69] Mawdudi's journal,

Tarjumanu'l-Qur'an, with its meager circulation, could hardly be of any influence far from the centers of Muslim political activity, and Hyderabad's cultural and academic life was not enough to keep him there. Punjab was the strategic, economic, and political heartland of the Muslim-dominated northwest provinces and at the time was also one of the most pro-British of the Indian provinces. The exceedingly anti-Western and revivalist Mawdudi believed that his *da'wah* would be of great significance to the fate of the northwestern provinces if he could take his battle for the hearts and minds of the Muslim intellectuals there.[70] Mawdudi became so convinced of the wisdom of moving to the Punjab that when Manazir Ahsan Gilani and Abu'l-Khayr Mawdudi tried to entice him into staying in Hyderabad with a lucrative offer of heading the department of Islamic studies at 'Uthmaniyah University, he flatly refused.[71]

Following their meeting with Iqbal, Mawdudi and Niyaz 'Ali agreed on the terms of Mawdudi's position as *waqf* overseer, and Niyaz 'Ali included Mawdudi in the *waqf's* governing committee, the Daru'l-Islam Trust.[72] Also included on the committee was Muhammad Asad, the Muslim scholar of Austrian origin.[73] Niyaz 'Ali guaranteed Mawdudi the autonomy he had asked for, but not the permission to involve himself in political activity, because their agreement with Iqbal regarding the nature of the *waqf's* projects precluded it. Mawdudi agreed to these terms.[74] In the November 1937 edition of the *Tarjuman,* it was announced that the journal would be moving from Hyderabad to Pathankot; Mawdudi arrived there on March 16, 1938.[75]

The story of Daru'l-Islam also brings to the fore another important and interesting aspect of Mawdudi's biography and, hence, his persona—namely, the exact nature of his relation to Iqbal. Iqbal has become the most popular poet of Pakistan and an infallible and omniscient philosopher and sage. His name bestows a legitimacy on all ideas and programs associated with him. He has gained an almost prophetic reputation in Pakistan, far exceeding the claims of the modest poet and thinker of Lahore.[76] His ideas and sayings are invoked to legitimate various policies, sanctify sundry views and decisions, and silence opposition and criticism. In short, for Pakistani people all across the political spectrum, from Left to religious Right, Iqbal became a figure larger than life, a repository of great wisdom and charisma. Mawdudi and the Jama'at-i Islami lost no opportunity to benefit from this by reitering their long affiliation with him.[77] The Jama'at's literature often related both Mawdudi's mission and his philosophy to Iqbal's influence. Especially when the Jama'at's critics charged it with anti-Pakistan activities, they counted on this association with Iqbal to redeem their political image. Because Daru'l-Islam was the source of this contact, it naturally became the basis for this connection.[78]

Before they were introduced by Chaudhri Niyaz 'Ali in Lahore, Iqbal had met Mawdudi once, in 1929 in Hyderabad where he was lecturing. He was later to know of Mawdudi through his *Al-Jihad fi'l-Islam* and through the *Tarjuman,* which Iqbal regularly received,[79] but there is no evidence that Iqbal was particularly enthralled by Mawdudi's revivalist agenda.

Jama'at-i Islami leaders claimed a connection on the grounds that Daru'l-Islam had been Iqbal's brainchild[80] and that Mawdudi referred to Iqbal as his "spiritual guide"[81] and the patron of and participant in his movement: "But alas! He [Iqbal] was the in last days of his life," Mawdudi later wrote. "The very next month [after Mawdudi came to Pathankot] he breathed his last, and I was left alone for the uphill task we had decided to undertake jointly."[82] In fact, privately Mawdudi limited the scope of Iqbal's influence, arguing that "the commonality of views between 'Allamah Iqbal and me are limited to our belief that Islamic law should underlie the revival of our religion; my thoughts and intellectual probing are my own."[83] Iqbal did not conceive of the Daru'l-Islam project as it eventually unfolded, and Mawdudi was not Iqbal's choice to lead it. Even after the two met again in 1937, Iqbal's opinion of Mawdudi was guarded. Mian Muhammad Shafi', Iqbal's secretary, recollected that he referred to Mawdudi as "just a mullah [low-ranking cleric],"[84] someone more suited to lead the prayers at the Badshahi mosque than to oversee a pioneering educational project.

When Daru'l-Islam began, it had a staff of some twelve people, not the educated leaders that Iqbal had intended (besides Mawdudi only four other educated men were involved), but mainly people from nearby towns and villages.[85] No person of consequence joined. When on April 21, 1938, Iqbal died, Mawdudi was greatly dismayed, but at least Iqbal's death freed him from the restrictions to which he had acceded in Lahore.[86]

When Mawdudi began, he was full of enthusiasm. He had set out to train a cadre of men who would be able to operate in the political arena, yet remain aware of their religious loyalties.[87] Mistri Muhammad Siddiq, who had been an associate of Abu'l-Kalam Azad, and had in fact been sent to Punjab on Azad's behalf to obtain *bai'ahs* in support of his plans to become the Amiru'l-Hind (leader of India's Muslims), was politically motivated and experienced in organization. Mawdudi's belief that the political failures of the Muslims in the past was due to their lack of organization and his conviction that organizations were essential to the success of any future Muslim political endeavors can be traced to Siddiq's company at this time.[88] In general, however, Mawdudi's coterie at Pathankot was limited when it came to establishing either an educational institution or a political movement. Daru'l-Islam therefore increasingly took the shape of an experiment at constructing an *ummah* (holy community), and even that was a Herculean task.[89] In July 1938, Mawdudi wrote that the project at Pathankot had been named Daru'l-Islam because its objective was to make India the *daru'l-Islam* and that Pathankot was the "nerve center" of the Muslim revival in India.[90] Mawdudi's agenda had found a manifestation and his political ambitions were now expressed more openly. This shift from ideas to practice had a cathartic impact on Mawdudi. For one thing, it forced him to resolve the contradiction between his prescriptions and his own behavior. His beard began to grow, and his conduct corresponded more exactly to his public pronouncements.

Daru'l-Islam was to provide the Muslim community of India with its leaders and to serve as the foundation for a genuine religious movement of political deliverance.[91] The project at Pathankot was to be both an intellectual and political force and an ideal Muslim community whose example would revolutionize Indian politics. In October 1938, Mawdudi wrote of his plans for Daru'l-Islam to forty of his peers and mentors, seeking their opinion and inviting them to join his cause.[92] Among them were the renowned Islamic scholars 'Abdu'l-Majid Daryabadi, Manazir Ahsan Gilani, and Zafaru'l-Hasan, along with some of India's most prominent ulama, Sayyid Sulaiman Nadwi, Mufti Kifayatu'llah, and Mawlana Ahmad Sa'id. Muhammad Manzur Nu'mani and Amin Ahsan Islahi were among the religious leaders who later joined the Jama'at-i Islami. Islahi was the editor of *Al-Islah* of Sara'i-i Mir; Nu'mani was then, and continues to be, the editor of *Al-Furqan* of Lucknow. Also included were Chaudhri Niyaz 'Ali, who was the patron of Daru'l-Islam, and Chaudhri Ghulam Ahmad Parwez, who was to become one of Muslim India's—and later Pakistan's—most controversial religious thinkers.[93] Zafaru'l-Hasan, Daryabadi, and Parwez responded, and eleven of the forty visited Mawdudi at Pathankot between October 14 and 16, 1938.[94] Manzur Nu'mani was among the participants. He recalled that at the time he did not find Mawdudi complying with the "pure Islamic way of life" and therefore did not join Daru'l-Islam. Mawdudi did listen to Nu'mani's criticism—a rare occurrence in his life—and promised that he would soon fully abide by the *shari'ah*.[95] Muhammad Asad, the Austrian scholar of Islam, also came to engage Mawdudi and Islahi in debate.[96] In October 1938, Mawdudi began to organize the Pathankot community. He divided it into categories of *rukn* (member), *shura'* (a consultative body consisting of five men), and *sadr* (president), who was to be Mawdudi himself. This tripartite organization was to serve as the basis for that of the Jama'at-i Islami.

Mawdudi then began preparing books and pamphlets to propagate his views and his project and to encourage people to join the Daru'l-Islam. These works, along with publications of Daru'l-Islam, were sent to all the major Muslim educational centers of India: Aligarh University, Deoband Daru'l-'Ulum, Jami'ah-i Milliyah University, Nadwatu'l-'Ulama, and Madrasatu'l-Islah.[97] Thus began the systematic propagation and dissemination of textual material that would help institutionalize Mawdudi's view of Muslim identity and his "imagined community"—the Islamic state—and plant them in the intellectual life of Indian Muslims.[98] He also continued to write on political issues in the *Tarjuman*.

To promote organized Muslim political activity and train leaders for his community, Mawdudi's attention had by this time turned from the Congress party to the Muslim League, from the enemy without to the rival within. Mawdudi opposed the league, though not yet on clear grounds; he simply did not like the pro-British and Westernized Muslims who constituted its intellectual and political leadership. After Mawdudi's turn to revivalism in 1932 and the league's growth in importance after 1937, his clash with it was in many ways unavoidable.[99]

Mawdudi's outspoken criticism of the Muslim League soon precipitated a disagreement between him and Chaudhri Niyaz 'Ali, a fervent Muslim Leaguer who was not happy with the increasing politicization of Daru'l-Islam. He told Mawdudi that his frequent use of the term *Islami hukumat* (Islamic government) in his discussions of Daru'l-Islam violated their original agreement,[100] and he sought to curb Mawdudi's politics and his anti-league activism by appealing to the trustees of the *waqf*, reminding them of Daru'l-Islam's apolitical purposes and Iqbal's specific instructions regarding the institution's educational objectives.[101] The trustees sided with Niyaz 'Ali and declared that Mawdudi had violated his own agreements with Iqbal and the *waqf*'s trustees. Mawdudi remained defiant, declaring that separation of religion from politics had no place in Islam and that if Niyaz 'Ali wished to distinguish between the two he should remove the title "Islamic" from his *waqf* and call it instead the "Niyaz 'Ali Trust."[102] Mawdudi in effect acknowledged his deviation from the original agreement but refused to acquiesce to Niyaz 'Ali's interference with his running of Daru'l-Islam and to restrict his activities in any fashion. Despite Mistri Muhammad Siddiq's intercession, this soon led to a confrontation between Mawdudi and Niyaz 'Ali. The members of the Daru'l-Islam sided with Mawdudi and voted to confirm him *sadr* and to move Daru'l-Islam elsewhere.[103] Consequently, in January 1939, Mawdudi resigned from his position in the *waqf* and left Pathankot for Lahore.[104]

Organizational Solution: The Jama'at-i Islami

In Lahore, Daru'l-Islam's existence was nominal but its spirit became reinvigorated. At first, Mawdudi and his followers from Pathankot collected money to reestablish Daru'l-Islam, but once in Lahore, a major metropolitan center with a large Muslim community, Mawdudi became more intensely political. Mawdudi, wrote Nu'mani, viewed the crisis before the Muslims as too acute to await long-term solutions; he hence saw no point in pursuing a cumbersome educational project at that time.[105] He became noticeably keener on organizational matters and increasingly interested in creating a *jama'at* (party).[106] Early in 1939 he had traveled to Mewat to observe the working of the Tablighi Jama'at,[107] where he met its founder, Mawlana Muhammad Iliyas (1885–1944).[108] Mawdudi was very impressed with Iliyas's work and his efforts to revive Islam and promote an Islamic order in Mewat. He prefaced his account of the trip by lamenting the fall of Islam and the deplorable decline of Islamic observance in Delhi. Contrasting this account of the fate of Islam in Delhi with the revival in Mewat, Mawdudi hailed Iliyas as the heir to Shaikh Ahmad Sirhindi and Sayyid Ahmad Shahid, both important figures in the tradition of revival and reform of Indian Islam.[109] Still, he was of the belief that more was needed. There were sociopolitical issues that required the efforts of a hierarchical organization. The Tablighi Jama'at could not serve that end; it was only a beginning, one that Mawdudi intended to improve.

Mawdudi was not the only one to consider forming a party; it was the subject of discussion among many Muslim leaders in Lahore.[110] It is evident that to give Muslims a new identity, to construct the Islamic state, and to define and realize the full potential of his authority, Mawdudi would have to find an organizational expression. In Punjab, Ahmadis, Hindus, and Sikhs had all organized by then, but Muslims had formed no notable organizations.[111] A new Muslim organization would level the playing field between communal rivals.

In the meantime, he continued his incessant fulminations against the Muslim League in the *Tarjuman*; they were published as the second and third volumes of *Musalman awr mawjudah siyasi kashmakash* in 1939 and 1940.[112] He also began to elaborate on his notion of *iqamat-i din* (establishment of a religious order) and to attack colonialism, which soon landed him in trouble with the provincial authorities, who censored the *Tarjuman* when it attacked the British directly. In September, he accepted a teaching position at Lahore's Islamiyah College but, wary of his experience with Niyaz 'Ali, refused to accept a salary.[113] His openly political lectures soon led the Punjab government to push the college's administration to dismiss him. Mawdudi refused to bend and left the college in the summer of 1940. This experience convinced him that the work of Islamic *da'wah* could not succeed as long as the political establishment was hostile to it; from that point onward, he believed that the fate of Islamic *da'wah* and the control of the centers of power were interdependent.

Mawdudi now began to work actively toward creating a Muslim political organization. He wrote and traveled extensively during this period, delivering numerous lectures on the relation of Islam to politics, some of which were later collected and published.[114] During these peregrinations, he spoke to Muslim intellectuals and visited such educational institutions as the Aligarh University, the Muslim Anglo-Oriental College of Amritsar, Islamiyah College of Peshawar, and Nadwatu'l-'Ulama in Lucknow, where in addition to articulating his political concerns he criticized the educational system, especially the absence of links between traditional and modern educational methods and subjects of study.[115]

Still opposed to the Muslim League and aware that no viable alternatives had surfaced, Mawdudi believed that the establishment of a new party was a prerequisite to a successful movement of *tajdid* (renewal of Islam).[116] A new and even somewhat modernized *tajdid* effort supported by an organization created and led by him would put him in a position of authority and give him wide-ranging powers. It can be argued that his ambitions in this regard actually superseded his concern for founding an organization that would remedy the problems of the Muslims of India. In August 1940, Mawdudi wrote to Abu'l-Hasan 'Ali Nadwi at the Nadwatu'l-'Ulama of Lucknow, requesting the services of an Arabist to translate his writings on *iqamat-i din* for the benefit of the Arab world.[117] Mawdudi's authority was tied to the power and reach of texts, for, as he put it, "there should be a literary force to mould the mind of the people on the pattern of Islam. There should be an organizational force to unite workers [who] may have accepted the literary force. Third [there] should be a moral force to put a check on any wrong activities of people."[118]

His high opinion of his own abilities seemed to be confirmed by the approval with which his works were received. Sayyid Sulaiman Nadwi was impressed with Mawdudi's 1939 *Tanqihat* (Inquiries); the famous Khilafat activist 'Ubaidu'llah Sindhi approved his articles in the *Tarjuman*.[119] Such accolades also encouraged him to air his views more directly and announce his plans more openly.

His organizational ideas were influenced by what he thought the Muslim League was doing wrong.[120] In a letter to Zafaru'l-Hasan, he complained of its failure to resolve the problems before Indian Muslims. The organization he had in mind would "serve as a 'rear guard' [the term was written in Latin letters] to the Muslim League."[121] The league was Mawdudi's bugbear and, as such, an important influence on his views. So was its leader, Muhammad 'Ali Jinnah (d. 1948), whom Mawdudi viewed as a rival in his drive to win over Muslims.

He was drawn into politics by Jinnah's example.[122] Mawdudi believed that Jinnah's popularity emanated from his appeal to Islamic symbols. If a secular Muslim could sway the masses in the name of Islam, surely Mawdudi could, and ought to, do better. Leadership in the Muslim community would be meaningful only if it was tied to the very roots of the community, Islam. He rejected appealing to the leadership of the *ashraf* (nobility) and the wealthy, although at the time privileged descent, wealth, and landed status were transformed to serve as the basis for the leadership of the Pakistan movement and the future Muslim state.[123]

This all showed that Muslim communalism/nationalism, although then associated solely with the Muslim League, was not a monolithic force: There were other competing versions of the Muslim nation. Mawdudi's version was by no means the dominant one but was and continues to be influential. This in part explains the depth and breadth of the Jama'at's rivalry with the founders of Pakistan.

The Jama'at-i Islami was finally established in August 1941 in Lahore, and from the very beginning, it was the platform for Mawdudi's ideas. Especially after the founding of Pakistan six years later, Mawdudi's career as an ideologue ended. His most important and influential works had been published by this time (nineteen of his most noted works on *tabligh*—propagation of religious doctrine—were written between 1933 and 1941)[124] and the years that followed would be dedicated to politics. By then his ideas had already found a niche in contemporary Islamic thought in South Asia and across the Muslim world.

The Pakistan Years: 1947–1979

Following the founding of Pakistan in 1947, the Jama'at set a new course and Mawdudi's career underwent a fundamental change. The party was caught up in the turbulance that followed the partition and soon found itself involved in politics. Mawdudi became more and more a politician and less and less an ideologue and a scholar, and the Jama'at changed from a religious movement to a political party. The Pakistan years were therefore not a time of great intellectual activity for the Jama'at. In Pakistan, Mawdudi and the Jama'at would leave their mark as political actors.[125]

In 1947 the Jama'at was split into Indian and Pakistani units. Along with the majority of its members, Mawdudi opted for Pakistan. The Jama'at-i Islami of India continued to function under an independent leadership but remained close to Mawdudi's works. At first Mawdudi had intended to educate the population in their religious obligations and convince them of the hollowness of the Muslim League's agenda. He expected that the Jama'at would inherit Pakistan once the people who had been moved by Islam to create a country would hear and understand his ideas. As a result, the Jama'at remained anti-state in these first years. It was intent on manipulating the country's susceptibility to religious activism to push it toward Islamization. It sought to preserve the place of Islam in society and politics, while it trained an Islamic vanguard who would oversee the revival of Islam at the national level and would cultivate support for its cause.

The party soon developed a tightly knit and well-structured network of activists and sympathizers not only to propagate Mawdudi's views but also to enable the party to project power in the political arena. It put forward a program in which political realities and social concerns found meaning in the context of its greater emphasis on the renewal and reform of Islam.

Although antagonistic toward traditional Islam, Mawdudi and the Jama'at quickly closed ranks with the ulama and other Islamic groups in demanding an Islamic constitution for Pakistan.[126] The Jama'at's ideas and policy positions defined the demands of the Islamic alliance and featured prominently in the debates between the government and the religious divines and parties from 1947 to 1956, when the country's first constitution was promulgated. For example, Mawdudi's demands as voiced by the ulama were clearly reflected in the Objectives Resolution of 1949, which outlined the government's aim with regard to the constitution. The Jama'at's activism in these years, especially given its anti-state posture, eventually culminated in an open confrontation with the government over the role of religion in politics.

After Pakistan's independence, the Jama'at forbade Pakistanis to take an oath of allegiance to the state until it became Islamic, arguing that a Muslim could in clear conscience render allegiance only to God.[127] The government was troubled by the Jama'at's challenges to its legitimacy, all the more so when they involved foreign affairs. In 1948, although officially observing a cease-fire with India, Pakistan resumed support of the insurgents in Kashmir by dispatching armed paramilitary units. The government had found a way to support such a move by calling the conflict a jihad. Mawdudi undermined these efforts by arguing that vigilante groups organized by the government to conduct a covert war in Kashmir could not be fighting a jihad, nor could the government surreptitiously support a jihad while outwardly professing to observe a cease-fire. Jihad had to be properly declared by a government to justify a legitimate war; it could not be tainted by "hypocrisy." Mawdudi claimed that the government should either declare war with India over Kashmir or abide by the terms of the cease-fire to which it had agreed; covert war and diplomatic sleights of hand were not acceptable in Islam.[128] The government did not take kindly to Mawdudi's position and accused the Jama'at of pro-Indian sympathies and anti-Pakistan activities. Several Jama'at leaders, including Mawdudi, were jailed, and the party was charged with sedition, a charge hitherto leveled only against Communist organizations.[129]

While the government tried to turn the tables on the Jama'at, it was clear that Mawdudi had damaged its position by questioning the wisdom of its policy toward India over Kashmir, as well as revealing its susceptibility to criticism from the religious quarter. Moreover, the entire episode confirmed that the Jama'at had a place in Pakistan's politics and the constitutional debates in Karachi, which only served to increase the government's hostility to religious activism. Retaliation by the Pakistani government did not suppress the Jama'at, nor did it diminish Islam's role in Pakistan's politics. Even while in prison, Mawdudi continued his activities by mobilizing the ulama and various other religious groups to press the Constituent Assembly to move Pakistan in the direction of Islamization.

When Mawdudi was released from prison in 1950, the party successfully revived the Islamic alliance, further anchoring constitutional debates in Islam. In 1951, it took part for the first time in a provincial election but did not do well. The Jama'at was more successful in promoting its cause on the streets, and this continued to generate tensions with the government.

The elections also proved consequential by demonstrating that electoral politics can interfere with the pious activities of members and lead them into actions not in keeping with the party's moral standards. For that reason, a number of the Jama'at leaders suggested the party should withdraw from politics, and the shura' passed a resolution to that effect but Mawdudi opposed it. The tussle led to serious dissension in the ranks, and Mawdudi resigned from the Jama'at pending resolution of the dispute at an open party meeting. At that meeting, he strongly defended the party's newfound interest in the political process, thereby reorienting it away from its anti-state and revolutionary posture and toward national politics. Politicization both tamed the Jama'at and confirmed the primacy of politics in its agenda.[130]

Several Jama'at leaders left the party in protest. Following their departure, Mawdudi's position became stronger because he had won and had been able to secure the support of members. With those senior enough and willing to challenge him gone and the powers of the amir over the shura' established, the Jama'at became an extension of his person and a cult of personality began to grow up around him. As the Jama'at became more a political party than a religious movement, Mawdudi's style began to change from scholar to politician.

The tensions between the Jama'at and the government came to a head in the anti-Ahmadi agitations in Punjab in 1953 and 1954. In 1953, agitators organized and led by the ulama and other religious activists demanded that the government dismiss Zafaru'llah Khan, Pakistan's Ahmadi foreign minister, and declare the Ahmadis to be a non-Muslim minority.[131] Passing these measures, the agitators argued, would serve as a litmus test demonstrating the government's commitment to Islam. Although these agitations were led by the ulama and religious groups such as the Anjuman-i Ahrar-i Islam (Society of Free Muslims), the Jama'at provided them with convincing justifications, especially in the form of a book called *Qadiyani mas'alah* (The Ahmadi question). In fact, the government viewed the Jama'at's support with greater alarm and as more invidious than the provocative activities of the Ahrar.[132] As a result, once the government clamped down on the agitiators, Mawdudi and a number of prominent Jama'at leaders were apprehended and put on trial. Mawdudi was found guilty of sedition by a military tribunal and sentenced to death; that sentence was later commuted by a civilian court to fourteen years in prison, and the verdict was eventually reversed by the country's supreme court in 1955.[133]

By pitting the Jama'at against the state over a popular cause, the anti-Ahmadi issue enhanced the party's political standing and following. Moreover, the agitations placed Islam more squarely at the center of the constitutional debates regarding the nature of the Pakistani state, all to the Jama'at's advantage. As a result, the Jama'at used its growing power to exert renewed pressure on the government, this time about the issue of the Constitution of 1956.

By the time the anti-Ahmadi issue was over, it had become clear that, despite the government's swift reactions, the Jama'at had successfully anchored national politics in the concern for the Islamicity of the state and convinced Pakistanis of Mawdudi's view of how to frame key questions about the role of Islam in the state. This was reflected in the final shape of the Constitution of 1956, which accommodated many of the demands of the Jama'at and its allies. Mawdudi was involved in drafting that constitution by his long-time friend Chaudhri Muhammad 'Ali, who was prime minister at the time.[134] Muhammad 'Ali had pushed for accommodation of Islamic groups despite his own precarious position and the objections of the secular elite led by the president, General Iskandar Mirza.[135] Aware of the opposition of the secularists, Mawdudi lost no time in endorsing the constitution and claiming victory for Islam, although some aspects of the document had been opposed by the Jama'at earlier. He was also instrumental in convincing the ulama to accept the new constitution as Islamic, thus precluding widespread opposition to it. The Islamic groups, led by the Jama'at, then concentrated their energies on pushing for the Islamization of state institutions.[136]

Acceptance of the constitution as Islamic paved the way for the Jama'at to become a full-fledged political party. In 1957, despite reservations in some quarters within the party, Mawdudi directed the Jama'at to participate in the national elections of 1958. The constitutional victory was short-lived, however. The armed forces of Pakistan, under the command of General Muhammad Ayub Khan (d. 1969), and with a modernizing agenda that opposed the encroachment of religion into politics, assumed power in 1958 and shelved the constitution.

Over the course of the following decade, the political establishment was dominated by the military and bureaucratic elite, who actively promoted Islamic modernism as a way of undermining the Jama'at and its allies; they appropriated the right to interpret Islam and slowed the drive for the Islamization of the country. Advocates of Islamic revivalism and an Islamic state were increasingly pressed into retreat. The Jama'at's offices were closed down and funds were confiscated; its leaders were excoriated in government-sponsored publications; and its activities, publications, networks, and operations were curtailed. Mawdudi himself survived an attempt on his life (which led to the death of a Jama'at worker) during a party meeting in 1963 and was imprisoned twice (in 1964 and in 1967) during Ayub Khan's rule. The government had launched an offensive against religious activism with the hope of freeing Pakistan and Ayub's modernization schemes from Islamic opposition.

Unable to advocate the cause of Islam in the political arena, the Jama'at turned to the task of removing Ayub Khan and restoring a political climate that would be conducive to religious activism. The Jama'at's experiences with Ayub Khan's government led them to look for new allies outside the circle of Islamic revivalists. Consequently, the Jama'at joined an alliance of secular political parties that advocated restoration of democracy and putting an end to Ayub Khan's hegemony of power in Pakistan. The Jama'at even went as far as supporting the anti-Ayub candidacy of Fatimah Jinnah in the presidential elections of 1965, an endorsement that ran counter to Mawdudi's views on the social role of women.

In any case Ayub Khan had not been entirely successful in marginalizing the Jama'at and was on occasion even compelled to temper his opposition to Islamic activism. As Pakistan faced numerous crises, its leaders and people turned more and more to Islam. At times, its government found itself beholden to those like Mawdudi who mobilized Islam and made its power available to the state. For example, in 1965 Ayub Khan—hitherto one of the Jama'at's most determined enemies—publicly appealed to Mawdudi for support in his war against India by declaring a jihad.[137] However, instances of government conciliation were rare, and, for the most part, Mawdudi and the Jama'at were kept under pressure,[138] which only politicized the party further. The result was clear in the Jama'at's policies in the post-Ayub period. In 1970 it participated in national elections with the aim of capturing power. Mawdudi toured the country, campaigning as Pakistan's new leader in waiting. The Jama'at fielded 151 candidates to contest the majority of the seats in the National Assembly, but the party's hopes were dashed when it won only four seats in the National Assembly and four seats in various provincial assemblies. In 1971, the Jama'at responded to the advent of civil war in East Pakistan by mobilizing its resources in defense of the government and by joining the conflict to prevent East Pakistan from becoming Bangladesh.

After the elections of 1970, Mawdudi developed second thoughts about the path he had chosen for the Jama'at. Participation in the political process had exacted a cost. The party had lost it innocence and had found itself in compromising moral dilemmas, most notably the rising number of violent incidents involving the Jama'at's student wing. The party had not been compensated for this moral loss with electoral victories. Politics had proven to be a dangerous gambit that Mawdudi was hesitant to pursue further. In 1975, he advised the Jama'at's *shura'* to reassess the party's course of action and to opt out of politics,[139] but by then the party was far too politicized to follow his counsel. By some accounts, Mawdudi was disappointed with what he had created: "If I had the stamina I would start all over again,"[140] he told his wife. To another friend he commented, "When historians write of the Jama'at, they will say it was yet another *tajdid* movement that rose and fell."[141]

The secession of East Pakistan and the rise of Zulfiqar 'Ali Bhutto (d. 1979) to power in 1971 intensified the Jama'at's political activism. The socialism of the Pakistan People's Party was particularly objectionable to the Jama'at, and this pushed it into action. Viewing Bhutto's populism as a direct challenge to the Islamic foundations of Pakistan and to its place in the country's political order, the party confronted the government on numerous occasions, most notably during the movement for nonrecognition of Bangladesh during 1972–1974 and the renewed anti-Ahmadi disturbances of 1974.[142]

Throughout the Bhutto years, the Jama'at spearheaded a political movement that appealed to religious sentiments with a view to weakening the Bhutto regime.[143] Whereas the opposition to Ayub Khan had brought Islamic groups into an alliance for democracy, opposition to Bhutto brought disparate parties, secular as well as Islamic, together under the banner of Islam. The Jama'at's program proved instrumental in giving shape to this alliance—the Nizam-i

Mustafa (Order of the Prophet) movement—and in managing its nationwide agitations. The struggle against Bhutto greatly bolstered the Jama'at's popular standing. In the elections of 1977, widely believed to have been rigged to favor Bhutto, the opposition won thirty-six seats, nine of which were won by Jama'at candidates. During the subsequent antigovernment protests, the party's popularity soared.[144] Both the Jama'at and the movement it led eventually undermined the Bhutto government and in July 1977 provoked a military coup. Mawdudi played an important role in that opposition. He had stepped down as amir of the Jama'at in 1972, but in 1977, with his successor in prison and Pakistan in the throes of a national crisis, Mawdudi returned to center stage. He became the de facto leader of the opposition to Bhutto's premiership. When on April 16, 1977, Bhutto decided to diffuse tensions and break the political impasse, he showed up at Mawdudi's house for consultations,[145] and before the National Assembly he referred to Mawdudi as the brain behind the opposition to his government.[146]

Because Islamic slogans proved so efficacious in galvanizing the opposition to Bhutto, after his fall from power, they became the basis for the new regime's program. The cause of the opposition, now enjoying widescale popularity, could not be ignored by the administration of General Muhammad Zia ul-Haq (d. 1988), who in his search to legitimize his military government was quick to appease the anti-Bhutto Nizam-i Mustafa movement. Zia accorded Mawdudi the status of a senior statesman, sought his advice, and allowed his words to adorn the front pages of the newspapers. Mawdudi proved receptive to Zia's overtures and supported his decision to execute Bhutto.[147] He also supported the military regime by approving the general's Islamization initiatives.[148] In Zia's regime, Mawdudi saw not only a breath of fresh air for the Jama'at— access to power and more room to maneuver—but also the possibility of realizing his vision: creation of a true Islamic state in Pakistan. This possibility became all the more real when in 1979 Ayatollah Khomeini carried out in Iran what Mawdudi had argued was feasible in Pakistan and had been the first to promise to do. He did not live to see where Khomeini's and Zia's experiments would lead.

In April 1979, Mawdudi's long-time kidney ailment worsened; by then he also had heart problems. He went to the United States for treatment and was hospitalized in Buffalo, New York, where his second son worked as a physician. Whatever his medical experience there, his time in Buffalo was intellectually productive. He spent many hours reviewing Western works on the life of the Prophet and meeting with Muslim leaders, their followers, and wellwishers.[149] Following a number of operations, he died there on September 22, 1979, at the age seventy-six. His funeral was in Buffalo, but he was buried in an unmarked grave in his garden in Lahore after a large funeral procession through the city.[150]

II

ISLAM
REINTERPRETED

If I had a hand in the universe like God;
I would remove it altogether.
I would create it anew so that,
to the free-spirited fulfillment would come easily.

Omar Khayyam

3

Faith and Ideology

The development of the Jama'at-i Islami and the success of Islamic revivalism depended in part on Mawdudi's ability to articulate his political program effectively. His writings disseminated his ideas far and wide, cultivating a following for his views, particularly among the educated, and placing his arguments at the center of Muslim intellectual and political debate. For his followers, these texts became the principal means of learning about Islam, distinguishing them from other Muslims, and defining the party. Given the pivotal role his writings played in spreading the revivalist interpretation of Islam and defining the Jama'at, it is important to know their general thrust.

Mawdudi's ideas were formulated at a time of colonial retreat and the rise of Indian national consciousness. Although they addressed political concerns, they were essentially cultural in orientation and divorced from socioeconomic considerations, which stands in sharp contrast, for example, to the case of Ayatollah Khomeini and Iran. Mawdudi's ideas emerged in response to problems that were intrinsic to a process of cultural and communal reassertion: first in debate with the colonial order and eventually in response to the ineluctable ascendancy of Hinduism in India.[1]

Although aware of the economic impact of imperialism on India,[2] Mawdudi did not view imperialism in Hobsonian terms. The problem with imperialism, which in Mawdudi's view had produced and hence encompassed the menace of Hinduism, was essentially cultural. Its evil lay in the propagation of such moral and ethical evils as women's emancipation, secularism, and nationalism, all of which ran contrary to the teachings of Islam and had caused them to be ignored or rejected. Undermining Islamic culture in India had in turn engendered Muslim's economic and political marginalization. He drew on conflicts in the Indian social context but gave them meaning in a more general framework—relations between Islam and the West. The revivalist response, which the two-fold problem of imperialism and Hindu ascendancy elicited from Mawdudi, was divorced from the kind of economic determinism associated with the emergence and unfolding of similar social movements. He worried less about economic liberation than about preserving dress, language, and customs, for they were essential to safeguarding Muslim culture. Mawdudi's expositions on Islamic revolution, state, and economics attested to the central role played by the drive for cultural authenticity, what he termed "intellectual independence"[3] (and his long time follower, Khurshid Ahmad, referred to as "intellectual decolonization"[4]) in the face of challenges from the colonial government and the Hindus. Having identified the problems, he described a solution that made sense by placing the problems in the context of larger issues and universal concerns. Whether or not he was successful is open to question: his transformation of Islamic life and thought into something altogether new is still not complete.

Mawdudi began by redefining a Muslim, providing Muslims with a new identity that would remove them from the colonial normative order and distinguish them from the emerging Indian one.[5] This redefinition was supposed to change Muslim popular values and lay the foundations for the type of collective action that would preclude a secular Indian identity and would strengthen communalist feelings.[6] The need to redefine a Muslim was born from Mawdudi's understanding of the structure of relations among Islam, Hinduism, and the West, and his desire to provide power and identity to Muslims by reversing the balance in relations between Islam and the other two.[7] Mawdudi went even further. He defined a Muslim in terms of differences from Hindus and Westerners, but, in doing so, he used ideas from the intellectual repertoire of the West, a tendency characteristic of movements that encounter ideas they regard as superior to their own.[8] Such a reaction is no doubt shaped by the relationship of power implicit in the perceptions of inferiority and superiority that produce the resentment. Whether the result of this reaction is viable hinges on the extent to which it resolves the feelings of inferiority and dissipates the resentment. If it is too great, the reaction will remain focused on those attributes that seem to determine the superiority of the other and will be shaped by its values. Hence, for Mawdudi,

> Islam was a "revolutionary ideology" and a "dynamic movement", the *Jama'at-e-Islami*, was a "party", the *Shari'ah* a complete "code" in Islam's "total scheme of life". His enthusiasm [for Western idioms and concepts] was infectious among those who admired him, encouraging them to implement in Pakistan all his "manifestoes", "programmes" and "schemes", to usher in a true Islamic "renaissance".[9]

To debate effectively with "modernity," Mawdudi had to accept many modernist assumptions, especially those involving scientific truths, which he saw as value neutral.[10] His views also involved a process of modernization, but under the guise and in the name of Islam. This modernizing impetus of Islamic revivalism was not limited to the use of tape recorders, facsimile machines, and other instruments of the modern world, as some observers of this phenomenon have contended,[11] but encompassed values, ideas, and institutions.[12] Revivalists are not only moderns but modernists.[13] He characterized his efforts in the following terms:

> We aspire for Islamic renaissance on the basis of the Qur'an. To us the Qur'anic spirit and Islamic tenets are immutable; but the application of this spirit in the realm of practical life must always vary with the change of conditions and increase of knowledge. . . . Our way is quite different both from the Muslim scholar of the recent past and modern Europeanized stock. On the one hand we have to imbibe exactly the Qur'anic spirit and identify our outlook with the Islamic tenets while, on the other, we have to assess thoroughly the developments in the field of knowledge and changes in conditions of life that have been brought during the last eight hundred years; and third, we have to arrange these ideas and laws of life on genuine Islamic lines so that Islam should once again become a dynamic force; the leader of the world rather than its follower.[14]

Mawdudi redefined being a Muslim to mean more than just following Islam; a Muslim was a modern creature with modern social links, political aspirations, and, ultimately, cultural outlook.

The directives and dynamics of this process of redefinition were present in Mawdudi's own political education and understanding of the political exigencies before his community. As a veteran of the Khilafat movement, Mawdudi was concerned with reestablishing the boundaries of the Muslim community to preclude the possibility of encroachment into its social and political life from the Hindu culture as well as the colonial one.[15] To do this, he revised the structure of relations between Islam and Hinduism and between Islam and the West.[16]

The erection of communal boundaries and the search for identity in Mawdudi's works increasingly cast the world in terms of good and evil, converting history into an arena for an apocalyptic battle between the two. In political terms, this meant both the rejection of British rule in India and the rejection of its replacement with any form of Hindu rule. In intellectual and ideological terms, the necessity of a reign of virtue—an Islamic order—set Mawdudi on a search for the means to reorganize Muslim society and imagine it anew. To do this, Mawdudi, as an intellectual who was not all that firmly rooted in tradition and who was in addition enamored of the achievements of the West, borrowed directly from the very culture he sought to evict from Muslim lands. The West provided a display of power in the modern world and hence could be emulated. This would take place within an Islamic framework based on a romantic view of the past. The result would be a uniform view of the objectives of the Muslim community, the task before it, and the role of the individual Muslims therein. Mawdudi's central concern was the restitution of power in Muslim society, so power was what related the ideal of the past to the reality of the modern West and made easier the infusion of the values of the West into the definition of Islam. Modernism was the path on which Muslims would be able to repeat the glories of the past. Mawdudi's ideal was in the *image* of the past but in the *nature* of the modern world.[17] In this view, Islamic revival had an atavist veneer. It was essentially a political struggle that could succeed only if its modernizing impulse refashioned Muslim life and thought. Mawdudi's binary vision—dividing the world into Islam and "un-Islam"—often obfuscated the intrusion of the culture of the "other" into the redefinition of the "us." Mawdudi's ideal Islamic order was far more tolerant of Western values, ideals, and institutions than his rejectionist rhetoric has suggested. This is an important aspect of Mawdudi's contribution to contemporary Islamic thought because it sets him apart from those who wish to simply reform Islam, and it sets the Jama'at apart from those forms of Islamic revivalism that pit Islam against modernization.

Islamic revivalism is usually thought to be a reaction to changes in the pattern of social interactions that followed modernization. Where these changes have produced limitations on cultural expression, they have resulted in feelings of anomie among those who have been exposed to modern society's working but have not as yet been fully assimilated into its structure. These Muslims believe that returning to traditional modes of social organization will allow them greater cultural expression and solve their predicament.[18] In these cases, Islamic revivalism is often the cultural and political manifestation of groping for the solace of the traditional order. Mawdudi was not concerned with the psychological impact of modernization. On the contrary, he considered traditional Islam to be the shackles that bound Muslims to an anachronistic existence in the modern world. Rather than consoling his community's anxieties about the dehumanizing nature of modern society, he fervently advocated the adoption of modern social thought and organization; failure to do this lay at the root of the political and economic weakness of Muslims. Maryam Jameelah, one of Mawdudi's most influential disciples, characterized Mawdudi's approach in the following terms: "We Muslims are therefore determined to make full use of modern knowledge but for our own purposes which will be in conformity to our cultural values and ideals."[19] Mawdudi did not masquerade modern ideas behind an Islamic veneer; he interpreted and assimilated the foundations of modern thought and social organization into an essentially new and integrated perspective. A change in the balance of power between Islam and the West was to come about through a revitalization of Muslim religious and cultural livelihood combined with assimilation of modern ideas into the structure of Islamic thought. Revivalism would be a vehicle for modernization of Islam and in turn would bring about and sustain a new Islamic order.

His opposition to things Western was manifest only when Western ideas came to Muslims through Western media and had the effect of subjugating Muslims to the political writ of the West: "The approach of the Islamic movement is to . . . modernize without compromising on Islamic principles and values. . . . It says 'yes' to modernization but 'no' to blind Westernization."[20] He saw modern ideas as universal truths to be distinguished from Western ones. He was unconcerned with the positivist philosophical underpinnings of modern science, seeing no problems in the coexistence of faith and modern scientific thought.[21] Once science, value neutral as Mawdudi assumed it was, became infused with Islamic ethics, it would readily turn into an "Islamic" scientific corpus: "even a bulldozer or computer would be 'Islamic' if used in the path of God."[22] This attitude was reflected in Mawdudi's response to a query regarding the use of loudspeakers at religious gatherings; technology and invention, he said, were "pure" in origin, only the way "Western rebellious civilization" has used them is "impure."[23]

According to Mawdudi, modern science was not based on any particular philosophical perspective, nor did it promote a set of values or require an attitude from Muslims that could interfere with their faith. Modern science as a "body" that could accommodate any "spirit"—philosophy or value system—just as a radio could broadcast Islamic or Western messages with equal facility.[24]

This idea did more to modernize the Islamic worldview than it did to Islamize modern science: "The process of 'wahy' or revelation might puzzle some persons, but there is nothing improbable therein. If we can communicate with one another through a long distance in no time, a process of communication with the invisible cannot be ruled out."[25] Faith was therefore not simply inductive; it could be deduced using scientific principles. The rejection of Western culture while appropriating its tools of progress was the cornerstone of Islamic revival. Although the two had different aims, little separated Mawdudi's position from that of the Islamic modernists.[26] He sought to appropriate modern scientific thought and Islamize it; they accepted modern scientific thought and attempted to interpret Islam according to it. The modernists wanted to modernize Islam whereas Mawdudi wanted to also Islamize modernity. The distinction was enough to permit Mawdudi to inveigh against his modernist rivals.[27]

It was with a view to assimilating the "pure" scientific truths, one of the most important of which was a modern conception of social organization, that he excoriated traditional Islam and its values, mores, and fractious institutional structure as retrogressive in spirit and the root cause of the plight of Islam.[28] Mawdudi therefore sought to modernize Islam (free of Westernism), to restructure its doctrines by consolidating his own syllogistic and rational reading of Islam into a coherent corpus of thought, to create a homogeneous Muslim community capable of united political action, and to gain access to the source of power that was available to the West and had once been a hallmark of Islamic history. Whereas revivalism elsewhere had been concerned with restoring the dignity of the individual before the dehumanizing edifice of modern society, Mawdudi was keen to erect exactly one such society so as to streamline Islamic culture and, hence, to concentrate the energies of Muslim faith on gaining worldly power and glory.

Need for Islamic Revival

Mawdudi spoke to the profound intellectual perplexity and political anxiety that was evident among the Muslims of India during the twilight of the British Raj. The source of that malady—loss of ground to the Hindus—lay, he thought, with relations between Islam and the colonial culture, which, he argued, had decided the distribution of power in Indian society. It was for this reason that, although the apprehension with which Muslims viewed the ascendance of the Hindu community informed Mawdudi's works with a sense of urgency, his discourse remained focused on freeing Muslims from colonial influence. The cultural imprint of the West was too pervasive to allow his attention to be diverted from it for long. It was Western thought and values that sustained the Hindu drive for power under the guise of Indian nationalism. In addition, loss of ground to the Hindu community followed loss of ground to the West and was therefore a product of it, especially in that the colonial patronage of the Hindus since 1857 had empowered the Hindu community. The Hindu challenge was merely a by-product of the "fall of Islam." Restoration of Muslim power in India could only follow a change in the balance of relations between Islam and the West.

Hinduism also had no intellectual allure; Mawdudi regarded it as a sociopolitical force rather than a culture. He saw no intellectual challenge in Hinduism as he understood it, nor did he believe that Hinduism as a religion had anything to do with the appeal of Indian nationalism. Mawdudi believed that once Muslims followed the true teachings of Islam they would become immune to the lure of Western thought as it was reflected in Indian nationalism. The inevitable rise of Islam would check and subdue Hindu power and eventually also win Hindus over to Islam. If the threat of Hindu supremacy necessitated a revival of Islam, the key to that revival rested in freeing Muslims from the clutches of traditional Islamic thought and the influence of the West.

At the heart of Mawdudi's approach was the belief that religious authenticity was a panacea. This led him to try to cleanse Muslims of Western influence by harping on Islamic dogma and to provide a viable alternative to Westernism by modernizing the structure and content of the Muslim faith. The problems before the Muslim community and the solution he supplied therefore imparted a distinctly missionary outlook to Mawdudi's worldview and were characteristic of his ideas.

Nowhere was the convergence of opposition to the West and fear of Hinduism more apparent than in Mawdudi's treatment of his erstwhile passion and newfound rival, nationalism. Mawdudi considered nationalism both a cultural and a political threat. He rejected secular nationalism because he considered it "polytheism,"[29] a demon that would be the undoing of Muslims, and because it was a facade for the Hindu drive for power. Thus, the struggle with the West— embodied in the challenge of secular nationalism—was superimposed on rivalry with the Hindus.

Mawdudi's response to the problem of imperialism and its corollary, the Hindu challenge, closely resembled the articulation of the Ahl-i Hadith idealism half a century earlier. The Ahl-i Hadith school was a puritanical reform movement that found a following among those who were anxious about their declining sociopolitical position in India in the nineteenth century.[30] They saw the reversal in the fortunes of the Muslims in apocalyptic terms and sought to establish a modicum of stability in their lives through a new interpretation of Islam, to cleanse their faith of cultural accretions, and to reduce it to its exoteric dimension. They were fiercely sectarian, permitting only a single interpretation of Islam, rejecting the four Sunni schools of law and the primary classical sources altogether, encouraging the practice of *ijtihad* (independent judgment in interpreting Islamic law) and maintaining a condescending attitude toward other Muslims. Moral rectitude and denunciation of traditional Islamic practices and beliefs had convinced the movement's followers of their superior religious stand in apocalyptic times.

Although Mawdudi also saw the need to reinterpret Islam in light of the problems put before Indian Muslims by the menace of colonialism, he was not content with moral rectitude as a guarantee of salvation at a time of impending doom. The new interpretation of Islam had to serve a purpose greater than merely saving the souls of individual Muslims: it had to restore Islam to its place of glory. For Mawdudi, there was nothing inevitable or irreversible in the fall of Islam, nor did he explain the Muslim predicament by pointing to the political might and material resources of the West or the numerical superiority of the Hindus. Rather, he looked to Muslims themselves for the source of the problem.

Mawdudi's synthesis began with individual Muslims, who were responsible for the occlusion of their religion and were the ultimate arbiter of its fate:

> The future of the whole world of Islam will depend upon the attitude that the Muslims ultimately adopt towards Islam. If, unfortunately, the present hypocritical attitudes . . . persist, I am afraid that the newly liberated Muslim nations will not be able to preserve their freedom for a long time.[31]

The cause of and, hence, the solution to the crisis lay with the Muslims. Because they had erred in their obedience to God, they had brought about the decay of Muslim societies and paved the road for Western supremacy and, later, the ascendance of the Hindu community. The Muslims had forfeited their access to the power and glory of which their history had shown them to be capable. The "fall of Islam," in Mawdudi's thinking, was not just the product of intellectual or institutional failures, or even of historical changes; it was more immediately the result of the "fall of individual Muslims." Above and beyond any other historical dynamic at work, the crisis of contemporary Islam and the resultant "pollution" of the relation between Muslims and the Qur'an was the doing of "partial" Muslims—those who were less than resolute in following God's commands.[32] For instance, Mawdudi believed that Turkey had abrogated the caliphate and adopted a secular state because it had accepted Islam "through obscurantist channels and after the occlusion of Islamic orthodoxy."[33]

It followed from Mawdudi's argument that the revival of the faith at the individual level was the first step in resuscitating Muslim social and political life. This proved intellectually to be the most complex dimension of his call. "Now the only way open for reform and resuscitation is to rejuvenate Islam as a movement and to revive the meaning of the word Muslim anew."[34] It was elaborated meticulously and systematically in the form of a "three-pronged offensive,"[35] which sought both to insulate Muslims from Western influences and to reaffirm their loyalties to their own faith: "I have ruthlessly attacked the ideological foundations of Western culture. . . . I have expounded as fully as I know how, the ideological bases of Islam. . . . I have offered practical Islamic solutions of important problems which previously even observant Muslims could see no alternative but to follow the West."[36] Some of Mawdudi's most renowned works on Islam, such as *Tafhimat* (Understandings, 1940–1965), *Purdah* (1939), *Islami tahzib awr uski usul'u mabadi* (Islamic culture and its norms and foundations, 1955), and *Risalah-i diniyat* (Treatise on religion, 1932), written between 1932 and 1965, were intended to free Muslim intellectuals from the clutches of Western influence, as were the writings of a number of his followers, most notably, Maryam Jameelah.[37] Mawdudi focused on purifying the Islamic faith, explicating its ethos, and putting its teachings into practice, all with a view to modernizing Islam while extracting Western influence from Muslim minds.

In accomplishing this feat, Mawdudi reduced the intellectual foundations and spiritual expressions of the Islamic faith that had supported the flowering of Muslim cultural and social life over the centuries to their most basic elements to produce a parsimonious and discrete "system"; this was an order that could serve as the common denominator for all Muslims. This reductionist view of Islam would not only promote unity but also resurrect the true faith. He would "scientifically prove that Islam is eventually to emerge as the World-Religion to cure Man of all his maladies."[38]

Mawdudi's *da'wah,* as the embodiment of his reinterpretation and revival of the Islamic faith, ultimately became a "movement" directed at regimenting the lives of all those who had accepted Islamic ideals and molded their lives accordingly, erecting an Islamic order, and, eventually, revolutionizing human thought by instilling Islamic values into it.[39] His scheme was holistic and all-inclusive; it began with the individual Muslim and culminated in a new universal order.[40]

Mawdudi defined his efforts in terms of the Islamic concept of *tajdid*; it was *tajdid* that served as the fulcrum of his synthesis, his struggle with traditional Islam, and his debate with the West. He described his agenda in great detail and with the compelling logic of a scientific formula. His reading of the doctrine of *tajdid* and the action sanctioned by it, however, parted with the classical understanding of the role of a revival of Islamic faith. Mawdudi rationalized the doctrine so that it closely approximated his *da'wah*. Throughout his exposition of *tajdid*, from his diagnosis of the predicament before Muslims to his plan for the intellectual revolution that would rejuvenate the Islamic order, Mawdudi remained focused on the intellectual and political struggle between Islam and the West. *Tajdid* thus found a dynamic role that would relate the past to the present, just as it forecast the future. That role began from the time of the rightly guided caliphs (Rashidun caliphate, A.D. 632–661) and extended to modern times, determining the nature and scope of the struggle for cultural authenticity along the way.[41]

For Mawdudi, *tajdid* rested at the heart of the Muslim historical experience, during which the struggle between good and evil, Islam and un-Islam, had marked history from the end of the prophetic era to modern-day India.[42] His reading of the doctrine had provided for a revolutionary interpretation of Islamic history that clearly bore the mark of Western historicism. He used *tajdid* not just as a religious doctrine but, more important, as a historical paradigm to relate political exigencies to faith, mobilize Muslims, and, above all, claim the authority to reinterpret and rationalize the Islamic faith. *Tajdid* was a process that began at the individual level by defining anew the term Muslim and eventually encompassed the whole society; it also involved a qualitative change in the traditional worldview, moving it toward modernity. Mawdudi called Muslims back to Islam but to an Islam that was rationalized and streamlined so that its social expression would be able to support a viable modern political order.

In traditional Islam there had been a balance between religion as individual piety and religion as social order. It was the piety of men that created and sustained a religious order. In Mawdudi's formula, although individual piety featured prominently, in the final analysis, it was the society and the political order that guaranteed the piety of the individual[43]: "a very large part of the Islamic system of law, however, needs for its enforcement in all its details the coercive power and authority of the state."[44] The logical implication of Mawdudi's position was a different balance between the individual and the society; the flow of Islamicity was not from the individual to the society but from the society to the individual.

Doctrine of Absolute Obedience to God

Mawdudi began his revival and reform of Islam by reexamining the structure of the Muslim faith. He emphasized links in the structure of faith as he deemphasized individual salvation as the objective of religious practice. Although this shift in emphasis was not total, it was significant in that it permitted a thorough reinterpretation of the notion of faith in Islam. Central to this endeavor was the concept of absolute obedience to God, which was developed and articulated by Mawdudi as the sole objective of the faith.

What distinguished Mawdudi's view of the relation between man and God from the traditional one was the fact that Mawdudi's theology did not revolve around the attributes or the conditions of the supremacy of God but was directed at explicating what that supremacy entailed—the incumbency of a particular mode of personal behavior and, more important, social organization. Mawdudi wanted to divert man's attention away from individual salvation and concern with spirituality, which he viewed as narcissistic anthropomorphism and the reason mankind neglected the nature of his or her relation to God. For whereas theology and philosophy provided humans with knowledge of God and the working of the world for solace, the power of ideology lay in its capacity to organize and activate its adherents, thus producing organization and action.[45] For Islam to produce social action it had to pose as ideology, which in turn demanded less attention to salvation and more to social action. He earlier had put this thought into verse:

> We believe in cash, not in credit,
> So why narrate to us the story of paradise.

Idealization of Islam at Mawdudi's hands thus began with the mobilization of individual Muslims around what he called an *active* submission to God, by which he meant rigorously implementing the teachings of Islam with the aim of establishing the ideal Islamic order. For Mawdudi, this was the spirit of the Islamic doctrine of *tawhid* (unity):[46] "Islam is nothing but man's exclusive and total submission to God. . . . True religion means total obedience and submission to God."[47] Such obedience was also the very raison d'être of human existence and a function of mankind's position as God's vicegerent on earth (*khilafatu'llah fi'l-arz*).[48] He wrote: "You must remember that you are a born slave of God. He has created you for His servitude only."[49] In effect, Mawdudi stripped man of volition in matters of faith.[50] He viewed absolute obedience to God as a fundamental right of God about which man had no real choice.[51]

> Man in this kingdom is, by birth, a subject. That is, it has not been given to him to choose to be or not to be a subject . . . nor is it possible for him, being born a subject and a natural part of this kingdom, to swerve from the path of obedience followed by other creations. Similarly he does not have the right to choose a way of life for himself or assume whatever duties he likes.[52]

It followed from this that absolute obedience to God was necessary for the healthy operation of the sociopolitical order.[53] The religious incumbency of absolute obedience to God, complemented by the compelling logic of its sociopolitical function, transformed Islam from a faith into a movement (*tahrik*). Denial of choice was implicit in his ideological position.

From this premise, Mawdudi proceeded to institutionalize his doctrinal position through an elaborate process of redefinition and interpretation of the pillars and fundamentals of the Islamic faith. The task began with the very term Islam, an Arabic word that means peace, submission, surrender, and obedience. "Islam requires complete submission and obedience to Allah—and that is why it is called 'Islam.'"[54] Being a Muslim went beyond adherence to the religion of Islam; it was an aspect of nature that encompassed all of God's creatures.[55] A Muslim, Mawdudi argued, was not someone who abided by the teachings of Islam, but someone who accepted obedience to God:

> Islam does not consist merely in bowing [*ruku'*], prostration [*sujud*], fasting [*sawm*] and pilgrimage [*hajj*]; nor is it found in the face and dress of a man. Islam means submission to God and the Messenger. Anyone who refuses to obey them in the conduct of his life-affairs has a heart devoid of the real Islam—"faith has not yet entered their hearts." His Prayers, his Fasting and his pious appearance are nothing but deception.[56]

In dividing Islam into "real" and "deceptive," Mawdudi parted with formal faith, tried to appropriate Islam in toto, and attempted to redefine it.[57] From this point on, the adjective Islamic did not define orthodoxy; it invoked the spirit of Mawdudi's *da'wah*—absolute submission to God.

Herein lay the source of Mawdudi's break with traditional Islam, for the doctrine of absolute obedience to God in lieu of human choice and volition in matters of faith subtly but surely challenged the traditional Islamic position. Its ostensible "radical orthodoxy" rejected the prevalent norms and institutions of Islamic life. It was exactly on this point that ulama such as the rector of the Nadwatu'l-'Ulama in Lucknow, Mawlana Sayyid Abu'l-Hasan 'Ali Nadwi, echoing the sentiments of the Islamic establishment of the Indian subcontinent, criticized Mawdudi's rigid interpretation in the strongest terms, accusing him of parting with the fundamental tenets of Islam.[58] Their debate elucidated the extent of Mawdudi's challenge to traditional Islam.

Nadwi argued that free will is a fundamental right bestowed on man by God; it is the crucial doctrine by which the whole notion of belief finds meaning in Islam. To deny man choice in matters of faith is a clear violation of the spirit of Islamic teachings. Mawdudi argued that choice has been the cause of both moral crisis and sociopolitical predicaments. For Mawdudi, the salvation of man did not rest with his acquisition of knowledge of God and, hence, exercise of his choice in matters of faith, but was the direct outcome of surrendering his will in absolute obedience to God. In effect, divine guidance was an undisputed necessity, and the exercise of choice was a possible source of evil. In Mawdudi's discourse, the virtuous society could not exist save by the intercession of God and the dissolution of the human faculties of reason and choice in the divinely ordained religious order. To Nadwi, Mawdudi's position truncated the scope of Islamic faith, reducing its complex spirituality to a command structure best suited for politics, and it was a radical break with traditional norms, which was tantamount to decreeing a new set of religious values.[59] The senior Deobandi *'alim* Muhammad Manzur Nu'mani wrote that Mawdudi misunderstood the aim of the Islamic revelation, which "is not an establishment of a government, but the promotion of faith and piety . . . [and the] gaining of God's favor [*Allah ke qurb'u raza*]."[60]

What Nadwi and other ulama saw as a new set of religious values, Mawdudi regarded as nothing short of the *tajdid* and *ihya'* (revival) of true Islam, the espousal of the very essence of the original faith that had been corrupted by later accretions, leading to *jahiliyah* (ignorance, paganism) and *kufr* (disbelief).[61] Covered by an aura of puritanism, Mawdudi's interpretive reading of Islam broke entirely with the traditional view to purge it of everything through which the Islamic revelation had been manifested over the centuries. Philosophy, literature, the arts, mysticism, and especially time-honored customs and cultural mores were all derided by Mawdudi as a syncretic and impure adulteration of the Islamic faith, diverting the attention of the Muslims from the divine to the mundane. Mawdudi accepted only politics as a legitimate vehicle for the manifestation of the Islamic revelation and as the sole means for the expression of Islamic spirituality, a position that correlated piety with political activity, the cleansing of the soul with political liberation, and salvation with utopia.

Obviously this was an approach to Islamic history very different from the traditional perspective found in most schools of Islamic theology.[62] From the earliest days, traditional Islam has accepted the unfolding of history as the will of God, arguing that mankind had no authority to question what lay in the realm of divine wisdom. Although traditional divines idealized the early history of Islam, they did not view what followed that era to be "un-Islamic," and although the subsequent history of Muslim societies has displayed many imperfections, it continues to manifest the Islamic truth to varying degrees, though never as fully as during the early years of the faith.[63] Islamic history possesses a sacred dimension. The traditional divines value tradition as cumulative and as a transmitter of truth, norms, and values. In the words of Nu'mani, their thought is the thought of the venerated religious thinkers over the ages [*tarz-i fikr . . . salaf'u halaf'ulama-i rabbani*].[64] This means that they have never rejected Islamic history or sought to destroy its continuity. They have enjoined the good and sought to influence society and politics but have not extended their efforts beyond this. This is also a major difference between the Jama'at and other revivalist expressions of Islam, such as the Tablighi Jama'at, which encourages the rigorous observance of Islamic teachings but does not seek to disrupt the historical continuity of the faith.

Like other contemporary Islamic revivalists, Mawdudi did not view Islamic history as the history of Islam but as the history of un-Islam or *jahiliyah*. Islamic history, as the product of human choice, was corruptible and corrupted. For him, Islamic history held no value and manifested no religious truths, except during its early phase. The history of Muslim societies was not so much a testimony of divine will as an account of the fall of Islam. In Mawdudi's view, which later shaped the thinking of a host of revivalist thinkers, the history of Islam stopped with the rightly guided caliphs, for the social and political institutions that followed were incapable of reflecting the ideals of Islam in any fashion. The revival of Islam, it followed, must entail the total rejection of what came after the rightly guided caliphs and would be realized by reconstructing that period. The Islamic state therefore had to stand outside the cumulative tradition of history of Muslim societies. Merely enjoining the good and admonishing those who transgress Islamic teachings in a setting that was altogether un-Islamic would be pointless. The resumption of the history of Islam would require Muslims to work diligently to stop the current unfolding history of Muslim societies—to wrest control of history, to do what must be God's command rather than accept what had occurred and continued to be accepted as His will. In effect, the history of Islam would resume, after a fourteen-century interlude, with the Islamic state.

This difference over the meaning of Islamic history was an important distinction that separated Mawdudi's views and those of other expressions of contemporary revivalism from the traditional conception of orthodoxy. The resulting principal point of contention was over the nature of the relationship between religion and politics. The inseparability of religion and politics has been a part of the teachings of all schools of Islamic law and theology; however, it has not necessarily been maintained in Islamic history. Throughout its course, institutions have been based on the de facto separation of religious and political authority.[65] Viewing history as the manifestation of God's will led traditional Islam to believe this separation to be acceptable and, indeed, divinely sanctioned. Revivalists who hoped to bring about a new social order had to end this practice in Islamic history and were therefore compelled to break with traditional Islam and formulate a fundamentally new perspective. The anticipated utopian order would be "not a form of state so much as a form of Islam."[66] The break with tradition occurred in tandem with the articulation of the revivalist agenda, the transformation of the old into the new and of faith into politics.

Renewal and reform in Mawdudi's thinking were "fundamentalist" in that they could be based solely on the Qur'an, the prophetic traditions, and the legal canon (*fiqh*) of Islam as repositories of divine truth. Yet this restricted outlook was not divorced from an interpretive effort to extend the purview of religious thought and function beyond its traditional boundaries. Religious sources served a dual function in Mawdudi's thinking—they were the primary means for reformulating the meaning of faith in Islam, and they legitimized the new perspective—thereby promising salvation in a way that tied piety to social action.[67]

Mawdudi therefore always prefaced his expositions with a reaffirmation of the authenticity of the sources of Islamic faith. This emphasis on authenticity set the stage for an exclusive monopoly of its interpretation and exposition. Mawdudi's definition of "true" Islam as solely the interpretation of the primordial religious truth found meaning in this reading of the religious sources.[68]

Mawdudi saw himself as the intermediary—and authority—whose mission it was to restore the relation between religious sources and the faithful.[69] He utilized what Khurshid Ahmad termed *fiqhi tafsir* (jurisprudential commentary) to discover the true spirit and intent of the Qur'anic revelation (*istinbat-i ahkam*) and to capture them in new social legislation.[70] The term *fiqhi* thinly disguised what was, in effect, a sociopolitical reading of the Qur'an. Mawdudi emphasized that the Qur'an was not literature to be read and enjoyed, but a socioreligious institution. Moreover, it was not *a* source but *the* source for all social legislation and not merely *an* aspect of faith but its *entire* focus. All along, he also reinterpreted the meaning and function of other sources of Islamic law so that they would lend themselves to the more assertive and worldly role that Mawdudi had intended for them. In interpreting the sources, Mawdudi deliberately avoided following any one school of Sunni law,[71] deemphasizing theological and legal differences in favor of a systemic reading and regimentation of the religious sources.

Questions pertaining to structure, style, and methodology featured prominently in Mawdudi's *tafsir* works, as did the links between Islamic teachings and social concerns relating faith to action, which is why his writings have been so instrumental in creating an activist consciousness in contemporary Islamic revivalism. The most noted example of his *tafsir* work is his commentary on the Qur'an (*Tafhimu'l-Qur'an*), where he introduced the four interrelated concepts, *ilah* (divinity), *rabb* (lord), *'ibadah* (worship), and *din* (religion).[72] These he argued, collectively captured the essence of religious experience, delineated the boundaries of faith, and defined its content. The four terms, general as they seem, were interpreted narrowly by Mawdudi, producing a structured definition of Islam that determined the attitude of the faithful toward God, religion, and the obligatory rites and duties (*fara'iz*).

The activist aim of the commentary was evident in its format, as well as in Mawdudi's literary style. It was written in modern Urdu and used such stylistic innovations as paragraphs and a subject index to facilitate access to the Qur'an and encourage its study and interpretation, as opposed to mere recitation.[73] Mawdudi regarded the Qur'an as constituting direct dialogue between God and mankind; each *ayah* (verse) constituted a separate conversation, all were inter-related and could be understood in the context of the four underlying concepts. This immediate relation between the Qur'an and Muslims conditioned the read-ing of the Qur'an in light of the imperatives suggested in the structure of the framework of *ilah–rabb–'ibadah–din*.

Mawdudi argued that the Qur'an was revealed in a piecemeal fashion, with each sura (chapter) reflecting the circumstances of the time and the particular needs of the nascent Islamic community.[74] This not only explained some of its stylistic variations and enigmatic contents but also attested to the fact that the Qur'an was sent down to mankind in response to the practical needs of the early Muslim community and, therefore, was and continued to be a socioreligious guide: "the real relation between al-Fatihah (the first chapter of the Qur'an) and the [rest of the] Qur'an is not that of an introduction to a book but that of a prayer and its answer."[75] The Qur'an, Mawdudi argued, was not merely to be recited, pondered, or investigated for hidden truths; it was rather to be read at face value and implemented. As an answer to mankind's prayers, the Qur'an would solve social maladies.[76] The Qur'an's innermost reality and ultimate func-tion were its insistence on absolute obedience to God, and it acted as a guide on how that might be attained.

Mawdudi subsumed the spiritual significance of the Qur'an, truncating the scope of the holy book in favor of a narrow interpretation that rejected the idea of the Qur'an as the fountainhead of perennial truths and the repository of spiri-tual knowledge. Mawdudi's systemic approach instead was informed by the urgency of sociopolitical exigencies, and he sought to base the historical and spiritual significance of the Qur'an on temporal contingencies.[77] In Mawdudi's conception, wrote Abu'l-Hasan 'Ali Nadwi, "theocracy replaces spirituality as the objective of Qur'anic revelation."[78] The Qur'an thus becomes a book about the world and, hence, a worldly book: "Insofar as it seeks to explain the ultimate causes of man's success or failure the subject of the Book [the Qur'an] is man."[79]

A similar outlook characterized Mawdudi's approach to the Islamic doc-trine of prophecy (*nubuwwah*) and the prophetic traditions (sunnah, hadith). Mawdudi's discussion of prophecy began with a reaffirmation of its authentic-ity. The confirmation of the sanctity of this fundamental article of faith then set the stage for an interpretive reading of its function. Authenticated, the doctrine of prophecy was cast anew, no longer as an autonomous source of spirituality and manifestation of divine reality, but as a constituent component of the sys-temic structure that was premised on absolute obedience to God and led to sociopolitical action. In Mawdudi's view, prophecy functioned to guide and educate man in truths that would lead him to believe in Islam and would elicit from him a commitment to his religion.[80] For Muslims, prophecy and the pro-phetic traditions serve as ideals for men to follow, determining the place of Islam in their lives; for Mawdudi, however, prophecy was also a historical paradigm, a model for leadership, and a guide to the ideal political order. The Prophet of Islam was not only the ideal Muslim or a hallowed subject of religious devo-tion, but the first and foremost Muslim political leader and, hence, a source of emulation in political matters. It was this appropriation of the fundamental sources of Islam and a single-minded reinterpretation of their role within the framework of the Islamic faith that permitted Mawdudi to extend personal piety into a quest for political power. Politicization of faith could only follow its rationalization, however.

Rationalization of Islamic Thought

Mawdudi's discourse on Islam extended beyond the revival of the religion and culminated in a rationalized and systemic view of the faith directed at shaping society and politics. Islam was not merely faith in God or a conglomeration of beliefs and values anchored in the spirituality that envelopes the practice of the faith; instead, it was a distinct and discrete worldview, premised on Islamic teachings and appealing to Islamic symbols, but directed at realizing specific sociopolitical objectives that lay beyond the purview of traditional religious concerns. Wahidu'ddin Khan, himself a one-time Jama'at votary, uncharitably described this as a distortion of the very purpose of Islamic piety[81] and saw an outlandish element in Mawdudi's puritanical scheme. The systematization of Islam was an "Islamic view of modernity" more than it was a reflection on the fundamentals of the Islamic faith. The religious underpinnings of Mawdudi's views camouflaged his subliminal modernization of thought and practice, which often worked in ways that were not readily visible.

The impetus for Mawdudi's exegetics was clearly sociopolitical: the Islamic revival was not intended to save individual souls, but to soothe anxieties born of social, economic, communal, and political crises before the Muslims of India. "True" Islam was predicated on a different relation between mankind and God, one that was not private and inward-looking but externalized and engaged. The relationship between mankind and God became increasingly a tool for achieving success in the world—a template that could provide meaning to the confusion that reigned in Muslim lives. The amorphous idea of faith had to be replaced with an ideology that would produce tightly knit and tangible relations of authority and provide a more concrete definition of community, political action, and even salvation. Rationalized and streamlined religion would prove more relevant to the fractious and yet exceedingly modern sociopolitical setting in which it was to operate. The ideological interpretation would also sequester Islam from the influence of the West in the intellectual realm and from Hinduism in the communal structure of Indian politics. The more engaging and worldly spirit of this new formulation could no longer be captured in the term Muslim; it was more appropriately expressed by the adjective Islamic.

This redefinition of Islam began with erecting impregnable boundaries around the religion, a necessary first step in constructing an Islamic ideology. In fact, the requirements of such an ideological formulation in good measure determined its nature and scope. The lines of demarcation that defined Islam were perforce steadfast: there was either Islam, as it was understood and defined by Mawdudi, or there was un-Islam.[82] To Mawdudi's audience, the psychological implications of such a dichotomy were many. Conscious of this fact, and eager both to inoculate Muslims against Hindu and Western viruses and to mobilize them in a religiopolitical movement, Mawdudi brought to bear the full force of the choice between true Islam and un-Islam, salvation and perdition, on individual Muslims: "A Muslim is *not a Muslim* by *appellation* or *birth*, but by virtue of abiding by holy law."[83] The distinction between true faith and nominal allegiance to it legitimized Mawdudi's ideology and vested his program of action with a sense of mission. In effect, revival of Islam began with the statement that of those who claimed to be Muslim, "not more than 0.001%" knew what Islam actually was,[84] implying that what was widely accepted as Islamic was, in fact, un-Islamic. Mawdudi's invitation to Islam was a daring challenge to traditional Islam.

The redefinition of Islam and its reorganization into a system required the use of a particular nomenclature that would relate the underlying assumptions and aims of the new orientation to the basic tenets of the Islamic faith and serve as key concepts for regimentation of the faithful. *Ilah, rabb, 'ibadah*, and *din*, were injected with new meaning, invoking a different worldview and capturing the essence of the structure of relations that set in motion the doctrine of absolute obedience to God in the form of a religiopolitical program. The four terms were interrelated. From *ilah* to *din*, the novel ideological perspective encompassed the gamut of religious experiences, all in the framework of a rationalized chain of authority from God to the individual believer.

Din was of particular significance in Mawdudi's discourse. It was the linchpin and the culmination of the links that constituted "true" Islam. Mawdudi used *din*—literally meaning religion—as a synonym for Islam *the system*, the "true" Islam. In traditional sources the term *din* underscored the social dimension of Islam's teachings, but Mawdudi used *din* in a new way—it no longer referred to Islamic practices or rituals, nor to the scope of Islam's teachings, but to an all-embracing ethos.[85]

Mawdudi defined *din* primarily as absolute obedience to God. The *shari'ah* as the content of the *din* in turn provided linkages between the individual and the society and, hence, the manner in which *din* was to fulfill its objective. The *shari'ah* set the guidelines for the performance of religious duties (*'ibadah*, the third pillar of Mawdudi's systemic approach) and governed the believer's social transactions. It perpetuated obedience to God—the purpose of *din*. Hence, the *shari'ah* extended beyond enactment of religious teachings, worship, or piety to serve as the means for reaffirmation of man's moral commitment to and acceptance of *din*.[86] *'Ibadah*, wrote Mawdudi, was etymologically rooted in the word *'abd* (slave); it was the profession of absolute obedience to God.[87] *'Ibadah* was "revering, serving and obeying God in our whole lives."[88] It had no other function than to facilitate the recognition of the true meaning of the concepts of *ilah* and *rabb*,[89] the first two pillars of Mawdudi's system. Mawdudi's views on a total and engaged obedience to God, also seen in Abu'l-Kalam Azad's concept of *rububiyat* (divinity), resembled, and was probably influenced by, the absolute and unwavering devotion to God that is the basis of mysticism in Islam.[90] *'Ibadah* was not to cherish or praise God, nor was it meant to serve as a source of spiritual benediction.[91] It was directed at acting out one's absolute obedience to God, hence giving meaning to the concept of *din*.[92]

Traditional Islamic scholars have taken strong exception to Mawdudi's exposition of the concept of *din* and have castigated him for tampering with the very foundation of the Islamic faith.[93] Abu'l-Hasan 'Ali Nadwi, for instance, rejected his suggestion that religious works and piety are directed at any objective other than the spiritual salvation of man. Muslims will be judged by God for their piety and performance of religious works, argued Nadwi, *'ibadah* should therefore be directed at the realization of that end and should not serve as a vehicle for establishing a theocracy, which was at best only a means to the higher end. Nadwi emphasized the devotional dimension of *'ibadah* and openly criticized Mawdudi for his omission of this aspect of the faith. Nadwi argued that *iqamat-i din*—the Islamic order about which Mawdudi had written much—should encompass every aspect of the faith and not just its social dimension.[94] Wahidu'ddin Khan also accused Mawdudi of misinterpreting the meaning of *'ibadah*. Religious worship, he said, was to serve as a means for personal reform and not as a vehicle for establishing worldly power.[95]

In some measure, the criticisms of both Nadwi and Wahidu'ddin Khan reflected their appreciation of the apolitical work of the Tablighi Jama'at.[96] The Tabligh movement directed its efforts toward invigorating the faith at the individual level; it had not conditioned the revival of Islam on acquiring worldly power. Nadwi's and Wahidu'ddin Khan's criticisms of Mawdudi amounted to confirming the Tabligh movement and its reinforcement of the traditional norms of piety as the paragon for Muslim activism.[97]

Implicit in Mawdudi's ideas about *din* and *'ibadah* was the belief that the faithful must be willing to break with the traditional Islam they had hitherto understood and practiced. Mawdudi's exegesis required an internal conversion that would commit them to struggle for the implementation of divine will. To become true Muslims, Mawdudi argued, the faithful must undergo a conversion, restate the *shahadah* (Muslim testimony of faith) in the spirit of the *din*, purge themselves of all other beliefs, and live by the holy law.[98] For "a corrupt will," argued Mawdudi, "cannot accept revelation, nor comprehend nature, nor reason effectively."[99] Erection of the ideal Islamic order would have to follow that conversion and was therefore predicated on a missionary outlook, one that began with individual Muslims and culminated in expanding the boundaries of Islam.[100] The proselytical endeavor was directed at increasing religious observance, purifying society, and ultimately reshaping Islam.[101]

Because conversion occurred within the framework of Islam, the new faith found its meaning through an added emphasis on a varied interpretation of Islamic teachings and doctrines in general and religious works in particular. Works in effect became the very harbinger of faith (*iman*), and the embodiment of the Muslims' new commitment.[102] The increased emphasis on works was also a natural conclusion to Mawdudi's definition of a Muslim. Islam, he wrote, was not a birthright, nor a simple proclamation of the *shahadah*, but the testimony to an individual's absolute obedience to God—Islam found meaning only in the context of works. The implications of this attitude in the communal setting of India, where the cultural basis of nationalism was syncretic, was far-reaching.

In traditional Islam, religion is "essentially a way of knowledge. . . . Islam leads to essential knowledge which integrates [a Muslim's] whole being."[103] Islamic spirituality is therefore predicated on knowledge of God, a realization that stands above and beyond the restrictions of esoteric religion. It presents the possibility of a transcendental religious dialogue with Hinduism.[104] It is for this reason that the revivalist discourse in the Indian subcontinent, insofar as it reflected communal consciousness, sought to close the door to such an eventuality. For Mawdudi, there existed no possibility of spirituality outside the *din* and no knowledge distinct from or transcendental to the obligatory duties.[105] The incumbency of the *din* was premised not on the knowledge of God, but simply on acceptance of absolute obedience to Him. For this position to be viable, the emphasis on works would have to be complemented with an interpretation of its constituent rituals and practices. Mawdudi's followers argued that his purpose in discussing the central practices of Islam, such as prayers or even recitation of the Qur'an, was not to offer juridical exposition, but to ascribe to those practices their correct place in the structure of his system.[106] Mawdudi's objective was to appropriate the meaning and significance of a central Islamic practice and thereby to relate the spirit and function of that practice and its associated doctrines to his conception of *din*.[107] The spirit of religious observance, argued Mawdudi, could be captured efficiently in a hierarchic gradation, beginning in *iman* (faith in God), then proceeding to *islam* (surrender to God), *taqwa* (faith and consciousness of God), and finally *ihsan* (benediction, but interpreted by Mawdudi as "godliness").[108]

Although this was a piecemeal effort, it nevertheless strove toward erecting a complete belief system. Moreover, investiture of the central Islamic practices with new meaning in the context of Mawdudi's greater emphasis on works made religious observance itself a medium for internal conversion: "That the prayer as such has extraordinary power to make us attain to greater and greater heights of obedience and worship is quite obvious."[109]

This formulation made full use of the believer's concern for salvation. Adherence to the *din*, Mawdudi had concluded, would be more compelling in light of the soteriological concerns of Muslims. Mawdudi's oeuvre was therefore very much informed by the content and meaning of Islamic eschatological doctrines and the religion's conceptions of salvation and perdition.[110] Unlike Ayatollah Khomeini or Sayyid Qutb,[111] Mawdudi did not argue exclusively for a utopian order in this world; he was more directly concerned with salvation. He never broke completely with the traditional position in the sense that his advocacy of the utopian order was tempered by his continued, although tentative, acceptance of the very possibility of salvation outside the purview of that order. This meant backtracking on, although not renouncing, his earlier position. The result of this contradictory posturing was to confuse the aim of his ideology and to check the chiliastic and revolutionary tendency of his formulation. Muslims should not be disheartened if their revolution did not materialize, Mawdudi wrote on occasion, for they would be rewarded in the hereafter.[112] In the final analysis, a Muslim was merely to fulfill the will of God, for which he would be rewarded in the hereafter.[113] Reference to divine punishment and, more frequently, to paradisiacal reward in the discussion of the *din* was so pervasive in Mawdudi's works that it at times obfuscated his original justification for the concept of the *din*—namely, the utopian Islamic sociopolitical order:

> *Iman* in Allah is not a mere metaphysical concept; it is in the nature of a *contract* by which man barters his life and his possessions in exchange for promise of Paradise in the Hereafter. God, as it were, purchases a Believer's life and property and promises, in return, the reward of Paradise in the life after death.[114]

Mawdudi's attempt to reinforce the *din* by appealing to Muslim eschatological doctrines and soteriological concerns in effect had moderated the pace and scope of his rationalization of Islam. As the utopian ideal was made to share the limelight with the Muslim quest for salvation, the urgency of the realization of that order and, hence, the revolutionary potential of the drive to realize it were checked. Mawdudi argued in later years that the Jama'at's objective from inception was "to erect a divine government (*hukumat-i ilahiyah*) in the world and hence to win God's favor in the afterlife."[115] Worldly utopia was enmeshed with the quest for salvation. Ironically, Mawdudi's arguments planted the seeds of traditional tendencies in his new approach, which accounts for both the Jama'at's ambivalent attitude toward revolution and Mawdudi's complex and enigmatic relation to traditional Islam.

Despite the confusion that his wavering over salvation caused, a worldly outlook and a concern for the political implications of religious exegesis continued to characterize his thinking and determine its course. Although his appeal to the theme of salvation suggested a traditionalization of his program, by the same token, his treatment of Muslim eschatological doctrines, true to his style, reinterpreted those doctrines with a view to the requirements of the *din* and his sociopolitical program. In Mawdudi's conception, man's fate in the afterlife, accepted as a primary motive and reward for religious observance, was decided not on the basis of his spiritual stature judged by God in His eternal wisdom, but was rationally understood as the automatic outcome of adopting a particular posture toward the world in light of a distinct interpretation of Islam.[116] Paraphrasing Mawdudi, Maryam Jameelah argued, "Paradise is not reward for *mere profession* of the bargain [covenant with God], it is the reward for the faithful's *execution* of it."[117]

The need to create clearly defined boundaries around the Muslim community, combined with the attitude toward the world demanded of Muslims by Mawdudi, increasingly limited the very definition of a Muslim. It was this aspect of Mawdudi's discourse that brought the discussion of the *din* to its logical conclusion—who is a Muslim?—and, moreover, related his intellectualized treatment of religion to the life and thought of average Muslims. Being a Muslim, Mawdudi had often argued, was a matter of volition.[118] The definition of a Muslim as it appeared in Mawdudi's expansion on the theme of the *din* was, however, premised on the notion of compulsion; in effect, volition in religious matters was applicable only to non-Muslims.[119] For Mawdudi, there was no compulsion in becoming a Muslim, but for those who were Muslim, fulfilling the demands of the *din* was not a matter of choice. Wrote Freeland Abbott, Mawdudi interpreted the Qur'anic injunction "there is no compulsion in religion" as "there is no compulsion in respect to adopting religion"; otherwise, "the various penalties and prohibitions found in the Qur'an [were] meaningless:"[120] "When you recite the Kalima [*shahadah*] . . . you relinquish your independence in favor of God."[121] More to the point, Mawdudi warned:

> All the Muslims resident in countries where the Islamic revolution is to take place should be given notice that they have discarded their faith. . . . They should declare themselves to be non-Muslims. . . . Those who are Muslims because they were born into a Muslim family . . . must be subjected to Islamic Law and be compelled to observe the *fara'iz* and *wajibat* [obligatory religious works].[122]

Concerned with safeguarding the boundaries of the Muslim community, Mawdudi did not permit apostasy, nor did he sanction individual choice in the manner and extent of orthopraxy.[123]

Mawdudi's views had precedents in the classical sources, but he arrived at them independently. Islam as a sociopolitical reality was more than just a set of religious beliefs; much like the "American Union," wrote Mawdudi, it, too, had the right to protect itself.[124] Therefore, the demand for strict adherence to the *din* was necessary for the preservation of the true Islamic community. In effect, the less than fully committed Muslim, and those who did not abide by Mawdudi's conception of the *din,* were depicted as apostates.[125] They fell short of fulfilling the requirements of *kalimah-i tayibbah* (pure profession of the Muslim testimony of faith), and lived by the *kalimah-i khatibah* (literally, professed testimony). The latter, Mawdudi argued, had its rooting in *shirk* (polytheism).[126] Such Muslims, Mawdudi argued, were as the Jews to Moses and no better than the followers of Emperor Akbar's eclectic *din-i ilahi* (divine religion).[127] In their self-centered obscurantism, they had neglected Islam and failed to defend the faith in the challenges with which it was confronted.[128] In Maryam Jameelah's words, "[A Muslim's] practical living [must provide] eloquent testimony to his non-Muslim neighbors that he subscribed to the Kalima. . . . A Muslim, in order to be worthy of the name, must actually live an Islamic life."[129] Conversely, the followers of the *din* were deemed to be "true" Muslims because they had "completely [merged] into Islam their full personality and entire existence." [130] They were responsible for the glories of Islam.[131] The only difference between an apostate and a "nominal" or "partial" Muslim was that Mawdudi prescribed severe punishment for an actual apostate but not for unobservant Muslims. Mawdudi never gave up on the latter; he tried to appeal to their religious, intellectual, and, ultimately, their political sensibilities. His concern lay with politics; hence, he needed to extend the reach of his message and persuade greater numbers to his cause.

Mawdudi's idealization of Islam, the dialectic of which articulated a rationalized and systemic view of the faith wherein the Islamic conceptions of God, society, and man were reinterpreted and woven into one whole, was thus complete. He pushed the boundaries of the revival of Islam beyond mere reaffirmation of orthodoxy to a new vision. Mawdudi's oeuvre had produced an all-inclusive worldview, an internally consistent ideological perspective, and a novel method of religious exegesis and political analysis. The resulting intellectual system in turn shaped the concept of the "Islamic state" and conditioned the nature of the struggle for realizing it.

4

The Islamic Revolution

Ever since the Iranian revolution of 1978–1979, the West has been apprehensive about the possibility of an Islamic revolution, which it has assumed to be the hallmark of Islamic revivalism, the object of the Islamic state, and the culmination of the *tajdid* and *islah* of Islam. The role revolution is to play in Islamic revivalism is not as clear as the example of Iran or the scholarly reflections on Islamic revivalism since its advent suggest, however.

In Mawdudi's view, and as expressed elsewhere in the revivalist literature, the Islamic state could not happen until the existing political order had been removed from the scene. As Mawdudi put it, "a tree [grown to bear] lemon[s] from its rudimentary stages right up to the state of its completion" cannot "all of a sudden begin producing mangoes."[1] Because any political order is bound to resist change, some form of direct action is necessary to topple it.

The history of Islam in India, Mawdudi believed, shows that the religion's success depended on controlling the centers of power. It was the decline of Muslim power after Awrangzeb that had straddled the boundary between Islam and Hinduism, arrested the spread of Islam, and ultimately caused the collapse of Muslim power in India. The Jama'at's trials and tribulations in Pakistani politics after 1947 showed the limits to the flexibility of a secular political order before the demands of Islamicity. Islam, according to Mawdudi, was not likely to survive its eclipse at the centers of power, especially when those at the helm were hostile to its interests. A complete change in the political setup was therefore central to Mawdudi's program of action. The pace and breadth of this change, and the manner in which the logic of Mawdudi's arguments have been reflected in the Jama'at's praxis are open to question, however. Mawdudi did not favor violent revolution; on the contrary, he wanted greater interaction with the authorities.

Mawdudi's teachings seemed to call for "a revolution in the social set-up": as long as the social system was based on immoral and atheistic precepts, and as long as its leaders were "disciples of Satan," abiding by such a system was against reason.[2] Still, entangled as it was in Pakistani politics, "abiding by such a system" was exactly what the Jama'at has been doing.[3] If the Jama'at has not been true to a revolutionary reading of Mawdudi's teachings, then what propels the party's political activism? How has the Jama'at understood and implemented Mawdudi's notion of complete and thorough political change? What is needed to attain an Islamic state? The questions, as well as the answers, point to Mawdudi's having a complex understanding of the concept of revolution that was not always in keeping with Western notions of the term.

A social revolution is a profound and often violent process of change. It involves a total rejection of and break with the established order, the destruction of the bureaucratic and military institutions of the old regime, elimination of class differences (especially in the Marxist definition), removal of cultural obstacles to social change, and the institution of fundamentally new relationships of power, distribution of wealth, and social structure.[4] A revolution begins when contenders organize to advance the program of action that will culminate in the process of radical change, and when they are willing and able to use violence to that end.[5]

The Jama'at had no such ideas of revolution, nor has it ever acted to set a social revolution in motion. On the contrary, it has avoided violent social change and has instead, viewed the path to the Islamic state as lying within the existing sociopolitical order:[6] "The Jamaat-e-Islami wants to bring about radical reform—in fact, a peaceful revolution—in this country. But this revolution can come about only gradually. It can be achieved step by step."[7]

Many regarded Mawdudi's Islamic state and his plan of action for attaining it as revolutionary because it was bent on overthrowing first the Raj and later the Pakistan state through radical means, and his rhetoric and use of such terms as Islamic ideology and Islamic revolution certainly did little to discourage the idea.[8] Especially after the 1978–1979 Iranian revolution, he came to be seen as an avatar of Islamic revolution.[9] Part of the problem was that the same ambiguities that appeared in his appropriation of other Western concepts turned up in his treatment of revolution. Mawdudi's program did indeed sound revolutionary in intent and possibly Marxist in origin when he wrote in *The Process of Islamic Revolution,* "Islam is a revolutionary ideology and a revolutionary practice, which aims at destroying the social order of the world totally and rebuilding it from scratch . . . and Jihad denotes the revolutionary struggle."[10] Reading on, however, we discover that Mawdudi described revolution in evolutionary terms, as a piecemeal effort predicated on the exact confluence of a set of social, cultural, and psychological prerequisites.[11] The exact requirements of this confluence preclude the kind of spontaneity that the liberating force of a true revolution denotes. Mawdudi conceived of revolution as a methodical and determinist process, that favored an orderly transfer of power, and he was ambivalent toward the political system that it challenged.[12] What Mawdudi wrote is not necessarily what the overall thrust of his ideas meant, nor did he define revolution consistently within the same book. Scraping away the Western political jargon, we find that Mawdudi issued directives that were not true to the spirit of those terms. He called the Prophet Muhammad "the greatest revolutionary," then in the same article went on to extol his "patience and pacifism."[13] In 1941, Mawdudi told the *shura'* of the Jama'at, "We desire no demonstrations or agitations, no flag waving, slogans, or the like. . . . [For us] such display of uncontrolled emotions will prove deadly. . . . You do not need to capture your audience through impassioned speeches . . . but you must kindle the light of Islam in your hearts, and change those around you."[14] Revolution was an axis around which Mawdudi conducted his debate. The definition of the term changed according to shifts in Mawdudi's ideological perspective. Revolution had no clear-cut definition but was one of the parcel of slogans and shibboleths that served his purpose.

In his battle with the leftists for the adherence of Muslims, Mawdudi used the idioms of revolution to conjure up a progressive image for Islam. The idiom related his program to the collection of ideas that had, and continues to have, currency among the very people in India and Pakistan who were the target of his ideology. In Mawdudi's conception, revolution and its corollary, ideology, had no class reference. They simply permitted Mawdudi to equip the Jama'at with a repertoire of terms that allowed the party to stand its ground in debates over what constituted progress, justice, and political idealism. In appropriating the myth of revolution, Mawdudi hoped to disarm his leftist rivals, to tarnish the gloss of their appeal, and eventually to render their agenda redundant.

In practice, Mawdudi steered clear of revolutionary activism. His harangues against the political order in India and, later, Pakistan never extended beyond expressions of dissent and were never systematized into a coherent revolutionary worldview:

> The nature and extent of despotism in the different Muslim countries is so varied that it is not possible to suggest any one standard procedure. But what I do feel is necessary in all these cases is the need to resist the temptation of resorting to the methods and techniques of secret underground movements and bloody revolutions.[15]

When pressed to define Islamic revolution, it was of evolution, rather than revolution, that he spoke. "Immediate revolution is neither possible nor desirable," said Mawdudi in 1948; instead, the Jama'at's objective was "gradual change, replicating the Prophetic era."[16] Mawdudi's revolution was essentially a process of reform:

> If we really wish to see our Islamic ideals translated into reality, we should not overlook the natural law that all stable changes in the collective life of a people come about gradually. The more sudden a change, the more short-lived it is. For a permanent change it is necessary that it should be free from extremist bias and unbalanced approach.[17]

Despite his use of terms associated with Marxist historicism and leftist praxis, Mawdudi's point of reference was Western liberalism:

> Living as slaves of an alien power and deprived of the Islamic influences for a long time, the pattern of our moral, cultural, social, economic and political life has

undergone a radical change, and is today far removed from the Islamic ideals. Under such circumstances it cannot be fruitful, even if it were possible, to change the legal structure of the country all at once, because then the general pattern of life and the legal structure will be poles apart, and the legal change will have to suffer the fate of a sapling planted in an uncongenial soil and facing hostile weather. It is therefore inevitable that the required reform should be gradual and the changes in the laws should be effected in such manner as to balance favorably the change in the moral, educational, social, cultural and political life of the nation.[18]

This process was modeled partly after the example of the Prophet's rule in Medina and later Mecca and partly after British rule in India, which had erected legal and social systems gradually and methodically.[19] The Islamic state had to emerge as a particular entity; it could not be the product of conjecture, nor could it be influenced by disparate forces, which were bound to be the result of anomie. Islamic revolution could not be realized through force because the Prophet persuaded the Arabs to accept the wisdom of his reforms; he did not force them.[20] Islam was established out of faith; hence, Islamization, Mawdudi insisted, must remain true to the prophetic example.[21] Reform on behalf of Islam should concern itself with substance rather than the pace and breadth of the reform process.[22]

The Jama'at and the Pakistan State

Because the Islamic revolution was a distant goal,[23] the Jama'at did not need to act, but it did have to create the exact circumstances that would bring about revolution. Because this could take many years to materialize, the Jama'at in the meantime had the task of preventing other systems of government from taking root too firmly. This feat was to be accomplished through political activism, which is why the Jama'at found itself moving from ideology to pragmatic politics. Political activism, although initially only a tactic to safeguard the prospects of the Islamic state, eventually became an end in itself. In later years, Mawdudi became even more convinced of the sagacity of this strategy: governments and constitutions had come and gone in the meantime and had proved capable of permanently institutionalizing the Pakistan state. The Jama'at had helped thwart any effort at consolidating power by any one of them. Mawdudi and his party outlasted all of their "anti-Islamic" rivals, from Liaqat 'Ali Khan to Chaudhri Ghulam Muhammad to General Ayub Khan and, finally, to Zulfiqar 'Ali Bhutto. The Jama'at remained on course, and Pakistan moved steadily in the direction of its aims. Before Mawdudi died in 1979, he could see tangible evidence that Pakistan was moving toward Islamicity without cataclysmic revolution.[24] In 1991, the Jama'at's vice-president (na'ib amir) 'Abdu'l-Ghafur Ahmad, declared that with the advent of democracy and the rise to power of the Islami Jumhuri Ittihad (Islamic Democratic Alliance),[25] revolution was no longer a necessity and, by implication, no longer an aim.[26]

Following the creation of Pakistan, Mawdudi forced the party, at the cost of dissensions and defections, to accept the legitimacy of the state.[27] As pragmatic political considerations began to replace revolutionary idealism, the Jama'at began to look like a controlled and responsible party, aiming to form a government and rule the country. In 1957, when he outlined the Jama'at's new policy, Mawdudi drove the last nail into the coffin of revolution by declaring that "transforming the political system can be done only through constitutional means: elections; . . . transformation of the political order through unconstitutional means is forbidden by the *shari'ah*."[28] Not long after that, the Jama'at's student organization, the Islami Jam'iat-i Tulabah (Islamic student association), declared that it did not wish to adopt the methods of the Muslim Brotherhood of Egypt, who at the time were engaged in a violent campaign against Gamal Abdel Nasser.[29]

Mawdudi did not waver from this stand, even when Ayub Khan pushed his party toward more and more radical options.[30] Ayub Khan did away with the electoral process to which the Jama'at had committed itself and systematically harassed the Jama'at itself, first by pushing the party out of politics and later by moving to eliminate it altogether. The government regarded the Jama'at as a subversive organization and followed policies that were likely to push it in that direction, but Mawdudi stayed his ground and kept the Jama'at in the mainstream of Pakistani politics:

> I am in principle opposed to all unlawful, unconstitutional and underground activities. I did not come to this opinion out of consideration of any expediency or in response to any challenge. My opinion is rather the product of contemplation and studying. . . . Support for the law is the basic tenet of a civilized society . . . covert activity is a greater menace to society than the one it seeks to remove.[31]

Elsewhere he insisted:

> Whatever I have done, I have always done it openly within the boundaries of the law and existing Constitution, so much that I have never violated even those laws which I have fought hard to oppose. I have tried to change them through lawful and constitutional means and never adopted the path of violence.[32]

"Creating a chaotic situation," argued Mawdudi, would only make it possible for "forces inimical to the interests of Islam [i.e., the Left] [to] find an opportunity to capture power."[33]

When in the late 1960s Ayub Khan's regime collapsed as a result of socioeconomic and political unrest, the support for leftist forces grew. Still, Mawdudi continued to adhere to his earlier conclusions,[34] and he did not allow the Jama'at to be provoked into clandestine activities when the People's Party government clamped down on its activities in 1972. In the five years that followed, a Jama'at member of the National Assembly, Nazir Ahmad, was assassinated, and Mian Tufayl Muhammad (the amir of the Jama'at) and a number of other Jama'at leaders and pro-Jama'at activists were jailed and, for the first time, seriously abused. Even then, Mawdudi urged the Jama'at not to waver from its commitment to the constitutional process.[35]

Mawdudi was unable to control the Jama'at completely, and its activists were eventually provoked by the People's Party to set in motion a chain of violence that damaged the party's moral standing. Mawdudi was gravely concerned about this turn of events and moved swiftly to prevent it from influencing the party's doctrinal position. In his eyes, the Jama'at was merely defending itself against government brutality and had not changed its mind about violence.[36] To his last days, Mawdudi continued to advocate the use of peaceful means in the pursuit of an Islamic state just as the Jama'at, and especially its student wing, the Jam'iat, steered in new directions and became increasingly involved in acts of violence.[37]

Jihad and Revolution

Mawdudi's position on such key Islamic doctrines as jihad was more conservative than those of other revivalist thinkers and limited revolutionary activism.[38] In 1948 he rejected the validity of a jihad declared by the government in Kashmir during a cease-fire with India. Pakistan had let it be known that the jihad was declared by local religious leaders and was undertaken by volunteer fighters. Mawdudi rejected the validity of a jihad so declared, stating that it could only be proclaimed by a government. Nor did Mawdudi accept purely political or revolutionary readings of the doctrine of jihad. He argued that it must not denote "a crazed faith . . . blood-shot eyes, shouting *Allah'u akbar* [God is great], decapitating an unbeliever wherever they see one, cutting off heads while invoking *La ilaha illa-llah* [there is no god but God]"[39]—the very terms in which jihad and its revivalist advocates are seen today. Jihad, Mawdudi went on to explain, was not war, but a struggle—a struggle not in the name of God but along the path set by God.[40] There is little here to distinguish Mawdudi's position from that of the ulama, who divided jihad into a greater and a lesser struggle, the former against one's soul and the latter against Islam's enemies.[41]

Over the years, Mawdudi's position softened further. In 1939 he declared the military jihad to be a weapon of last resort when it pointed to a path of victory for Islam.[42] In 1954 he told Justice Muhammad Munir and the Court of Inquiry into the Punjab Disturbances that jihad could only be declared when the country was actually, and not potentially, at war, and then only if the war was with *daru'l-harb* (abode of non-Muslims).[43]

Populism and Revolution

Mawdudi was more or less oblivious to the socioeconomic issues that are generally at the heart of mass support for a revolutionary movement. More often than not, he even seemed to swim against the current. In the 1950s, when he openly opposed Prime Minister Liaqat 'Ali Khan's land reform in the Punjab,[44] he went so far as to justify feudalism (*jagirdari*) by pointing to Islam's protection of property rights and to caution the government against punishing all property owners for the excesses of a few.[45] Mawdudi later moderated his defense of feudalism by arguing that the issue should be dealt with in full compliance with Islamic law and the protection for right to property, thus shifting the emphasis from the merits of feudalism to the Islamicity of government actions.

Then, however, he again cautioned the government not to tamper with "lawful *jagirdari*";[46] this was hardly an attitude in keeping with a popular revolutionary agenda.

The ambiguity inherent in Mawdudi's use and misuse of Western terms also caused confusion among his coterie. Kaukab Siddiq, a onetime Jama'at stalwart and translator of Mawdudi into English, understood the *mawlana* in clearly Marxian terms, and Siddiq's translations of Mawdudi bear the imprint of that bias, possibly confusing what Mawdudi actually meant. In an interpretive extrapolation from Mawdudi's ideas, Siddiq wrote that the Islamic state would be "a society in which everyone is a Caliph of God, and an equal participant in this caliphate, [and] cannot tolerate any class divisions of birth and social position. All men enjoy equal status and position in such a society."[47] The differences between Mawdudi and Siddiq on that point finally led to a parting of the ways.[48] Mawdudi did not like Siddiq's openly Marxian rendition of his views, and Siddiq realized that in his search for revolution he had entangled himself in the wrong movement. The ambiguity caused by the use of the term revolution continues to generate contradictory formulations and actions to this day.

After the revolution in Iran and, later, the advent of the war in Afghanistan between its people and the Soviet Union, in 1980–1981 the debate over revolution sharpened. The Iranian revolution broke out the year Mawdudi died, so the debate that followed was based on various interpretations of his teachings. By virtue of its success, the Iranian revolution put the Jama'at's passive notion of Islamic revolution in question, as did the Afghan war that followed.[49] Qazi Husain Ahmad, amir of the Jama'at since 1987 and formerly a liaison of the Jama'at with the Afghan mujahidin, argued that "the Afghan case stands as the only tangible victory for Islam"; the Jama'at can boast no such victory.[50]

Jama'at members today seem to talk of revolution more than they once did, reflecting the greater visibility of the debate over the issue in the party's ranks. Still, references are often qualified by the explanation that revolution does not necessarily involve cataclysmic social upheaval, only a drastic change in society's conception of religion and its aims. Some of Jama'at's leaders, notably Sayyid As'ad Gilani (the amir of Lahore), favor the Iranian model. Gilani believes that Mawdudi's ideas should be reinterpreted to allow the Jama'at to pursue real revolution.[51] If the Jama'at espouses an Islamic revolution, it should also commit itself to a revolutionary struggle.[52] The examples of Iran and Afghanistan have proven to this group that revolution works.

The difference with the Iranian and Afghan models is that they could require the Jama'at to dissociate itself from the state and to reject an order it had recognized for the past four decades as sufficiently legitimate for it to support. The Jama'at would have to emulate Sayyid Qutb and declare Pakistan a thoroughly pagan society. Not only is such an about-face difficult, but many Jama'at activists think it would cause more damage than any gain it could generate. 'Abdu'l-Ghafur Ahmad and his followers are committed to the political process in Pakistan. They believe that the Jama'at has gained from its commitment to the electoral process and see no benefit in rekindling revolutionary fervor in a party that has already routinized its revolutionary zeal.[53] The position of this group is strengthened by the ever-present power and influence of Mawdudi's teachings among a great number of both the rank-and-file and the leadership.

Revolutionary action has time and again been placed before the Jama'at's *shura'* and is also widely debated in the party ranks.[54] Thus far, the Jama'at has not been successful in any election and is unlikely to be so, as long as elections are controlled by the traditional elite—landlords and their patronage systems; therefore, the upshot of the debate has been that the Jama'at is not yet ready to turn revolutionary but remains open to such a possibility. Its objectives are definite (*qat'i*), argue the Jama'at leadership, and its methods can remain open to interpretation and adaptation (*ijtihadi*) based on the exigencies of the moment.[55] This issue underlines the uncertainty that surrounds the concept of revolution in the Jama'at. More important, it attests to the fact that what Mawdudi meant by revolution is not the same thing as what many observers of Islamic revivalism have understood him to mean.

What Is Islamic Revolution?

It is clear from the foregoing that Mawdudi, despite his frequent use of the idiom and symbols of revolution, did not advocate sociopolitical change on the kind or scale that can be described as revolution in Western terms. It is also apparent that he imparted a particular meaning to the term. The question that arises, then, is if Mawdudi did not mean revolution as it is commonly understood in the Western world when he used the word, what did he mean? His Islamic revolution was to be a gradual and evolutionary process of cultural, social, and political reform, whose objective was to be *'adl* (justice) and *ihsan* (benevolence), understood not in socioeconomic terms, but in ethical ones. The obstacles to Islamic revolution were not social consciousness, distribution of resources, or any other of the usual postulates of Western thinkers, but *fahsha'* (immorality) and *munkarat* (forbidden acts).[56]

Mawdudi's focus on the ethical nature of revolution, rather than the economic and political natures of it, flew in the face of conventional notions. Having appropriated the myth of revolution, he then eviscerated it by applying it to a utopian sociopolitical order that existed in some indefinite future. Action was no longer decisive; zeal was to be sublimated. This is in direct contrast with Iran, where Islamic revolutionary ideology appropriated all the paraphernalia of Western ideological movements and political religions, to which it added the promise of otherworldly salvation.[57] Mawdudi's discourse on revolution resembled the Iranian model in that it sought to produce an ideological outlook that utilized Western ideas, but instead of invoking revolutionary activism, his "promise of otherworldly salvation" suspended it. Muslims, he said, should not be disheartened by the lack of tangible success. Their efforts on behalf of the Islamic state had not been in vain; they would be rewarded in the hereafter.[58] It was more important that they stay the course: "Even if the current methods of struggle takes a century to bear fruit, a nonviolent movement shall be our way."[59]

Hence, what Mawdudi meant by the term revolution was a process of changing the ethical basis of society, which should begin at the top and permeate into the lower strata. It was a process of cultural engineering based on definite criteria and postulates, which not only would shape the society in the image of the *din*, but would also prepare the ground for an Islamic state. Other social dialectics or aspirations, such as changes in the social structure, were not central to this process and, at any rate, could be accommodated within the framework of the Islamic state.

If his message was directed at any class or social stratum, it was to the society's leaders. Revolution, he told a Jama'at gathering in 1945, did not involve the society as a whole; it was *inqilab-i imamat* (revolution in leadership).[60] "It is not the people's thoughts which changes society," argued Mawdudi, "but the minds of the society's movers and leaders."[61] Mawdudi held to the belief that "societies are built, structured, and controlled from the top down by conscious manipulation of those in power."[62] Inherent in this view is a greater emphasis on human resolve and volition than Western interpretations of revolution allowed:[63] "Strengthening the faith and moral ethics of Muslims in Pakistan is our primary concern and problem. Unless this feat is accomplished no scheme of reform, regardless of how attractive it may look on paper, would be attainable."[64] Change in the hearts and minds of individuals from the helm of the society downward through an educational process—a *da'wah* effort—and without any other sociopolitical catalysts would ipso facto culminate in an Islamic revolution.[65]

This attitude probably arose from Mawdudi's own change of heart and reconversion to Islam during the 1928–1932 period. It was first introduced by him during the convocation ceremonies of the Muslim Anglo Oriental College of Amritsar in 1940.[66] His proposals at Amritsar were translated into policy guidelines during the Jama'at's first forum on education, held in Pathankot in 1944.[67] It certainly predated the creation of Pakistan and was therefore not rooted in the vicissitudes of Pakistani politics.

Mawdudi used education not so much to rejuvenate religious observance as to train a cadre of dedicated and pious men who would be charged with initiating, leading, and subsequently protecting the Islamic revolutionary process. Mawdudi predicted that they would ultimately assume the reins of government and thenceforth oversee the process of Islamization:

> An Islamic state does not spring into being all of a sudden like a miracle; it is inevitable for its creation that in the beginning there should grow up a movement having for its basis the view of life, the ideal existence, the standard of morality, and the character and spirit which is in keeping with the fundamentals of Islam.[68]

Education was a primary agent in Mawdudi's conception of revolution; it gave shape to the leadership cadre and served as the impetus for the unfolding of the revolution from the apex of the society to its base. It lay at the heart of the Islamic revolutionary ideology and had to precede the revolution because it prepared the ground for the successful institution of the Islamic state: "A state-system based on belief in the sovereignty of God and in a sense of responsibility to Him requires for its successful working a special type of individual mass-character and peculiar mental attitude."[69] It was also with a view to fulfilling this objective that the Jama'at created its student union, Islami Jam'iat-i Tulabah, to spread Mawdudi's influence to Pakistan's future leaders. There are interesting parallels here with fundamentalist Protestant movements and Catholic movements of re-Christianization. The Jama'at's emphasis on education as the means for infiltrating the power structure and thus influencing future socio-political developments brings to mind the cases of Jerry Falwell's Liberty University and the Oral Roberts University in the United States, as well as the numerous institutions of higher learning affiliated with the Opus Dei in Spain.

Mawdudi's demand that society first be educated in Islam and prepared for the Islamic revolution and the Islamic state stood in clear contrast to the approaches of Ayatollah Khomeini and General Zia ul-Haq, both of whom used state power to carry out Islamization and therefore placed primary importance on the struggle for political power. Mawdudi did not share their enthusiasm for a singularly political solution and saw Islamization as an organic process that should emerge from the social culture and only then culminate in the Islamic state. In contrast to Khomeini, Mawdudi regarded the Islamic revolution as essentially a peaceful process. Education would guarantee greater adherence to the *din* and harmonize society, thereby reducing the need for force in the revolutionary process. The Islamic revolution, Mawdudi implied, would become more, not less, peaceful as it unfolded; however, the specter of force to guarantee Islamicity, especially after the success of the revolution, lurked in the background of this peaceful process.

By education, Mawdudi meant the process that would encourage revolution, a process whereby Muslims would be reconverted to true Islam—the *din*—and develop firm loyalties to it.[70] It was the means by which Muslims would be trained to produce a leadership cadre, a vanguard movement, and, eventually, a religiously conscious citizenry. For this reason, the Jama'at invested heavily in producing and disseminating publications to facilitate a far-reaching program of cultural change.

But education was not merely the locomotive of the Islamic revolution or simply a *da'wah*; (it was a process of learning, of filling minds with a particular body of knowledge conveying a distinctive worldview. Education as cultural engineering lay at the heart of Mawdudi's call; it was the primary vocation of the Jama'at and a primary mechanism for instigating a revival of Islam. To this end, it had to combine Islamic learning with knowledge of modern subjects so that the religious, intellectual, and political leaders and, subsequently, the citizenry it produced, would be both culturally authentic and at home with modern scientific thought. Education therefore possessed both Islamizing and modernizing objectives.[71] Mawdudi's views here are close to the Nadwi educational model, which also began as an effort to relate Islamic and modern educational methods and subjects of study and to train a leadership equally versatile in Islamic and modern fields. Mawdudi extolled the Nadwi model as a sensible medium between the traditional and the modern systems of education and as a representative example of what he had in mind for Muslim education.[72]

Although the political enfranchisement of the Jama'at that resulted from the party's decision to participate in the Pakistani electoral process in 1951 was tantamount to resorting to political means to nudge society toward the Islamic state, at the doctrinal level the Jama'at remained loyal to the idea of revolution through education—Islamizing society by impressing Islamic values on its leaders and members.

Despite the Jama'at's departure from this position in practice, Mawdudi's discourse on revolution was sufficiently compelling to be adopted by the rival revivalist movements that have emerged in Pakistan since the 1970s. Israr Ahmad, a one-time member of the Jama'at who left the party in 1957 in protest of the party's decision to participate in national elections, has organized Tanzim-i Islami (Islamic Order) on the pattern of the original Jama'at and based it on an ideological outlook similar to Mawdudi's. The Tanzim differs from the Jama'at only in that the former adheres strictly to Mawdudi's doctrinal position of revolution through education and has thus far remained aloof from politics.[73]

Muhammad Tahiru'l-Qadri founded the Minhaju'l-Qur'an (Path of the Qur'an) organization and the Pakistan Awami Tahrik (Pakistan People's Movement) party in a different response to Mawdudi's discourse on revolution. Qadri discerned a fundamental problem in the Jama'at's two-tier approach to revolution—advocating revolution through education at the doctrinal level and utilizing the electoral process to hasten the advent of the revolution on the practical—and concluded that the inconsistency was sufficiently debilitating to inhibit the Jama'at's ability to attract support and cash in on its electoral potential. He decided to fill the void by forming two organizations to resolve the inconsistency. He separated education from politics and established separate organizations for each: Minhaju'l-Qur'an acts as a *da'wah* movement, the Pakistan Awami Tahrik as a political party.[74] All these organizations attest to Mawdudi's influence. Both Israr Ahmad and Tahiru'l-Qadri faithfully support Mawdudi's irenic view of revolution, which has withstood the challenge of the Iranian revolution and found roots in Pakistani revivalist thought.

5

The Islamic State

At a glance, Mawdudi's conception of the Islamic state and his views on the place of Islam in politics appear to be a modernization of the classical doctrine of the caliphate. On closer examination, however, it appears that he was less concerned about the caliphate and more about the problems of enforcing the writ of the *din* while at the same time running a modern state. His principal intellectual challenge was to devise a state that would encompass his concept of the true Islamic community. For him, enforcement of the *din* and managing the state were ineluctably tied to one another. Much like John Calvin who, "as a prelude to admitting the state to the world of religious purpose . . . admitted politics to religion,"[1] Mawdudi began by interpreting Islam in political terms. Islam, argued Mawdudi, could not be understood through mere contemplation; it could only find meaning when implemented by what he termed *'amali shahadat* (testimony of faith through practice).[2] Religious truth was predicated on social action, which was also the supreme expression of piety.[3] Reiterating his stock argument in favor of revivalism, Mawdudi time and again asserted that Islam recognized no boundaries between the spiritual and the mundane, between faith and politics: "The *chief* characteristic of Islam is that it makes no distinction between the spiritual and the secular life."[4] Suggestions to the contrary were rejected as Western plots against Islam.[5] Mawdudi consistently defended the principle of Islam's role in politics as being both fundamental and logical. In fact, he regarded it as true of all religions. To the chagrin of many of his followers, he endorsed the effort to base India's legal code on the Hindu Manu laws, even though this would have been detrimental to the Muslim community. He had no objection to implementation of Manu laws even "if the Muslims of India . . . [are] treated in that form of Government as *shudras* or *malishes* (*mlecchas*, outcasts) . . . depriving them of all share in the Government and the rights of a citizen," although he also asserted, almost as an afterthought, that "such a state of affairs already exist[ed] in [secular] India."[6]

To him, the logic of his position was self-evident: ethical concerns emanated from the heart of Islam and were superior to worldly concerns; they must therefore supersede all other considerations in shaping mankind's social life.[7] Furthermore, Islam must assert its claim to politics and inform social relations with its teachings and values: "Man's status in the universe having thus been determined, it follows logically that he has no right to lay down the law of his conduct and decide the right and wrong of it. This is a function which properly belongs to God."[8] The Islamic state was needed because Islam would never be fully implemented unless it controled the centers of power. Without the Islamic state, Islam would most likely become marginalized. The revival of Islam hinged on its control of politics. The *shari'ah*, argued Mawdudi, had to lay equal claims to the public and private lives of Muslims. To do that, it would have to be rationalized to strengthen its hold over Muslim social conduct and to reaffirm the fusion of Islam and politics.[9]

This logical end to Mawdudi's exegesis was supported by such Qur'anic verses as "His verily is all creation and commandment" (7:54) and "Establish the religion and be not divided therein" (42:13).[10] This latter verse was interpreted by Mawdudi as calling for the establishment of an Islamic political order to which Muslims were obliged to give unwavering obedience,[11] because establishment of Islamic rule would not be possible, nor would it hold any meaning, if it were based on political fiat. The political order must be a clear manifestation of the sovereignty of God. The corollary of the establishment of the religion (*iqamat-i din*) was virtuous leadership (*imamat-i salihah*) and divine government (*hukumat-i ilahiyah*).[12]

If there were no Islamic state, the whole reason for revelation would come into question, for religious teachings were not sent by God to be ignored.[13] Hence, not only did true faith automatically lead to political action, but the very existence of religion was predicated on a political goal. Islam could have no glory unless it was true to its ethos, which, in turn, could not fully blossom in the absence of a truly Islamic order.

Being a Muslim, as defined by the *din*, was predicated on the struggle for an Islamic state, for only within the framework of that state could the Muslim identity find shape.[14] This would be the practical testimony of faith, the denial of which would be tantamount to refusing to live fully as a Muslim.[15] Because there was no possibility of salvation for Muslims outside the structure of their faith and because faith could not be fully implemented without the Islamization of the political order, Mawdudi concluded that making politics sacred was a religious obligation:[16] "If you believe in God and His Prophet and accept the Qur'an as the Book of God, then inevitably you have to use moral principles which Islam teaches and will have to accept the political principles which it has given."[17] If there were to be an Islamic order, it would have to arrive on the heels of an Islamic state. The kind of Islamic existence that Mawdudi had in mind could only emerge with the support of an Islamic government. After all, Islam had survived in India for as long as the Muslims had occupied the seats of power.[18] Maryam Jameelah wrote, "Once I asked Maulana Maudoodi why the Jama'at-e-Islami is so intensely involved in political activity. The Maulana replied that preaching, printed literature and even education is of little avail unless Islam can be implemented practically in a full-blooded Islamic state."[19]

Mawdudi had arrived at this position gradually. He began with the idea that the *shari'ah* must be preserved and the faithful mobilized if the interests of Muslims in India were to be safeguarded. His ideology was originally premised on the need for religion to inform politics with a sense of the sacred. This conclusion was eventually supplanted by the realization that only political power could guarantee the preservation and implementation of religious norms and values: "In the Muslim world, secularism means anti-religion and state-sponsored persecution of the religious elements."[20] Without political power, concluded Mawdudi, true Islam would remain only an ideal, forever threatened with annihilation. The Islamic state could not be only a utopian order—the end result of Islamization—it had to be the beginning of Islamization, the guarantor and harbinger of the entire process. This politicized Mawdudi and the Jama'at more completely.

Mawdudi's idea that Islam's future depended on politics had immediate bearing on the Jama'at's mode of operation and determined the final shape of its activism. In 1956 and 1957, for example, when a number of Jama'at leaders objected to the idea of participating in the national elections, Mawdudi retorted that the activities of the Jama'at had no meaning outside of politics and that politics was the logical end of the Jama'at's activities. Politics, he declared, was not merely a means to an end but the end itself. As politics came to be the raison d'être for the Jama'at, the concept of the Islamic state found new meaning. The transformation of the Jama'at from a politicized religious movement to a religiously conscious political party required a new understanding of the Islamic state. In the final analysis, the Islamic state was not merely a means for creating an Islamic order of life, but a model for perfect government with universal application—a political end for a political movement. In this light, the political teachings of Islam and, subsequently, the Islamization of politics would have to be implemented, even through coercion.[21]

This argument extended the discussion of the Islamic state further: if politics were to be subject to religious values, then religion could only be understood in light of politics. Islamization of politics in a logical continuum led to the politicization of Islam. For the Islamic state to function, it would have to be premised on an interpretation of Islamic law that would be able to justify and, more importantly, sustain the functioning of that state.[22]

> Acknowledging that someone is your ruler to whom you must submit means that you have accepted his Din. He now becomes your sovereign and you become his subjects. . . . Din, therefore, actually means the same thing as state and government; Shari'ah is the law of that state and government; and 'Ibadah amounts to following and complying with that law.[23]

The continuity between Islam and politics, argued Mawdudi, was akin to the relation of "roots with the trunk and the branches with the leaves [of a tree]"; it was a symbiotic relationship wherein the religious informed the political and the political sustained the religious: "In Islam the religious, the political, the economic, and the social are not separate systems; they are different departments and parts of the same system."[24]

The convergence of Muslim piety and religious values with political objectives found its embodiment in the doctrine of jihad. The traditional view of the doctrine distinguished between *jihad-i kubra* (the greater jihad), man's struggle with his soul in a quest for spiritual purity, and *jihad-i sughra* (the lesser jihad), defense of Islam against the religion's physical enemies. In Mawdudi's view, the lesser jihad overrode the greater.[25] The identification of faith with politics, spiritual gain with worldly power, and salvation with social utopia was thus complete:

> Of all the factors of social life which impinge on culture and morality, the most powerful and effective is government. . . . Hence the best way of putting an end to the *fitna* [mischief] and purifying of life of *munkar* [that which is reprehensible] is to eliminate all *mufsid* [corrupt] governments and replace them with those which in theory and practice are based on piety and righteous action, the objective of Islamic Jihad is to put an end to the dominance of the un-Islamic systems of governments and replace them with Islamic rule.[26]

Mawdudi's position over the years consolidated into a distinct notion that political power was the logical objective of faith. Faith in turn became an active and dynamic process of becoming, and the struggle for religious salvation became manifest in a quest for a virtuous order whereby the *ummah,* community of the faithful, would be converted into the *hizbu'llah,* party of God.[27] The *din* thus found clear political connotations because it was defined in overtly political terms: as the "organization" of the true faith. "Ours is not a party of the enlightened or the religious missionaries. It is a party of God's soldiers. This party therefore, has no option but to take control of political power."[28]

Nature of the State

The concept of the Islamic state, the end point and crowning achievement of Mawdudi's discourse, tied his interpretation of Islam to the political exigencies from which his movement drew inspiration. The Islamic state was not so much a utopian order or a romantic conglomeration of disparate religious dicta as it was a model for governance, formed as a result of debate with the concept of the Western state. In his proposals and discussions, Mawdudi seldom made comparisons with the ethical teachings of other religions, but he did with various Western theories and systems of political organization and government, from communism to democracy.[29] The comparisons served as the locus for the formulation of an Islamic ideological orientation that above and beyond its nativist idealism incorporated concepts, values, and ideas from the corpus of thought with which it was in debate. It should not be examined, therefore, only as a means for putting Islamic teachings on society and politics into practice, but also with a view to gauging the efficacy of an ideology rooted in Islam but defined in contrast to the West.

Mawdudi understood the Islamic state not as territorial but as a cultural and ethical entity. Its boundaries, values, goals, and citizens were defined in Islamic terms. It was this emphasis on ethical and cultural factors that distinguished his conception of the Islamic state from the pan-Islamic formulations that preceded his ideas; formulations that had espoused a territorial unity of Muslim lands.

The ethical and cultural basis of the Islamic state also made its choice of leaders an issue of great concern. The Islamic state was anchored in the idea of *imamat-i salihah* (virtuous leadership) in place of the existing *fussaq'u fujjar ki imamat* (leadership of the corrupt) of the "godless" political order.[30] The nature of the leadership of the Islamic state was expected to confirm that it was based on the sovereignty of God. Those outside the Jama'at regarded a state that vested sovereignty in God to be intrinsically authoritarian.[31] Mawdudi and his followers went to great lengths to assure their audience of the democratic nature of the Islamic state. The results often revealed a "dislocation between the outward argument and the inner train of reasoning."[32] The debate with the critics of the Islamic state was a serious effort at anchoring the state in democracy. This debate motivated the Jama'at to define the concept of the Islamic state more clearly and to make it compatible with Western conceptions of the state in general and liberalism in particular. As a result, democracy found multiple levels of meaning in Mawdudi's works, which coalesced to produce a complex definition of that ideal.

Mawdudi insisted that the Islamic state would be democratic because its leadership would be duly elected and bound by the writ of divine law. He captured the gist of this argument in the terms "democratic caliphate" and "theo-democracy," which he coined to describe how the Islamic state would work. At first glance, the synthesis between Islamic symbols and Western political ideals may seem to be a tactical ploy designed to manipulate the political sensibilities of educated Muslims by hiding unpalatable proposals behind a veneer of democracy. Mawdudi's synthesis is more complex. His debate with Western political thought was antagonistic, but it also assimilated Western ideas into his interpretation of Islam and the Islamic state. Mawdudi was not concerned with liberal values but solely with a means for promoting and safeguarding an Islamic social order. Whether or not the state would be a democracy or a dictatorship was secondary. The preoccupation with democracy was a later development, the inevitable outcome of his debate with Western political thought and the Jama'at's involvement in electoral politics in Pakistan.

The complexity of Mawdudi's treatment of democracy perhaps has to do with the context in which he first encountered it. Indian nationalism was emancipatory in its spirit and promised democracy in a pluralistic society.[33] The Congress party, however, failed to convince Muslims that it would carry out its promise. Many Muslims saw Indian nationalism as a vehicle for Hindu supremacy. For example, the Muslim thinker Chaudhri Rahmat 'Ali argued that Indian nationalism was simply an effort by caste Hindus and the British to enslave the followers of other religions and cultures of India, Muslims in particular.[34] This led many Muslim leaders to distance themselves from Indian nationalism, to envision a Muslim identity separate from Indian identity, and to demand communal and, ultimately, national rights.[35] Muhammad 'Ali Jinnah left the Congress party to lead the Muslim League to Pakistan, arguing that for Muslims a secular state had no meaning except in a Muslim state; only in such a state would their social progress and political rights be divorced from their identity. Although Jinnah remained content with questioning the inclusive and secular nature of the Congress party, Mawdudi went further, questioning the wisdom and ethical basis of the emancipatory, democratic, and inclusive order that the party promised.

Although Islamic activists like Mawdudi never became as prominent as Muhammad 'Ali Jinnah, their Islamic discourse was of importance to the success of Muslim communalism. In fact, Mawdudi's views on a host of issues was shaped by his communalist inclination.[36] Because Islamic thinkers resisted Indian nationalism, emancipation and democracy were either irrelevant or dangerous to its aims. The victory of numbers would mean Hindu rule; in an Indian democracy, Muslims would be outnumbered and would have no power. Consequently, Mawdudi, who believed that Muslim power was justified by Islam's moral superiority, was suspicious of democracy. He could not simply dismiss the much vaunted ideals of emancipation and democracy, however. The new Muslim identity had to have its own vision and then argue that it alone would bring true emancipation and true democracy; it had to reject democracy's values and cultural foundations and promote its own vision of freedom. It was therefore also anti-West, claiming that Western freedom would mean prostitution, decay, servitude, and extinction. Anti-Westernism thus was a function of the competition—first with Indian nationalism and its promise and then with the Muslim League's Muslim nationalism, which had developed along similar although less collectivist lines than Mawdudi's own. Mawdudi's position on democracy therefore had its roots not merely in Islamic doctrine, but in Indian history. It reflected his disdain for Indian nationalism, which, needless to add, greatly complicated his accommodation of democracy. It also meant that for Mawdudi revivalism was less an expression of idealism and more the pragmatic use of faith for a political end.

Mawdudi conceived of the Islamic state in ahistorical terms as an ideal type, not because it produced the most efficient machinery for governance, but because it created conditions most conducive to living according to the *din*. The state was neither democratic nor authoritarian, for it had no need to govern in the Western sense of the term. Concern for that kind of government was generated by crises of governability and legitimacy, which were in turn generated by demands for political participation and mass mobilization and the need to manage the economy effectively. In a polity in which there were no grievances and both the government and the citizenry abided by the same infallible and inviolable divine law, there would be no problems with democratic rights and procedures. The question of democracy would not arise, for democracy and authoritarianism were defined as opposites. If the populace did not feel itself oppressed, it would not dream of democracy. The Islamic state was based on the society envisioned by the *din*. The ideals of the *din* would not only cure Muslim society

of those maladies that produced cleavages in other societies, it would also dis-
tribute resources and power equitably. It would produce a society that would
make both government fiats and individual rights unnecessary. Mawdudi's conception was idealistic. It echoed German romanticism, which had defined citizenship in the context of its need to foster homogeneity in its ethnonational
community and, in turn, limited the scope of civil, political, and even social
rights.

In Mawdudi's writings, therefore, democracy was merely an adjective used
to define the otherwise undefinable virtues of the Islamic state. The state was
defined as democratic because it was an ideal state. Mawdudi used the term
democratic to express the virtues of the Islamic state and embellish it because
in Western political thought the term had positive connotations. Mawdudi later
featured democracy in his discussions as a concern he had to contend with before
the Islamic state was established. These discussions encompassed both the ideal
state and the path leading to it; therefore, he had to deal with democratic rights
because Muslims were concerned with them, especially once critics began to
point to the authoritarian tendencies that were implicit in Mawdudi's views on
social organization.

Mawdudi's discourse on the *din* and the Islamic state produced an image
of society that blended the individual Muslim into a collective unit in which
social interactions were rationalized and turned into contractual arrangements
as determined by the *din*. It was this modernization of social structure through
collectivism—which would follow the institution of the Islamic state—that
made both Western and traditional critics apprehensive about Mawdudi's
agenda. Those who remained skeptical about the democratic nature of the
Islamic state were wary more of the authoritarian tendencies inherent in the kind
of social modernization that Mawdudi advocated than they were of its Islamic
content.

As the debate over the nature of the Islamic state continued, Mawdudi began
to target particular social strata. Because Mawdudi was compelled to directly
address the question of the nature of authority in the Islamic state if he was to
win Westernized intellectuals over, he used democracy to deal with their concerns. He did so more as a concession to this audience than out of conviction,
however, especially after the Jama'at became involved in the political process in
Pakistan and began to target the educated classes.[37]

By becoming involved in the elections in Pakistan in the 1950s, the Jama'at
postponed its efforts on behalf of realizing the ideal Islamic state, substituting
pragmatic politics for the chiliastic zeal of the movement.[38] Earlier, Mawdudi
had argued that the Islamic state could only be produced when particular religious, social, and political factors came together, at the right time and under
the right circumstances.[39] The determinism inherent in this view and the exact
nature of the revolution that would bring it about precluded entrusting the fate
of the Islamic state to the vicissitudes of a political process that was based on
un-Islamic principles and over whose course the Jama'at had no control. This
kind of idealism had to give way to a more pragmatic and flexible approach to
Pakistani politics, however, if the Jama'at were to survive at all. As a result, prac-

tical decisions became more important than ideological discourse. Because Mawdudi's idea of the Islamic state was relegated to a distant utopia as he became engaged in political debate and the electoral process, he had to concern himself with this question of democracy. Increased concern for democracy was also a function of the routinization of the Jama'at's idealism, the politicization of its program, and the replacement of outright revolution by incremental Islamization. Throughout its existence in Pakistan, moreover, the Jama'at had to contend with the government. As a consequence, Mawdudi's interest in the protection of individual rights, due process of law, and freedom of political expression became a matter of personal concern. Democracy was no longer just a concession to those who were skeptical about the Islamic state, it was increasingly also the guarantor of the Jama'at's survival.

Mawdudi's new focus on democracy also intensified the cycle of criticism and apologia reflected in the Jama'at's program. The more Mawdudi sought to depict his program as democratic, the more his critics found reasons to use democratic yardsticks to scoff at his plans for Pakistan. The democratic pretension made him vulnerable to criticism, which, in turn, intensified his apologetic attempts to assuage his critics.

Democracy thus was featured in different ways at different stages in the evolution of Mawdudi's thought: first as part of an ideal type and then as part and parcel of introducing Islamic norms and values to the existing political order to which the Jama'at committed itself in the 1950s. As a means of gauging the efficacy and allure of Mawdudi's political program, democracy both obfuscated the actual dialectic of his discourse and revealed the influence of political imperatives on his ideological formulation. For Mawdudi, politics was as much shaped in the image of ideology as ideology was shaped by the needs of politics. Hence, despite Mawdudi's clear logic and systematic argumentation, the concept and goal of the Islamic state had produced confusing directives for the Jama'at.

Defining the Islamic State

Throughout his works, Mawdudi showed little interest in the actual workings of institutions. He was more concerned with abstract theoretical formulations and lessons in moral philosophy. The incorporation of the myth and certain features of Western democracy into the Islamic state elicited objection from traditional thinkers and from the ulama because they regarded it as a secular concept that had no place in the Islamic state, if there were to be one. Mawdudi, however, regarded democracy as a neutral ideal that could be Islamized without surrendering any ground to the West.[40] Undaunted by the castigations of the ulama, the pace and breadth of his assimilation of democratic ideas and values into his concept of the structure of the Islamic state increased over the years, producing more liberal versions of his model.

This model also incorporated the idea of the Prophet Muhammad's state in Medina. The example of Medina generally has been viewed by Muslims as a perennially valid historical model, one with relevancy to their social life and politics; it thus also had relevance to the Islamic state. Mawdudi's aim was to emulate the prophetic example in shaping the Islamic state and its mode of governance but remain true to the goal of a democracy. As democratic symbols and slogans begin to crop up in Mawdudi's writings, the prophetic model was used in increasingly Western terms in his later works, until the Islamic state finally became a "God-worshipping democratic Caliphate, founded on the guidance vouchsafed to us through Muhammad."[41]

History therefore ceased to be the mere narration of events and lives and became idealized to embody modern values about power and authority.[42] As the term democratic caliphate suggests, the idea of Islamic state also had its creative dimension, part romantic and atavist, and part modern. It was neither a thing of the past nor an entirely modern phenomenon but, instead, a modernizing one. The term democratic caliphate and its corollary, theodemocracy, both coined by Mawdudi, best captured this modernizing spirit. Even within Mawdudi's lifetime, the concept of the Islamic state evolved along exceedingly modern lines, becoming filled with values, ideals, and mechanisms borrowed from the West. Through the debate with democracy, Mawdudi's Islamic state was drawn to democratic ideals and principles to an increasing extent until in the end, democracy was both an objective and an attribute of the Islam state. For Mawdudi, a religious and democratic Islamic state would be superior to secular democracy[43]; however, any comparison between the two would show that the evolution of the Islamic state toward democracy remained far from complete. Despite its democratic aims, the Islamic state remained anchored in doctrines that hindered an acceptance of pluralism. In spite of changes made in its structure and objectives, the state as Mawdudi conceptualized it remained fundamentally antithethical to pluralism, though not to other aspects of secular democracy. In the words of Khurshid Ahmad,

> We have certain reservations about Western democracy on ethical/moral principals, especially over where sovereignty lies. But that does not mean that Muslims are "fascists." Muslims believe in the rule of law, human rights, shura', all of which are also important to a democracy. We have problems of accommodating democracy, but our faith is not antithetical to it.[44]

No doctrine was a greater impediment to democratization than the belief that sovereignty belonged to God alone. The Islamic state could not accept the relativity of truth, which is an essential tenet of Western democracy.[45] This idea was so central to Mawdudi's thinking that no compromise was possible. Yet, he saw this as no deterrent because he posed the problem differently. Making no effort to hide the Islamic state's theocratic inclination, he instead presented as true democracy what the West regarded as theocracy. The popular slogan of Islami Jam'iat-i Tulabah—"Rule of man over man is exploitation; submission to Allah the Creator is the only way to emancipation"—best captures the essence of Mawdudi's argument. This, as Amir Arjomand remarked, showed that Mawdudi "made no distinction between legislation and jurisprudence, between law-finding (by religious jurists) and law-making (by popular assemblies), and none between the Roman conception of the republic and the Islamic conception of the *umma*."[46]

Providing theocracy with a veneer of democracy, whether to assuage criticism or to appropriate democratic myths and symbols to further the cause of the Islamic state, was not free of problems. In theory, as well as in practice, the democratic rather than purely theological justification for the Islamic state led Mawdudi and the Jama'at into a maze of complex, muddled, and often contradictory arguments. The Jama'at consequently became entangled, on the one hand, in apologetic responses to its critics, who have persisted in exposing the inherent inconsistency of Mawdudi's position, and, on the other hand, in warding off the scorn of the traditional establishment who found Mawdudi's use of a secular idea to define the Islamic state insupportable.

In defining the Islamic state, Mawdudi sought to tailor the Islamic doctrines of *tawhid* (unity of God), understood as the absolute sovereignty of God, *risalat* (prophecy), understood as the ideal Islamic state;[47] and *khilafat* (caliphate), understood as a vicegerency of mankind on behalf of God and, hence, the reproduction and perpetuation of the Islamic state in the post-prophetic era, to support his position.[48] Although *tawhid* and *risalat* are immutable Islamic beliefs that were used to explicate and legitimize the concept of the Islamic state, it was *khilafat* that governed the intellectual and practical formulations on which Mawdudi based the working of the state.

Mawdudi's scheme for the Islamic state was premised on the absolute sovereignty of God, who held the role of Law-Giver and was the de jure head of the sociopolitical order.[49] The executive branch in the Islamic state would serve as vicegerent to God—a political interpretation of the Islamic belief that man is *khalifatu'llah* (God's vicegerent) on earth.[50] In this conception, God became the raison d'être, the guarantor, and an integral part of the sociopolitical order. As the Islamic state was the sole medium of interaction between man and God,[51] God's role and image were temporalized.

The absolute sovereignty of God furthermore would act to mold the Islamic state in a particular cast. Because the state would operate essentially as vicegerent[52] to the "legal sovereignty"[53] of God, it would be a managerial and praetorian state—a "caretaker" state, in the words of E. I. J. Rosenthal.[54] For Mawdudi, the Islamic state was not an evolving model, but an already perfect one, requiring no changes. Man could not improve upon it; he was merely enjoined to institute it and, subsequently, preserve it. Hence, politics, elections, or legislations could only play secondary roles in such a state.[55]

The liberal notion of the state is based on the centrality of the individual citizen. In this theory, the state's legitimacy is directly related to its accountability vis-à-vis the individual; that is, the state is regarded as legitimate only as long as it serves the public interest as freely expressed. The Islamic state, on the other hand, requires the depoliticization of the public sphere to make it subject to the designs of the state, a feat that can be accomplished through the education of the citizenry in Islam—in the *din,* to be specific. This will harmonize public opinion, reduce the role of competing interests in forming political programs, and produce a unified view on what constitutes the good of the state and the interests of the citizenry. The effort to depoliticize the citizenry also justifies the right of the state to intervene in society as arbitrator.

According to Mawdudi, individual expression would also be curtailed by the primacy of the legal and, by implication, political sovereignty of God, lest it counter the divine mandate of the state. As the embodiment and seat of divine will and man's vicegerency, the state would become the supreme authority and the sole political actor, as well as the embodiment of the popular will. The individual would have to relinquish his own vicegerency to the Islamic state, which is the expression of a collective vicegerency.[56] The individual therefore would be bound by the writ of the state, backed by the full force of religious law and the more paramount power of the collective vicegerency. Mawdudi concluded his argument with a Qur'anic injunction: "O ye who believe! Obey Allah, and obey the messenger and those of you who are in authority" (4:59).[57] He identified "those . . . in authority" (*ulau'l-amr*) as the guardians of the Islamic state—the executive branch.[58] The example of the Prophet's rule in Medina, the model for the Islamic state, moreover, confirmed that the Islamic state was a centralized body politic with an omnipotent executive branch.[59]

Mawdudi also conceived of the Islamic state as having a legislature and a judiciary, but their functions would be limited to advising the executive.[60] The task of legislative and judicial oversight, should the need arise, would be vested in the state itself and, by implication, in the state's overseer, the executive. The tasks of legislation and interpretation were limited matters that pertained only to worldly affairs and could not infringe on the sovereignty of God.[61] As the vicegerent of God, the state could exercise *ijtihad* (independent inquiry to establish the ruling of the *shari'ah*),[62] which traditionally had been the domain of the ulama. Mawdudi favored wresting the exclusive right to this practice from the doctors of religious law and vesting it in the state.

When Mawdudi defended the Islamic state from charges of theocracy, the influence of Western political thought on his views could be seen. The Islamic state, ideally above mundane political slogans, was given shape through the use of unmistakably Western terminology and theoretical constructs. It was a seemingly Islamic system that was in fact premised on a modernizing ethos. The issue of the absolute sovereignty of God aside, Mawdudi's assimilation of Western ideas in his discourse flowed without interruption. The Islamic state duplicated, assimilated, and reproduced Western political concepts, structures, and operations, producing a theory of statecraft that, save for its name and its use of Islamic terms and symbols, showed little indigenous influence. The synthesis, although systematic and consistent in its method, was not always free of theoretical inconsistencies and operational handicaps.

The Islamic state relied heavily on the *shari'ah* and the office of the amir or caliph: one set the boundaries of the state by determining its laws, and the other oversaw its affairs. The titular head of the state, the amir, was to be elected by the citizenry, but no one would be allowed to put forward his candidacy or to engage in electioneering. Mawdudi also did not countenance the operation of more than one political party in the state because more than one correct position could not exist, and it was religious law rather than popular vote that was to decide what the truth was. How democracy was to take its course, thus remained unclear.[63]

The *shari'ah* guaranteed the equality of all citizens before the law and provided the proper channels for expressing popular grievances against the executive. Grievances had to be based on stipulated criteria that would be in accord with the aims of the state. Freedom of political expression was limited because it could have currency only during the formative stages of the Islamic state when, in the absence of the rule of divine law, inconsistencies might persist that required protection of individual rights. After the formative years, dissent in a polity based on divine law could only be construed as apostasy. With this in mind, Mawdudi further curbed individual rights by stipulating that unless the citizenry of the Islamic state was able to prove inappropriate intentions or deeds on the part of the executive body, it was bound by its decisions.[64] More significant, he argued that should a legitimate grievance arise among the citizenry regarding the affairs of the state, and it be demonstrated that the government had erred from the path of the *din*, care should be taken not to confuse the state, which always remained virtuous, with the holders of office, who were fallible.[65] Dissent thus was also restricted to the government and was diverted away from the state. With the legislature and the judiciary occupying merely advisory positions, it was not certain what channels were open for an orderly expression of dissent or for forcing a transfer of power should the dissent be justified.

In Mawdudi's works, discussions of popular consultation were theoretical and diffuse. Concrete procedures and mechanisms were supplanted by emphasis on the famous prophetic saying "My community will never agree over error" and its corollary doctrine of consensus.[66] The Islamic state would employ these concepts not as a mechanism for consultation and expression of popular will, but as the means to reinforce its legitimacy and policy decisions. The individual was, in effect, excluded from political activity unless he could prove it was necessary for him to interfere in the affairs of the state. The burden of proof in such circumstances was with the dissident, who could participate in governance only at the helm of an irrefutably popular movement of dissent, if there were a clear consensus regarding a particular program. *Ijma'*, by stipulating the possibility of change only as a result of popular consensus, the extent and nature of which was open to interpretation, strengthened the status quo and vested power in the Islamic state. In short, the individual, though given the right to dissent, would be hard pressed to express it. Dissent would be irrelevant to the working of the state unless it were expressed by the overwhelming majority of its citizens.

Mawdudi saw nothing undemocratic in all these propositions. He argued that the election of the amir, albeit divorced from a free electoral process, would provide a democratic state whose continuity would be guaranteed by a sacrosanct code of law, which by definition was just and therefore required obedience.[67] Absent from Mawdudi's list of democratic features were guarantees for democratic procedures, protection of individual rights, and, most important, a mechanism for translating popular interest into policy. By discouraging electioneering, Mawdudi divorced the election of leaders from popular concerns and cast a shadow on the manner in which the state could reproduce itself and gain continuity.[68]

In effect, Mawdudi had understood democracy as static, involving only elections and equality before the law. Democracy as a dynamic process through which social, economic, and political concerns could be relayed to political actors and find expression in their programs, policies, and decisions had no place in Mawdudi's thinking. He understood democracy in parts, rather than as a whole, as a concession by the state and not as a system.

Perhaps Mawdudi thought that in an ideal state no grievances could exist that would require a leader's attention. Where the citizenry willingly submitted to the state and turned its attention from the affairs of the world to spiritual concerns, democracy could easily be reduced to elections and the rule of Islamic law. Mawdudi assumed that a powerful and centralized state, whose institutions were based on Islamic law and reflected Islamic values, would be democratic in spirit, provided it was the ideal state.

The picture that emerged from Mawdudi's discourse was of a state with commanding authority, based on mass support that was guaranteed as long as the state remained true to Islamic norms. Mass support would be ensured by the education of the population in the true teachings of Islam, which would reduce the burden of the government because the use of compulsion in enforcing its authority would be unnecessary.[69] A state guided by the tenets of the *shari'ah* was unlikely to wield power unjustly or to resort to the oppression of its citizens. Corruption had been introduced by the Umayyads, argued Mawdudi, who had converted the historical institution of the caliphate into a tyrannical regime.[70] Until then, the Islamic polity had been free of authoritarian tendencies. Islam in its pure form could never support despotic rule because by its very nature it was attuned to the needs of man and was the best guarantor of his rights. The human rights people in the West had to fight for, Mawdudi argued, already existed in the *shari'ah*. The advent of the Islamic state would resolve rather than generate the problem of guaranteeing human rights.[71]

Human rights were considered in terms of the objective of Islamic law and not in relation to the epistemological and political basis of the concept. The basic human right was the right to demand an Islamic order and to live in it, not the right to differ with the rulers of the Islamic state or defy its authority. Rather than providing concrete safeguards for individual rights, Mawdudi entrusted the state with the supervision of the *shari'ah*, the implementation of which was seen as synonymous with protecting fundamental rights. As long as the Islamic state and its executive branch abided by the *shari'ah*, their democratic character would be preserved.[72] The influence of Islam on the state was such that democracy, a concept and myth that bore positive connotations for Mawdudi, could be appropriated to describe its working. The Islamic state was democratic because its virtues could best be captured by that term: it is a mark of adulation rather than a point of fact. Islam as the embodiment of the highest moral values and democracy as the most cherished political ideal were blended into the language of Mawdudi's discourse. Thus Mawdudi's Islamic state, although it grappled with the notion of democracy, remained at odds with it. As the embodiment of the will of the masses and the realization of an ideological vision, the Islamic state approximated the setup of a "popular democratic republic" more than it did a liberal democratic polity.

Although his assurances failed to calm anxieties about the Islamic state's authoritarian tendencies, Mawdudi suggested that the primary concern was Islamicity, not democracy. The Islamic state was to be judged by its adherence to the *din* and not by its mode of government. Ideally, Islam and democracy should both shape the state, but Islam was the more important. For that reason— to protect and perpetuate Islamic rule, to enforce Islamic law, and to ward off "corruption" and "decay" from within[73]—Mawdudi gave the state broad coercive powers and a monopoly over such key Islamic doctrines as jihad. The division of power in the state between the various branches reflected the same objective: to augment the power of the executive and therefore bolster stability and order in the system. Such thinking echoed the position of medieval Islamic political thinkers, for whom order was the highest ideal and anarchy an evil that should be avoided at all costs, even if it meant support for an unjust ruler. The disdain shown for the political will by Muslim thinkers from al-Mawardi (d. 1058) to al-Ghazzali (d. 1111) found their regeneration in Mawdudi's Islamic state.

The election and duties of the amir in the Islamic state were modeled after those in the rightly guided caliphate. Elections provided legitimacy[74] because although the state was legitimized by Islam, its leader received his mandate from the people. The contradiction inherent in applying democratic mechanisms to an ideological state structure is self-evident. In both the Islamic state and the Jama'at-i Islami—where elections have been institutionalized as the principle mechanism for transfer of power—discouraging candidates to preserve the ideological purity of the party vitiated the implementation of a democracy.[75] Democracy without a choice of candidates is impossible, and Mawdudi's insistence on it created numerous difficulties for the Jama'at when the party decided to take an active part in Pakistani politics. It had to be abandoned, therefore, and since 1957, although candidates are not put forward in the Jama'at's internal elections and are not incorporated into its theory of the Islamic state, they have been allowed in national elections. This discrepancy is just one example of the distinction Mawdudi was forced to make between the tenets of the Islamic state and actions permissible during the struggle to achieve it. It also underscores once again the difficulties of accommodating democracy in such a state.

Once in office, the amir was supposed to emulate the rule of the Prophet in Medina and the rightly guided caliphs,[76] a model that, Mawdudi argued, had been tested and found viable. Because traditional thinkers regarded the prophetic era and the reign of the rightly guided caliphs as unique in history, and were suspicious of anyone who claimed to re-create that period, Mawdudi was careful to avoid that claim by identifying the social mechanisms and political institutions he believed had supported the early Islamic polity. With the rigor of a sociologist, he sought ways and means to make his idealized order relevant to and operable in modern times.[77] The result was the "democratic caliphate," a hybrid combining early Islamic history and modern political concepts.

One example is the emphasis on elections, which, in some measure, was a way to guarantee against a dynastic usurpation of power in the Islamic state. Mawdudi believed just such an event had caused the corruption and decline of the caliphate in the seventh century. He disapproved of primogeniture and thought that elections would avoid any eventuality of hereditary rule.[78] The tenet that the interests of the state were more important than the interests of either its leader or any of its constituent branches stemmed from the same concern. In Mawdudi's concept, the amir was more clearly bound by the law and more accountable to the people than were the Prophet and the rightly guided caliphs.[79] He avoided the dependence on the leader that typified the prophetic and early caliphate states and, subsequently, all Muslim rule, instead seeking to anchor all authority in the state itself, and, symbolically at least, to delegate more power to the judiciary and the legislature.[80] As the mainstay of the virtuous order, it would be the state and not its leader that would serve as the object of loyalty and adulation of the citizenry.

Mawdudi replaced the charismatically charged office of the caliph as successor to the Prophet with the "impersonal collective autonomous reality"[81] of his Islamic state, thereby doing away with the traditional criteria for leadership. The classical sources, for example, specified that the caliph must be a member of the Quraysh tribe to which Prophet Muhammad and all subsequent caliphs had belonged. Mawdudi argued that any Muslim, regardless of caste, color, race or any other affiliation, was eligible to become the amir of the Islamic state.[82]

Aside from these changes, Mawdudi continued to appeal to the emotive power of the classical doctrine of the caliphate to avoid a total break with tradition and to legitimize his model. This coexistence of the idealized past with a more modern revision led to confusion about the source of authority and legitimacy. This ambivalence also surfaced in the Jama'at with regard to authority within the party and the extent of Mawdudi's powers.

As Mawdudi saw it, the amir was the omnipotent head of the Islamic state, and his source of authority rested in the ideological content of the state. His power emanated from his function as the protector of the Islamic state and from the electoral mandate he received from the citizenry. His office demanded the loyalty of the citizenry, although it was implicitly in competition with the loyalty demanded by the state itself, a confusion evident in the dynamics of Mawdudi's own position in the structure and political praxis of the Jama'at-i Islami, the forerunner of the Islamic state. This accounts for the Jama'at's equivocal approach both to pragmatic politics and to Islamic revolution. The contradiction in Mawdudi's plan for the Islamic state obviated the possibility of its consolidation into a revolutionary movement.

Mawdudi's ideas about the legislature had similar problems. It was based on the concept of *shura'* (consultative assembly) and on the institution of *ahl al-hall wa'l-'aqd* (those who unbind and bind).[83] Throughout Islamic history, both had performed consultative and legislative functions. The *shura'*, which figured prominently in the Jama'at, was compared by Mawdudi to a Western parliament.[84] Its role was to reflect the popular will, reinforce the democratic proclivities of the state, and be the source for new legislation. However, it had no power and could act only in an advisory capacity. Membership was open only to pious Muslims; the criterion of piety, although ambiguous, reinforced the Islamicity of the state and was supposed to eliminate the possibility of discord in the ranks and limit the extent of legislative autonomy vis-à-vis the executive. The criterion of piety would also exclude "undesirable" ideas, politicians, and policies. This criterion undoubtedly limited the democratic intent of Mawdudi's formulation as ideological concerns of the state overrode democracy.

The legislative powers of the *shura'* would be based on the practice of *ijtihad*, which would be limited by Mawdudi to a select few—pious men well-versed in modern subjects, the religious sciences, and Arabic.[85] The activities of the *shura'* were therefore limited, both by the constitution and by the criteria governing membership. Mawdudi regarded the legislature as a legal organ, not as a political one; although it had Western connotations, it was equated with the time-honored social and religious functions of the ulama and doctors of Islamic law (*ahl al-hall wa'l-'aqd*). The relationship of the legislature to the executive branch was similar to the relation of the ulama to the caliphate. The legislature would assist the executive branch and preserve the ideological purity of the state but would not translate popular demands into policy positions. Mawdudi favored limiting the contacts between legislators and their constituencies by advocating a system of proportional representation that would place greater importance on the ideological orientation of the contestants and reduce the contact between the electorate and its representatives.[86] Proportional representation, moreover, would allow for elections without candidates, which Mawdudi always favored.

The *shura'* was limited in its powers by the executive branch and the amir. Mawdudi recognized that the functions of the executive and the legislature in the Islamic state would overlap so that one should be made clearly subservient to the other; he did not necessarily see this as a conflict of interest because he assumed that in ideal circumstances (which he deemed attainable if the *din* reigned supreme in the state) no discord could arise. The unity of the *din* would preclude disagreement over policy because disagreements could only result from deviations from the *din*. Discord was both unnatural and religiously reprehensible (it was seen as *nifaq*, seditious discord).[87]

The state was not designed to manage discord, but to minimize its occurring. Checks and balances and mechanisms for ironing out differences did not feature prominently in Mawdudi's exposition. As a result, the Islamic state was susceptible to discord: with no viable means to resolve disagreements, aside from the reiteration of the ideological ethos of the state, the *din* was the only glue that bound the otherwise fragile structure of the state together. As a result, the state would be more viable "once society is educated in Islam . . . [then] . . . this [Islamic] view of the state would appear most natural."[88] One implication of Mawdudi's argument was that the Islamization of the society, in contrast to the preaching of other revivalist thinkers such as Ayatollah Khomeini, had to precede the establishment of the state.[89] That inference caused much confusion about the aims and agenda of the Jama'at in Pakistani politics because participation in politics meant that the Jama'at sought to establish the Islamic state before the Islamization of the society.

Mawdudi's ideas about how the Islamic state worked were put to test in 1956 and 1957. When dissent arose in the Jama'at over the party's participation in Pakistani politics,[90] a number of its members, backed by the resolutions of the party's *shura'*, opposed Mawdudi's decision. Their opposition was overruled by Mawdudi, who, true to his teachings on the working of the ideal Islamic state, refused to accept the legitimacy of their dissent and openly rejected the decisions of the party's *shura'* as unwarranted infringements on the amir's powers. The merits of the argument were overshadowed by concerns for unity of purpose and the rights of the amir. Mawdudi argued that the success of the party hinged on "unity of thought, heart, spirit, and most important, action," and that the position of the amir should be as supreme as a military commander in the battlefield.[91] This episode pointed to the inherent weakness of Mawdudi's essentially authoritarian orientation. It also showed how fidelity to the ideological aim of the state could be used to augment the powers of the executive and limit those of the legislature.

The Islamic Constitution

Islamization was to take place within the framework of a *da'wah* movement, directed at popularizing adherence to the *din*. It had to transform the existing apparatus and mechanisms of the secular state into Islamic ones. An Islamic constitution, as it was shaped in Pakistan between 1947 and 1956, was supposed to provide a path to the Islamic state that would replace the Islamic revolution. An Islamic constitution thus became the Jama'at's main agenda and the way it would carve a niche for itself in Pakistani politics. It would be the mechanism used to move the struggle for the Islamic state away from revolutionary activism and toward pragmatic politics in the existing political order.

The Islamic constitution was to be an evolving document; it was neither the *shari'ah*, nor any other ready-made document. It was to be the axis along which the existing polity would be reformed and reconstituted:

> When we say that this country should have an Islamic Constitution, we do not mean that we possess a Constitution of the Islamic state in a written form and the only thing that is required to be done is to enforce it. The core of the problem is that we want an unwritten Constitution to be transformed into a written one. What we term as Islamic Constitution is in reality an unwritten Constitution. It is contained in certain specific sources, and it is from that we have to evolve a written Constitution in keeping with the present-day requirements of our country.[92]

Constitution making was therefore integral to the struggle for the creation of an Islamic state. It also implied the acceptance of the principle of a gradual change that would replace British laws, institutions, and judicial procedures. Mawdudi placed a great deal of emphasis on proceeding gradually, lest the entire process be jeopardized. The population first had to be prepared in the ways and means of the new order through Islam, a path fraught with difficulties, especially in view of the machinations of the imperialist powers.[93] "If we wish to promulgate Islamic law here [in Pakistan], it would mean nothing less than the demolition of the entire structure built by your British masters and the erection of a new one in its place."[94] The Islamic constitution would be a religious document based on the Qur'an, hadith, conventions of the rightly guided caliphs, and the canonized verdicts of recognized jurists (i.e., the *shari'ah*).[95] It was not, however, the same thing as the *shari'ah*: although the *shari'ah* would serve as the basis of the legal code, it was not structured in the fashion of a constitution.[96]

The divine law had two parts, one immutable and binding, and the other open to interpretation and change.[97] New laws would have to be incorporated into the body of the *shari'ah* through *ta'wil* (hermeneutic interpretation), *qiyas* (logical reasoning), *ijtihad* (independent inquiry into Islamic law), *ijma'*[98] (collective consensus), and *istihsan* (invoking the spirit of the shari'ah in novel circumstances), all in keeping with the precepts of the *din*. Such legislative endeavors were open only to the learned men of the religion or "vanguard" movements such as the Jama'at.[99] The law-making process, moreover, was complemented by the institution of ancillary changes in the infrastructure of society in general and its educational system in particular. Mawdudi argued that, for the constitution-making process, an "academy of law" should be established that would relate knowledge of Islamic sources to the contemporary needs of the society and the polity.[100] This academy would consist of legal minds versed in the religious sciences and familiar with modern subjects. The latter requirement would disqualify the ulama. Mawdudi prescribed education in Arabic and law for the people as a corollary to constitution making. Islamic legal education would be reformed to create a milieu that would enable an Islamized legal and political order to work. All this should take place in tandem with reforms in the existing legal and constitutional structures of Pakistan, to bring them closer to the Islamic perspective.[101]

The *shari'ah* also had to be streamlined, reinterpreted, and expanded to accommodate the needs of the state. In its classical form, it did not address questions of governance to the extent required for a state to function. For instance, it did not make clear the relation between the various branches of government. Safeguards would have to be added to the existing Islamic legal code.

Mawdudi was particularly keen on guaranteeing the autonomy of the judiciary and of lawyers such as Allahbakhsh K. Brohi (who at the time was critical of Mawdudi) from the executive.[102] This did not appear in his earliest works. The charge was not because because he was influenced by Western political thought; it came about because of his experiences with the strong-arm tactics of Pakistani governments. In the beginning, Mawdudi had rejected both the adversarial system and the role of lawyers as immoral and un-Islamic, arguing that Islam accepted only an inquisitional system in which the judge was the final authority.[103] Mawdudi said that during the time of the Prophet, *qadis* (judges) implemented the *shari'ah* without discussion or the interference of lawyers, who could obfuscate the truth.[104] Then in 1948, 1953, and again in 1963, when the Pakistan government tried to crush the Jama'at, it had been the judiciary that rescued the party. Mawdudi and the Jama'at consequently favored the autonomy of the Pakistani judiciary and accepted the adversarial system and the right to appeal as beneficial (the Jama'at subsequently even formed an Islamic Lawyers

Association.) What the Jama'at advocated for Pakistan soon appeared in the model for the Islamic state. As a manifestation of equity, itself a cardinal Islamic virtue, justice was the *condito sine qua non* for the Islamic state.[105]

Many were skeptical of this view, however. At the center of the debate were the *hudud* (singular, *hadd*) laws, which were unpalatable to the Westernized classes whom Mawdudi sought to attract to his cause, because these laws entailed punitive prescriptions for such crimes as theft, adultery, or murder, and were criticized as retrogressive, cruel, and in violation of international human rights. Mawdudi tried to mollify this opposition by instituting limits to the law's applicability, but he defended them in principle, arguing that the cruelty in the West that resulted from the absence of punitive measures far outweighed the barbarity of the *hudud* laws.[106] Shortly after that, however, he suspended their application. The *shari'ah*, argued Mawdudi enjoined certain practices, *ma'rufat,* and forbade others, *munkarat*. As long as Muslims remained ignorant of the teachings of their faith, they could not be punished for the *munkarat*. When a society was imperfect, individuals could not be held entirely accountable for deeds that might have been provoked either by their social and economic circumstances or by their ignorance of the faith.[107] *Hudud* laws, Mawdudi argued, only made sense in the Islamic state, where the individual had no legitimate excuse for committing the *munkarat*. Even in the Islamic state, however, the *hudud* laws were not likely to be a problem because once Muslims were educated in the *din,* they would not err, and the laws would fall into disuse.[108]

Mawdudi's views on the *hudud* laws also changed over the years. He first regarded these laws' function not as punitive, but as a deterrent, but he moved away from this position by linking their implementation to the elimination of the causes of crime. When General Zia ul-Haq enacted his Hudud Ordinances of 1979, this caused difficulties in the Jama'at's alliance with the general's government and led to costly doctrinal compromises by the party.

Practical politics in Pakistan and modification in his treatment of the Islamic state forced Mawdudi to modify a number of other doctrinal issues. Some of his conclusions were implemented in policy; others remained mere guidelines yet to be reflected in the Jama'at's program. In his later writings and speeches he seemed to have grown weary of the centralization of power in the executive branch. He gave greater scope to the rights of the citizenry to "protest against tyranny" in the Islamic state,[109] which is in contrast with his earlier declaration that the Islamic state had the right to expect obedience from its subjects, whether its orders were "palatable or unpalatable, easy or arduous."[110]

Later on, however, his proclamations on Pakistani politics were a good deal more liberal than his prescriptions for the Islamic state. The Jama'at demanded from Pakistani governments rights that in principle it would not itself grant in the Islamic state. For example, Mawdudi favored neither a party system in the Islamic state, because in an ideal state there would be no need for intermediaries between the state and its citizens, nor a mechanism to translate popular demands into policy.[111]

In 1963, when Ayub Khan abrogated the multiparty system in Pakistan in favor of his Basic Democracies—something akin to what Mawdudi intended for the Islamic state—the Jama'at was in the forefront of those struggling to restore the multiparty system. In 1978, Mawdudi gave the Islamic state a one-party system but found it inappropriate for any other state until the society was fully committed to Islam.[112] As the Jama'at became more and more political, Mawdudi adopted party politics as a tool in the struggle to achieve the Islamic state, but he saw it as one to be discarded when the goal had been reached.

Citizens of the State

Mawdudi's concern for the collective left little place for the individual.[113] The citizenry was bound by the legal code of the state, enjoined to obey the executive, and, as devout Muslims, invoked to follow the *din*. In defining the citizen, insofar as he did, Mawdudi was influenced not only by Islamic sources, but also by the polyglot society of India. His political consciousness and religious thinking were molded during an era of increasing communal strife following the collapse of the Khilafat movement. From his revivalist exordium, *Al-Jihad fi'l-Islam,* to his desperate attempts to salvage the rule of the nizam in the predominantly Hindu Hyderabad, to his support of the anti-Ahmadi agitations in Pakistan in 1953 and 1954, Mawdudi's religious and political notions were shaped by the idea of the threat from outside, which in theory was the West, but in practice was Hindus, Sikhs, Ahmadis, and a host of parochial others who influenced his thinking and intensified the pace of his debate with Western thought. Mawdudi's Islamic state, although an ideal, was intended for India and only later for Pakistan. At first, therefore, it had to confront cultural pluralism, communalism, and minorities.

Generally, Mawdudi divided the Islamic state into four groups: male Muslims, female Muslims, *zimmis* ("protected subjects," followers of a religion recognized by Islam), and non-Muslims, a residual category for those who did not fit the other three, for example, the Ahmadis. In practice, Mawdudi only accepted those who fit into the first two categories as citizens of the Islamic state, with men enjoying full citizenship rights and women only partial rights.[114] Any Muslim anywhere, irrespective of his or her country of origin, would be entitled to citizenship.

Muslim men in turn were further divided into subcategories: those who followed the *din* and those who were only nominally Muslim. In a different gradation, there were Hanafi Sunnis, to which most Muslims of the subcontinent belonged, whom Mawdudi distinguished from followers of other schools of law, as well as from the Shi'is. A similar distinction was made between followers of the Deobandi, Brelwi, Nadwi, and the Ahl-i Hadith schools, the first three of which were Hanafis. These gradations were important because the structure of authority and social organization in the Islamic state would rest on them. True Muslims, followers of the *din*, would stand at the helm, guiding the course of the Islamic state. After Pakistan was founded, however, the need for a united religious front before the greater threat of secularism muted the idea of a gradation. Mawdudi simply assumed that as all Muslims would follow the *din*, the distinctions on which the gradations were based would disappear.

The *zimmis* were also more important in the early years, first in India and then when Pakistan had a sizable Hindu minority. Even today, however, any discussion of the Islamic state, whether of the Jama'at variety or not, immediately lapses into a debate about the rights of Pakistan's Shi'i, Ahmadi, Parsi, and Christian minorities.[115] The Jama'at has become more tolerant, especially of the Shi'is, thanks both to their importance in elections and to pressures exerted by the Islamic Republic of Iran since 1979. Still, the rights of *zimmis* continues to be a central and sensitive issue, and any draft proposal for such a state always has its carefully worded section on them.

Mawdudi's views on the subject were grounded in the *shari'ah*, but in essence they were an attempt to assuage the concerns of the minorities themselves. The Islamic state, Mawdudi argued, would not be a national democratic state, nor one defined by a territorial boundary; it would be an ideological state, with Islamic ideology serving as its protector and raison d'être. Hence, preservation of the purity of the ideology that undergirded this state was its foremost concern,[116] and one that justified excluding from authority or from any position that could influence the working of the state (e.g., the right to vote) those who did not subscribe to its ethos and ideology.[117] No one (except, possibly, women) was permanently excluded from political life, however, for conversion to Islam and adherence to the *din* were open to all.[118] Because the *din* was the highest form of existence, all would gravitate naturally to it, and dissent from it would be undeserving of protection. For that reason, non-Muslims could have limited civil rights, as defined by their own religious laws as well as those of the *shari'ah,* but no political rights. They would have only a marginal role in the society and the polity as citizens, if they could be called citizens at all.

The prohibitive criteria for citizenship in the Islamic state and the emphasis on the *shari'ah's* injunctions regarding *zimmis* have a curious history. They can be traced to Mawdudi's opposition to the Congress party's overtures to Muslims in the 1937–1947 period, when that party sought to attract Muslims to its cause. The Islamic state and the *zimmi*-Muslim dichotomy were used by Mawdudi to discourage Indian Muslims from joining the Congress party. The Islamic state was not just a source of communal identity, it was a way totally separate from a secular Indian state.

The *zimmi*-Muslim dichotomy found reinforcement in the possibility of basing Indian law in Hindu Manu laws, which Mawdudi supported. The rejection of secular nationalism encouraged recognition of the idea of a religious state in general and of a political division of society along religious lines. Obviously, Mawdudi favored Muslim domination, but, given the demographic realities of India, in effect he was sanctioning a Hindu domination of Muslims in a Hindu religious state as being preferable to no religious state at all. Advocating a society based on the *zimmi*-Muslim dichotomy was the flip side of the imposition of Hindu Manu laws on Muslims. The two drew on the same logic: the primacy of religious considerations in the conduct of politics and the religious incumbency of communalism. Promoting the one ensured the legitimacy of the other. Secular nationalism could only be snuffed out by religious entrenchment, by a joint pincer attack from Islamic and Hindu revivalism. The logic of this strategy made the two surreptitious allies as long as there was no possibility for the Islamization of the whole of India. In 1954 Mawdudi was to admit before the Court of Inquiry into the Disturbances of Punjab that he defended the incumbency of a religious state completely and in all instances, even if it meant the imposition of the writ of Hindu Manu laws on the Muslim population.[119] Hindus should establish a Hindu state, implied Mawdudi, for it justified and encouraged the institution of an Islamic state. He would not have defended the idea of a Hindu state if he had believed in the unity of India.

Jinnah had undergone a similar shift. The founder of Pakistan, who had at one time been the ambassador of Hindu-Muslim unity,[120] had turned to communalism and advocated partition after the Congress party and the nationalist movement were "Hinduized" by Gandhi. Jinnah, too, at first had favored a united India, but wary of a Hindu Raj, he became a staunch advocate of Muslim communalism, campaigning for Pakistan with an enthusiasm that blinded him to the perilous consequences of his cause for the scores of Muslims who lived in Hindu-dominated provinces.

For Mawdudi, the zimmi-Muslim dichotomy satisfactorily molded the structure of Hindu-Muslim relations in India in favor of Islam, protecting the religion against self-defeating political alliances with the Congress party and what he regarded as the corrupting influence of Hinduism. Social segregation sanctioned by Islamic law would not only close the door to insidious Hindu overtures to Muslims, but also set the stage for a thoroughly communalist approach to politics. Hence, separate electorates and, eventually, some form of partition became natural choices for those who subscribed to Mawdudi's views. His ideas about the rights of minorities in an Islamic state were therefore rooted in his desire to prevent the Congress party from dissolving communal boundaries in India and to reinforce those boundaries that separated Muslims from Hindus until the only logical conclusion was the partition of India.

Once Pakistan existed, however, Mawdudi had to pacify the liberal critics of the zimmi-Muslim dichotomy. Although his arguments reiterated the *shari'ah's* teaching on zimmis and referred to the Ottoman Empire's *millet* (nationalities) system,[121] he mainly justified the zimmi-Muslim dichotomy in Western terms. He implied that modern democracies and communist regimes alike treated their "national and ideological minorities" in similar fashions, although they might not admit it.[122] He denied that the zimmi-Muslim dichotomy was undemocratic. To force the majority to abide by the dictates of the minority, argued Mawdudi, would be "undemocratic."[123] If the majority of Muslims decided to live by the *shari'ah*, which demanded the segregation of society based on religious identity, then to prevent them from doing so would be a violation of their fundamental democratic rights.[124]

In an ideological state, curtailing the rights of those who did not subscribe to the official ideology was a matter of national security and state interest, an assertion that to some extent was pertinent in the xenophobic and anti-Hindu climate of Pakistani politics. The same argument could have been used by Indians to restrict Muslim rights in India, but Mawdudi was unmoved by such a possibility because separation of Muslims and Hindus was the paramount concern.

In 1956 these ideas brought Mawdudi into conflict with Prime Minister Shahid Husain Suhrawardi of Pakistan, who advocated joint electorates for Muslims and non-Muslims (mainly the Hindus in East Pakistan) in the elections scheduled for 1958. Mawdudi regarded Suhrawardi's proposal as a hinderance to the establishment of an Islamic state in Pakistan and fought tooth and nail with the government to safeguard the separation of the electorates along religious lines.[125]

Mawdudi's advocacy of zimmi-Muslim separation was no doubt popular with the Jama'at's constituency, especially the Muhajirs (migrants), those who had immigrated to Pakistan from the Hindu majority areas of India after partition and had settled in Punjab, Sind, and East Pakistan where—in Sind and East Pakistan in particular—sizable Hindu minorities continued to live. For the Muhajirs, the zimmi-Muslim dichotomy had conveniently diverted attention from the problems that surrounded the large-scale migration of Urdu-speaking people to regions with distinct linguistic and cultural traditions. It appealed to their anti-Hindu sentiments and echoed the popular cause of separation advocated by the Muslim League before partition. Although for all practical purposes the Hindu minority of Pakistan has ceased to exist, separate electorates remain a demand in the Jama'at's political program and are yet another mark of the Islamic state's uneasy interaction with democracy.

The Islamic State and Modernization of Islamic Political Thought

Mawdudi's views on the Islamic state reveal the influence of Western values and ideas. The very notion of a state with an elaborate machinery of government, a due process and the apparatus to oversee it, a system of checks and balances, and codification and centralization of law and its application are all modern imports. The process of appropriation and assimilation did not produce a harmonious political theory nor an efficient working model, however, as has been shown. Still, his use of the idiom and symbols of democracy represented more than just rhetoric. It was idiosyncratic, but it was one link in an intellectual and ideological chain that preceded Mawdudi and will no doubt continue to shape Muslim societies in the future. In and of itself, Mawdudi's Islamic state was imperfect and incongruous, authoritarian by nature and democratic by claim. But its significance lay not in its promise as a viable model for government, but in what it purported to do—find a more rational, consistent, and democratic formulation that would remain open to change. Mawdudi's synthesis was an opening in the structure of traditional Islamic thought, beginning a debate with Western ideas and assimilating them wholesale. Khurshid Ahmad argued that Islamic revival was only a "phase" in the history of the Muslim people; it was not so much a return to the past as a bridge to the future.[126]

In fact, it is the very inconsistency intrinsic to the concept of an "Islamic democracy" and the practical problems that it has created for the Jama'at that will continue to push Mawdudi's ideology and the party's political program toward greater rationalization and clearer understanding of the ideas that have been borrowed and debated. Time and again, throughout the Jama'at's history, realities have justified disputable political choices. The dynamics of these compromises have by and large determined the course of the Jama'at's development and the changes its ethos and worldview have undergone.[127]

Economy of the State

Mawdudi was perhaps as renowned for his theory of Islamic economics as he was for his views on the Islamic state.[128] He wrote about economics often, although not as the systematizing of a scientific discipline or for classifying Islam's teachings on economics,[129] but as a corollary to his discussion of the *din* and the Islamic state. He viewed Islamic economics as the totality of the teachings of the *shari'ah*.

His views were cast in the mold of the Islamic state and, therefore, were concerned with the interests of the collective rather than those of the individual. Because the state was the embodiment of the will and interests of the society as a whole, it rather than the individual, served as the principal economic actor.[130] Mawdudi's discussion of economics remained within the workings of a free market. He walked the same tightrope between state control of the economy and individual initiative that the classical Islamic sources did. Islamic law had always protected individual economic rights, but it also charged the political order to oversee and regulate the economy with a view to the interests of the society as a whole. Mawdudi's *via media*, however, did not so much reflect his doctrinal fidelity to the classical position as it underlined his attempt to carve a space for Islam's approach to economics vis-à-vis both capitalism and socialism—the main rivals of the Islamic state in the battle for the hearts and minds of Muslims. Mawdudi was critical of what he saw as the callousness displayed by both capitalism and socialism toward individual rights and needs.[131] He believed that capitalism and socialism were extremist positions that disturbed the natural equilibrium of social relations and were bereft of ethical values; they were secular worldviews that could not satisfactorily organize human life. Mawdudi believed that Islam, on the other hand, was based on an ethical perspective that could strike a tenable balance between the good of the many and the interests of the individual. The classical Islamic position on economics was therefore understood by Mawdudi as an alternative to both capitalism and socialism, embodying all the virtues of the two systems and none of their shortcomings. Although expressed through the medium of modern economic thought, Islamic economics found an existence separate from capitalism and socialism. It was not a marriage of the two Western economic systems, but a superior system all its own, elaborated on a higher plane. This was a Third Worldist conception of sorts, which aspired to rise above the two poles of capitalism and socialism but never fully eluded their magnetic pull.

In the political realm, the Islamic state placed its greatest emphasis on the collective interests of the Muslim community; in the economic realm (in its effort to strike a balance between capitalism and socialism), it came closer to the traditional balance between the society and the individual. Mawdudi wanted to institute Islamic practices such as *zakat* (an alms tax) and inheritance laws and to eliminate the *munkarat* practices, such as *riba'* (usury), from modern society. Should the *shari'ah* prove inapplicable in certain circumstances, he permitted the use of *ijtihad* to adapt Islamic law to the requirements of a modern economic system.[132] These suggestions were not divorced from his communalist agenda. For instance, his insistence on abolishing *riba'*—which he succeeded in convining Islamic economists who followed him to be synonymous with Islamic economics—had its roots in his attempts to safeguard Indian Muslims from Hindu influences. Abolition of *riba'* in Punjab and Hyderabad, where Mawdudi had lived, had the effect of limiting interactions of Muslims with moneylenders and, more generally, financial institutions, which were dominated by Hindus. Mawdudi's aim was to limit Muslim economic dependence on Hindus as a way of making communal autonomy and a separate Muslim normative order possible. In fact, why Mawdudi chose to summarize Islamic economics in the idea of abolishing *riba'* can only be explained by the fact that moneylending was the domain of Hindu financiers. There were other more convincing ways of conceptualizing Islamic economics than as simply an interest-free economy.

Mawdudi was aware that the enforcement of Islamic practices and institutions would make the state active in the economic arena. He was not perturbed by this prospect because the role of the state in the economy was another of those transient phenomena that were bound to diminish as the citizenry became educated in the teachings of Islam and eager to follow them. Implementing Islamic practices would then require no fiat. The citizenry would not be driven by greed; they would not engage in practices that were ethically wrong.[133] By virtue of their grounding in the *din*, they would have a different "marginal utility" and concern for consumption and production than otherwise expected. They would be guided not by the desire to maximize their interest in the market, but by their quest for spiritual gratification. Islam, concluded Mawdudi, would provide a strong moral compulsion, which as a new factor in economic transactions would foster economic change and social welfare without the need for continuous state intervention in market operations and would avoid the kind of distortion and injustices associated with free-market capitalism.[134]

Mawdudi again underlined the importance of education in Islam as a prerequisite for the Islamization of society and politics and as the guarantor of the efficient functioning of the Islamic state. This idea was in direct opposition to the "Islamization first" approach of General Zia ul-Haq. Although he relied on the state to promote Islamic teaching in the conduct of economic transactions, Mawdudi was careful not to institutionalize the state's control over the economy, which occurred in Pakistan under the guise of Islamization during Zia's regime (1977 to 1988)[135]: "Islam does not make it binding on society to provide employment for each and every one of its citizens, since this responsibility cannot be accepted without thorough nationalization of the country's resources."[136] The state's role, he argued, should not extend to that of economic regulator; it should limit itself to preserving the economic rights of individuals.[137] Islam's teachings on economics, he once said, were tantamount to a "bill of social rights" and the basis for a "social contract."[138] The same ambiguity that characterized Mawdudi's approach to democracy turned up in his vacillation between an etatist economic outlook and collectivist tendencies and his support for free-market operations and individual rights.

The question of ownership of economic resources and economic justice had important implications for the Jama'at's political program. The rampant economic inequalities and the chasm between the rich and the poor in Pakistan gave populist themes political appeal, as demonstrated by the success of Zulfiqar 'Ali Bhutto and his Pakistan People's Party in 1969–1971. But Mawdudi was reluctant to exploit economic inequalities for political gain, and the Jama'at under his command remained indifferent to them. Throughout his career, Mawdudi remained a staunch defender of private property, in spite of clear signals that it was doing his cause no good. He objected to land reform in the Punjab throughout the 1950s, although at that time the backlash was so pronounced that he never again was openly antipopulist. During the last years of the Ayub Khan era, when industrialization had generated discontent among the country's labor force, the People's Party successfully tapped this discontent in its drive for power, but Mawdudi and the Jama'at remained indifferent to national politics and ill at ease with such popular political issues as land reform and the rights of labor. The Pakistani electorate reciprocated in the elections of 1970, handing the Jama'at a humiliating electoral defeat.

Mawdudi's position was based on classical sources, which he interpreted conservatively in keeping with the position of the ulama.[139] Because the Islamic state was the panacea for all sociopolitical problems, all other movements were unnecessary and redundant. This conservatism, combined with his horror of socialism, shaped his response to all social and economic problems.

Mawdudi went to great lengths to prove that Islam's teachings on equity and justice were not tantamount to egalitarianism.[140] He argued, as had traditional thinkers before him, that Islam was tolerant of difference in income and wealth as long as it reflected differences in effort and skill.[141] By giving this Islamic injunction political life, the Jama'at shirked responsibility for blatant socioeconomic injustices, relegating them to the domain of divine will. As a result, it remained oblivious to the staggering economic inequalities and deepening social cleavages in Pakistan.[142]

Mawdudi's dislike of socialism and the fear that populist politics would encourage "godlessness" at the cost of Islam dated from his days in Hyderabad, when he associated socialism with the Hindu challenge to the nizam's rule.[143] Socialism, Mawdudi had concluded, was inherently opposed to the interests of Islam and was the ideology most likely to gain a following among educated Muslims. His reactions to socialism and communism were emotional and vehement; he did not argue the merits of the case but began and ended with a discussion of atheism.[144] Concern with checking the growth of the Left at times even overshadowed all other concerns of the Jama'at,[145] a tendency that grew with the rising popularity of the Pakistan People's Party in the late 1960s. Mawdudi's antagonism to the Left distinguished him from Ayatollah Khomeini, who incorporated the slogans and praxis of the Left into his ideological perspective and movement, producing a politically successful populist reading of Islam.[146]

Although he rejected socialism, Mawdudi was fully aware of its lure.[147] In fact, he regarded it as a serious rival to Islam, and his invective against its ideas and policies were a response not only to its atheism but also to its political encroachments. He sought to carve out a space for his movement divorced from populism, which he saw as the means for mobilizing Muslims along socialist lines, facilitating their political acculturation into that "godless" ideology. Socialism, argued Mawdudi, caused ambiguity among Muslims regarding the true source of their predicament—the un-Islamic nature of society—and, hence, diverted their attention from the task before them.[148] Opposition to populist politics, like the *zimmi*-Muslim dichotomy, was another way to establish boundaries around Muslims. Eager to immunize Muslims against the lure of socialism, Mawdudi challenged the efficacy of its program and the truth of its message, presenting in its stead Islam as the only viable ideology for sociopolitical change: "There is social justice in Islam only." Islam would deliver all that socialism promised but would be unable to realize.[149]

Islam's promises were neither immediate nor tangible, however, and the Jama'at made no effort to respond to the demands of the underprivileged, whose problems would ipso facto be resolved by the creation of the Islamic state. Relations between social classes, the distribution of wealth, and the ownership of the means of production in society were never subjects of concern. No promises were forthcoming from Mawdudi, and therefore the masses failed to support his apolitical approach to social change and had no interest in his indirect solution to their immediate needs. Workers and peasants were understandably not pleased to be told, "You must never take the exaggerated view of your rights which the protagonists of class war present before you,"[150] and the Jama'at took the brunt of their displeasure time and again at the polls.

The idea of an Islamic state was developed systematically by Mawdudi. It was the logical conclusion to predicating faith on social action. Over the years, he embellished the model of this state, fine-tuning its various features. Although the Islamic state was never put in place in Pakistan, nor has it been accepted as a viable model by those outside the Jama'at, it served as the means for inquiry into Western ideas. The encounter led to adoption of some ideas and values from the West, which have resulted in the gradual transformation of the concept of the Islamic state. More than a form of state, Mawdudi's model was a window into both the nature and scope of modernizing change within Islam and the manner in which this process involved systematic enmeshing of faith and power.

6

A New Islam?

The scope and extent of Mawdudi's rationalization and modernization of Islamic thought and the manner in which he incorporated Western ideas and concepts into his ideology set him apart from the traditional perspective based on time-honored Islamic norms and institutions.[1] As a result, Mawdudi's ideology has often been regarded by traditional scholars and divines as unorthodox. The Jama'at and the traditional institutions in South Asia certainly have competing and mutually exclusive definitions of religious truth, as each vies to shape social institutions in its own image—posturing as "sect" before a "church," to use terms from the sociology of religion.[2] Although the traditional religious leaders insist that social transactions reflect Islamic values, the Jama'at promises a process of sweeping change that will reform Islam, though obviously it has not succeeded in realizing that aim so far.

Even when proclaiming a fundamentally new worldview, Mawdudi did not reject traditional values and institutions completely. To the contrary, he continued to remain tied to the traditional perspective, which led him into a complex process of interpretation that would fall within the pale of the traditional worldview and would interact with it. A case in point is his views on *ijtihad*, which could have served as the means for breaking with the traditional perspective by creating a space that would serve to radically reinterpret the tenets of the faith. But by permitting the resumption of the practice only in principle, and only when it served the needs of the Islamic state, Mawdudi limited that possibility. Only those who had faith in the *shari'ah*; had knowledge of the Qur'an, the prophetic traditions, and other sources of religious law; and were proficient in Arabic would practice *ijtihad*,[3] and these requirements have limited the extent of the Jama'at's break with the traditional perspective. In initiating his reforms, Mawdudi kept the Jama'at at a distance from traditional Islam, but, by restricting the scope of those reforms, he avoided a complete break. As a result, he distanced himself somewhat, but not decisively, from traditional teachings. The Jama'at's reform of Islam thus has been limited.

Mawdudi's teachings on the *din* and the Islamic state parted with the traditional perspective to a significant degree: he defined faith, the meaning of spirituality, and the nature of the relations between Islam and society very differently from the traditional view. The revitalization of Islam in Mawdudi's works came essentially from modern Western thought, and this is what separated Mawdudi's perspective from that of traditional Islam.

The difference between sect and orthodoxy has not always been defined in doctrinal terms. On occasion, "it is the political success of a given interpretive reading that renders a religious position 'orthodox,'"[4] and, by implication, the political failure of a position that renders it "heterodox" or sectarian. The case of the Jama'at illustrates this: Mawdudi's interpretation of Islam did not score a political victory and therefore did not become the orthodoxy. But this political failure, rather than institutionalizing the Jama'at's beliefs by forming a separate sect, has simply pushed the Jama'at back into the traditional order from which it emerged. The Jama'at was not able to go beyond its ideals to a working model that others found relevant and was therefore unable to expand its base of support. To survive, it had to change.

Unable to translate its zeal into political victory, over the years the Jama'at has gradually drifted back toward tradition, moving closer first to the position of the ulama and eventually to popular Islam as it has been manifested in South Asia. Participation in the political process underscored the shortcomings of its program. Just as perception of political success gave shape to the Jama'at's new interpretive reading of Islam, failure to realize its aims pushed it back to traditional Islam.

Whether a particular interpretive reading of doctrine is identified as constituting a new sect has much to do with the attitude of the reigning religious establishment. As the case of the Jama'at will show, rejecting new interpretations of Islamic doctrines and denouncing its protagonists provided a clear demarcation between established views and the new perspective.

The attitude of the new approach may be far more equivocal. In spite of its break with many of the values and practices of traditional Islam, the Jama'at remains attached to the traditional order from which it emerged. Rather than a completely new Islam, it has served as "a vision that [is] pitted authoritatively against the established order, not as a replacement but as a conceptual space in which new modes of behavior could be considered."[5] Its Islamic revivalism has been bound by the fundamental teachings of Islam, which have limited its development along sectarian lines and checked its reformist potential. If revivalism is distinguished from the traditional order in some measure by its radical interpretation of the fundamental tenets of Islam, with a view to orienting the faithful toward the realization of a political end, its concern with the fundamentals keeps it poised toward the traditional order and not away from it.

The Jama'at's case suggests that an element of choice may be involved in drawing back from a sectarian tendency. Implicit in Mawdudi's revivalist goal for Islam was the need to conquer all the faithful. There were greater gains in conquering the whole of traditional Islam than in parting with it.[6] The Jama'at has not claimed completely new truths, only a better understanding of the original ones. It is this that distinguished Mawdudi's views from those of the ulama. The Jama'at has perforce tried to reshape that tradition in its own image—to realize its existence, not outside the boundaries of the traditional order, but in place of it. Mawdudi was therefore content with keeping a certain distance from traditional Islam but avoiding a complete break; this proved ultimately untenable, requiring the Jama'at either to break with tradition or routinize its activist zeal and collapse back into it. The political imperatives before the party have been an important source of pressure in this regard. Under Mawdudi's direction, the party slowly but surely retreated toward traditional orthodoxy and popular Islam.

This development was, in part, a consequence of Mawdudi's confrontation with other self-styled thinkers and movements, from Ghulam Ahmad Parwez to Muhammad Asad and Khalifah 'Abdu'l-Hakim on the one hand, and the Tahrik-i Khaksar (Movement of the devoted; founded in 1931) and the Anjuman-i Ahrar-i Islam (Society of Free Muslims; founded in 1930), on the other.[7] Mawdudi's ideology was adumbrated at a time of experimentation that produced a number of schools of Islamic thought, movements, and parties, most of which also appealed to the Jama'at's constituency. They were espousing interpretations of Islam that competed with those of Mawdudi and the Jama'at. Mawdudi often looked to traditional Islam for ways of contending with his competition, guarding his flanks, and providing himself with institutional support against competing schools of thought, some of whom enjoyed the support of the modernist and secular bureaucratic and military elite. The appeal to traditional Islam was particularly effective in dealing with Islamic modernist thinkers, whose views on many issues were often quite similar to Mawdudi's own.[8] By moving closer to the traditional order, Mawdudi could accuse his competition of obscurantism and heterodoxy, accusations that could only be made from a position of established orthodoxy. For instance, competition with those modernists who rejected the authenticity of the hadith as a means of making Islam amenable to change led Mawdudi to a debate with the "deniers of hadith" (*munkirin-i hadith*)—Ghulam Ahmad Parwez and a number of his disciples in the Bazm-i Tulu'-i Qur'an (Celebration of the dawn of the Qur'an), such as Dr. 'Abdu'l-Wudud.[9] The debate was later extended to include all deniers of the authenticity of the hadith and those whose reading of the hadith was innovative or unorthodox—from Chiragh 'Ali (the companion of Sayyid Ahmad Khan); to the Ahl-i Qur'an leaders, Mawlvis 'Abdu'llah Chakralwi, Ahmadu'ddin Amritsari, and Mawlana Aslam Jairapuri; to self-styled thinkers such as Pirzadah Ibrahim Hanif and justices Shafi' and Rahman.[10] By placing those who denied the authenticity of the hadith or those who interpreted it in unorthodox ways beyond the pale of Islam, Mawdudi found himself squarely in the camp of traditional religious leaders. The dynamics of the Jama'at's competitive relations with other self-styled groups and thinkers pushed Mawdudi, who had himself parted with traditional norms of hadith analysis by permitting intuitive authentication of hadith, into the bosom of the traditional orthodoxy.[11]

Break with Traditional Islam

Differences between Mawdudi's interpretive reading of Islam and the traditional Islamic perspective had been part of Mawdudi's works since 1932, when he first launched his broadside against Islamic customs and mores, the ulama, and the Sufi *pirs*. His break with traditional Islam, however, was, perhaps most evident in the manner in which the Jama'at was founded and subsequently developed. It was launched as a "new community of believers."[12] All members, including Mawdudi, uttered the *shahadah* when they joined, in a symbolic gesture of conversion to a new Islamic perspective. They were what Clifford Geertz has termed "oppositional Muslims," whose intellectual and religious attitudes were defined in contradistinction to those of traditional Islam.[13] The Jama'at's mandate as a "new community of believers" vested with missionary zeal was subsequently underscored through Mawdudi's continual confrontations with the ulama and the *pirs* and his claim that he spoke for Islam.[14] The notion of a new community also implied that anyone else who claimed to be Islamic in fact was not. The Jama'at stood before Muslim society as Islam before *jahiliyah*.

The spokesmen for traditional Islam recognized Mawdudi's challenge for what it was, and so were not charitable in their response. What to Mawdudi was Islam versus *jahiliyah* was to the ulama the reverse: Islam versus innovation (*bid'at*) and sectarianism. No sooner had the Jama'at formed than the ulama began to air their opinion of Mawdudi's enterprise. Amin Ahsan Islahi, the young *'alim* of the Islahi school of thought who later joined the Jama'at, commented after his first meeting with Mawdudi, *la farq bainahu wa bain Parwez* (there is no difference between him and Ghulam Ahmad Parwez);[15] needless to say, the ulama did not hold the controversial Parwez in high esteem. The ulama also pointed to Mawdudi's use of the title *amir* as proof of his sectarian pretensions, a charge that was sufficiently damaging to compel Mawdudi to explain his use of the title in a rather lengthy speech during the Jama'at's annual session in Muradpur and in a lecture to the Jama'at in Lahore in 1946.[16] Mawdudi explained that the terms *amir* and *jama'at* (society/party) did not denote sectarianism, but served to consolidate a political organization.[17] Mawdudi's attempt to assuage the ulama's anxiety regarding his intentions pushed him into suppressing the Jama'at's sectarian inclinations and presenting his movement in political terms.

The ulama, however, were not interested in Mawdudi's denials or his protestations of fidelity to orthodoxy. Their purpose was not to bring the Jama'at into their fold, but to unmask its heterodoxy. Their use of the sobriquet Mawdudiyat (Mawdudism) when referring to the Jama'at's doctrinal position was more damaging and derogatory than at first glance it appeared to be.[18] The same suffix, -*iyat* (-*ism*), was used by the Deobandi ulama in the nineteenth and early twentieth centuries to denounce the teachings of Mirza Ghulam Ahmad, the founder of the Ahmadi sect.[19] Terms such as Qadiyaniyat and Mirzaiyat were used to convey the un-Islamic nature of Mirza Ghulam Ahmad's ideas; a whole *fatwa* (religious decree) could be implied by the use of the -*iyat* suffix. Deobandi and Ahl-i Hadith ulama and their followers joked among themselves that "Mawdudi had migrated to Punjab [in 1938] to become a prophet,"[20] again a reference to Mirza Ghulam Ahmad, who was from Punjab. To this day, traditional divines continue to denounce Mawdudi with the vehemence otherwise reserved for more clearly sectarian expressions of Muslim faith.

Over the years, the Jama'at has mended fences with various ulama groups at the institutional level and political alliances have even been forged in Pakistan and India with the aim of promoting political objectives they share. Still, the differences between Mawdudi and the spokesmen of traditional Islam run deep, and the cleavages between them are real.

At its foundation, Mawdudi's ideological orientation departed from the "cumulative tradition" of Islam in India.[21] His holistic approach, "demonstrating the rational interdependence of Islamic morality, law and political theory"[22] stood in opposition to the cultural foundations and worldview of traditional Islam. Its overtly and exclusively political reading was distinguished from the essentially soteriological and spiritual concerns of traditional Islam. Mawdudi was conscious of these differences; they were, in fact, proof of the doctrinal authenticity of his views, and the very raison d'être of his movement. Maryam Jameelah wrote:

> In launching his [Mawdudi's] Islamic movement in the Indo-Pak Subcontinent, his aim was not a mere patch-work of reforms, much less did he intend to attempt any restoration of traditional Islamic civilization as it had existed in the pre-colonial days. His goal was a total revolutionary break, with the medieval past and its so-called Muslim society. . . . He strived to build a better universal order.[23]

Mawdudi's "better universal order" was based on the fundamental sources of Islam and was religiously authentic; yet, in its exclusive reliance on fundamentals, especially in his particular interpretation of their intent and meaning, it negated all other component parts of the edifice of traditional Islam, from parochial customs and mores to philosophy, the arts, and an approach to Islamic history. It was in the rejection of the traditional approach to history that Mawdudi's authority as a *mujaddid* was articulated and the sectarian tendency of his movement was made clear.[24] The doctrine of *tajdid* had its basis in Islamic sources; its use, however, had been largely suspended. As a result, Mawdudi's appeal to the doctrine and the manner in which he sought to mobilize it ran counter to the traditional perspective.

Traditional Islam, although perturbed by its decline, did not develop the kind of cognitive dissonance that propels revivalists into reinterpretation and action. Traditionalist thinkers, wrote S. H. Nasr, explained the occlusion of the political power of their religion within the structure of Islamic theology, philosophy, and eschatological doctrines, acknowledging that "something had gone wrong with the world as God Himself had mentioned in His Book concerning the end of the world and the Blessed Prophet had described in his traditions. In such a case the eclipse of Islam was itself a proof of the validity of the Islamic message."[25] Although few traditional thinkers have remained steadfast in adhering consistently to this line of reasoning, it has remained the doctrinal position of traditional Muslim thinkers who have dabbled in politics but have not substituted political concerns for spiritual ones. More important, although aware of community interests, these theorists have not tried to alter the course of history or to break off its continuity to realize a worldly ideal that would ostensibly fulfill the directives of their faith. For traditional divines, Islamic history has never ceased to embody the truth of their faith: The quality of the society's leadership is not by itself a gauge of the Islamicity of society; the Islamicity of a society is rather an aggregate of individual pieties, and for this reason medieval jurists accepted unjust rule as long as it manifested order and permitted the practice of the faith by individual Muslims. In the same vein, traditional ulama believe that orthodoxy by itself would produce the political results favored by the Muslim community. If more were required to establish a religiously acceptable political order, the traditional divines could act through the leaders of society. They have advised, petitioned, admonished, and, on occasion, challenged them, but they have not traded in their holy mantle for the garb of a politician. It is accepted that political change may, at times, be by Islam, but this order has not been reversed. Islam cannot be reinterpreted with a view to the needs of political change. This, more than any other belief, distinguishes the piety-minded and the orthodox from the revivalist.[26]

Since the nineteenth century, when Islam found itself in competition with the West, the problem of the decline of Islam's worldly power has become an issue of paramount concern. Muslims became aware that their civilization and power were declining, as was all too evident in the lives of their caliphs and sultans and in the ebb and flow of history. This decline in Muslim power in the climate of political rivalry with the West created a sense of confusion and of discrepancy between the ideal and the real. Revivalist thinkers such as Mawdudi responded to the sociopolitical consequences and psychological pressures of this observation by parting with the traditional position, seeking instead to reason what was in the domain of God's will and even to venture to alter it.[27] They ceased to be concerned with Islamic history as the history of Muslim lives, spiritual as well as mundane, and instead looked upon it as the arena in which the Islamic community lost its power and glory. For them, Islamic history was the history of dynasties, caliphs, and sultans, in which power was the measure of all achievement, even spiritual achievement.

The traditions of Islamic philosophical inquiry (*falsafah*), Sufism, and gnostic illumination (*'irfan*) have always been a constituent part of the culture and religious life of Muslim India and, at least since the time of Shah Waliu'llah of Delhi (1703–1762), have made inroads even into the doctrinal positions of the ulama in South Asia. The philosophical and mystical perspectives also supported the direction of Islamic theology.[28] The transcendental theosophy (*hikmat-i muta'aliyah*) of Sadru'ddin Shirazi or Mulla Sadra (d. 1640), which is the dominant school of Islamic philosophy in the Indian subcontinent and has woven the Islamic philosophical and mystical tradition into a single theosophical inquiry, has further underlined the direction of Islamic theology.[29] Muslim philosophers have argued that, in order to contemplate Himself, God created the world. If He is the perfect good, the universe that has issued from Him is, by definition, less perfect and increasingly drawn to imperfection, which on its own plane appears as evil. But because evil is inevitable in the very creation of the universe, discrepancies between ideals and realities do not lead to confusion or connote cognitive dissonance, nor does the possibility of reasoning into the nature of evil, on which the revivalist discourse is predicated, present itself.

Sufis have similarly discouraged preoccupation with rationalization to explain the nature of evil. In Sufism, which is premised on a metaphysical view, evil is a part of the very existence of the world. Earthly existence, as privation of divine truth, is naturally prone to evil. Because only God is good, the world must be open to evil. Still, evil is not an independent reality to be contrasted with good. As was the case with the teachings of Islamic philosophy, confusion and cognitive dissonance cannot plausibly present themselves where evil is justified as inherent to the order of the world. Moreover, as the world by definition is the privation of God and, hence, the source of evil, it cannot possibly serve as the complete vehicle for the realization of the divine truth, nor as its embodiment, as Mawdudi intended the Islamic state to be. In fact, the very notion of a worldly utopian order is inconsistent with the logic of Islamic mysticism. Mankind, the Sufis and the theosophers have argued, can only combat evil by transcending the worldly reality, escaping from the trappings of the terrestrial order and thus beginning the journey back to God. It is only in Him, and outside the worldly order that issued *away* from Him, that divine truth may be realized.[30]

Nu'mani, himself a Deobandi *'alim*, believed that this metaphysical perspective, as it was reflected in the works of mystics such as Hasan al-Basri (the patriarch of Islamic mysticism, d. 728), Shaikh 'Abdu'l-Qadir Gilani (founder of the Qadiri Sufi order, d. 1166), and Shaikh Ahmad Sirhindi (an important figure in Naqshbandi Sufism, d. 1624) is central to the traditional Muslim perspective. They serve as models for the "correct" interpretations of the aim of the Islamic revelation, as seen in Mawlana Iliyas's Tablighi Jama'at, and insofar as Mawdudi's views clearly violated their spirit, accounted for his departure from the norms of traditional orthodoxy.[31]

The confluence of the theological, philosophical, and mystical positions on the source of evil and the decline in Muslim worldly power determined the approach of traditional Islam toward politics in the Indian subcontinent. The directives of the three had, moreover, been absorbed into the thinking of the Indian ulama through the aegis of Shah Waliu'llah, who fused theology, philosophy, mysticism, and Hanafi law into a coherent tradition of Islamic learning.[32] The tradition of renewal and reform associated with Shah Waliu'llah took shape within the bounds of this construct. It maintained an active approach toward the world but did not lose sight of the spiritual connotations of religious life and activities; a worldly utopia became neither a surrogate for spiritual realization nor the objective of religious practice.[33]

The Waliu'llahi tradition has been central to the culture and worldview of the ulama in India. As Hanafi jurists, but also as theologians, philosophers, and Sufis, Indian ulama have been the quintessential representatives of traditional Islam in its entirety. It is for this reason that Mawdudi's departure from the norms of traditional Islam found shape in a debate with them.

Mawdudi sought to enunciate an all-inclusive school of Islamic thought premised on a different response to the psychological implications of the "fall of Islam." To Mawdudi, Islamic history was essentially a failure.[34] There were both concrete reasons and remedies for that failure. Some of the ulama had similar feelings and had also been politically active, but Mawdudi parted with them in his conviction that Muslim glory was not merely a means to realize greater spirituality but an end in itself. Politics was not a passing concern necessitated by force of circumstance; it lay at the very heart of religious belief and practice. This attitude was conditioned by the communalist climate of Indian society and politics, and it had been thoroughly translated into a religious position. The "fall of Islam" had, by far, greater communal implications than religious ones. By equating (or confusing) the two, Mawdudi was shaping religion so that it would address a communalist need. The Islamic state would not only guarantee greater religiosity, it would be the very embodiment of religiosity. Muhammad Manzur Nu'mani claimed that such an argument was a *tahrif* (purposful misreading) of the Islamic concept of *tawhid* (unity of God).[35] This *tahrif* led Mawdudi to concoct a doctrine of *hikmat-i 'amali* (practical wisdom), which Nu'mani argued was neo-Khariji in outlook and 'Abdu'l-Majid Daryabadi claimed was the product of a *marizanah zihniyat* (sick mind).[36] Drawing a parallel between the Jama'at and the Khariji movement was no doubt prompted by the obvious similarity between the Jama'at's discussion of theodemocracy and divine government and the Khariji's motto of *la hukmah illa'llah* (rule belongs to God alone).[37] Drawing such parallels also placed the Jama'at beyond the pale of Sunni Islam on account of its "rigid" and "radical" puritanism, as was also the case with the Kharijis.

Mawdudi's critics among the ulama argued that *hikmat-i 'amali* reduced faith into worldly activism and a drive for political power and it converted Islam into an "-ism" indistinguishable from any other.[38] In devising such an openly political reading of Islam, wrote Nu'mani, Mawdudi fundamentally misrepresented the aim of the Islamic revelation by overlooking Islam's philosophical and theological traditions.[39] The boundaries between Mawdudi's views and traditional Islamic thought were thus ovbious and required divorcing the one from the other. This dissociation was clearly manifested in Mawdudi's break with the Hanafi school of law. Although Mawdudi claimed fidelity to the Hanafi rite, in practice he developed an independent legal approach, one that was "not bound by any school of law."[40] It incorporated elements from other schools, notably Hanbali law and the eminent jurist Ibn Taimiyah's (d. 1328) reading of it, and from Shi'ism to broaden Sunni law and attract "modern-educated Muslims."[41] The implications of these endeavors were significant enough to cause a showdown between the Jama'at and the ulama.

The ulama and other spokesmen of traditional Islam defined Mawdudi and the Jama'at in sectarian terms. Although the lines of demarcation between the traditional perspective and Mawdudi's ideology were quite clear at the doctrinal level, this was not true in the political arena. Doctrinal debates cast the Jama'at in a sectarian mold; political imperatives pushed it back toward tradition.

Struggle with the Ulama

It was the Jam'iat-i 'Ulama-i Hind's inability or unwillingness to cross the bound-aries of its traditional stand to accommodate Mawdudi's perspective, more than its support for the Congress party, that forced Mawdudi to break with it in the 1920s. It was also for this reason that, following his resignation from *Al-Jam'iat* and despite his formal education in the religious sciences, he parted with tradi-tional scholarship and enunciated his religious perspective in a new style. He was not of the ulama: his authority emanated from the tradition of Ibn Taimiyah and Shah Waliu'llah, as he understood them, and was to replace that of the ulama.[42]

The ulama clearly recognized the implications of Mawdudi's position. They fully understood that Mawdudi was posing as a *mujaddid* and firmly opposed his program. When the Jama'at was formed in 1941, Mawdudi wrote to some seventy-five ulama, including Manazir Ahsan Gilani, 'Abdu'l-Majid Daryabadi, Qari Muhammad Tayyib, and Husain Ahmad Madani, inviting them to join the Jama'at. A handful replied, but only to register their disapproval.[43] The younger among them were more receptive, however, and a number joined the Jama'at, to the dismay of their elders. Amin Ahsan Islahi and Abu'l-Hasan 'Ali Nadwi recollected that Mawlana Sayyid Sulaiman Nadwi, who had praised Mawdudi's book on jihad and helped publish it, was distressed to learn that the two had joined the Jama'at.[44] Some of them subsequently parted company with Jama'at and returned to the fold of the ulama.

As Mawdudi elaborated his ideas, moreover, his conflict with traditional Islam and its spokesmen came into sharper focus. He regarded them as an im-pediment to the success of his *da'wah*. Unlike the *pirs,* whom he dismissed as "heterodox," and, hence, incapable of resisting reforms of a truly *da'wah* move-ment, the ulama, as guardians of orthodoxy, operated in the same exoteric realm as Mawdudi's program. The institutional rivalry over turf was immediate. As a result, Mawdudi revealed his scheme for the future of Muslims in tandem with a concerted attack on the ulama. His discourse on the Islamic state deliberately sidestepped the ulama, depicting them as an anachronistic institution that had no place in a reformed and rationalized Islamic order. A resuscitated caliphate and a modern Islamic state would leave no room for the ulama as leaders, judges, and guardians of the community. By encouraging the independent study of Arabic, the Qur'an, hadith, and other religious sources, Mawdudi rendered them superfluous[45]—Muslims worthy of the name did not require ulama to guide them. Similarly, by stipulating the modern subjects needed for those practicing *ijtihad,* Mawdudi rendered the ulama obsolete as religious functionaries and as contemporary thinkers.[46] This attack was directed to educated Muslims rather than the masses. Mawdudi derided the ulama for their moribund scholastic style, servile political attitudes, and ignorance of the modern world.[47] Remarked Sayyid As'ad Gilani:

> The Modern age is an age of inventions, technology and discoveries. In this age, the inventions and political, economic and social change have created perplexing problems of human life. The new demands of life require modern solutions in the

light of Islamic teachings. The old-fashioned *ulema* or religious scholars who are produced by the traditional madrassahs, suffer from a limited intellectual horizon restricted to the old books of Hanafi *fiqh*.[48]

Mawdudi's attitude in some measure was retaliation for their having dismissed his educational credentials. The upshot of the rivalry, however, was to form a gap between the ulama and the Jama'at. The ulama, who were rooted in tradition, were ambivalent toward politics, the Jama'at, which was modernist in outlook, had an overtly political orientation.[49]

Once he had parted with tradition, Mawdudi still remained focused on traditional Islam and continued to make forays into the domain of the ulama, which underscored both his differences with them and his continued concern with traditional Islam. In numerous books, Mawdudi outlined the tenets of Islam and reinterpreted Islamic history in ways that refuted the traditional position. Works such as *Khilafat'u mulukiyat* (Caliphate and monarchy) and *Qur'an ki char buniyadi istilahain* (The four basic Qur'anic terms), cornerstones of Mawdudi's conception of *din*, undermined the ulama's status. Mawdudi saw the ulama as unequipped to contend with the problems of the modern world, and he believed they misunderstood Islam. The Jama'at was therefore given a form distinct to that of traditional Islam, with a view to replacing it. The ulama were blamed for sanctioning the wrongful deeds of the Mughals, who had alienated Hindus from Islam, and were subsequently in an alliance with the Congress party, whose aim was erecting a "Hindu Raj."[50] History bore testimony to their failure and the modern world had no place for them.

Mawdudi's invective found a target in the political choices of his former mentors in the Jam'iat-i 'Ulama-i Hind. He cast aspersions on their religious sagacity and knowledge, communal fidelity, and political judgments.[51] Needless to say, the religious and social ramifications were momentous.

Mawdudi's attitude toward the ulama underwent a drastic change after Pakistan was established. Pakistan presented the Jama'at with new political circumstances, choices, and exigencies. The Jama'at found that its political interests converged with those of the ulama, and, faced with the heavy hand of the Muslim League, Mawdudi now saw the divines as valuable allies.[52] In February 1947 he told two of his lieutenants, Amin Ahsan Islahi and Sibghatu'llah Madrasi, to contact various ulama groups and inform them of the Jama'at's political position.[53] Faced with the obduracy of Liaqat 'Ali Khan's government before the Jama'at's demands in January 1948, the party began to form tactical alliances with its erstwhile enemies. In a public speech in Karachi in April 1948, Mawdudi made a direct appeal to the ulama to cooperate in the demand for an Islamic state.[54]

From the Objective Revolution (1949) to debate over the Interim Constitutional Report (1952) to the ulama's twenty-two-point constitutional proposals (1952), the anti-Ahmadi agitations in Punjab (1953–1954), the ulama convention of 1960, and opposition to the Family Law Ordinance (1961–1962), the Jama'at and the ulama found common points that enabled them to form an alliance directed at preserving the place of Islam in Pakistani politics. The Jama'at saw this alliance as crucial to its survival and to the success of its program. When Mawdudi was incarcerated in 1948 on charges of treason over the issue of jihad in Kashmir, Jama'at leaders 'Abdu'l-Ghaffar Hasan and 'Abdu'l-Jabbar Ghazi actively lobbied with the ulama, especially with Pakistan's preeminent 'alim at the time, Mawlana Shabbir Ahmad 'Uthmani (d. 1952), on his behalf. Indeed, 'Uthmani proved instrumental in obtaining his release from prison.[55]

Following this confrontation over jihad, it became increasingly difficult for the Jama'at to maintain its influence in the constitution-making process.[56] Mawdudi then decided that the ulama could be turned into a convenient mouthpiece for the Jama'at, which was being squeezed out of politics.[57] The Jama'at, confident of its own intellectual superiority, saw no dangers in this arrangement; the ulama had the means and the Jama'at the knowledge to build an Islamic state. Mawdudi fostered unity through such measures as the twenty-two-point proposals. This unity, Mawdudi concluded, would augment the power and reach of the Islamic lobby in affecting the new constitution. When in 1950 Sayyid Sulaiman Nadwi came to Pakistan, Mawdudi openly endorsed his spiritual leadership, a symbolic but nevertheless significant gesture. Mawdudi's endorsement was brought about by Mas'ud 'Alam Nadwi, a close companion of Mawdudi and a favorite student of Sayyid Sulaiman. Mas'ud 'Alam arranged for Sayyid Sulaiman to visit Mawdudi in Lahore[58] and continued to keep the venerable Sayyid Sulayman conciliatory toward the Jama'at. This relationship and that of 'Abdu'l-Jabbar Ghazi with Mawlana Shabbir 'Uthmani suggest that, among the Jama'at's leaders, the young ulama acted as a link between their mentors and the party and were also a force in the Jama'at that prevented a complete rupture with tradition.

The ulama were indeed receptive to Mawdudi's overtures and helped return the Jama'at closer to traditional Islam. In 1951, when Mawlana Ihtishamu'l-Haq Thanwi, 'Uthmani's successor and putatively an enemy of the Jama'at, convened a conference of thirty-one ulama, Mawdudi was one of those invited.[59] Although in his invitation Ihtishamu'l-Haq did not address Mawdudi with the title Mawlana, which was commonly reserved for ulama (he called him *janab*, a generic mark of respect),[60] he nonetheless conferred coveted status upon him by inviting him; by coming, Mawdudi recognized the ulamas' traditionalizing influence on the Jama'at's political activism.

Despite the political incentives for cooperation between the ulama and the Jama'at, along with the concrete steps the two made toward a modus vivendi, tensions persisted and erupted from time to time in the form of denunciations and recriminations. The Jama'at retained its doctrinal independence, as confirmed by its periodic attacks on the ulama.[61] Many ulama, unrestrained by political considerations, continued to view the Jama'at with disdain. Between 1948 and 1950, years when the Jama'at was allied with the ulama in Pakistan, a number of senior religious scholars living in India—notably, Sayyid Sulaiman Nadwi in 1948 and Manazir Ahsan Gilani and 'Abdu'l-Majid Daryabadi in 1950—criticized Mawdudi's views and denounced him for his break with traditional orthodoxy. By 1952 the trickle of criticism had been converted into a flurry of *fatwas*. The *daru'l-'ulum* at Deoband initiated a *fatwa* campaign led by

Mawlana Sayyid Mahdi Hasan and Mawlana Aizaz 'Ali in March 1951 against the Jama'at.[62] The campaign soon gathered support from notable Deobandis; Mufti Kifayatu'llah, Mawlana Husain Ahmad Madani, Mawlana Ahmad Sa'id, and Mawlana Qari Muhammad Tayyib also joined the fray. The first three, having received the brunt of Mawdudi's attacks on the Jam'iat-i 'Ulama-i Hind in the years from 1938–1947, had a particular axe to grind. Additional *fatwas* came from Saharanpur, Malabar, and Lucknow accusing Mawdudi of giving unorthodox Qur'anic and hadith interpretations, departing from the norms of Hanafi law, issuing unorthodox religious verdicts, belittling the importance of the Prophet, insulting the companions of the Prophet, indulging in Wahabbism, sympathizing with the Ahmadis, having Mahdiist pretensions, and, in some cases, demonstrating Khariji tendencies.[63]

In the Jama'at's view, and justifiably so, the *fatwa* campaign was initiated at the behest of the Pakistani government, eager to weaken the alliance between the ulama and the Jama'at. The government may have been culpable, but the Jama'at only encouraged it. In June 1951, soon after the initial *fatwas* were issued at the Deoband *daru'l-'ulum* and in response to the query of a reader of the *Tarjumanu'l-Qur'an*, Mawdudi, true to his earlier communalist vision, declared India *daru'l-kufr* (land of blasphemy), forbidding Pakistanis to marry anyone from India and to accept any inheritances from there. Indian ulama understandably took umbrage, as did many Muslim Indians and Pakistanis.[64]

The institutional links between Indian and Pakistani ulama did not favor Mawdudi's case. The *fatwa* campaign gained momentum and soon spread to Pakistan. The Brelwi religious organization Jam'iat-i 'Ulama-i Pakistan in 1952 published a book entitled *Khatrih ki ghanti* (Bell of alarm),[65] in which Mawdudi was accused of harboring Mahdiist and "Mirza'i" (i.e., Ahmadi) tendencies. The Brelwi offensive started a widespread discussion over the Jama'at's doctrinal position among the ulama, which, to the delight of the government, was not politically productive. Mawdudi soon came under attack from all the schools and groups of ulama in India and Pakistan.[66]

The Jama'at was clearly perturbed by the invidious campaign and took great pains to refute the charges leveled against it. In areas of Pakistan such as the North-West Frontier Province, where the Deobandi ulama had particular importance, the *fatwa* campaign greatly damaged the Jama'at. Mawdudi, who had always condemned such *fatwa* campaigns, saw the hand of the Pakistan government behind the entire episode and refused to consider it seriously. He simply condemned the criticisms and recriminations by the ulama as unproductive and damaging to Islam.[67] He saw no reason that his controversial religious proclamations should interfere with the Jama'at's alliance with the ulama. In 1952 he wrote, "It is also wrong that, if someone disagrees with my research he should stop cooperating with me on religious issues."[68] Mawdudi did not involve himself in this imbroglio and consigned the task of responding to the charges leveled against him to other Jama'at leaders. In India, Mufti Muhammad Yusuf, later the amir of the Jama'at-i Islami of India, took the lead in the attempt to exonerate Mawdudi. In Pakistan, the task fell to the ulama votaries of the Jama'at, who had already acted as links between the party and the ulama.[69]

In these altercations, the Jama'at sought neither to justify its particular interpretive reading of Islam nor to defend what Mawdudi had stated. Instead, it
settled on defending itself against charges of obscurantism and denying that its
members had departed from traditional orthodoxy. All such suggestions were
either the result of insidious machinations on the part of a few ill-wishers or of
misunderstandings: "We have made no undue claims for the position of our
Jama'at; we claim no monopoly of truth. What we say is this: We recognized
our duty; therefore, we have formed an organization."[70] No mention was made
of Mawdudi's cavalier attacks on the ulama and their vision of Islam or of the
novel ideas that had been at the center of Mawdudi's message. When confronted
with the reality of its stand vis-à-vis traditional orthodoxy, the Jama'at tended
to reaffirm rather than loosen its links to it. The thinker who had labored to
distance himself from traditional Islam, faced with the prospects of a real break,
balked and reasoned his way back into it.

The Jama'at's conciliatory tone helped somewhat, and the immediacy of the
political question before the ulama-Jama'at alliance dampened the ulama's zeal.
Cooperation between the two was soon resumed, although disagreements continued to appear. As long as the Jama'at remained suspended between tradition
and a sectarian break with it, political alliances between the ulama and the Jama'at
were bound to be complicated by denunciations and recriminations. The Jama'at
remained close to the ulama, but the party's separate identity was periodically
reiterated by Mawdudi through his interpretive reading of Islamic doctrines.

Mawdudi's reaffirmations invariably invited the disapproval of the ulama,
which at times manifested itself in the form of renewed public denunciations.
The government, keen to both weaken the ulama-Jama'at alliance and under-
mine the Jama'at, did not remain altogether uninvolved. In 1963 when the
Jama'at decided to support the candidacy of Fatimah Jinnah for the presidency[71]
and again in 1966 following publication of Mawdudi's book *Khilafat'u mulukiyat*
the government was quick to point out Mawdudi's folly and his innovative reading of the orthodox position and to mobilize a group of the ulama, some from
the government camp, in another anti-Mawdudi *fatwa* campaign.

Khilafat'u mulukiyat presented a dilemma that had the potential to be particularly divisive. In it, Mawdudi made no bone about his independent legal
outlook and his departures from the norms of Hanafi law. The book presented
an uncharitable view of Caliph 'Uthman (one of the rightly guided caliphs),
which, regardless of its historical accuracy, was found to be sacrilegious by a
number of the ulama.[72] The venomous tone of the *fatwa* campaign, however,
acted to vindicate Mawdudi at times. For instance, one critic accused Mawdudi
of "Husain *parasti*" (worshiping Husain ibn 'Ali, i.e., being sympathetic to the
Shi'i), a charge that was construed as illogical by most observers. Still, the Jama'at
was hurt by the ulama's invective.[73] The book opened the door for a more serious discussion of Mawdudi's perspective and reexamination of some of his earlier writings, notably, *Qur'an ki char buniadi istilahain*, which produced further
criticism of his thought by his erstwhile followers Abu'l-Hasan 'Ali Nadwi,
Wahidu'ddin Khan, and Muhammad Manzur Nu'mani, all of whom are prominent Muslim scholars of India.[74]

Relations between the Jama'at and the ulama became complicated in the late 1960s, when the Jama'at's political activism intensified and its chances of success appeared to be improving. The Jama'at had politicized the ulama and it now had to contend with the results. As the parties of the ulama—the Jam'iat-i 'Ulama-i Islam and the Jam'iat-i 'Ulama-i Pakistan (and later the Jam'iat-i 'Ulama-i Ahl-i Hadith as well) developed distinct identities and vested political interests, organizational rivalry between the Jama'at and these parties became entrenched and relations between the Jama'at and the ulama were increasingly strained. Wary of the Jama'at's potential for a solid electoral showing in the elections of 1970 and no longer restrained by the need for political unity, the various ulama groups increased their attacks.[75] These attacks were aimed not just at Mawdudi's thinking, but at the work of the Jama'at itself. In May 1970, the Jama'at's Yaum-i Shaukat-i Islam (Day of Islamic Glory) rally, designed to shore up electoral support for the party, met with the passionate objections of Jam'iat-i 'Ulama-i Islam's Mufti Mahmud and Mawlana Hizarwi.[76] The Jam'iat-i 'Ulama-i Pakistan contested forty-two tickets in the elections of 1970 where there was a Jama'at candidate. The new political and institutional direction of the ulama's attacks on the Jama'at cost the party dearly in those elections.[77]

Eager to appeal to the mainstream Pakistani voter, the Jama'at could not afford to be cast in a sectarian mold or identified as an enemy of the ulama. In its effort to silence the ulama, it downplayed its controversial doctrinal teachings and placed increasing emphasis on the imminent danger to Islam from the secular leadership, hoping to persuade the ulama to re-create the alliance that the two had enjoyed soon after Pakistan was formed. The Jama'at sought to curb the attacks of the ulama by becoming increasingly like them, a de facto ulama party. Yet, a strong Islamic alliance under the Jama'at's leadership has been slow in forming. In 1992, when factions within Jam'iat-i 'Ulama-i Islam and Jam'iat-i 'Ulama-i Pakistan broke with their parties to form Islami Jumhuri Mahaz (Islamic Democratic Front), Mawlana Fazu'l-Rahman and Mawlana Shah Ahmad Nurani prevented the Jama'at from joining.[78] Again in 1993, when the Jama'at announced the formation of the Pakistan Islamic Front as an umbrella Islamic organization and invited all Islamic parties to join, pool their resources, and maximize the power of the Islamic vote bank, none of the ulama parties responded. Instead, they divided up and gathered under two other Islamic umbrellas, the Islami Jumhuri Mahaz and the Muttahidah Dini Mahaz (United Religious Front).

The Jama'at also sought to counter the threat posed by the ulama through infiltrating their institutional structure and, at the same time, creating ideological and institutional links. In 1962, with this objective in mind, it founded the Jam'iat-i Tulabah-i 'Arabiyah (Association of Arabic Students) in Dhaka, a movement to organize seminary students.[79] The Jam'iat-i Tulabah-i 'Arabiyah was charged with the task of recruiting seminary students from *madrasahs* (traditional religious seminaries) and *daru'l-'ulums* across Pakistan, along the lines of student organizations in the universities.[80] The Jama'at hoped that the Jam'iat-i Tulabah-i 'Arabiyah would be able to impress the Jama'at's perspective and influence on the next generation of Pakistani ulama and thereby establish good relations between the two.

In 1963, the Deobandi *'alim* and Jama'at stalwart Mawlana Gulzar Ahmad Mazahiri founded the Jam'iat-i Ittihad-i 'Ulama (Association of unity among the ulama). This organization was to act as a liaison between the Jama'at and the various ulama factions in Pakistan.[81] Mazahiri was also charged with the task of promoting unity among the ulama concerning the idea of Islamic revolution and the protection of the place of Islam in Pakistan. In 1976 Mazahiri founded another Jama'at organization, the 'Ulama Academy, which, in addition to working toward a common platform with the ulama, acted as a *daru'l-'ulum*, training Jama'at ulama. It opened its doors in 1979 with 125 students.[82] These Jama'at ulama have carried the message of the party to mosques and seminaries in cities, towns, and villages across Pakistan, reaching hitherto untouched ground to create a new sodality, which would compete with the existing schools of religious thought. Convinced of the futility of ad hoc alliances with the ulama, Mawdudi decided to infiltrate them, pressure them from within, and, if possible, replace them with ulama of his own. It was a daring offensive, which the Jama'at had also pursued vis-à-vis the bureaucracy and would eventually adopt for the army. The idea of Jama'at-i Islami ulama, however, violated Mawdudi's own arguments against institutional Islam. To unseat the ulama the Jama'at once again found itself retracting into the fold of traditional Islam.

Over the years, and especially since Mawdudi's death, the purview of the activities of the Jam'iat-i Ittihad and the 'Ulama Academy have been extended still further. The Jama'at now operates a number of *daru'l-'ulums* across Pakistan, the most important of which is the 'Ulama Academy in Lahore. At party headquarters in Lahore it also established a seminary, the Jam'iatu'l-Muhsinat (Society of the virtuous), for training women as preachers and ulama. The idea is to reduce the influence of the traditional ulama among women by creating a network of women ulama, a first in Islam. As a result of these undertakings, the Jama'at has intensified its interactions with the ulama.[83] This liaison is now overseen by a vice-president of the Jama'at, Jan Muhammad 'Abbasi, who regards it as promoting unity among the ulama as a whole. He has sought to obfuscate the Jama'at's problems by underlining the fractious nature of the institutional structure of the ulama, a strategy that had proved successful in the 1950s, when the Jama'at acted as the broker for unity among the ulama. He has also sought to rally the ulama to the support of Jama'at-sponsored causes, such as resistance to the invasion of Western culture and defense of gains made for Islam during the Zia period, all in the framework of various Jama'at-sponsored ulama conventions, the Muttahidah 'Ulama Council (Council of united ulama) or the Nifaz Shari'at (Protection of the *shari'ah*) movement.[84] Under 'Abbasi, who took over the Jama'at's projects on the ulama following Mazahiri's death in 1980, the Jama'at has made a number of significant concessions to the ulama, repressing Mawdudi's departures from Hanafi law and bringing the Jama'at squarely into the Hanafi tradition.[85] Pakistani ulama, however, have not been entirely convinced and are demanding that the Jama'at renounce a number of Mawdudi's works.

Following the retirement of Mian Tufayl Muhammad as amir in 1987, relations with the ulama emerged as a major consideration in the election of a new amir. Qazi Husain Ahmad, who succeeded Mian Tufayl, comes from a Deobandi background. His brothers are Deobandi ulama and his father was a devotee of the Jam'iat-i 'Ulama-i Hind leader (and Mawdudi's old foe) Husain Ahmad Madani, who is also Qazi Husain Ahmad's namesake.[86] In his capacity as amir and as part of his program of widening the political base of the Jama'at, Qazi Husain has moved the party closer to the ulama. This strategy has borne some fruit, as the party has been able to cultivate a following in the predomi- nantly Deobandi North-West Frontier Province. However, the increasingly political character of Pakistan's ulama parties, each with its own distinct iden- tity and set of political goals, his precluded unity among them and is likely to be a source of continuing rivalry and confrontation unless religious parties as a whole are challenged by other political forces. The elections of 1993 bore testi- mony to this fact.

The Jama'at's answer has been to shift back toward traditional Islam but to remain adamant about retaining a certain distance from tradition in its capacity as vanguard of the Islamic revolution. The Jama'at has made conciliatory over- tures to the ulama, with traditionalizing effects, has infiltrated ulama organi- zations, and has itself produced ulama, but ones who bear the imprint of Mawdudi's ideological perspective. The Jama'at's ulama policy, especially under 'Abbasi and Qazi Husain, is a testimony to the ultimate failure of the Jama'at's original vision and to the tenaciousness of traditional Islam.

The Struggle against Sufism and Popular Islam

The Jama'at's schismatic relations with traditional Islam were at least in part a result of Mawdudi's attitude toward Sufism. Like some Islamic reformers who preceded him, and true to the spirit of contemporary revivalist thought, Mawdudi and the Jama'at were disdainful of Sufism and the traditional institu- tions associated with it.[87] In a lecture at the Islamiyah College of Lahore in 1939, he argued that the spiritual powers of the Sufi masters were as relevant to the fundamental questions of existence as were the physical attributes of a wres- tler.[88] Elsewhere, he held Sufism accountable for causing the decline of Islam throughout history, referring to it as *chuniya begum* (lady opium).[89] He believed that Sufism had misled Mughal rulers like Emperor Akbar and his son Dara Shukuh into gravitating toward syncretic experiments. Their accommodation of Hinduism, as is evident in Akbar's *din-i ilahi* (divine religion) and Dara Shokuh's book *Majma'u'l-bahrain* (Conglomoration of the two seas),[90] which relied on an esoteric marriage between Islam and Hinduism, was not just reli- giously suspect, but caused the Mughals to miss a unique opportunity to con- vert the whole of India to Islam.

True to his modernizing perspective, Mawdudi found Sufism to be incom- patible with his own scheme of things. Sufism was of great importance to the major ulama groups in Pakistan, the Deobandis and the Brelwis, and they found Mawdudi's attacks on Sufism just as contentious as his exegeses on juridical and theological matters. In Punjab and Sind, Sufism played an important role in the popular culture of the masses and eventually in their politics.[91] Mawdudi's anti-Sufi rhetoric thus soon ran into trouble in Pakistan, and once again the Jama'at was compelled to explain and exculpate its position to minimize political damage and reduce the distance between Mawdudi's perspective and traditional Islam.[92] Both Mawdudi and Amin Ahsan Islahi went on record as denying that the Jama'at was antagonistic toward Sufism.[93] Mawdudi claimed that he had Sufi ancestors, which would by itself prevent him from denouncing Sufism. References to this Sufi ancestry, hitherto absent in his official biographies, began to appear in Jama'at publications on his life and thought from this time onward. In correspondence with 'Alau'ddin Shah, a Naqshbandi *pir* in Punjab who was also a relative, Mawdudi accepted the truth of Sufism, though only as practiced by the venerated shaikh, not the popular Sufism of the Chishti and the Qadiri orders, whose structures of authority were based on Sufi shrines and the festivals and rituals associated with them.[94]

Implicit in Mawdudi's qualified acceptance of Sufism was a definition of what he understood Sufism to be and a rejection of Sufism's beliefs concerning where the spiritual path led. A drastic redefinition of Sufism had been a part of Mawdudi's program of reform from its inception. Unable to spurn Sufism altogether, he had looked to redefine it.[95] Mawdudi attempted to infuse it with values and aims that would convert it into an aspect of the *din*, making it merely a component part of his message:

> *Fiqh* deals with the apparent and observable conduct, the fulfilling of a duty in letter. What concerns itself with the spirit of conduct is known as *Tasawwuf* [Sufism]. For example, when we say our prayers, *Fiqh* will judge us only by fulfillment of the outward requirements such as ablution, facing toward the Ka'ba . . . while *Tasawwuf* will judge our prayers by our concentration . . . the effect of our prayers on our morals and manners.[96]

For members of the Jama'at, this redefinition was a reform of Sufism and the restoration of its true spirit and intent.[97] Mawdudi's redefinition, however, imparted entirely new meaning to Sufism. Sufism was not an esoteric dimension of Islam, but merely a gauge to measure "concentration" and "morals."[98] It existed, Mawdudi conceded, but not in the form and spirit Muslims had thought it did. Recently, Khurshid Ahmad said, "Sufism is a sister—parallel—movement to ours. In earlier history it had sought to protect Muslim youth from corruption caused by monarchies."[99] By saying this, he implied that it might have been relevant to the early development of Islam but is of little relevance now.

By placing the redefinition of Sufism in tandem with emphasis on Mawdudi's own Sufi lineage, the Jama'at has suggested that he had the authority to (re-)interpret Sufism. Sufi terms such as cleansing the soul (*tazkiyah-i nafs*), dedication to God (*ta'alluq bi'llah*), spiritual charisma (*karamat*); reflections (*tajalliyat*), epiphanies (*mazahir*), and realizations (*mushahadat*) of God gradually found their way into Mawdudi's discussions, and his ideological formulation became his Sufi path (*suluk*). His organizational thinking concerning the Jama'at also showed the influence of Sufism.[100]

His reinterpretation of Sufism did little to end the admonitions of the ulama, and it did not expand the party's base of support among the masses. The Jama'at needed to accede more ground to Sufism, and from the mid-1960s onward, redefinition increasingly gave way to outright recognition of Sufism.[101] Mian Tufayl Muhammad translated *Kashf al-mahjub* (Discovery of the hidden) of the great mystic and the patron saint of Lahore, Sayyid 'Ali Hujwiri (Data Ganjbakhsh, d. 1072) into Urdu. The Jama'at's Jam'iat-i Ittihad-i 'Ulama was expanded to include the *mashayikh* (sing. *shaikh*, Sufi masters), as it sought to foster greater understanding between various Sufi orders and the Jama'at.[102]

The political incentives behind all this became clearer in 1987, when Qazi Husain Ahmad launched his tour, the Karvan-i Da'wat'u Muhabbat (Caravan of invitation and benevolence), to gather mass support for the Jama'at with a visit to the Hujwiri's shrine in Lahore. The visit was of great significance: by engaging in the most "obscurantist" aspect of Sufi devotion—visitation of the shrine of a saint—the Jama'at appeared to accept popular Sufism at face value. The event was a testament not only to the political motivation of the Jama'at and its traditionalizing influence, but also to the success of traditional Islam in stopping revivalism. Qazi Husain's lead has been followed by the Jama'at's student organization, Islami Jam'iat-i Tulabah, which now holds an annual conference on Hujwiri, and frequently sponsors sessions of *na't* (devotional reading of poetry about the Prophet, usually associated with Brelwis).

Mawdudi's ideology and the idea of the Jama'at were products of the politics during the partition years in India. Anxiety in the Muslim community elicited a number of responses, one of which took the shape of Islamic revivalism, which was given a new conception of authority and leadership and a new form of organization. It purported to give Muslims a new identity rooted in an interpretive reading of Islam. Through the use of texts and organizational power, this new Islam grew roots, not just in India, but elsewhere across the Muslim world. It did not manage to control Muslim political choices in South Asia, but it did find a following and, more important, it institutionalized its views on authority and religiopolitical organization.

The direction of development of this reading of Islam is far from clear. It was articulated with the aim of replacing traditional Islam and wresting monopoly of social and religious interpretation from its spokesmen. It is apparent that Mawdudi's interpretive reading of Islam, after its initial break with tradition, was unable either to dominate Muslim life and thought or to satisfactorily institutionalize a sectarian position, and it has been gradually collapsing back into traditional Islam. This process has been controlled by political imperatives before the Jama'at. The need to expand its base of support led the party to move away from divisive doctrinal issues and closer to traditional Islam. Doctrinal disputes were overshadowed by political necessities. This means that traditional Islam, in South Asia at least, is vigorous and powerful enough to withstand the challenge of Islamic revivalism, subdue it, and force changes on it.

This is a development of great significance, but it is not the end of the Jama'at and its ideology. In turn, traditionalization has in turn provided the Jama'at with a way to influence traditional Islam from within. By staying inside the pale of traditional Islam, the Jama'at has the opportunity to modernize it. The Jama'at's influence on the ideas and mode of operation of an array of ulama groups in Pakistan is indicative of this trend. The Jama'at's significance may finally rest not in its successful institutionalization of a new school of thought, as the party's leaders had originally intended, but in changing the structure of traditional Islamic thought and worldview so that it may win the struggle for the soul of Islam.

7

An Old Mandate in a New Age: Mawdudi's Authority

The Jama'at-i Islami and Mawdudi's prolific writings have given his ideology the reach it needed to become known in Muslim society. Their importance suggests that, ultimately, Mawdudi's authority was legal-rational in nature.[1] Many were drawn to Mawdudi by his intelligence, erudition, creativity, and self-reliance. He was not from the beginning the hardened leader that his followers later found him to be. In his earlier years, he had a different disposition, reflected, for example, in his love of poetry, especially that of Ghalib.[2] But as the years wore on, frustration at the political quandary of Indian Muslims, the eclipse of Islam in the city of his youth, and the demanding task of resolving these predicaments that he had set for himself changed him.

Mawdudi did not base his claim to leadership in any Islamic institution. In fact, he repudiated all institutional notions of authority, such as those of the ulama or the *pirs*; he did appeal to the concept of the *mujaddid*, however. As a model of religious leadership and source of authority, the *mujaddid* has been particularly important in Indian Islam since the time of Shaikh Ahmad Sirhindi, who was known as Mujaddid-i Alf-i Thani (the renewer of the faith in the second millennium).[3] Since Sirhindi's time, generations of Muslim figures of authority have drawn on his tradition of renewal and reform of Islam to revive the faith. Much like them, Mawdudi based his claim to leadership on his promise to deliver Muslims from their political impotence. He was more a Muslim political leader than he was an Islamic figure of authority, although it is not always easy to separate the Islamic ingredients from the purely political ones of his inspiration. The Islamic basis for his claim to authority often concealed the greater power that came from extending hope to a community that had been declined in stature, if not robbed of its power. There were flaws in his religiopolitical persona; however, these affected the nature of his authority, which in the end prevented him from leading a successful political movement.

An Aristocrat and a Mujaddid

Mawdudi was viewed first and foremost as a man of principle, a man motivated by his beliefs and ambitions and not by monetary gain. He strove for recognition, not wealth, and this quality fueled his untiring dedication to realizing his ambitions.[4] A case in point was his decision to leave the cosmopolitan city of Hyderabad for the village life of Pathankot. So drastic was this change of venue that in later years some of his more dramatic biographers equated it with the exile of Ram Chandra, Buddha's "decision to forsake his palace to seek salvation in a forest,"[5] and the Prophet Muhammad's *hijrah* (migration) from Mecca to Medina in A.D. 632. The decision to move to Pathankot was not an easy one, but for Mawdudi, forgoing a career at the 'Uthmaniyah University and the arduous challenges of this undertaking were rewarded in other ways. He believed that his sacrifices bore great religious significance. For him, the Daru'l-Islam experiment was a historic undertaking—a significant episode in the cavalcade of events that had shaped Muslim history in India since 1857 and would continue to do so thenceforth.[6] To his audience, these sacrifices were the proof of his dedication and moral rectitude, both of which were important leadership qualities.

Mawdudi was always known for his self-reliance, which at times bordered on haughtiness but allowed him a single-minded dedication to his cause and a selflessness in realizing it. In a poem he wrote on July 18, 1932, he reflected,

> You have a hidden fire within you
> So you don't need the candle.
> O, the burning desire of the moth become a radiant flame yourself.[7]

It was Mawdudi's burning desire that would rekindle the flame of Islam. Mawdudi worked long hours every day throughout his life, studying, writing, reading, and attending to the affairs of his party.[8] Immersed in his work, he was never much of a family man. Although close to his wife, he did not spend much time with his six sons and three daughters, using the excuse that once he had succeeded in creating the Islamic state—the panacea for all of the ills of the Muslim society—his children, like everyone else, would benefit by becoming true Muslims.[9] Not surprisingly, he was disappointed in his children. For the most part, their lives did not reflect his lifetime of *da'wah*; only one of them ever joined the Jama'at. Except for his second daughter, Asma, who was very close to him, none of his children ever showed any scholarly promise.[10]

Throughout most of his life, Mawdudi suffered from a kidney ailment, but it never retarded the pace of his efforts. In 1945 and 1946, he was often bedridden, and in 1969, amidst the national electoral campaign, he was forced to travel to England for treatment.[11] In later years he also suffered from severe arthritis, which at some points virtually paralyzed him.[12] He was a practical man and accepted responsibilities, even if they were not in keeping with the image of an intellectual. In 1947, when the predominantly Hindu and Sikh area of Pathankot was embroiled in the violence of the partition, some two thousand Muslim peasants took refuge at the Daru'l-Islam. Mawdudi distributed the three guns in the possession of the Jama'at at the time among his followers and defended his establishment.[13] In later years he wrote of that experience: "At that time I felt that it was the angels who were protecting us. There was a veil which kept us from seeing them. I wished so much the veil may be lifted, so that I would be able to see our protectors."[14]

Mawdudi wanted to be both a scholar and a politician. He was seen by his admirers as an "analyst," a "critic," and a "reformer." Although this image was a tribute to Mawdudi and a source of pride to the Jama'at, it also posed problems. Mawdudi did not try to solve them, nor did he attempt to consolidate his various functions. At least until 1972, politics superseded his scholarly and intellectual interests, but they interfered with his political instincts.[15]

In 1971, disappointed that the Jama'at has been defeated at the polls, Mawdudi returned to his scholarship. Even throughout his years of political activity, however, he continued to produce books (seventy-three at the time of his death)[16] and articles. His most important work was his Urdu translation and commentary on the Qur'an, *Tafhimu'l-Qur'an,* which he began in 1942. This voluminous work (sections of which were written in jail) was finally completed in 1972, after he ceased to be the Jama'at's leader in the wake of the election.[17] Then he began yet another major undertaking, a life of the Prophet (*sirah*), two volumes of which were completed in the remaining seven years of his life (it is still unpublished).[18] In 1979, just before he died, he received the King Faisal Award in recognition of his scholarship and his contributions to Islam; the proceeds went to the Jama'at's research institute Idarah-i Ma'arif-i Islami (Institute of Islamic studies).[19] Whatever his shortcomings as a politician, his written works brought his views into contemporary Muslim discourse on society and politics, and his charismatic appeal rested in great part on them.

Mawdudi was proud of his knowledge of Western culture and modern subjects, thereby deliberately dissociating himself from the ulama. In his last years, however, he showed a greater interest in serving in traditional modes of authority, which he previously had shunned. Throughout his life, he had practiced *unani tibb* (traditional medicine)—a tradition he inherited from his family[20]—as a *hakim* (practitioner of traditional medicine), though not openly until the end of his life. The Jama'at has also utilized *unani* medicine in its dispensaries since the creation of Pakistan. *Unani* medicine, a facet of traditional Islam in India, is sometimes practiced among Deobandi ulama[21] but more generally by a class of quasi-religious leaders closely tied to popular Islam.

Over the years, Mawdudi also became less opposed to Sufism and devotional religious practices. In the 1970s he would often be engaged in *nawafil* (nonobligatory religious practices) and would spend evenings in *tahajjud* (nonobligatory prayers offered during late hours of the night), practices not usually associated with Islamic reformers and revivalists.[22] Nor was he averse to adopting the mantle of a Sufi master. When Hakim Ni'mat 'Ali from Pattuki, a Jama'at member, wrote a book interpreting Mawdudi's *iqamat-i din* in terms of the Sufi concept of *tazkiyah-i nafs,* Mawdudi initiated the Hakim and another man into Sufism by the authority of his Chishti lineage[23] rather than object to the interpretation.

Although these traditional practices surfaced late in Mawdudi's career, they no doubt had existed in his persona earlier, however concealed. He was always associated with modernity as a thinker, scholar, and politician, and even more in his personal and public style and in the impressions they made on his audience.

Followers often said of Mawdudi that he had an impressive but impassive face, aristocratic demeanor, and impeccable manners (*adab*). He was not warm, but he was sincere and open. He spoke in beautiful Urdu, enunciated in the Delhi accent. He had a pleasant voice, a poignant sense of humor, and a taste for metaphors. He was very alert and always displayed great presence of mind. He was, at least in private, a tolerant man, "strict but not rigid."[24] He never forced his views on his family or on his skeptical visitors—his style on such occasions was one of persuasion. He was patient in the face of adversity, calm and composed, yet unyielding and uncompromising.[25] His stubbornness, a mark of his confidence and a sign of his power, had a pronounced effect on his followers.[26] He was reserved, not easily excitable, taciturn, and poised, but not altogether immune to fits of anger. When one time his tonga was stopped by a drunken Sikh in Pathankot, an enraged Mawdudi lashed the Sikh and berated his faith.[27]

Mawdudi remained in close contact with Jama'at members. Every day, during the time between dusk and evening prayers, he conducted informal discussions at his house with his fellow members, responding to questions and explaining his views on a multitude of religious issues. It was his practice to patiently listen to all arguments before giving his opinion. Sayyid As'ad Gilani recalled that Mawdudi always spoke last in a discussion and, therefore, always had the last word, although his opinion would include points others had raised. When the Jama'at's *shura*' met, he also listened silently to debates and then would speak at the very end, pointing out the strengths and weaknesses of each argument, encompassing points from each in his final opinion.[28] Similar tendencies was present in his scholarship. Muhammad Saeed wrote that when visiting Mawdudi in the early 1940s in Lal Kuan, he found him with some ten different English translations of the Qur'an, including ones by M. Pickthall, Yusuf Ali, and J. M. Rodwell, spread out around him.[29] Mawdudi began his own translation shortly thereafter.

Many were too intimidated by his demeanor to challenge him; those who were brave enough to do so found him far from accommodating.[30] In his earlier years, said Malik Ghulam 'Ali, he had a more receptive ear and was fond of debates, as his heated exchanges over theological questions with Jama'at leaders such as Mawlana Mu'inu'ddin of Banu, Mawlana Sayahu'ddin of Kakakheil, and Mawlana 'Abdu'l-'Aziz of Baluchistan showed.[31] Even then, however, he would lose patience with those whom he could not convince, and on occasion he grew angry.[32] As the years progressed, some believed he was less open and less interested in convincing others of his views. If asked a question, he would answer, but if presented with an argument or a challenge, he would remain silent: "He no longer encouraged discussions, only questions."[33] This was especially true after disputes over party policy in 1956 and 1957 led to a schism in the Jama'at's ranks. Islahi complained to Mawdudi that "if someone criticizes you they have criticized the Jama'at, and if they criticize the Jama'at they have criticized Islam."[34] Mawdudi was not interested in the emergence of any independent intellectual poles within the Jama'at, nor was he willing to relinquish any of his religious authority by acknowledging the intellectual worth of those around him.[35]

For some who knew Mawdudi from his earlier days, these later traits were not really new developments. He had always shocked his peers and mentors with his supercilious self-confidence and his audacity in criticizing those above his station. Even when a political neophyte in Delhi, Mawdudi recognized no equal; he was the "know-it-all" ('aql-i kull), an "intellectual autocrat."[36] Whereas those in the Jama'at readily succumbed to Mawdudi's authority, others did not. For example, his brother, on reading the first installment of Tafhimu'l-Qur'an, was not afraid to tell him, "You do not as yet have the profundity to be a commentator on the Qur'an [mufassir]." When Mawdudi finished it in 1972, Abu'l-Khayr told him he had finally acquired the acumen to be a mufassir and should start again.[37]

In public, Mawdudi was compelling. His views were always presented with great authority and in an articulate and rational style that appealed to logic rather than the emotions of his audience.[38] His expositions relied on the authority of Islamic edicts and manipulated the fears and expectations that would compel the faithful to action. He would lead his audience step by step through the structure of the idea that he had posited, using rationally discussed and interconnected arguments, the conclusions to each of which would carry his audience to the next argument and eventually to the grand conclusion, the sum total of the arguments presented and the idea that he had sought to prove. During the early part of his career, ideas were articulated through catechisms[39]; in his later years, he would carry his audience, without interruption in pace or line of thought, from assumptions and premises to conclusions. His final conclusions, however, invariably connected "understanding" to "action." Mawdudi never remained content with mere intellectual proof; he demanded action from his audience.[40] His argumentation gave the Jama'at texts a distinct style, which has since been emulated widely, but during the party's early years gave it a character that set it apart from the pack of Islamic movements that were competing for popular support.

Mawdudi deliberately erased areas of compromise, dividing issues into right and wrong, Islamic and un-Islamic.[41] By putting everything in black and white, he brought moral pressure to bear on his audience, manipulating the psychological impulse that is inherent in a consequential choice between such diametric opposites as truth and falsehood, salvation and perdition. Wuthnow found this approach to be central to development of ideologies and consequential to emergence of new intellectual traditions.[42] By dramatizing the conflict between good and evil, Mawdudi decided how social or theological issues were interpreted, what issues were of relevance, and how and in what manner they would be discussed. He thus brought together two central and interrelated aspects of contemporary Islamic revivalism: social critique and salvational dimension.[43] The structure of his argumentation was simple, but its implications for articulating an ideological perspective was both complex and far-reaching.

Discussing the relationship between Islam and science, Sayyid Ahmad Khan said that "true reason is Islamic"[44]—that is, not only is faith predicated on reason, but, more important, reason leads to faith. Mawdudi used this basic premise to interpret Islam, but in his interpretation reason was not merely the means for fostering a dialogue between Islam and modern science, it was a hermeneutic tool. In Mawdudi's works, however, rationalism was often modified by his apologetic posturing vis-à-vis Western thought. The need to defend Islam using the rational method often led him to what H. A. R. Gibb called a "[shocking] . . . method of argument and treatment of facts . . . [and] *writing to a predetermined conclusion*."[45] He stretched rationalism to its limits and, at times, found himself in rather untenable positions.

The clearest example can be found in his discussion of the purdah system. In his celebrated work, *Purdah and the Status of Women in Islam* (1972), he deviated from his customary ratiocinations and harangued his audience on Islam's advocacy of absolute segregation of society and the correlation between women's emancipation and the fall of civilizations.[46] Although he had otherwise rejected the sanctity of the writ of Islamic history in favor of strict adherence to the unadulterated teaching of the primary Islamic sources, here he sought to prove his arguments by confirming the sanctity of custom, going so far as to claim that the practice of purdah was sanctioned by the Qur'an. This departure from his customary line of reasoning was a direct consequence of his apologetic posture, which was most evident when it came to defending women's status in Islam. Compelled to defend Islam's position using Western criteria of liberty, justice, and rationality, Mawdudi resorted to "writing to a predetermined conclusion." The result was "a dislocation between the outward argument and the inner train of reasoning."[47] Although the reader may find Mawdudi's approach confusing, to say the least, Mawdudi did not find it at all problematic, for, as H. E. Chehabi pointed out with regard to Iranian Islamic modernists, "What [he says] may or may not be true or accurate, but what [he] means is that Islam is viable, even superior to all other systems."[48] His argument was rational because its intent was rational. Weaknesses in his line of reasoning did not detract from the rationality of his overall argument. Much of Mawdudi's discourse with the West suffered from the consequences of this apologetic posturing and, therefore, was found less than rational, despite its pretense of rationality.

Mawdudi's polemics often tied his views on religious issues with political concerns, attaching the full weight of soteriological anxieties to political choices. Faced with Mawdudi's piecemeal presentation of an idea, his audience, essentially made to participate, albeit passively, in his deductive reasoning and forced to confront a choice between truth and falsehood, was often taken in by his presentations.[49] Mawdudi's powerful command of Urdu reinforced the compelling logic of his arguments. His style had been deliberately honed to serve his agenda. He insisted on using Urdu as a vehicle for the propagation of his ideas in order to free Muslim minds from the influence of English.[50] Text was more than a vehicle for disseminating his ideas; it was an agent of cultural liberation.

Mawdudi's prose style was innovative. In religious debating, he was influenced by the didactic writings of the Deobandi *'alim* Mawlana Muhammad Qasim

Nanautawi, and the Ahl-i Hadith 'alim, Mawlana Thanau'llah Amritsari, but his literary style, although he denied it, bore the mark of Azad's journal, Al-Hilal (Calcutta) and Shibli Nu'mani's writings as reflected in his articles in Al-Nadwah (Lucknow), the journal of Nadwatu'l-'Ulama. Mawdudi's analytical approach utilized modern concepts and terminology, and language and methodology of modern scientific thought, in an attempt to cast Islam in a scientific light so as to attract educated Muslims.[51] It was Mawdudi's pen that accounted for his following and, in particular, for membership in the Jama'at.[52]

Mawdudi was not a great orator. He never sought to excite his audience, and he seldom delivered a talk extemporaneously. His reserve contrasted powerfully with the impassioned populist style of religious oratory developed among South Asian Muslim leaders since the last century, from Azad to Sayyid 'Ata'u'llah Shah Bukhari of the Anjuman-i Ahrar-i Islam (Society of free Muslims) to contemporary activists such as Muhammad Tahiru'l-Qadri. It also stands in contrast to those of his secular political rivals in Pakistan—men such as Zulfiqar 'Ali Bhutto and Shaikh Mujibu'l-Rahman. Siddiqi noted that in a speech in Amritsar in 1940, Mawdudi explained to his audience that he avoided the flowery and impassioned styles of Shibli Nu'mani or Azad that were in vogue then because he wished to attract students and to pose questions academically.[53]

All of this limited Mawdudi's appeal to the masses. On rare occasions, he resorted to populist themes, as when he wrote:

> Consider these brahmins and pirs, these nawwabs and ru'asa [sing. ra'is, leader], these jagirdars and feudal lords, these money-lenders and usurers. They all view themselves as superior to the common folk. They are the privileged ones. . . . They are the lords and the others their serfs. . . . They have the privilege to rob, while others are meant to be robbed. To satiate the selfish demands of these it is the life and honor of the common folk which is being sacrificed.[54]

In later years, Mawdudi appealed to populist themes by emphasizing Islam's demand for economic justice and equity, but the extent of these appeals remained limited as he continued to espouse the sanctity of private property and economic justice but not egalitarianism.[55] His support of populist themes was far too intermittent to identify him with any popular mass causes. Mawdudi also discouraged the type of activity that the manipulation of populist themes entailed. He was always reluctant to cross the boundaries of the law and was especially opposed to violence.[56] On occasion, the Jama'at ended up in clashes with rival forces or the police, increasingly so from the late 1960s onwards, but Mawdudi was careful to see to it that the practice was not reflected in the party's official position. He never considered violence a policy tool: "I do feel it is necessary in all these cases [of striving against despotism] to resist the temptation of resorting to the methods and techniques of secret underground movements and bloody revolutions."[57] It was not until he left office that the Jama'at and its student organization, the Islami Jam'iat-i Tulabah, became more routinely involved in violence. Unwilling to break with the established order or unleash the potential force of populist politics, Mawdudi was ultimately guided not by idealism but by the sensibilities of the traditional patrimonial order in which he operated. Khurshid Ahmad called him a "practical idealist,"[58] a leader whose idealism was checked by his rational pragmatism. Mawdudi's political ambitions never thoroughly overrode his traditional values, nor did they weaken his loyalty to his objectives. Convinced of the inherent superiority and eventual success of his vision, Mawdudi never saw any reason to engage in agitational politics, which would compel him to compromise the values he espoused and, hence, would blemish the image of the utopian order that he advocated. This attitude distinguished him from many other revivalist leaders, notably Ayatollah Khomeini.

The Jama'at, however, did not remain altogether immune to the temptations of power and occasionally did resort to means that vitiated its envisioned end,[59] but these incidents never found doctrinal expression in the Jama'at's ideology and the party remained surprisingly resistant to the lure of populist politics. Its activism required compromises, for which Mawdudi felt compelled to resort to complex and apologetic interpretations.[60] In 1956 and 1957, when the party was deadlocked over whether or not to recognize the legitimacy of the state and join the political process, and in 1963, when the Jama'at supported the candidacy of Fatimah Jinnah in the presidential elections, Mawdudi was forced, first, to justify participation in politics in lieu of religious works and shoring up the Jama'at's moral character and, second, to support a woman's bid for the presidency against the principle of purdah.[61] In both cases, political considerations won, and, in both cases, Mawdudi argued that the end justified the means, even if it violated the Jama'at's teachings. Although damaging to the Jama'at, these incidents underscored Mawdudi's religious authority, which he successfully used to justify these compromises and confirm his essentially political outlook.

The Nature of Revivalist Authority

Although Mawdudi sought to change the political order, his discourse was more immediately concerned with reshaping the structure of relations between Islam and Muslims—in part, by opening Islamic sources up to the believers. His written works (his Qur'anic commentary in particular) were written in a simple language, avoiding traditional scholastic terminology and style.[62] He reduced intellectual discussions to a level where they could be understood by a greater number of people and not become monopolized by any one class or group. The objective of this undertaking was to popularize religion and to facilitate greater participation of the Muslim masses, especially lay intellectuals, in religious discussions. It also had the effect of standardizing the scope and extent of the Islamic discourse and, hence, made it increasingly mundane. Mawdudi's significance does not lie in his scholarly contributions per se, but in creating an intellectual medium—in the form of a large number of texts—wherein modern sociopolitical themes could be discussed and addressed in an Islamic context. He produced a new vocabulary and novel social and religious references, which proved to have great success and staying power. In effect, he set an example for independent religious thinking and activism.

Authority in South Asia is closely tied to the oral tradition and its central role in the transmission of knowledge.[63] Because Mawdudi relied solely on texts to propagate his views and establish his claim to authority, he limited his audience to those who could read—precisely those few who would be least likely to be swayed by his authority and discourse.[64] Although the use of the written text clearly defined the boundaries of his movement and gave it its identity and character, it also limited its reach. If reliance on text is a sign of Western influence on Muslim society, then Mawdudi's failure to effectively use the paradigm of *tajdid* was a result of the extensive Western penetration of India.[65] The limits imposed by the use of the written text on public acceptance of Mawdudi's authority perhaps explains the importance of Iqbal and Azad, two of the most important users of text to articulate a revivalist message in modern times. Their importance was acknowledged by Khurshid Ahmad when he declared, "There is a direct line from Azad to Iqbal to Mawdudi."[66]

In many ways, Mawdudi's discourse, authority, and plan of action were influenced by, and drew upon, the tradition of revival and reform in Islam. From the time of Sayyid Ahmad Sirhindi to the present, this tradition has been an important component of Muslim history in India and has provided a powerful paradigm for activism.[67] Mawdudi viewed himself as a part of this tradition, and was viewed as a part of it by his followers, as their documentation of all of his statements and his every decision attests. The legacy of renewal and reform in British India, especially among the Deobandi and Ahl-i Hadith ulama and Khilafat activists such as Muhammad 'Ali, but more directly in Abu'l-Kalam Azad's career during the *Al-Hilal* days were of more immediate relevance to the articulation of Mawdudi's program.[68] It was through Azad that Mawdudi tapped into the revivalist tradition. Mawdudi was influenced by Azad's vision and style and was the same type of Muslim leader. Their backgrounds, ideas, and modes of operation show such an uncanny resemblance that S. M. Ikram concluded that, should the Jama'at succeed in its objectives in Pakistan, the state would be the embodiment of Azad's ideals.[69] Similarities in the life histories, educations, and careers of the two, frequently referred to in the Jama'at's literature and reinforced by Mawdudi's emulation of Azad's style, views, and approach, have created a direct link between them that is an important pillar of Mawdudi's authority. Mawdudi's biographers emphasize that, like Azad, Mawdudi was a brilliant child with poetic and literary predilections who discovered his faith through study and reflection. He had a Sufi background that he renounced, was a product of an eclectic education that combined modern and Islamic methods and subjects, had a romantic view of past Muslim glories in India and advocated a revival of them, was critical of the ulama, was aloof and supercilious, and harbored notions of being chosen amir and savior of Muslims. Both combined the professions of journalist, thinker, scholar, and political leader, and both were prolific writers with scholarly ambitions.[70] Both saw the *shari'ah* as a holistic system and favored the introduction of rationalism to the study of Islam. Both viewed organizations as essential to political aspirations; both gained political experience and education in the Khilafat movement. The two men used literary style and rhetorical prowess to further their cause, although Mawdudi's restrained style stands in contrast to Azad's flowery and impassioned prose.[71]

These parallels were of great benefit to Mawdudi because it associated him with Azad in popular minds.

Azad had so convincingly presented an ideal image of a leader and the path that he should follow that, even after he himself parted with it his image and ideas, he continued to capture the imagination of Muslim thinkers and activists. The Azad of the *Al-Hilal* days, "part journalist, part orator, part holy man" who combined "elements of East and West—not to imitate the culture of the conqueror, but rather to revitalize Muslim cultural and social life and to publicize his ideas of how it should be done through educational institutions, cultural organization, and the press"[72]—became a role model. He continues to be the archetype of the ideal leader, revered for his articulate argumentation, political zeal, faith, erudition, and the power of his prose. His ideas formed the foundation for all subsequent expressions of Islamic revivalism in the Indian subcontinent.

Simplifying the language and style of religious discourse was at the heart of Mawdudi's effort to challenge the ulama.[73] Having denied his own affiliation with them, Mawdudi instead said that he "belong[ed] to that school of Islamic Jurisprudents [*fuqaha*] who claim that everyone who is duly lettered must have his own, direct access to the Holy Quran and the Sunnah to seek Commandments and exemplification." He challenged the affiliation of the South Asian ulama, especially his mentors among the Deobandis, with the Hanafi school of Islamic law. A believer, he said, "should respect all the Imams of Ijtihad and the famous four: Abu Hanifa, Shafi'i, Maalik, and Hanbal (may Allah be pleased with them all'). A duly lettered and learned man ought not to resort to *taqlid* [obeying one particular imam]. Follow one Imam, if you will, but do not vow that you shall never obey the others."[74] He questioned the usefulness of the ulama in the modern world. "The poor students" wrote Mawdudi, "if they go to old institutions they will become a prey to religious traders—the ulama—and if they followed their views and programs they were bound to go astray."[75] Tirades against the ulama helped Mawdudi's own claim to religious authority.

Mawdudi aspired to an authority that would encompass religion and politics and would reign unchallenged. He did not express this ambition openly, but referred to it in such passages as the following:

> Unfortunately, I cannot claim the high degree of learning and knowledge that we would need to guide the community back to the path of redemption, nor do I have the power to reform such a large community out of such a hopeless desperation. But God has endowed me with a sensitive and sympathetic mind which prompts me to press into service the little knowledge and insight that I have. . . . I am determined to extend the scope of my endeavour as far as I can.[76]

Such expressions of humility intermittently appeared in Mawdudi's speeches, which were usually full of his high opinion of his own abilities and his belief in the primacy of his authority.

This claim to unrivaled authority was most clearly manifested in his use of the paradigm of *tajdid* in Islamic history, which at times bordered on aspirations to Mahdiism.[77] Mawdudi's examination of *tajdid*, its historical role, and the qualities and powers of the *mujaddid*, although couched in scholarly terms, sanctioned the pursuit of a political goal under the aegis of religion. Biographical sketches of Mawdudi place great importance on every episode in his life and openly associate him and the Jama'at with the tradition of *tajdid* in Islam. They legitimize Mawdudi's claim to consummate authority, bestowing historical significance on his movement's agenda.[78]

The use of the paradigm of *tajdid* is probably most clearly evident in Mawdudi's own writing. He regarded Islamic history from the end of the rightly guided caliphs onward as essentially a period of decline and of *jahiliyah*. Except for periodic surges of orthodoxy in the guise of revivalist movements, Muslim life had been defiled by syncretic concessions to heathen tendencies and the godless practices that were associated with them.[79] Obscurantism had so dominated Islam that three-quarters of the faith was defective and incorrect. The need to renew (*tajdid*) and reform (*islah*)[80] to reinstate orthodoxy is self-evident. Mawdudi identified a number of *mujaddids* to emphasize his point: the Umayyad caliph, 'Umar ibn 'Abdu'l-'Aziz (d. 720); the founders of the four schools of Sunni law, Abu Hanifah (700–767), Malik ibn Anas (716–795), al-Shafi'i (767–820), and Ahmad ibn Hanbal (780–855); al-Ghazzali (1058–1111); Ibn Taimiyah (1263–1328); Shaikh Ahmad Sirhindi; and Shah Waliu'llah. Establishing a chain of *tajdid* extending from the heartland of Islam to India, he argued that all of these great *mujaddids* were distinguished for their insight into problems before Muslims, for their reform of religious practices, for initiating an intellectual revolution and defending Islam in the political sphere, for establishing the primacy of the *shari'ah*, and for their opposition to the ostensibly orthodox practices of the ulama.[81] Mawdudi accorded a *mujaddid* interpretive powers and authority in keeping with his views of his own role and authority:

> Though a *mujaddid* is not a Prophet, yet in spirit he comes very close to prophethood. He is characterized by a clear mind, penetrating vision, unbiased straight thinking, special ability to see the Right Path [*al-sirat al-mustaqim*] clear of all extremes and keep balance, power to think independently of the contemporary and centuries-old social and other prejudices, courage to fight against the evils of the time, inherent ability to lead and guide, and an unusual competency to undertake *ijtihad* and the work of reconstruction.[82]

In fact, the only difference between a *mujaddid* and a prophet was that the latter received revelation "a *mujaddid*, on the whole, has to undertake and perform the same kind of work as is accomplished by a Prophet."[83] Mawdudi thought this work should be not so much the transmission of revelation as education.[84] Not surprisingly, *Tajdid'u ihya'-i din* (A short history of the revivalist movement in Islam, 1952) was denounced by the ulama in the strongest terms, and Mawdudi was criticized severely for his arrogation of the title of *mujaddid*.

Mawdudi believed that the role of the *mujaddid* encompassed the messianic doctrine of Mahdiism. He not only defined the Mahdi as a *mujaddid* but, more important, the reverse—that *tajid* was synonymous with Mahdiism. Throughout the *Tajdid'u ihya'-i din* Mawdudi used the two interchangeably, thereby associating some of the functions of the Prophet with both: "The ideal

Mujaddid (or *Imam-al-Mahdi*) can be a true successor to Prophethood."[85] The identification of *tajdid* with Mahdiism was no doubt of great consequence. Its utility became apparent once Mawdudi began to associate himself with the tradition of *tajdid* in Islam. This association at times had a clear Mahdiist tone, especially when premised on the identification of the millenarian circumstance as understood in religious and cultural terms,[86] which Mawdudi believed the Muslim world to be in: "If the expectation that Islam eventually will dominate the world of thought, culture, and politics is genuine, then the coming of a Great Leader under whose comprehensive and forceful leadership such Revolution is to come about is also certain."[87] Mawdudi's description of the Mahdi from this point on is unclear; he wrote of the Mahdi and his movement in terms that suggest that Mawdudi not only coveted these positions of authority but also permitted his identification with the Mahdi himself:

> In my opinion the Coming One [the Mahdi] will be a most modern Leader of his age possessing an unusually deep insight in all the current branches of knowledge, and all the major problems of life. . . . Most probably he will not be aware of his being the promised Mahdi. People, however, will recognize him after his death from his works to be one who was to establish "Caliphate after the pattern of prophethood" as mentioned in the prophecies.[88]

The implications of passages such as this in which he streamlined the image of the Mahdi can best be understood when read in conjunction with accounts of Mawdudi's own role.[89] Although Mawdudi articulated his views in light of the doctrine of *tajdid*, his authority appealed indirectly to the more emotionally charged millenarian doctrine of Mahdiism, which created the bases for the articulation of his authority.[90]

Mawdudi openly broke with the traditional order by claiming independence from traditional education.[91] His avowed "reconversion" to Islam and his self-styled hermeneutics cast him in a messianic role. Although his authority was based on traditional religious sources of legitimacy, it emanated from his claim to proficiency in modern subjects, which he also cited as a quality of the awaited Mahdi. Mawdudi's break with tradition was even clearer in his challenge to the hadith tradition, with an authority based on its chain of transmission going back to the Prophet and which had been canonized by generations of *muhaddithin* (relaters of hadith) and regarded as the foundation of Islamic religious sciences. Mawdudi introduced novel perspectives on hadith transmission. "With extensive study and practice one can develop a power and can intuitively sense the wishes and desires of the Holy Prophet. . . . Thus . . . on seeing a Hadith, I can tell whether the Holy Prophet could or could not have said it."[92] Mawdudi referred to this ability as *mizajshinasi rasul* (knowing the temperament of the Prophet). In part at least, the claim was designed to challenge the deniers of hadith who claimed there was no way in which authentic and forged hadith can be distinguished from one another. Mawdudi's attempt to argue that he was able to do so defended the traditional view of hadith, but it also put forward a highly controversial claim. In a similar manner, he wrote of his Qur'anic translation and commentary: "I have not tried to render the Arabic text of the Qur'an into another language. Instead I have tried to express in my own words, and as faithfully as possible, the meaning conveyed to me by the Qur'anic passages and the impression they make upon me."[93]

To use the paradigm of *tajdid* successfully, Mawdudi posed as a charismatic leader. Although not clearly divorced from the trappings of traditional Islam, Mawdudi was an innovator. He imposed a new set of obligations on Muslims in general, and on his followers in particular, based on the distinction between traditional Islam and Mawdudi's interpretation of it. Others may hesitate to define Mawdudi as a charismatic leader, for he never excited the masses, nor did he break with tradition clearly enough to fit the Weberian typology. That his authority in later years was closer to Weber's "legal-rational" type casts further doubt on his charisma. Still, his authority was defined in opposition to traditional institutions of authority: "I recognize no king or ruler above me; nor do I bow before any government; nor do I view any law as binding on me . . . nor do I accept any tradition or custom."[94] Mawdudi's embrace of modernity, combined with his opposition to the ulama, constituted an independent approach to Islam and, by implication, cast Mawdudi in the role of a "missionary" expressed through the paradigm of *tajdid*.[95] The acceptance of reconversion to Islam as the first step toward restoring the political fortunes of Indian Muslims was tantamount to invoking *tajdid*, but Mawdudi's insistence on presenting a qualitatively different interpretation of the faith distinguished his attempt at *tajdid* from the attempts of those who had preceded him. He argued that his intent was not only to revive Islam but also to propagate true Islam, the absence of which accounted for the failure of earlier efforts at *tajdid*.[96] The notion of true Islam, which first appeared in Mawdudi's writings around 1932, reinforced the appeal of *tajdid* as it invested Mawdudi with a charismatic potential and defined the boundaries of his movement.

Mawdudi's biographers have tended to recount his life in hagiographic style, writing about his *karamat* (special gifts) and *haybah* (great presence)[97] in the manner of hagiography about Sufi saints written in the 1960s under the patronage of shrines and the various governments in Pakistan.[98] This genre had popularized the style, and the Jama'at found it useful for establishing Mawdudi's authority. In the Jama'at's literature, he is venerated not simply as a leader endowed with great gifts, but as one who has embarked on a divine mission, as "the sage awaited by Muslims."[99] His aristocratic demeanor, Delhi accent, and style of attire were regarded as signs of his leadership qualities. His birth had been foretold, his life had been spared in what should have been fatal accidents and assassination attempts, God responded to his prayers, and his movement was protected while the Jama'at's enemies—from Liaqat 'Ali Khan to Ghulam Muhammad, Shahid Husain Suhrawardi to Ayub Khan, and Nawab of Kala Bagh to Zulfiqar 'Ali Bhutto—fell from grace or died dishonorably.[100] The "Ibn Taimiyah of his era" and the "*lisanu'l-'asr*" (tongue of the age),[101] he was Imam Mawdudi, "the founder of a school of thought," on a par with the founders of the four schools of Sunni law and the "*da'i-i 'awwal*" (the foremost missionary, a term with Isma'ili connotations), the true bearer of the mantle of Sayyid Ahmad Sirhindi, Shah Waliu'llah, Sayyid Ahmad Shahid, and even Sayyid Ahmad

Khan.[102] One Jama'at votary even wrote a posthumous biography of Mawdudi entitled *Hayat-i javidan*, a title similar to one selected by the poet Altaf Husain Hali (d. 1914), *Hayat-i javid*, for his biography of Sayyid Ahmad Khan.[103]

Mawdudi's courage was the most vaunted of his virtues. He was the courageous "sayyid," whose uncompromising stand in the face of opposition attested to his staunch faith and exemplary leadership.[104] Upon hearing the news of his death sentence in 1953, he responded with a simple "all right,"[105] then added, "If God has so willed, I shall gladly accept this fate, but if it is not His will that I die now, no matter what they try to do, they cannot inflict the least harm upon me."[106] Mawdudi remained unapologetic and, despite advice from Islahi and other Jama'at workers, refused to ask for clemency. The impact of this behavior on his followers was immense;[107] one wrote, "You are marching toward the gallows because you led the Ummah of the Holy Prophet." Chaudhri 'Abdu'l-Rahman 'Abd went further: "It seems as if, with his bowed head, he is humbly and submissively in discourse in the presence of the Almighty."[108] When Mawdudi's sentence was reversed in 1954 and he was freed without compromising his position, the event was interpreted by his followers as the victory of Islam over un-Islam and, as 'Abd concluded, the result of the Prophet's direct intercession.[109] Similar displays of composure typified Mawdudi's later encounters with adversity; in 1963, following an attempt on his life and the ensuing clashes with agitators during a Jama'at meeting, and in 1964, when he was again sent to prison.[110] Gilani compared his travails to those of Christ before the Romans, to Husain ibn 'Ali, martyred at Karbala in 680, before the Umayyad caliph, Yazid (d. 683), and to the struggles of the founders of the Sunni schools of law with the Umayyad and Abbasid caliphs.[111]

The millenarian content of Mawdudi's authority is best demonstrated in the writing of the American Jewish convert and pro-Jama'at thinker Maryam Jameelah.[112] Drawing on hadith references that describe the preconditions for the emergence of the Mahdi, Jameelah carried Mawdudi's directives to their logical conclusion. In her biography of Mawdudi, she identified his time as the Mahdi's time and, by implication, identified him as the promised Mahdi:

> The Holy Prophet predicted that a time would come when the Muslims, although numerous, would be devoid of faith, when they would imitate the Jews and Christians in their mode of life and pious Muslims would suffer severe persecution. The Hadith tells us that in the midst of these calamities, an immensely powerful man would arise in the area now controlled by Israel, deceiving the world. . . . Eventually the Jews and their friends would so much adore him as their hero, they would worship him as God. The Holy Prophet called this man as the *Masih al Dajjal* (the Anti-Christ of the Christian tradition).
>
> The former Commander-in-Chief of the Israeli army and now Israeli Defense Minister, *General Moshe Dayan*, has now become the most popular and revered Jewish leader of our day. It will be not surprising if after he becomes the virtual leader of the Zionist state, he proclaims himself as the *Messiah* the Jews have awaited for more than two thousand years. General Moshe Dayan's physical appearance and his works strikingly correspond to the Hadith's description of the *Masih al Dajjal*. The Holy Prophet tells us that from the creation of Adam until the Day of Resurrection, mankind would suffer no greater trial.

Muslims must beware of the coming of the *Masih al Dajjal* and combat this
menace by scrupulously abiding by the Quran and the Sunnah, by upholding the
Shariah as the law of the land, by enthusiastically supporting all movements working for Islamic revival and by uniting against our common enemy in a zealous spirit
of Jihad.[113]

The messianic call here is clear. The time is that of the messiah; the anti-Christ
has arrived, and so will the messiah. That the messianic call happens in a biography of Mawdudi leaves little doubt as to who is the messiah and what is the
messianic movement.

Although some members of the Jama'at disapproved of this sanctification
of Mawdudi,[114] and open references to him as the Mahdi have not been com-
monplace, they have been pervasive enough in the Jama'at literature to worry
the ulama, and they forced Mawdudi on a number of occasions openly to deny
any messianic pretensions. His denials were far from convincing, however,
because he qualified them with his own messianic claims. "*Mahdawiyyat*
[Mahdiism] does not involve a proclamation," he wrote, "it is something which
is achieved in action," and added that the Mahdi might only be recognized after
his death.[115] He ignored requests from his critics to order his followers not to
refer to him as the Mahdi after he died.[116]

The Jama'at's limited growth over the years suggests that Mawdudi was not
able to construct a charismatic image that would be universally accepted or to
effectively use the paradigm of *tajdid*. He has yet to be called Mahdi. His fourth
son, Haidar Faruq, has sought, although thus far unsuccessfully, to establish a
form of *sajjadah-nishini* (hereditary religious authority associated with Sufi
shrines) based on Mawdudi's venerated image, centered in his house and burial
place, 5-A Zaildar Park in Ichrah, Lahore.

On the other hand, Mawdudi's success in establishing the Jama'at and his
ideas in contemporary Islamic thought suggest that he was successful with at
least some Muslims. The Jama'at has continued to portray Mawdudi as a charismatic leader and a *mujaddid*, to reaffirm his authority within the Jama'at, and
to extend the boundaries of the party by convincing other Muslims of it. For
Jama'at's votaries, Mawdudi is not only a revered scholar, politician, and thinker,
he is a hallowed *mujaddid*. Beyond the Jama'at, Mawdudi's authority has become
the basis for the systematic articulation of an all-encompassing reinterpretation
of Islam that forms the foundation for a novel religious and intellectual orientation that has been institutionalized in Muslim life and thought. From his
authority came a new Islam.

Appendix: Mawdudi's Poetry

Mawdudi composed these two poems on July 18 and 24, 1932, under the pen name Talib (seeker). They were kept with his personal papers and were not published until after his death, when they were printed first in *Sayyarah Digest* (Lahore), Mawdudi Number (December 1979), pp. 75–76, and later in Ahmad Munir, *Mawlana Abu'l-A'la Mawdudi* (Lahore, 1986), p. 125. Given the style of the poems, a number of Jama'at leaders initially denied that they were the work of their former amir, but his friends, family, and close companions confirmed their authenticity. Both poems are my English translations.

July 18, 1932

Indeed, the world has always considered the wise one
A fool!

Nay, the fool at his highest station
Is to them the wisest!

How novel are the ways
Of people in love:
Here, sober in their senses
There, enraptured fools!

With a drop bring commotion in the world; with a mouthful of liquor create a whole
    tavern.
In this realm of existence why do you seek tranquillity; why not continuous tumult
    and a manly struggle?

Give to the drinkers, O wine bearer, the wine which promotes rapture.
Disturb the wine shop with every drunkard slip.

You have a hidden fire within you,
So you don't need the candle.
O, the burning desire of the moth become a radiant flame yourself.

We believe in cash, not in credit,
Then why narrate to us the story of paradise.

Despair not, O, drunkard, if the wine bearer passes you by.
Your turn will come.
It is in the nature of the wine cup to circulate.

In every manifestation of the idol You are reflected.
You worship Yourself, O creator of the house of idols.

O Talib! Satiation of the heart and the soul is difficult
But still attainable if you have manly courage.

July 24, 1932

Friendship is reciprocated with betrayal.
They require faithfulness along with treachery.

Why do You inquire about the destiny of this miserable patient
Who is a play thing for the Healer?

O, thou who is dying of thirst, do not beg the river.
Death is continuous if love is accompanied with dignity.

The poison and antidote are both in one cup;
Flowers rain along with sparks.

Ignoring one on the one hand;
On the other, cotton and ointment go together with every blade cut.

In the robe of success, failures are hidden.
My destiny is asleep with a wakeful stride.

It is not possible that the wilderness of the heart could be inhabited for a long time
Since by its nature it destroys all that it constructs.

The ecstasies of that drinker are jealousy of wisdom
Who has his access to the divine throne despite all his drinking.

All thy efforts, O Talib, are of no use, you have lost your senses.
Gain is your desire, loss is your practice!

Notes

Introduction

1. Said Amir Arjomand, "The Emergence of Islamic Political Ideologies," in James A. Beckford and Thomas Luckmann, eds., *The Changing Face of Religion* (London, 1989), pp. 111–112.

2. On Mawdudi's impact on expressions of Islamic revivalism in the West, the Arab World, Afghanistan, Iran, and Malaysia, see Larry Poston, *Islamic Da'wah in the West: Muslim Missionary Activity and the Dynamics of Conversion to Islam* (New York, 1992), pp. 64–93; Philip Lewis, *Islamic Britain: Religion, Politics and Identity among British Muslims* (London, 1994), pp. 102–112. Emmanuel Sivan, *Radical Islam: Medieval Theology and Modern Politics* (New Haven, Conn., 1985); John L. Esposito, *The Islamic Threat: Myth or Reality?* (New York, 1992), pp. 154–155; Ahmad S. Mousalli, *Radical Islamic Fundamentalism: The Ideological and Political Discourse of Sayyid Qutb* (Beirut, 1992); Abdelwahab El-Affendi, "The Long March from Lahore to Khartoum: Beyond the 'Muslim Reformation,'" *British Society for Middle Eastern Studies Bulletin* 17.2 (1990): 138–139; Abdel Azim Ramadan, "Fundamentalist Influence in Egypt: The Strategies of the Muslim Brotherhood and the Takfir Groups," in Martin E. Marty and R. Scott Appelby, eds., *Fundamentalisms and the State: Remaking Politics, Economies, and Militance* (Chicago, 1993), pp. 156, 161; Olivier Roy, *Islam and Resistance in Afghanistan*, 2nd ed. (New York, 1990), pp. 68–70, 80; Said Amir Arjomand, *The Turban for the Crown: The Islamic Revolution in Iran* (New York, 1988), p. 107; and Zainah Anwar, *Islamic Fundamentalism in Malaysia*, 2nd ed. (Kuala Lumpur, 1989).

3. Seyyed Vali Reza Nasr, "Communalism and Fundamentalism: A Re-examination of the Origins of Islamic Fundamentalism," *Contention* 4.2 (winter 1995): 121–139.

4. The term "imagining" is used here as employed by Benedict Anderson in *Imagined Communities: Reflections on the Origin and Spread of Nationalism*, 2nd ed. (New York, 1991).

5. For more on the impact of print on the Muslim society of South Asia, see Francis Robinson, "Technology and Religious Change: Islam and the Impact of Print," *Modern Asian Studies* 27.1 (February 1993): 229–251. For more on the use of texts to define Muslim identity and community, see Timothy Mitchell, *Colonising Egypt* (Cambridge, 1988), pp. 128–160; David B. Edwards, "Summoning Muslims: Print, Politics, and

Religious Ideology in Afghanistan," *Journal of Asian Studies* 53.3 (August 1993): 609–628; and Barbara D. Metcalf, "Living Hadith in the Tablighi Jama'at," *Journal of Asian Studies* 53.3 (August 1993): 584–608.

6. For a theoretical discussion of this issue, see Robert Wuthnow, *Communities of Discourse: Ideology and Social Structure in the Reformation, the Enlightenment, and European Socialism* (Cambridge, Mass., 1989), pp. 3, 10, and Robert Wuthnow and Matthew P. Lawson, "Sources of Christian Fundamentalism in the United States," in Martin E. Marty and R. Scott Appleby, eds., *Accounting for Fundamentalisms* (Chicago, 1994), p. 23.

7. For a discussion of the role of Islam in shaping social movements, see Ira M. Lapidus, "Islamic Political Movements: Patterns of Historical Change," in Edmund Burke III and Ira M. Lapidus, eds., *Islam, Politics, and Social Movements* (Berkeley, 1988), pp. 3–16.

8. Farzana Shaikh, *Community and Consensus in Islam: Muslim Representation in Colonial India, 1860–1947* (Cambridge, 1989), p. 6

9. Paul Brass, "Elite Groups, Symbol Manipulation and Ethnic Identity among the Muslims of South Asia," in David Taylor and Malcolm Yapp, eds., *Political Identity in South Asia* (London, 1979), pp. 35–77.

10. Francis Robinson, "Islam and Muslim Separatism," in Taylor and Yapp, *Political Identity*, pp. 78–112.

11. Shaikh, *Community and Consensus*, pp. 22–23.

12. Ibid.

13. For explanation of Muslim communalism as a reaction to the prospect of permanent subjugation to Hindu rule, see Khalid bin Sayeed, *Pakistan: The Formative Phase, 1857–1948* (London, 1968).

14. This was also the agenda of the Tablighi Jama'at established in 1926 by Mawlana Muhammad Iliyas (d. 1944). Iliyas established this Jama'at to work in Mewat, near Delhi, among Muslim peasants who had maintained close cultural ties to Hinduism. Iliyas sought to purify their faith from Hindu influences and to make them immune to the overtures of Shuddhi activists; see I. S. Marwa, "Tabligh Movement among the Meos of Mewat," in M. S. A. Rao, ed., *Social Movements in India* (New Delhi, 1979), 2:96–98.

15. A number of studies have argued that Indian Muslims have been assimilating into a larger Indian society exactly along the lines Mawdudi had wished to avert; see Imtiaz Ahmad, ed., *Caste and Social Stratification among the Muslims* (Delhi, 1973); Ahmad, *Modernization and Social Change among Muslims in India* (Delhi, 1983); and Muhammad Mujeeb, *The Indian Muslims* (London, 1967).

16. For accounts of Mawdudi's ideology, see Charles J. Adams, "The Ideology of Mawlana Mawdudi," in Donald E. Smith, ed., *South Asian Politics and Religion* (Princeton, N.J., 1966), pp. 371–397; Adams, "Mawdudi and the Islamic State," in John L. Esposito, *Voices of Resurgent Islam* (New York, 1983), pp. 99–133; Erwin I. J. Rosenthal, *Islam in the Modern National State* (Cambridge, 1965), pp. 221–272; John L. Esposito, *Islam and Politics*, 3rd ed. (Syracuse, N.Y., 1991), pp. 142–150; Syed Asad Gilani, *Maududi: Thought and Movement* (Lahore, 1984); Mumtaz Ahmad, "Islamic Fundamentalism in South Asia: The Jamaat-i-Islami and the Tablighi Jamaat," in Martin E. Marty and R. Scott Appleby, eds., *Fundamentalisms Observed* (Chicago, 1991), pp. 457–530.

17. William A. Graham, "Traditionalism in Islam: An Essay in Interpretation," *Journal of Interdisciplinary History* 23.3 (winter 1993): 499.

18. Seyyed Hossein Nasr, *Traditional Islam in the Modern World* (London, 1987), and Nasr, ed., *Islamic Spirituality*, vol. 1 (New York, 1987).

Chapter 1

1. For more on the Chishtis, see Khaliq Ahmad Nizami, "Čishtiyya," in *EI*, and Sayyid Athar Abbas Rizvi, "Chishtiyyah," in Seyyed Hossein Nasr, ed., *Islamic Spirituality* (New York, 1991), 2:127–143.

2. Chaudhri 'Abdul-Rahman 'Abd, *Mufakkir-i Islam: Sayyid Abu'l-A'la Mawdudi* (Lahore, 1971), pp. 46–47, and Sayyid Abu'l-A'la Mawdudi, *Watha'iq-i Mawdudi* (Lahore, 1984), p. 97.

3. *KN*, p. 24.

4. Ibid., and Jalil Ahmad Rana and Salim Mansur Khalid, eds., *Tazkirah-i Sayyid Mawdudi* (Lahore, 1986), p. 3. Mawdudi traced his lineage to both grandsons of the Prophet Muhammad, Hasan ibn 'Ali (d. 670), and Husain ibn 'Ali (d. 680).

5. Rana and Khalid, *Tazkirah*, p. 5, and *KN*, p. 25.

6. Mawdudi wrote that Khwajah Mu'inu'ddin's Sufi master was 'Uthman Harwani, whose master was Jami Sharif Zindani, whose master was Qutbu'ddin Mawdud; *KN*, p. 24.

7. Abad Shahpuri, *Tarikh-i Jama'at-i Islami* (Lahore, 1989), 1:184; and 'Abd, *Mufakkir-i Islam*, pp. 46–47.

8. *KN*, p. 27; Ahmad Munir, *Mawlana Abu'l-'Ala Mawdudi* (Lahore, 1986), p. 13, and Sayyid Asad Gilani, *Maududi: Thought and Movement* (Lahore, 1984), p. 25.

9. Abu Mahmud Mawdudi, "Hamara khandan," in Munir, *Sayyid Abu'l-A'la Mawdudi*, p. 11.

10. *KN*, p. 27.

11. For more on Ahmad Khan and the Aligarh experience, see David Lelyveld, *Aligarh's First Generation: Muslim Solidarity in British India* (Princeton, N.J., 1978).

12. *KN*, p. 27.

13. Ibid., pp. 27–28.

14. Ibid.

15. Gilani reported that Mawdudi's mother, Ruqiyah Begum, was also a Sufi. It is quite possible that she had embraced Sufism at the same time as her husband, and that the two followed the same master; see Gilani, *Maududi*, p. 28. Regarding Mawdudi taking the *bai'ah*, see *KN*, p. 28.

16. *KN*.

17. Mawdudi's opposition to Sufism was no doubt in part a reaction to these excesses of his father; see Gilani, *Maududi*, pp. 25–28.

18. *KN*, p. 28.

19. Mawdudi echoed his father's sentiments when in 1948 he declared that defending those at fault was religiously reprehensible and argued that the adversarial system and the whole institution of legal representation had no place in Islam, for it would allow wrong to prevail over right; see Sayyid Abu'l-A'la Mawdudi, *Islamic Law and Constitution* (Karachi, 1955).

20. Leonard Binder, *Religion and Politics in Pakistan* (Berkeley, 1961), p. 79.

21. Abu Mahmud Mawdudi, "Hamara khandan," p. 12.

22. 'Abd, *Mufakkir-i Islam*, p. 47.

23. *KN*, p. 26.

24. Revivalist thinking at this time was closely associated with scions of eminent families whose fortunes had been reversed during British rule. The puritanical Ahl-i Hadith school of thought, wrote Metcalf, emerged and grew in the nineteenth century among those who had descended from the Mughals or other princely families or traced their lineage to the landed or literary families that had been associated with Muslim

rule, and whose social status and economic prowess had declined during the colonial era. See Barbara D. Metcalf, *Islamic Revival in British India: Deoband, 1860–1900* (Princeton, N.J., 1982), pp. 268–269.

25. *KN*, p. 29.

26. This fact was related by Mawdudi's full brother, Sayyid Abu'l-Khayr Mawdudi, through an interview with Ja'far Qasmi. See also, Sayyid Abu'l-A'la Mawdudi, "Mera bachpan," in Muhammad Yusuf Buhtah, ed., *Mawlana Mawdudi: apni awr dusrun ki nazar main* (Lahore, 1984), pp. 17–22.

27. *KN*, p. 27.

28. Mawdudi, "Mera bachpan," pp. 17–22.

29. *KN*, pp. 29–30.

30. Ibid., p. 30.

31. Ibid.

32. Ibid.

33. Mujibu'l-Rahman Shami, "Kiran se aftab tak," in *HRZ*, p. 31.

34. *KN*, p. 30.

35. Ibid. See also Mawdudi, "Mera bachpan," pp. 19–20.

36. Gilani explained that Fauqaniyah was the name of a new system of high school education, which was initiated by Nawab 'Imadu'l-Mulk Bilgirami, the curriculum of which was drawn up by Shibli Nu'mani and Mawlana Hamidu'ddin Farahi. The medium of instruction was Urdu and the subjects of study included Arabic, *fiqh*, hadith, and *mantiq*, as well as natural sciences. See Gilani, *Maududi*, p. 36.

37. Ibid., pp. 36–37.

38. *KN*, p. 38.

39. Mawdudi, "Mera bachpan," pp. 21–22.

40. *KN*, p. 31.

41. For more on this institution, see J. Jomier and A. S. Bazmee Ansari, "Dar al-'ulum," in *EI*.

42. For more on Farahi's life and his school of thought, see Mustansir Mir, *Coherence in the Qur'an* (Indianapolis, 1986), pp. 6–7, 42–44.

43. *KN*, pp. 31–32.

44. Ibid., p. 32.

45. Ibid., p. 38.

46. Ibid.

47. Ibid., pp. 38–39.

48. Ibid., p. 31. See also Sarwat Saulat, *Maulana Maududi* (Karachi, 1979), p. 3.

49. Mawdudi remembered himself as a voracious reader, who spent all his money on books. See Sayyid Abu'l-A'la Mawdudi, "Mera mutala'ah," reprinted in *SSMN*, pp. 390–391. Mumtaz Ahmad kindly pointed out to me that *taraqqi-pasand* here refers to the Anjuman-i Taraqqi-Pasand Musannifin, or Progressive Writers Association. In Delhi, Mawdudi became acquainted not only with the writings of Sayyid Ahmad Khan, but also with the works of the Khayri brothers with whom, Abu'l-Kayr Mawdudi recalled, his younger brother was greatly impressed; from an interview with Ja'far Qasmi. The Khayri brothers, 'Abdu'l-Sattar and 'Abdu'l-Jabbar, were German-educated socialists who were prominent in the intellectual circles of Delhi in the 1920s; they also were proponents of Muslim self-determination. For more on them, see K. K. Aziz, *A History of the Idea of Pakistan* (Lahore, 1987), 1:88–92.

50. For an example of Mawdudi's analysis of the works of Marx and Lenin, see his interview in *Al-Nadwah*, Book Number (1943), pp. 14–18.

51. Mawdudi noted that he began to learn English when he was fifteen or sixteen and that he was proficient in the language by the age of twenty-two; see 'Asim Nu'mani, ed., *Makatib-i Sayyid Abu'l-A'la Mawdudi* (Lahore, 1977), 2:348.

52. See, Safir Akhtar, "Mawlana Mawdudi awr ma'arif," in Rana and Khalid, *Tazkirah*, pp. 141–142.

53. Metcalf wrote that this approach was used by those associated with Delhi College and was also typical of Sayyid Ahmad Khan's earlier writings on Islam; see *Islamic Revival*, pp. 320–23.

54. See, for instance, Mawdudi's enthusiastic reaction to the first landing on the moon; interview with *Asia*, July 25, 1969, p. 2.

55. *KN*, p. 32.

56. The article on Malawiyah is reprinted in *Khudabakhsh Library Journal* 50 (1989): 1–32. See also *Takbir*, November 30, 1989, p. 42. The information about Mawdudi's biography of and attitude toward Gandhi is from an interview with Maryam Jameelah and is also noted in *KN*, pp. 32–33.

57. *JIKUS*, pp. 6–7.

58. *KN*, p. 33, and Sayyid Abu'l-A'la Mawdudi, *Da'wah awr 'amal* (Lahore, n.d.), p. 3.

59. *KN*, p. 33.

60. Ibid.

61. Ibid, p. 34.

62. Mawdudi, *Da'wah*, p. 3.

63. *KN*, pp. 34–35.

64. Ibid., p. 34.

65. *SAAM*, 1:41–45.

66. For more on this movement see, F. S. Briggs, "The Indian Hijrat of 1920," *Muslim World* 20.2 (April 1930): 167–186. On Mawdudi's role in this movement, see Khurshid Ahmad and Zafar Ishaq Ansari, "Mawlana Sayyid Abul A'la Mawdudi: An Introduction to His Vision of Islam and Islamic Revival," in Khurshid Ahmad and Zafar Ishaq Ansari, eds., *Islamic Perspectives: Studies in Honour of Mawlana Sayyid Abul A'la Mawdudi* (Leicester, 1979), p. 361.

67. *KN*, p. 35.

68. 'Abd, *Mufakkir-i Islam*, p. 65.

69. *KN*, p. 35.

70. For more on this, see Metcalf, *Islamic Revival*, p. 31, and Shaikh Muhammad Ikram, *Rud-i kawthar*, 12th ed. (Lahore, 1988), pp. 605–609.

71. 'Abd, *Mufakkir-i Islam*, p. 61; Shahpuri, *Tarikh*, 1:197–199.

72. Rana and Khalid, *Tazkirah*, p. 834, and Ja'far Qasmi, "Mujhe yad hey sab zara zara," *Nida*, April 17, 1990, pp. 28–34.

73. *KN*, p. 35.

74. Concerning relations between Mawdudi and Muhammad 'Ali, see Ra'is Ahmad Ja'fari, *Ali baradaran* (Lahore, 1963), pp. 22–25. Mawdudi's eulogy of Muhammad 'Ali is reprinted in *SSMN*, pp. 408–411.

75. *KN*, pp. 35–36.

76. Shahpuri, *Tarikh*, 1:197–199.

77. See Gail Minault, *The Khilafat Movement: Religious Symbolisms and Political Mobilization in India* (New York, 1982), pp. 28, 30.

78. In Mawdudi's *ijazah*, Mawlana Kandihlawi wrote that Mawdudi had studied texts on *madarij-i sama'* (gradations of mystical ecstacy) under his supervision. See

Mawdudi, *Watha'iq*, p. 13. For the other subjects he studied, see 'Abd, *Mufakkir-i Islam*, p. 62; 'Asim Nu'mani, *Tasawwuf awr ta'mir sirat* (Lahore, 1972), p. 4; and Rana and Khalid, *Tazkirah*, pp. 945–947.

79. For reproductions of the two *ijazahs*, see Mawdudi, *Watha'iq*, pp. 12–14.

80. Peter Hardy, "The Ulama in British India," unpublished paper cited in Francis Robinson, *Separatism among Indian Muslims: The Politics of the United Provinces' Muslims, 1860–1923* (Cambridge, 1974), p. 263.

81. Farzana Shaikh, *Community and Consensus in Islam: Mulism Representation in Colonial India, 1860–1947* (Cambridge, 1989), pp. 181–183.

82. See Metcalf, *Islamic Revival*, pp. 252–258.

83. *JIKUS*, p. 19.

84. The discussion of a middle path in Muslim education surfaced on numerous occasions in Mawdudi's writings and was a reason why he viewed the Nadwatu'l-'Ulama favorably. Examples of some of Mawdudi's early writings on the subject can be found in the very first issue of *Tarjumanu'l-Qur'an*, which he edited in March 1933. For the text of a lecture he delivered on this subject at the Nadwatu'l-'Ulama in Lucknow in January 1941, see *TQ*, December 1940–January 1941, pp. 347–371. For more on the Nadwatu'l-'Ulama, see Metcalf, *Islamic Revival*, pp. 315–347.

85. Cited in Abu'l-Afaq, *Sayyid Abu'l-A'la Mawdudi: sawanih, afkar, tahrik* (Lahore, 1971), p. 73.

86. *KN*, p. 36.

87. Cited in *SAAM*, 1:40; see also Saulat, *Maulana Maududi*, pp. 3–4, and *KN*, p. 36.

88. On 'Ubaidu'llah Sindhi's influence on Mawdudi, see Maryam Jameelah, "An Appraisal of Some Aspects of Maulana Sayyid Ala Maudoodi's Life and Thought," *Islamic Quarterly* 31.2 (1987): 118.

89. See Minault, *Khilafat Movement*, pp. 7–8, who pointed out that the Khilafat movement should be understood as an attempt to create a "pan-Indian Islam."

90. 'Abdu'l-Ghani Faruqi, "Hayat-i javidan," *HRZ*, p. 25.

91. *JIKUS*, p. 8.

92. These criticisms appeared in *Nigar* and *Al-Jam'iat* in Delhi throughout 1925 and 1926; see *SAAM*, 1:41–45.

93. *JIKUS*, pp. 19–20.

94. Minault, *Khilafat Movement*, p. 42.

95. *JIKUS*, pp. 19–20.

96. *KN*, p. 36.

97. For more on the Ahmadis, see Yohanan Friedmann, *Prophecy Continuous: Aspects of Ahmadi Religious Thought and Its Medieval Background* (Berkeley, 1989).

98. Interview with Khurshid Ahmad.

99. On the Arya Samaj, see Kenneth Jones, *Arya Dharm* (Berkeley, 1976); for a discussion of the Shuddhi campaign, see pp. 202–215. On Muslim reaction to the Shuddhi movement, see Minault, *Khilafat Movement*, pp. 193–195.

100. *JIKUS*, pp. 11–12. Swami Shradhanand had appeared at the Jami' mosque in April 1919 for a Hindu-Muslim unity meeting regarding Gandhi's nonviolent resistance (*satyagraha*); see Minault, *Khilafat Movement*, p. 70.

101. Some three decades earlier, in 1897, another Hindu revivalist leader, the Arya Samajist Pandit Lekh Ram, was assassinated for inveighing against Muslim beliefs following the publication of *Jehad or the Basis of Mohammedi Religion*, his attempt to depict Islam as a religion of the sword and his invitation to Muslims to reconvert to their Aryan heritage. Shradhanad's death also generated a debate on the question of jihad. See Jones, *Arya Dharm*, pp. 194–202.

102. Cited in *JIKUS*, p. 15, and in Binder, *Religion and Politics*, p. 82. Binder, however, claimed that Gandhi did not say it, but that later attempts to mythicize Mawdudi's role ascribed the quote to Gandhi. Mawdudi referred to this episode in *JIKUS*.

103. Cited in Muhammad Salahu'ddin, "Tajziah," *Takbir,* September 28, 1989, p. 31. Allahwala cited the same episode but quoted Muhammad 'Ali as saying, "would none rise up to explain Islam's true position"; see Mahmud Ahmad Allahwala, "Mard-i haqq agah," *Takbir,* September 28, 1989, pp. 41–43.

104. Allahwala, "Mard-i haqq agah," p. 41. The author underscored the fact that Mawdudi did not display a beard, which then—as now—was a mark of commitment to the religious path.

105. On the Ahmadi view of jihad, see Hazrat Mirza Bashir-ud-Din Mahmud, *Invitation to Ahmadiyyat* (London, 1980), p. 52, and Yvonne Y. Haddad and Jane I. Smith, *Mission to America: Five Islamic Sectarian Communities in North America* (Gainesville, 1993), p. 58.

106. Sayyid Abu'l-A'la Mawdudi, *Al-Jihad fi'l-Islam,* reprint (Lahore, 1986).

107. For references cited by Mawdudi in this book see *Al-Jihad,* see also Mawdudi, *Watha'iq,* p. 92, where the original drafts are reproduced.

108. Faruqi, "Hayat-i javidan," p. 23.

109. Ahmad and Ansari, "Mawlana Sayyid Abul A'la Mawdudi," p. 361. Reprints of the first and last installments of the article can be found in Mawdudi, *Watha'iq,* pp. 90–91.

110. Mawdudi, *Watha'iq,* p. 90; Ahmad and Ansari, "Mawlana Sayyid Abul A'la Mawdudi," p. 361; and Faruqi, "Hayat-i javidan," p. 23. Daru'l-Musannifin was established by Shibli Nu'mani and was closely associated with the Nadwatu'l-'Ulama in Lucknow.

111. Gilani, *Maududi,* pp. 43–44; Shahpuri, *Tarikh,* 1:204; and Malik Ghulam 'Ali, "Ik rafiq ke ta'athurat," in Buhtah, *Mawlana Mawdudi,* p. 253.

112. Cited in *JIKUS*, p. 17, and in Shahpuri, *Tarikh,* 1:206.

113. *KN,* p. 36; Shahpuri, *Tarikh,* 1:205–206. Reference is probably to Ibn Khallikan's *Wafayat al-a'yan wa anba' al-zaman.* See J. W. Fück, "Ibn Khallikan," in *EI.*

114. *KN,* p. 36.

115. Sayyid Abu'l-A'la Mawdudi, *Tahrik-i azadi Hind awr musalman* (Lahore, 1973), 2:22–23; see also *RJI,* 1:4.

116. *SAAM,* 1:75.

117. For more on the *Asfar,* see Fazlur Rahman, "Al-asfar al-arba'a," in Ehsan Yarshater, ed., *Encyclopaedia Iranica* (London and Boston, 1982).

118. Mawdudi's biographers suggested that he translated either all the text or the last two *safars* (which were never published); *SAAM,* 1:74, and Faruqi, "Hayat-ijavidan," p. 26, but, in fact, he worked on only a few segments in cooperation with another translator named Miranbakhsh, as is stated in the published volumes. Sadra's *Asfar* and *Sharh al-hidayah al-athariyah* are taught at the Farangi Mahal, Jama'-i Sultaniyah and the Daru'l-'Ulum of Deoband; see Seyyed Hossein Nasr, *Ma'arif-i Islami dar jahan-i mu'athir* (Tehran, 1969), pp. 123–132. The importance of Sadra is perhaps best reflected in the fact that the term *Sadra-khandah* (well-read in Sadra) continues to be a hallmark of intellectual advancement among members of the Muslim religious sodalities in India. On *Asfar* in the curriculum of Muslim religious schools, see Nasr, *Ma'arif,* pp. 123–132, and Francis Robinson, "Scholarship and Mysticism in 18th Century Awadh," in A. L. Dallapiccola and S. Z. Lallemant, eds., *Islam and Indian Religions,* vol. 1: *Texts* (Stuttgart, 1993), pp. 394–398.

119. On Sadra's views, see Seyyed Hossein Nasr, *Sadr al-Din Shirazi and His Tran-*

scendent Theosophy (Tehran, 1978). Similar influences on Ayatollah Khomeini can be detected; see Alexander Knysh, "*Irfan* Revisited: Khomeini and the Legacy of Islamic Mysticism," *Middle East Journal* 46.4 (autumn 1992): 631–653.

120. James Morris, *The Wisdom of the Throne: An Introduction to the Philosophy of Mulla Sadra* (Princeton, N.J., 1981), pp. 121–122.

121. Hamid Dabashi, "Didgahi bar afkar-i ijtima'i-i Mulla Sadra: nizami ijtima'i dar jahani sarmadi," *Iran Nameh* 3.3 (spring 1985): 407–428.

122. This is an important dimension of contemporary Islamic revivalism; Hasan al-Banna (d. 1949) of the Muslim Brotherhood of Egypt had ties to the Hasafiyah Sufi order; see Richard P. Mitchell, *The Society of the Muslim Brothers,* 2nd ed. (New York, 1993), pp. 2–3. Similarly, the Syrian Muslim Brotherhood leader Sa'id Hawwa (d. 1990), based his concept of *ihya'-i rabaniyah* (divine revival) on the teachings of the Naqshbandi order to which he had belonged; see Itzchak Weismann, "Sa'id Hawwa: The Making of a Radical Muslim Thinker in Modern Syria," *Middle Eastern Studies* 29.4 (October 1993): 607–611. For a discussion of the general impact of Sufism on revivalism, see John O. Voll, "Conservative and Traditional Brotherhoods," in Charles E. Butterworth and I. William Zartman, eds., *Annals of the American Academy of Political and Social Science* 524 (November 1992): 66–78.

123. The poems are reprinted in Munir, *Mawlana Abu'l-A'la Mawdudi,* p. 125.

124. Cited in Annemarie Schimmel, *Mystical Dimensions of Islam* (Chapel Hill, N.C., 1975), p. 289.

125. At the time, for instance, several of Hyderabad's leading ten families were Hindu and the rest were Shi'i; Karen Leonard, "The Hyderabad Political System and Its Participants," *Journal of Asian Studies* 30.3 (May 1971): 581–582.

126. On the nizam's failure to forge a viable Hyderabadi identity to justify Muslim rule, see Karen Leonard "The Deccani Synthesis in Old Hyderabad: A Historiographic Essay," *Journal of the Pakistan Historical Society* 21.4 (October 1973): 205–218. The comments by Mawdudi about Hyderabad are in *JIKUS,* pp. 21–22. On the domination of Hindus over Hyderabad's commerce, see Karen Leonard, "Banking Firms in Nineteenth-Century Hyderabad Politics," *Modern Asian Studies,* 15.2 (April 1981): 177–201.

127. *JIKUS,* p. 18.

128. Said Amir Arjomand, "Shi'ite Islam and the Revolution in Iran," *Government and Opposition* 16.3 (summer 1981): 293–316, and Ervand Abrahamian, *Khomeinism* (Berkeley, 1993).

Chapter 2

1. Abad Shahpuri, *Tarikh-i Jama'at-i Islami* (Lahore, 1989), 1:209.

2. In later years, Mawdudi held Muslim rulers responsible for failing to convert all of India to Islam and failing to protect Islam from the influence of Hinduism. For elaboration of this theme by Mas'ud 'Alam Nadwi, see *RJI,* 6:173–206.

3. Leonard Binder, *Religion and Politics in Pakistan* (Berkeley, 1961), p. 82.

4. Sarwat Saulat, *Maulana Maududi* (Karachi, 1979), p. 5.

5. Shahpuri, *Tarikh,* 1:194.

6. Ra'is Ahmad Ja'fari, "Mawlana Sayyid Abu'l-A'la Mawdudi," in *SSMN,* p. 214.

7. Cited in M. R. Khan, *The Delusion of Grandeur: Maulana Maudoodi and His Jamaat* (Karachi, 1964), p. 16.

8. See, Mawlana Muhammad Manzur Nu'mani, *Mawlana Mawdudi mere sath rifaqat ki sarguzasht awr ab mera mu'qaf* (Lahore, 1980); see also Seyyed Vali Reza Nasr, *The Vanguard of the Islamic Revolution: The Jama'at-i Islami of Pakistan* (Berkeley, 1994),

pp. 24–26, and interviews with Mawlana Amin Ahsan Islahi, Mawlana 'Abdu'l-Ghaffar Hasan, and Mawlana Seyyid Abu'l-Hasan 'Ali Nadwi.

9. For more on this concept, see M. Canard, "Da'wa," in *EI*.

10. *SAAM*, 1:90.

11. Ahmad Munir, *Mawlana Abu'l-A'la Mawdudi* (Lahore, 1986), p. 125; for the full text of these poems, see the appendix in this book.

12. Interview with Begum 'Abidah Gurmani.

13. *RJI*, 1:5–6.

14. Muhammad Yusuf, "While Green in Age: Maulana Maudoodi's Childhood," in *The Universal Message* (Karachi, 1980), pp. 5–6.

15. Shahpuri, *Tarikh*, 1:213–214.

16. Mahiru'l-Qadri, "Tarikhsaz shakhsiyat," in *SSMN*, p. 216.

17. *SAAM*, 1:107.

18. Shahpuri, *Tarikh*, 1:214.

19. In its early years, for example, *TQ* passionately opposed listening to music; see *SAAM*, 1:108.

20. *TQ*, August 1936, p. 483.

21. *SAAM*, 1:107.

22. See for instance, *TQ*, April 1935, pp. 82–91; May 1935, pp. 162–170; and June 1935, pp. 242–252.

23. Sayyid Asad Gilani, *Maududi: Thought and Movement* (Lahore, 1984), p. 172.

24. At the turn of the century, a market in Hyderabad—still known as Medina market—donated its earnings to Medina for the welfare of that city; Akbar S. Ahmed, *Discovering Islam: Making Sense of Muslim History and Society* (London, 1988), p. 163.

25. Nu'mani, *Mawlana Mawdudi mere sath*, pp. 20–23. See also Khurram Jah Murad's foreword to Sayyid Abul-A'la Mawdudi, *Let Us Be Muslims* (Leicester, 1985), p. 37.

26. *TQ*, March 1936, pp. 4–5.

27. Mawdudi was involved in several government offices and affiliated institutions, including the Directorate of Education and the 'Uthmaniyah University. The deputy commissioner of Hyderabad, Nawab Nisar Jang, was his friend, as was Nawab Zulqadr Jang, who was the one who had arranged for the government to purchase three hundred copies of the *Tarjuman*; see Mahiru'l-Qadri, "Tarikhsaz," p. 216, and *SAAM*, 1:107.

28. Cited in Muhammad Yusuf Buhtah, ed., *Mawlana Mawdudi: apni awr dusrun ki nazar main* (Lahore, 1984), pp. 54–55.

29. Cited in Khurshid Ahmad, "Jama'at-i Islami kiya hey, uski zarurat kiya thi," in *Haftrozah Zindagi*, November 10–16, 1989, p. 13.

30. *TQ*, July 1933, p. 275.

31. *SAAM*, 1:122–123.

32. See Khurram Murad's forward in Mawdudi, *Let Us Be Muslims*, p. 37, and Nu'mani, *Mawlana Mawdudi mere sath*, pp. 24–25.

33. Interview with Mian Tufayl Muhammad. The story of this incident is also cited in *CRTIN*, p. 299, and in *JIKUS*, p. 23. On his decision never to live under a Hindu regime, see Chaudhri 'Abdu'l-Rahman 'Abd, *Mufakkir-i Islam: Sayyid Abu'l-A'la Mawdudi* (Lahore, 1971), pp. 200–201.

34. 'Abd, *Mufakkir-i Islam*, pp. 106–120; *JIKUS*, p. 23, and Nu'mani, *Mawlana Mawdudi mere sath*, pp. 24–25. The essays that later constituted *Musalman awr mawjuda siyasi kashmakash* first appeared in *TQ*, December 1937, and were then elaborated further in *TQ* January 1938, which was a special issue dedicated to this topic.

35. Cited in Gilani, *Maududi*, p. 65.

36. Cited in Ishtiaq Husain Qureshi, *Ulema in Politics: A Study Relating to the Political Activities of the Ulema in South Asian Subcontinent from 1566–1947* (Karachi, 1972), p. 351.

37. For a fuller discussion of this issue, see this author's "Communalism and Fundamentalism: a Re-examination of the Origins of Islamic Fundamentalism," *Contention* 4.2 (winter 1995): 121–139.

38. These views were reflected in Mawdudi's *Musalman awr mawjudah siyasi kashmakash* and in another of his works, *Mas'alah-i qaumiyat*, reprint (Lahore, 1982).

39. Qureshi, *Ulema in Politics*, p. 352.

40. Ibid., pp. 351–53.

41. Mahiru'l-Qadri, "Chand nuqush-i zindagi," in Buhtah, *Mawlana Mawdudi*, pp. 241–242. Qadri said that Mawdudi had purchased an entire set of the *Encyclopaedia Britannica* and was busy studying its volumes.

42. For a discussion of this tendency in Third World ideologies, see Partha Chaterjee, *Nationalist Thought and the Colonial World: A Derivative Discourse* (Tokyo, 1986).

43. Benedict Anderson, *Imagined Communities: Reflections on the Origin and Spread of Nationalism*, 2nd ed. (New York, 1991), especially pp. 104–107.

44. 'Abd, *Mufakkir-i Islam*, p. 47, and *SAAM*, 1:122–123.

45. Interview with Begum Mahmudah Mawdudi. The wealth of the family came from its business dealings, notably money lending. Abu'l-Khayr Mawdudi is quoted as saying that Mahmudah Begum was the daughter of Delhi's "biggest Muslim usurer (*sudkhar*)"; cited in Ja'far Qasmi, "Mujhe yad hey sab zara zara," *Nida*, April 17, 1990, p. 31.

46. Begum Mahmuda Mawdudi, "Mawlana Mawdudi apne ghar main," in Buhtah, *Mawlana Mawdudi*, p. 263; *SAAM*, 1:327; and Muhammad Yahya, "Sikandarpur se Lahore tak," in *QDMN*, pp. 169–189.

47. Interviews with Mawlana Amin Ahsan Islahi and Mawlana Sayyid Abu'l-Hasan 'Ali Nadwi. See also Nasr, *Vanguard of the Islamic Revolution*, pp. 24–26.

48. Interview with Begum Mawdudi.

49. Begum Mahmudah Mawdudi, "Mawlana Mawdudi"; also interview with her. Begum Mawdudi continued to shun observance of purdah as late as the 1960s. Maryam Jameelah, who lived at the Mawlana's house at the time, ran afoul of Mawdudi after she protested Begum Mawdudi's lax attitude toward purdah; interviews, Lahore.

50. Begum Mahmudah Mawdudi, "Mawlana Mawdudi," pp. 261–265. She furthermore said of him: "I was not what his view of a perfect Muslim wife was. But I admire his patience with me and that he did not force me. I came to his ways gradually"; interview with Begum Mawdudi. Begum Mawdudi's lax attitude in observing purdah, and the evident exception accorded to her by Mawdudi, were cited by Nu'mani as a reason for leaving the Jama'at. See Nu'mani, *Mawlana Mawdudi mere sath*.

51. From the text of a note written by Mawdudi on April 16, 1938; reproduced in Sayyid Abu'l-A'la Mawdudi, *Watha'iq-i Mawdudi* (Lahore, 1984), p. 61.

52. Mawdudi, *Watha'iq*, pp. 61, 62, and *SAAM*, 1:122.

53. Sabir Khalhwarvi, "Sayyid Mawdudi awr Iqbal," in *SDMN*, p. 102.

54. The correspondence and plans for the Shabbanu'l-Muslimin are in the archives of the Institute of Islamic Culture in Lahore.

55. For more, see J. Pederson-[G. Makdisi] et al., "Madrasa," in *EI*.

56. Interview with Javid Iqbal.

57. Javid Iqbal, *Zindarud*, 3rd ed. (Lahore, 1989), pp. 980–982. The letter was drafted in Arabic by Mawdudi at the behest of Niyaz 'Ali. It was dated August 15, 1937,

four months after Mawdudi had informed Niyaz 'Ali about his own plans for an Islamic institution.

58. Ibid.

59. For 'Ali's offer to Thanwi, see Shahpuri, *Tarikh*, 1:372–374. For his attempt to get Mawdudi to move to Punjab, see Rahman Siddiqi, "Mawlana Azad awr Mawlana Mawdudi ke mabain ik gumshudah kari," *Nida*, February 7–13, 1990, p. 21, and Mawdudi, *Watha'iq*, p. 62.

60. Shahpuri, *Tarikh*, 1:372–373.

61. *JIKUS*, pp. 21–22.

62. Mawdudi, *Watha'iq*, p. 62. See also letters dated May 25, 1932, and June 7, 1937, in Shahpuri, *Tarikh*, 1:380.

63. Shahpuri, *Tarikh*, 1:382–383.

64. Mawdudi, *Watha'iq*, p. 63.

65. *SAAM* 1:122–123, and Shahpuri, *Tarikh*, 1:394.

66. Cited in Asim Nu'mani, *Makatib-i Sayyid Abu'l-A'la Mawdudi* (Lahore, 1977), 1:206. In later years, in response to a letter from Hafeez Malik, dated March 3, 1967, Mawdudi provided yet another reason for his decision; he wrote that he agreed to go to Pathankot to work on the codification of Islamic law; cited in *SAAM*, 1:128.

67. For more on the meaning of this concept, see A. Abel, "Dar al-Islam," in *EI*.

68. See, for instance, Mawdudi, *Watha'iq*, pp. 62–64, and *TQ*, December 1937, pp. 40–51, where, in an article entitled "The Malady and the Remedy," Mawdudi reiterated his original objective.

69. See the text of a letter by Mawdudi, dated June 2, 1937, reproduced in Mawdudi, *Watha'iq*, p. 83.

70. Gilani, *Maududi*, p. 66.

71. *SAAM*, 1:138.

72. Mawdudi, *Watha'iq*, pp. 65–66.

73. Shahpuri, *Tarikh*, 1:409.

74. Gilani, *Maududi*, p. 67.

75. Shahpuri, *Tarikh*, 1:405.

76. For more on Iqbal, see Aziz Ahmad, *Iqbal and the Recent Exposition of Islamic Political Thought* (Lahore, 1950); Annemarie Schimmel, *Gabriel's Wing* (Leiden, 1963); and Hafeez Malik, ed., *Iqbal: Poet-Philosopher of Pakistan* (New York, 1971). Iqbal's image has grown in stature steadily over the course of the years. Today he is routinely referred to as *'allamah* (the most learned), a title that did not accompany his name during his lifetime or immediately after. There are two government-supported research institutions concerned with the life and works of Iqbal, the Iqbal Academy of Pakistan and Bazm-i Iqbal, both situated in Lahore. *Iqbal-shinasi* or *Iqbaliyat* (Iqbal studies) have become self-contained fields of study, offered at universities as a discipline.

77. Some studies of Mawdudi have emphasized his relation to Iqbal, tracing the evolution of Mawdudi's revivalism to Iqbal's own sentiments. See, for instance, Freeland Abbott, "The Jama'at-i-Islami of Pakistan," *Middle East Journal* 11.1 (winter 1957): 38; Aziz Ahmad, "Mawdudi and Orthodox Fundamentalism in Pakistan," *Middle East Journal* 21.3 (summer 1967): 369; Ahmad, *Islamic Modernism in India and Pakistan, 1857–1964* (London, 1967), pp. 156, 175; Erwin I. J. Rosenthal, *Islam in the Modern Nation State* (Cambridge, 1965), p. 206; and Maryam Jameelah, "An Appraisal of Some Aspects of Maulana Sayyid Ala Maudoodi's Life and Thought," *Islamic Quarterly* 31.2 (1987): 119–120.

78. See, for instance, Sayyid As'ad Gilani, *Iqbal, Daru'l-Islam awr Mawdudi* (Lahore, 1978).

79. *SAAM*, 1:67–68, 121, 129. On Iqbal's familiarity with the *Tarjuman*, see Mawdudi's letter to Mawlana 'Aziz Zubaidi, dated April 7, 1951; cited in Abu Rashid Faruqi, *Iqbal awr Mawdudi* (Lahore, 1977), pp. 77–79.

80. See, for instance, Na'im Siddiqi, *Al-Mawdudi* (Lahore, 1963), p. 33, and Sayyid As'ad Gilani, "Ta'limi nazariyat-i 'Allamah Iqbal awr Daru'l-Islam ki ta'limi iskim," in Ja'far Baluch, ed., *Iqbal-Shinasi awr Sayyarah* (Lahore, 1989), pp. 74–86.

81. Abu Tariq, ed., *Mawlana Mawdudi ki taqarir* (Lahore, 1976), 1:182–187.

82. Sayyid Abu'l-A'la Mawdudi, *Islamic Law and Constitution* (Karachi, 1955), pp. 203–204.

83. Cited in a letter dated March 2, 1967, reprinted in Faruqi, *Iqbal awr Mawdudi*, p. 83.

84. Interviews with Mian Muhammad Shafi' and Javid Iqbal.

85. *RJI*, 1:10; *SAAM*, 1:143-145; and *Jasarat*, August 6, 1973, p. 2.

86. Saulat, *Maulana Maududi*, p. 8. In *TQ*, March 1938, p. 3, Mawdudi had written of Iqbal's importance to both the *Tarjuman* and Daru'l-Islam.

87. Shahpuri, *Tarikh*, 1:362–363, 367–368, and *TQ*, December 1937, p. 299.

88. Shahpuri, *Tarikh*, 1:424–425, and Siddiqi, "Mawlana Azad awr Mawlana Mawdudi," p. 21.

89. Mawdudi, *Watha'iq*, p. 82.

90. *TQ*, July 1938, pp. 3–4.

91. Shahpuri, *Tarikh*, 1:415–416. Mawdudi compared Daru'l-Islam's function to one of "providing water to the thirsty."

92. Ibid., p. 423.

93. Chaudhri Ghulam Ahmad Parwez (d. 1979) was a famous contemporary thinker on Islam, whose ideas regarding the hadith caused much controversy and dismay among the ulama. For more on Parwez, see Freeland Abbott, *Islam and Pakistan* (Ithaca, N.Y., 1968), pp. 212–213; see also Ishtiaq Ahmed, *The Concept of an Islamic State: An Analysis of the Ideological Controversy in Pakistan* (New York, 1987), pp. 128–133, 177–190.

94. Shahpuri, *Tarikh*, 1:423.

95. Nu'mani *Mawlana Mawdudi mere sath*, pp. 28–30.

96. Yahya, "Sikandarpur," p. 80.

97. See Shahpuri, *Tarikh*, 1:429, and *SAAM*, 1:149.

98. On the scope and reach of this campaign, see Nasr, *Vanguard of the Islamic Revolution*, pp. 78–80.

99. Ibid., pp. 103–115.

100. Iqbal Ahmad Nadwi's editorial in *Zindagi-i Naw* (April 1978), p. 12.

101. Cited in *Mahnamah-i Zikri*, Ihya'-i Islam Number (January 1982), p. 174.

102. Sayyid 'Abdu'l-'Aziz Sharqi, in Jalil Ahmad Rana and Salim Mansur Khalid, eds., *Tazkirah-i Sayyid Mawdudi* (Lahore, 1986), p. 294.

103. Ibid.

104. Shahpuri, *Tarikh*, 1:429.

105. *CRTIN*, pp. 85–88.

106. Nu'mani, *Mawlana Mawdudi mere sath*, pp. 30–33; also interview with Malik Ghulam 'Ali.

107. Account of this trip is narrated in *TQ*, October 1939.

108. Mawlana Muhammad Manzur Nu'mani, *Tablighi Jama'at, Jama'at-i Islami, awr Brelwi hazrat* (Lucknow, 1980), p. 44.

109. Ibid.

110. Nu'mani, *Mawlana Mawdudi mere sath*, pp. 32–33.

111. Kenneth W. Jones, *Socio-Religious Reform Movements in British India* (Cambridge, 1992), pp. 87–121.

112. See, for instance, Mawdudi's editorial in *TQ*, February 1939.

113. 'Abd, *Mufakkir-i Islam*, pp. 152–164, and Rana and Khalid, *Tazkirah*, p. 107.

114. See, for example, Sayyid Abu'l-A'la Mawdudi, *The Process of Islamic Revolution*, 8th ed. (Lahore, 1980). The book is based on lectures presented at Aligarh University on September 12, 1940, and was first published in 1947.

115. *SAAM*, 1:176.

116. Mawdudi cited the collapse of efforts of Muhammad 'Ali and Hakim Ajmal Khan (1863–1928) in regard to viable alternatives, see *TQ*, May 1939, pp. 2–13. Regarding *tajdid*, see Sayyid Abu'l-A'la Mawdudi, "Ihya'-i nizam-i Islam," *Al-Furqan*, Shah Waliu'llah Number (1940), p. 18.

117. Shahpuri, *Tarikh*, 1:466.

118. From *Short Proceedings of the 2nd Annual Conference, Jamaat-e-Islami, East Pakistan, March 14–16, 1958* (Dacca, 1958), p. 2; enclosed with U.S. Consulate, Dacca, Dispatch no. 247, April 3, 1958, 790D.00/4-358, United States National Archives.

119. 'Abd, *Mufakkir-i Islam*, pp. 96–97, 156–157.

120. Nasr, *Vanguard of the Islamic Revolution*, pp. 20–21.

121. The letter was dated 23 Rabi'u'l-Thani, A.H. 1357 (1938–1939); reprinted in *Al-Ma'arif* 18.2 (April–May 1985): 249–250.

122. Nasr, *Vanguard of the Islamic Revolution*, pp. 20–21, 103–115.

123. David Gilmartin, "Democracy, Nationalism and the Public: A Speculation on Colonial Muslim Politics," *South Asia* 14.1 (June 1991): 126.

124. Sayyid Abu'l-A'la Mawdudi, *Jama'at-i Islami: tarikh, maqsad awr la'ihah-i 'amal*, reprint (Lahore, 1963), pp. 26–27.

125. For accounts of Mawdudi and the Jama'at's activities in Pakistan, see Mumtaz Ahmad, "Islamic Fundamentalism in South Asia: The Jamaat-i-Islami and the Tablighi Jamaat," in Martin E. Marty and R. Scott Appleby, eds., *Fundamentalisms Observed* (Chicago, 1991), pp. 457–530; Rafiuddin Ahmad, "Redefining Muslim Identity in South Asia: The Transformation of the Jama'at-i Islami," in Martin E. Marty and R. Scott Appleby, eds., *Accounting for Fundamentalisms: The Dynamic Character of Movements* (Chicago, 1994), pp. 669–705; Kalim Bahadur, *The Jama'at-i Islami of Pakistan* (New Delhi, 1977); and Nasr, *Vanguard of the Islamic Revolution*.

126. On the Jama'at's activities on behalf of the Islamic constitution and in opposition to the new state, see Binder, *Religion and Politics in Pakistan*, and Nasr, *Vanguard of the Islamic Revolution*, pp. 141–46.

127. Nasr, *Vanguard of the Islamic Revolution*, pp. 119–120.

128. *SAAM*, 1:225.

129. For details of these events, see Nasr, *Vanguard of the Islamic Revolution*, pp. 120–123.

130. For more on this debate, see ibid., pp. 28–43.

131. See ibid., pp. 131–141, and Ayesha Jalal, *The State of Martial Rule: The Origins of Pakistan's Political Economy of Defence* (Cambridge, 1990), pp. 144–51.

132. Zafaru'llah Khan and General Iskandar Mirza, in a conversation with the American consul in Karachi, characterized Mawdudi as the "most dangerous man in Pakistan"; see U.S. Consulate General, Lahore, Dispatch no. 103, January 4, 1955, 790D.00/1-455, United States National Archives.

133. Abdur Rahman Abd, *Sayyed Maududi Faces the Death Sentence*, reprint (Lahore, 1978), and Nasr, *Vanguard of the Islamic Revolution*, pp. 140–141.

134. See 'Abdu'l-Ghani Faruqi, "Hayat-i javidan," *Haftrozah Zindagi*, Mawdudi Number (September 29–October 5, 1989), p. 29.

135. For General Mirza's objections to Muhammad 'Ali's "flirtation with the mullah," see the general's unpublished memoirs, pp. 109–110.

136. *TQ*, January–February 1956, pp. 2–8.

137. Altaf Gauhar, "Pakistan, Ayub Khan, awr Mawlana Mawdudi, *Tafhimu'l-Qur'an* awr main," *Haftrozah Zindagi*, Mawdudi Number (September 29–October 5, 1989), pp. 41–45.

138. *SAAM*, 2:128–187.

139. Personal correspondences with Mawlana Wasi Mazhar Nadwi, 1989–1990. Mawlana Nadwi was then a member of the *shura'* and was present during Mawdudi's address before that body.

140. Interview with Begum Mahmudah Mawdudi.

141. Interview with Khwajah Amanu'llah.

142. *Ijtima' se ijtima' tak (1963–1974): rudad-i Jama'at-i Islami, Pakistan* (Lahore, 1989).

143. Kausar Niazi, *Zulfiqar Ali Bhutto of Pakistan: The Last Days* (New Delhi, 1992).

144. 'Abdu'l-Ghafur Ahmad, *Pher martial law a-giya* (Lahore, 1988), and Kawthar Niyazi, *Awr line kat ga'i* (Lahore, 1987).

145. Interview with Kawthar Niyazi.

146. See, for instance, Bhutto's remarks before the parliament on April 28, 1977; cited in Niazi, *Zulfiqar Ali Bhutto*, p. 91.

147. Sarwat Saulat, *Maulana Maududi* (Karachi, 1979), p. 101.

148. Nasr, *Vanguard of Islamic Revolution*, p. 191.

149. *SAAM*, 1:368.

150. *SDMN*, pp. 39–40. Mawdudi's grave was left unmarked, in keeping with Mawdudi's last will and testament; this was interpreted by some to reflect Wahhabi sentiments; interviews.

Chapter 3

1. For discussions by Mawdudi of imperialism, see Sayyid Abu'l-A'la Mawdudi, *Islam Today* (Beirut, 1985), pp. 16–48; Mawdudi, "Saw baras pahle ka Hindustan," in Muhammad Yusuf Buhtah, ed., *Mawlana Mawdudi: apni awr dusrun ki nazar main* (Lahore, 1984), pp. 149–161.

2. Mawdudi, "Saw Baras," pp. 149–161, and *Al-Jihad fi'l-Islam*, reprint (Lahore, 1986), pp. 19, 21.

3. Sayyid Abu'l-A'la Mawdudi, *'Asr-i hazir main ummat-i muslimah ke masa'il awr unka hall*, 2nd ed. (Lahore, 1988), pp. 88–95; Mawdudi, *Musalman ka mazi, hal awr mustaqbal* (Lahore, 1962), 1:18–42, 3:291–294; and Abu Tariq, ed., *Mawlana Mawdudi ki taqarir* (Lahore, 1976), 2:284–331. Mawdudi was influenced in this regard by his reading of Iqbal. He interpreted Iqbal's concept of *khudi* (selfhood) and his "reconstruction of Islamic thought" as the defense and reassertion of Islam before other "-isms" and the Western thought that lay behind them; see *SAAM*, 1:130–32, and Ahmad Munir, *Mawlana Abu'l-A'la Mawdudi* (Lahore, 1986), pp. 129–132.

4. Khurshid Ahmad's talk at the University of South Florida and World and Islamic Studies Enterprise conference, Tampa, Florida, May 1993.

5. In this regard, Mawdudi followed in the tradition of Islamic revival among the ulama in the nineteenth century; see Barbara D. Metcalf, *Islamic Revival in British India: Deoband 1860–1900* (Princeton, N.J., 1982).

6. On the role of popular culture in shaping collective action in South Asia, see Sandria Freitag, *Collective Action and Community: Public Arenas and the Emergence of Communalism in India* (Berkeley, 1989).

7. Gran and Arjomand found similar intellectual processes at work in new interpretive readings of Islam that were born of the encounter with the West in Iran and Egypt and were directed at rationalizing the amorphous corpus of religious thought with a view to the needs of the times. See Peter Gran, *Islamic Roots of Capitalism: Egypt 1760–1840* (Austin, Tex., 1979); and Said Amir Arjomand, "History, Structure, and Revolution in the Shi'ite Tradition in Contemporary Iran," *International Political Science Review* 10.2 (1989): 111–119.

8. See Liah Greenfeld's discussion of the origins of nationalism in her *Nationalism: Five Roads to Modernity* (Cambridge, Mass., 1992), p. 16.

9. Maryam Jameelah, "An Appraisal of Some Aspects of Maulana Sayyid Ala Maudoodi's Life and Thought," *Islamic Quarterly* 31.2 (1987): p. 127.

10. See Peter van der Veer, *Religious Nationalism: Hindus and Muslims in India* (Berkeley, 1994), pp. 133–134.

11. Bruce Lawrence, *Defenders of God: The Fundamentalist Revolt against the Modern Age* (San Francisco, 1989), and Mark Jurgensmeyer, *The New Cold War? Religious Nationalism Confronts the Secular State* (Berkeley, 1993).

12. Theodore P. Wright Jr., "Inadvertent Modernization of Indian Muslims by Revivalists," *Journal of the Institute of Muslim Minority Affairs* 1.1 (1979): 80–89. For discussions of this theme in the case of the Iranian revolution, see Mangol Bayat, "The Iranian Revolution of 1978–79: Fundamentalist or Modern?" *Middle East Journal* 37.1 (winter 1983): 30–42, and Said Amir Arjomand, *The Turban for the Crown: The Islamic Revolution in Iran* (New York, 1988), pp. 177–88.

13. The term *moderns* is used by Lawrence, who wrote that revivalists "are moderns but not modernists"; Lawrence, *Defenders of God*, p. 17.

14. Muhammad Yusuf, *Maududi: A Formative Phase* (Karachi, 1979), p. 35.

15. For more on this issue, see Seyyed Vali Reza Nasr, "Communalism and Fundamentalism: A Re-examination of the Origins of Islamic Fundamentalism," *Contention* 4.2 (winter 1995): 121–139.

16. *TQ*, September 1934, pp. 9–24; Sayyid Abu'l-A'la Mawdudi, *Nationalism in India* (Pathankot, 1947), pp. 6–7; Mawdudi, *Tanqihat*, 22nd ed. (Lahore, 1989), pp. 177ff.; Mawdudi, *Musalman ka mazi*, pp. 8ff. Mawdudi's work was followed by a number of his disciples, especially 'Abdu'l-Hamid Siddiqi and Maryam Jameelah; see 'Abdu'l-Hamid Siddiqi, *Iman awr akhlaq* (Lahore, n.d.); and Maryam Jameelah's *Islam and Modernism* (Lahore, 1988), *Islam and Orientalism* (Lahore, 1987), *Islam versus the West* (Lahore, 1988), and *Is Western Civilization Universal?* (Lahore, 1969).

17. On the relation of such notions of religious reform to religious nationalism in South Asia, see van der Veer, *Religious Nationalism*, pp. 56–58.

18. In this regard, see important studies by Şerif Mardin, *Religion and Social Change in Turkey: The Case of Bediüzzaman Said Nursi* (Albany, N.Y., 1989), and Roy Mottahedeh, *Mantle of the Prophet: Religion and Politics in Iran* (New York, 1985).

19. Maryam Jameelah, *A Manifesto of the Islamic Movement* (Lahore, 1969), p. 42.

20. Khurshid Ahmad, "The Nature of Islamic Resurgence," in John L. Esposito, ed., *Voices of Resurgent Islam* (New York, 1983), p. 224.

21. *TQ*, September 1934, pp. 2–9, and March 1938, pp. 38–54; Mawdudi, *Tanqihat*, pp. 272–276. See also, Muhammad Riyaz Kirmani, *Basa'ir-i Mawdudi: Tafhimu'l-Qur'an main jadid 'ulum se istifadah* (Lahore, 1988), on the place of modern scientific thought in Mawdudi's Qur'anic commentary.

22. Interview with Maryam Jameelah.

23. Cited in Jameelah, "An Appraisal," p. 122.

24. *TQ,* December 1937, pp. 301–302.

25. Cited in *SAAM,* 1:96. Mawdudi sought to prove scientifically the existence of God on numerous occasions in his writings; see, for instance, *TQ,* December 1933, pp. 239–254; Sayyid Abu'l-A'la Mawdudi, *Tafhimat* (Lahore, 1965), 1:36; and Mawdudi, *Tawhid'u risalat awr zindagi ba'd mawt ka 'aqli subut* (Lahore, n.d.).

26. On modernist thought, see Fazlur Rahman, *Islam and Modernity; The Transformation of an Intellectual Tradition* (Chicago, 1982); Albert Hourani, *Arabic Thought in the Liberal Age, 1798–1931* (Cambridge, 1962); Malcom Kerr, *Islamic Reform* (Oxford, 1966); Aziz Ahmad, *Islamic Modernism in India and Pakistan, 1857–1964* (London, 1967); and Seyyed Vali Reza Nasr, "Religious Modernism in the Arab World, India and Iran: The Perils and Prospects of a Discourse," *Muslim World* 83.1 (January 1993): 20–47.

27. On Mawdudi's criticism of Islamic modernism, see Charles J. Adams, "The Ideology of Mawlana Mawdudi," in Donald E. Smith, ed., *South Asian Politics and Religion* (Princeton, N.J., 1966), p. 386. The distinction that Mawdudi made between Islamic modernism and his own ideas was reflected in his eulogy of Iqbal, which praised him for remaining a true Muslim, not in spite of his Western education, but because of it; cited in Munir, *Mawlana Abu'l-A'la Mawdudi,* pp. 129–131.

28. Jameelah, "An Appraisal," p. 121, and Abad Shahpuri, *Tarikh-i Jama'at-i Islami* (Lahore, 1989), 1:261–262.

29. Mawdudi, *Nationalism in India,* pp. 48–49.

30. The following discussion of the Ahl-i Hadith is based on the analysis presented in Metcalf, *Islamic Revival,* pp. 268–80.

31. Mawdudi, *Islam Today,* p. 7.

32. See Sayyid Abu'l-A'la Mawdudi, *Let Us Be Muslims* (Leicester, 1985), pp. 116–117, and Khurshid Ahmad's preface to *TUTQ,* 1:xii.

33. *TQ,* January–February 1936, pp. 388–400.

34. Sayyid Abu'l-A'la Mawdudi, *Musalman awr mawjudah siyasi kashmakash* (Lahore, 1940), 3:31.

35. See letter from Mawdudi to Maryam Jameelah dated May 19, 1961, cited in Maryam Jameelah, *Correspondences, between Maulana Maudoodi and Maryam Jameelah,* 4th ed. (Lahore, 1986), p. 30.

36. Ibid., pp. 30–31.

37. 'Abdu'l-Ghani Faruqi, "Hayat-i javidan," in *HRZ,* p. 26. Even in Mawdudi's seminal Qur'anic translation and commentary, *Tafhimu'l-Qur'an* (Understanding the Qur'an, 1949–1972) it can be seen that he was aware of the Western perspective on the Qur'an in general and the Orientalist allegations regarding the Jewish and Christian origins of Islam in particular. It was a defense of the Qur'an before Muslims. Also instructive in this regard is Mawdudi's correspondence with Pope Paul VI in December 1967, in which he complained of Christian belligerence toward Islam and the Prophet Muhammad and of Christianity's excessive missionary activity in Muslim lands; cited in Mawdudi, *'Asr-i hazir,* pp. 274–284.

38. Sayyid Abu'l-A'la Mawdudi, *A Short History of the Revivalist Movement in Islam,* reprint (Lahore: Islamic Publications, 1963), p. iii.

39. Ibid., p. 25, and Sayyid Abu'l-A'la Mawdudi, *Witness unto Mankind: The Purpose and Duty of the Muslim Ummah* (Leicester, 1986), pp. 46–50.

40. Mawdudi, *Tanqihat,* pp. 33ff.

41. Mawdudi, *A Short History,* pp. 36–38.

42. For Mawdudi's historiography of Islam in this context, see *TQ,* September 1934, pp. 2–9, and October 1934, pp. 96–106; and Mawdudi, *Tanqihat,* pp. 23–32; see also Mas'ud 'Alam Nadwi, cited in *RJI,* 6:173–206.

43. Mawlana Wahidu'ddin Khan, *Ta'bir ki ghalti* (Delhi, 1975); and Mawlana Wahid-u'addin Khan, *Din kiya hey* (Delhi, 1978).

44. Sayyid Abu'l-A'la Mawdudi, *Islamic Law and Constitution* (Karachi, 1955), p. 31.

45. Michael Walzer, *The Revolution of Saints: A Study in the Origins of Radical Politics* (Cambridge, Mass., 1965), p. 27.

46. Sayyid Abu'l-A'la Mawdudi, "Foundations of Culture," *Criterion* 6.4 (July–August 1971): 9–11, and Mawdudi, *Qur'an ki char buniyadi istilahain: ilah, rabb, 'ibadat, din* (Lahore, 1988). For Mawdudi's thoughts on *tawhid,* see his *Towards Understanding Islam,* reprint (Indianapolis, 1977), pp. 65–77.

47. Mawdudi, *Let Us Be Muslims,* p. 94.

48. Mawdudi, *Qur'an ki char,* p. 10.

49. Sayyid Abu'l-A'la Mawdudi, *Fundamentals of Islam,* reprint (Delhi, 1985), p. 101.

50. See, for instance, the critique of Sayyid Abu'l-Hasan 'Ali Nadwi in *'Asr-i hazir main din ki tafhim'u tashrih* (Karachi, n.d.), and Syed Athar Husain, trans., *Appreciation and Interpretation of Religion in the Modern Age* (Lucknow, 1982).

51. Mawdudi, *Towards Understanding Islam,* pp. 117–120.

52. Muhammad Yusuf Buhtah, *Mawlana Mawdudi: apni awr dusrun ki nazar main* (Lahore, 1984), p. 102.

53. Mawdudi, *Let Us Be Muslims,* p. 100; Mawdudi, *The Islamic Way of Life* (Leicester, 1986), p. 9; and Mawdudi, *The Religion of Truth* (Delhi, 1972), pp. 8–17.

54. Mawdudi, *Towards Understanding Islam,* pp. 1–2.

55. Ibid., pp. 3–4.

56. Mawdudi, *Let Us Be Muslims,* p. 104.

57. In Iran, 'Ali Shari'ati and Ayatollah Khomeini made similar distinctions between true and "corrupted" Shi'ism, with similar aims; see Nikki Keddie, *Roots of Revolution* (New Haven, Conn., 1981), pp. 218–220.

58. On criticisms of Mawdudi by Nadwi and Wahidu'ddin Khan, see Christian W. Troll, "The Meaning of Din: Recent Views of Three Eminent Indian Ulama," in Christian W. Troll, ed., *Islam in India: Studies and Commentaries* (Delhi, 1982), 1:168–177; Khan, *Din kiya hey;* and Nadwi, *'Asr-i hazir.* The traditional perspective has been outlined by reasserting the views of the eminent Deobandi *'alim,* Mawlana Ashraf 'Ali Thanwi. Thanwi's dates preceded the debate precipitated by Mawdudi, but his works, which are a lucid exposition of the traditional position, have been reprinted by the Deobandis in Pakistan in response to Mawdudi's views; see, for instance, Mawlana Muhammad Taqi 'Uthmani, "Hakimu'l-ummat ke siyasi afkar," *Al-Balagh,* March 1990, pp. 23–53.

59. Nadwi, *'Asr-i hazir,* pp. 15–16. See also Troll, " Meaning of Din," p. 170.

60. Mawlana Muhammad Manzur Nu'mani, *Tablighi Jama'at, Jama'at-i Islami, awr Brelwi hazrat* (Lucknow, 1980), p. 37.

61. Mawdudi, *Fundamentals of Islam,* pp. 53–54.

62. See, for instance, Nadwi, *'Asr-i hazir,* and 'Uthmani, "Hakimu'l-ummat"; see also Seyyed Hossein Nasr, *Traditional Islam in the Modern World* (London, 1987).

63. See for instance, Sayyid Abu'l-Hasan 'Ali Nadwi, *Islam and the World,* reprint (Beirut, 1983).

64. Nu'mani, *Tablighi Jama'at,* p. 37.

65. See Said Amir Arjomand, "The Emergence of Islamic Political Ideologies," in James A. Beckford and Thomas Luckmann, eds., *The Changing Face of Religion* (London, 1989), pp. 109–123; Hamid Dabashi, "Symbiosis of Religious and Political Authorities in Islam," in Thomas Robbins and Ronald Robertson, eds., *Church-State Relations: Tensions and Transitions* (New Brunswick, N.J., 1987), pp. 183–203; Eqbal Ahmad, "Islam and Politics," in Yvonne Haddad et al., eds., *The Islamic Impact* (Syracuse, N.Y.: 1984), pp. 7–26; Ira M. Lapidus, "The Separation of State and Religion in the Development of Early Islamic Society," *International Journal of Middle East Studies* 6 (1975), pp. 363–385; Nazih Ayubi, *Political Islam: Religion and Politics in the Arab World* (New York, 1991); John O. Woll, "Religion and Politics in Islamic Africa," in Matthew Moen and Lowell S. Gustafson, eds., *The Religious Challenge to the State* (Philadelphia, 1992), pp. 211–213; Olivier Roy, *The Failure of Political Islam* (Cambridge, Mass., 1994), pp. viii–ix; and Nasr, *Traditional Islam*. For examinations of this theme in Islamic history, see Said Amir Arjomand, *The Shadow of God and the Hidden Imam: Religion, Political Order, and Societal Change in Shi'ite Iran from the Beginning to 1890* (Chicago, 1984); Hamilton A. R. Gibb, *Studies on the Civilization of Islam,* 2nd ed. (Princeton, N.J., 1982); and Ann K. S. Lambton, *State and Government in Medieval Islam: An Introduction to the Study of Islamic Political Theory: The Jurists* (London, 1981).

66. Wilfred Cantwell Smith, *Islam in Modern History,* 2nd ed. (Princeton, N.J., 1977), p. 213.

67. For a discussion of this attitude among revivalists, see Martin Riesebrodt, *Pious Passion: The Emergence of Modern Fundamentalism in the United States and Iran* (Berkeley, 1993), p. 18.

68. See, for instance, Mawdudi's introduction to his *Tafhimu'l-Qur'an,* in *TUTQ,* 1:7–31.

69. See Khurshid Ahmad's preface in *TUTQ,* 1:xiii–xiv.

70. Ibid., p. xi.

71. Ibid., p. xvi.

72. Ibid., pp. xiv–xv.

73. Sayyid Abu'l-A'la Mawdudi, *Introduction to the Study of the Qur'an* (Delhi, 1971), pp. 36–41, and Khurshid Ahmad's preface to *TUTQ,* 1:xv–xvii.

74. *TUTQ,* 1:4–5.

75. Mawdudi, *Introduction to the Study of the Qur'an,* pp. 12–19. The quote is from p. 44; see also *TUTQ,* 1:34–35.

76. Mawdudi, *Introduction to the Study of the Qur'an,* pp. 43–48.

77. *TUTQ,* 1:17–20.

78. Nadwi, *'Asr-i hazir,* p. 16.

79. *TUTQ,* 1:12.

80. Mawdudi, *Towards Understanding Islam,* pp. 30–36.

81. Khan, *Din kiya hey,* p. 22.

82. Mawdudi, *Towards Understanding Islam,* pp. 4, 11–12, 18–19; Mawdudi, *Let Us Be Muslims,* pp. 53–55; *TQ,* September 1946, p. 59; and *RJI,* 6:347–418.

83. Mawdudi, *Fundamentals of Islam,* p. 21.

84. Sayyid Abu'l-A'la Mawdudi, *Tahrik-i azadi Hind awr Musalman* (Lahore, 1973), 2:140.

85. See Mawdudi's *Qur'an ki char.* Mawdudi's conception of din has been accepted and institutionalized in the revivalist discourse in the Indian subcontinent; it is seen as expressing Islam's omnipresence in man's social and political activities. Muhammad Tahiru'l-Qadri, a self-styled Brelwi revivalist thinker and activist based in Pakistan, echoed Mawdudi when he asserted, "Islam is not a religion, it is a *din*"; interview with

Tahiru'l-Qadri; see also Muhammad Tahiru'l Qadri, *Minhaju'l-afkar* (Lahore, 1990), 1:405–416.

86. Mawdudi, *Fundamentals of Islam*, pp. 66–67, 93–100.

87. Ibid., pp. 93–97, and Sayyid Abu'l-A'la Mawdudi, *Tafhimat*, 1:46–73.

88. Mawdudi, *Let Us Be Muslims*, p. 145.

89. Mawdudi, *Qur'an ki char*, pp. 10ff.

90. On the devotion of mystics to God in Islam, see Annemarie Schimmel, *Mystical Dimensions of Islam* (Chapel Hill, N.C., 1975), pp. 289–292, and Seyyed Hossein Nasr, "God," in Seyyed Hossein Nasr, ed., *Islamic Spirituality* (New York, 1987), 1:311–323. For a discussion of this issue in the philosophy of Mulla Sadra, see James Morris, *The Wisdom of the Throne: An Introduction to the Philosophy of Mulla Sadra* (Princeton, N.J.: 1981), pp. 94–129.

91. Mawdudi, *Let Us Be Muslims*, p. 145, and Mawdudi, *Fundamentals of Islam*, p. 97. In a commentary on the first chapter on the Qur'an, Mawdudi wrote that *'ibadah* had three meanings: worship and devotion, submission and obedience, and subjection and servitude; see Mawdudi, *Introduction to the Study of the Qur'an*, p. 47.

92. Mawdudi, *Fundamentals of Islam*, p. 97; Mawdudi, *Tafhimat*, 1:46–73; and *RJI*, 6:121–134.

93. Nadwi, *'Asr-i hazir*, pp. 57–74; Khan, *Din kiya hey*; and 'Uthmani, "Hakimu'l-ummat," pp. 23–53.

94. Nadwi, *'Asr-i hazir*, pp. 82–83.

95. Khan, *Din kiya hey*; Khan, *Din ki siyasi ta'bir* (Lahore, n.d.); and Khan, *Ta'bir ki ghalti*.

96. See, for instance, Sayyid Abu'l-Hasan 'Ali Nadwi's biography of the founder of the Tablighi Jama'at, Mawlana Muhammad Ilyas: *Life and Mission of Maulana Mohammad Ilyas*, reprint (Lucknow, 1983), and Mawlana Wahidu'ddin Khan, *Tabligh Movement* (n.p., 1986).

97. See Nu'mani, *Tablighi Jama'at*.

98. Through this testimony one becomes a Muslim. On the notion of "internal conversion" in the Jama'at, see Israr Ahmad, *Tahrik-i Jama'at-i Islami: ik tahqiqi mutala'ah* (Lahore, 1966), p. 85. "Reconversion" to Islam was stipulated as a basic criterion for joining the Jama'at in 1941; see *RJI*, 1:45.

99. Cited in Sheila McDonough, *Muslim Ethics, and Modernity: A Comparative Study of the Ethical Thought of Sayyid Ahmad Khan and Mawlana Mawdudi* (Waterloo, Canada, 1984); p. 68.

100. *SAAM*, 1:250; *RJI*, 5:101, and 6:173–206; Sayyid Abu'l-A'la Mawdudi, *Hikmat-i tabligh* (Lahore, 1987); *JIKUS*, p. 13; and Ahmad, *Tahrik-i Jama'at*, pp. 51–54. Ahmad argued that the attention of the Jama'at was diverted from converting non-Muslims after the partition of the Indian subcontinent, *Tahrik-i Jama'at*, pp.114–115.

101. Mawdudi, *Hikmat-i tabligh*; and *RJI*, 1:12–13. Absence of a proselytical posture had been viewed by the Jama'at as the cause of eclipse of Islam in India and hence lay at the heart of the solution to its predicament; see *RJI*, 6:173–206.

102. Mawdudi, *Let Us Be Muslims*, pp. 26–33.

103. Seyyed Hossein Nasr, *Ideals and Realities of Islam*, 3rd ed. (London, 1975), p. 22.

104. The possibility of an understanding between Islam and Hinduism has been explored since the time of Emperor Akbar (d. 1605) and Prince Dara Shokuh (d. 1658), mainly through the aegis of Sufism; see Daryush Shayegan, *Hindouisme et Soufisme* (Paris, 1979). Similar attempts were made in modern times by Abu'l-Kalam Azad; see Ian Henderson Douglas, *Abul Kalam Azad: An Intellectual and Religious Biography* (Delhi,

1988); and in the aftermath of the Ayodhya crisis, see Niranjan Desai, ed., *Contemporary Relevance of Sufism* (New Delhi, 1993).

105. Mawdudi, *Islamic Way*, pp. 52–58.

106. See Khurram Murad's introduction to Mawdudi, *Let Us Be Muslims*, pp. 23–24.

107. Mawdudi, *Fundamentals of Islam*, pp. 109–134, 141; Mawdudi, *Towards Understanding Islam*, pp. 100–103; and Mawdudi, *Tafhimat*, 1:46–73.

108. Sayyid Abu'l-A'la Mawdudi, *The Islamic Movement: Dynamics of Values, Power and Change* (Leicester, 1984), pp. 111–121.

109. Mawdudi, *Let Us Be Muslims*, p. 165. *Hajj* (pilgrimage to Mecca) and *zakat* (obligatory almsgiving) were also treated in the same fashion.

110. Mawdudi, *Fundamentals of Islam*, pp. 42–43, and Mawdudi, *Towards Understanding Islam*, pp. 16–17.

111. For an interpretive examination of Qutb's ideas and their comparison with Mawdudi's works, see Leonard Binder, *Islamic Liberalism: A Critique of Development Ideologies* (Chicago, 1988), pp. 170–205.

112. Mawdudi, *Towards Understanding Islam*, p. 96.

113. Maryam Jameelah, *Who Is Maudoodi?* (Lahore, 1973), pp. 58–60.

114. Cited in ibid., pp. 12–13.

115. From the text of a speech delivered in February 1957, published as Sayyid Abu'l-A'la Mawdudi, *Tahrik-i Islami ka a'indah la'ihah-i 'amal* (Lahore, 1986), p. 38.

116. *RJI*, 6:434–440.

117. Jameelah, *Who Is Maudoodi?*, p. 15.

118. Mawdudi, *Islamic Law*, p. 22, and Mawdudi, *Islami tahzib awr uske usul'u mabadi* (Lahore, 1966), pp. 106–109.

119. Freeland K. Abbott, "Maulana Maududi on Qur'anic Interpretation," *Muslim World* 48 (1958), pp. 10–12. Abbott said that Mawdudi's position was most clearly evident in his treatment of the Ahmadis.

120. Freeland K. Abbott, "The Jama'at-i-Islami of Pakistan," *Middle East Journal* 11.1 (winter 1957): 39.

121. Mawdudi, *Fundamentals of Islam*, p. 22.

122. Sayyid Abu'l-A'la Mawdudi, *Murtad ki saza*, reprint (Lahore, 1981), p. 75.

123. Ibid., pp. 9–11.

124. Mawdudi, *Islamic Law*, pp. 13–46.

125. McDonough, *Muslim Ethics*, p. 70, and Mawdudi, *Musalman awr mawjudah*, 3:134.

126. Mawdudi, *Fundamentals of Islam*, pp. 33–40.

127. On the first example, see *RJI*, 2:17–18; on the second, see Mawdudi, *Tanqihat*, pp. 23–32, and Sayyid Abu'l-A'la Mawdudi, *Shakhsiyat* (Lahore, n.d.), pp. 155–156. *Din-i ilahi* was conceived by Emperor Akbar as a creed that would encompass elements from both Islam and Hinduism and work to unite the two communities.

128. Mawdudi, *Fundamentals of Islam*, pp. 68–70.

129. Jameelah, *Who Is Maudoodi?*, pp. 5–6.

130. Ibid., p. 69.

131. Ibid., p. 70.

Chapter 4

1. Sayyid Abu'l-A'la Mawdudi, *The Process of Islamic Revolution*, 8th ed. (Lahore, 1980), p. 17.

2. From Sayyid Abu'l-A'la Mawdudi, *Come Let Us Change the World* (Washington, D.C., 1972), pp. 142–143.

3. Kaukab Siddiq believes that before 1947 Mawdudi was openly leftist and far more supportive of revolution; see preface to Mawdudi, *Come Let Us Change*. Binder is also of the opinion that the Jama'at's attitude toward revolution changed after 1949, when Mawdudi accepted the Pakistani state as the basis for a future Islamic state. Binder regarded the Objectives Resolution as a harbinger of this change, for by committing Pakistan to Islam, it legitimized the existing state as the basis for a future one; Leonard Binder, *Religion and Politics in Pakistan* (Berkeley, 1961), pp. 194–195.

4. Arendt defined revolution as a process whereby "change occurs in the sense of a new beginning, where violence is used to constitute an altogether different form of government, to bring about the formation of a new body politic, where the liberation from oppression aims at least at the constitution of freedom"; Hannah Arendt, *On Revolution* (New York, 1965), p. 35. Huntington's definition closely parallels that of Arendt. He defined revolution as "the rapid and violent destruction of existing political institutions, the mobilization of new groups into politics, and the creation of new political institutions"; see Samuel P. Huntington, *Political Order in Changing Societies* (New Haven, Conn., 1968), p. 266.

5. Charles Tilly, *From Mobilization to Revolution* (Reading, Mass., 1978), pp. 191–192.

6. See A. Rashid Moten, "Pure and Practical Ideology: The Thought of Mawlana Mawdudi (1903–1979)," *Islamic Quarterly* 28:4 (1984), pp. 235–236.

7. *Short Proceedings of the 2nd Annual Conference, Jamaat-e-Islami, East Pakistan*, (Dacca, 1958), p. 8; enclosed with U.S. Consulate, Dacca, Dispatch no. 247, April 3, 1958, 790D.00/4-358, United States National Archives.

8. See, for instance, his vituperative language against the ruling political order in India in his Iqbal Day lecture in 1939; cited in *SAAM*, 1:168–169. See also *TQ*, March 1939, pp. 2–13.

9. For instance, having read Mawdudi's works in Arabic translation and in the context of Islamic revivalism in the Arab world, Lerman found him to be an avid revolutionary; see Eran Lerman, "Mawdudi's Concept of Islam," *Middle Eastern Studies* 17.4 (October 1981): 492–509.

10. Ibid., p. 500.

11. Enayat argued that emphasis on the need for an exact confluence of factors for effecting social change suggests the influence of al-Ghazzali and Ibn Khaldun on Mawdudi; see Hamid Enayat, *Modern Islamic Political Thought* (Austin, Tex., 1982), pp. 102–103.

12. Sayyid Abu'l-A'la Mawdudi, *Islam Today* (Beirut, 1985), pp. 16–48.

13. *TQ*, February 1936, p. 119.

14. *RJI*, 1:49–50.

15. Cited in Maryam Jameelah, *Islam in Theory and Practice* (Lahore, 1973), pp. 318–319. In his first book, Mawdudi had condemned the use of violence, see Sayyid Abu'l-A'la Mawdudi, *Al-Jihad fi'l-Islam*, reprint (Lahore, 1986), pp. 25–26.

16. *TQ*, August 1948, pp. 236–237.

17. Sayyid Abu'l-A'la Mawdudi, *Islamic Law and Constitution* (Karachi, 1955), p. 48.

18. Ibid., p. 52.

19. Ibid., pp. 48–52. See also his *System of Government under the Holy Prophet* (Lahore, 1978), pp. 9–10. Mawdudi cited the Prophet's gradual reform of the existing Arabian practices regarding intoxicants, slavery, and polygamy as examples of his reformist approach to legal and social change; cited in Freeland Abbott, *Islam and Pakistan* (Ithaca, N.Y., 1968), pp. 215–216.

20. Mawdudi, *Process of Islamic Revolution*, pp. 5–8, 25.

21. Mawdudi, *System of Government*, pp. 9–10, where he went to great lengths to

convince his readers of the peaceful nature and gentle enforcement of the Prophet's reforms and the society he had established.

22. Mawdudi, *Islamic Law*, pp. 99, 102. Again, Mawdudi's understanding of revolution had become institutionalized in the discourse on revivalism in Pakistan and found an echo in the proclamations of later movements such as Israr Ahmad's Tanzim-i Islami; see Israr Ahmad, *Minhaj-i inqilab-i nabawi* (Lahore, 1987). Although Ahmad, unlike Mawdudi, refused to renounce violence, he reiterated Mawdudi's position when he asserted that by the term revolution he merely meant a significant and qualitative change between the existing circumstances and the sought-after ones—what would result from revolution.

23. Mawdudi, *Process of Islamic Revolution*, pp. 25–26; and Mawdudi, *Istifsarat* (Lahore, n.d.), 1:157–158.

24. *SAAM*, 2:444–445.

25. Islami Jumhuri Ittihad was a Muslim League–led coalition of right-of-center and Islamic parties that was formed in 1988 in opposition to the Pakistan People's Party. The coalition formed a government in Pakistan in 1991–1993.

26. Interview with 'Abdu'l-Ghafur Ahmad in *Takbir*, August 15, 1991, p. 15.

27. Seyyed Vali Reza Nasr, *The Vanguard of the Islamic Revolution: The Jama'at-i Islami of Pakistan* (Berkeley, 1994), pp. 28–44.

28. Sayyid Abu'l-A'la Mawdudi, *Tahrik-i Islami ka a'indah la'ihah-i 'amal* (Lahore, 1986), p. 205.

29. Cited in an interview with Khurshid Ahmad, in Mutaqqiu'l-Rahman and Salim Mansur Khalid, eds., *Jab vuh nazim-i a'la the* (Lahore, 1981), 1:126.

30. Nasr, *Vanguard of the Islamic Revolution*, pp. 147–170.

31. Interview with Mawdudi in *Nawa'i Waqt*, November 11, 1963, p. 4.

32. This statement, which was made in 1963, is cited in Jameelah, *Islam in Theory and Practice*, p. 334.

33. Cited in Muhammad Saeed, *Lahore: A Memoir* (Lahore, 1989), pp. 224–225.

34. Interview with Mawdudi in *Chatan*, April 14, 1969, p. 3. Throughout this period, Mawdudi distinguished the Jama'at from the parties of the left by noting that the former advocated revolution without violence, whereas the latter favored a violent path to revolution. Cited in *SAAM*, 2:371–372.

35. *SAAM*, 2:444.

36. Interview with Khwajah Amanu'llah and Begum 'Abidah Gurmani.

37. Interview with Mawdudi in *Nawa'-i Waqt*, October 25, 1978, p. 1.

38. Ahmed believed that Mawdudi essentially wanted to support its use, see Ishtiaq Ahmed, *The Concept of an Islamic state: An Analysis of the Ideological Controversy in Pakistan* (New York, 1987), p. 103.

39. From the text of the Iqbal Day speech of 1939, published as Sayyid Abu'l-A'la Mawdudi, *Jihad fi sabil Allah*, reprint (Lahore, 1989), p. 3.

40. Ibid., p. 11.

41. Seyyed Hossein Nasr, "The Spiritual Significance of Jihad," *Parabola* 7.4 (fall 1982): 14–19.

42. Mawdudi, *Jihad fi sabil*, pp. 14ff. Binder wrote that Mawdudi did not see jihad as a way of converting non-Muslims to Islam, but only as a weapon to guarantee the right to proselytize. Muslims attacked the Byzantine, Persian, and Egyptian empires in the seventh century, said Mawdudi, not to force them to convert Islam, but to preserve the right to spread Islam; Leonard Binder, *Islamic Liberalism: A Critique of Development Ideologies* (Chicago, 1988), p. 181.

43. *Report of the Court of Inquiry Constituted under Punjab Act 11 of 1954 to Enquire into the Punjab Disturbances of 1953* (Lahore, 1954), pp. 221–223.

44. On the opposition to Liaqat 'Ali Khan's plan, see Binder, *Religion and Politics*, p. 211, and Abu Tariq, ed., *Mawlana Mawdudi ki taqarir* (Lahore, 1976), 2:73–77. On the opposition to Malik Firuz Khan Noon's plan, see U.S. Consulate General, Lahore, Dispatch no. 34, September 17, 1953, 790D.00/9-1753, United States National Archives, p. 3.

45. Sayyid Abu'l-A'la Mawdudi, *Sunnat'u bid'at ki kashmakash* (Lahore, 1950), pp. 33–39.

46. Interview with *Tasnim* (June 26, 1950) reprinted in S. Zakir Aijaz, *Selected Speeches and Writings of Mawlana Mawdudi* (Karachi, 1981), pp. 78–79.

47. Kaukab Siddique, "Islam and Social Change," *New Trend,* July 1977, p. 6.

48. Cited in S. Abdullah Schleifer, "Jihad: Sacred Struggle in Islam IV," *Islamic Quarterly* 28.2 (1984): 98. Siddiq himself admitted that Mawdudi was not keen on class analysis, but he believed that this was a later policy adopted after the creation of Pakistan; see Siddique, "Islam," p. 6. References to class analysis are extremely rare in Mawdudi's works, even before 1947; one of the rare occasions was Mawdudi's Iqbal Day lecture of 1939, cited in *SAAM*, 1:168–169.

49. Khurram Murad recalled that during his trip to Paris to meet with Ayatollah Khomeini, members of Khomeini's entourage, with the help of an American professor who served as the translator, severely criticized the Jama'at's approach to revolution, arguing that the Jama'at should engage forthwith in open revolutionary activism against the Pakistan state; interview with Khurram Jah Murad.

50. Interview with Qazi Husain Ahmad. Qazi Husain repeated this observation in several rallies as a justification for the Jama'at's support for the jihad in Kashmir since 1989.

51. Interview with Sayyid As'ad Gilani.

52. Interview with Sayyid Munawwar Hasan. See also Muhammad Salahu'ddin, "Qa'din-i Jama'at-i ki khidmat main chand ma'ruzat," *Takbir,* November 16, 1989, pp. 11–13.

53. Interview with 'Abdu'l-Ghafur Ahmad.

54. Interview with Sayyid As'ad Gilani in *Nida,* April 17, 1990, p. 12.

55. Interview with a number of Jama'at leaders, especially Khalil Ahmadu'l-Hamidi.

56. Sayyid Abu'l-A'la Mawdudi, "Three Virtues and Three Vices," *Muslim Digest* 9.12 (July 1959): 14–15.

57. Said Amir Arjomand, *The Turban for the Crown: The Islamic Revolution in Iran* (New York, 1988), p. 210.

58. Cited in Maryam Jameelah, *Who Is Maudoodi?* (Lahore, 1973), pp. 58–69.

59. Interview with Jan Muhammad 'Abbasi.

60. Sayyid Abu'l-A'la Mawdudi, *Tahrik-i Islami ki akhlaqi buniadin* (Lahore, 1968), p. 3.

61. Reprinted in Sayyid Abu'l-A'la Mawdudi, *Tahrik-i Pakistan awr Jama'at-i Islami* (Multan, n.d.), p. 16.

62. Charles J. Adams, "The Ideology of Mawlana Mawdudi," in Donald E. Smith, ed., *South Asian Politics and Religion* (Princeton, N.J., 1966), pp. 388–389.

63. Enayat, *Modern Islamic Political Thought*, p. 103.

64. Sayyid Abu'l-A'la Mawdudi, *Dakter ka nishtar ya daku ka khanjar* (Lahore, n.d.), p. 5.

65. Na'im Siddiqi, *Al-Mawdudi* (Lahore, 1963), pp. 216–233.

66. For proceedings of that convocation, see Sayyid Abu'l-A'la Mawdudi, *Ta'limat*

(Lahore, n.d.), pp. 66ff. Mawdudi himself attributed his views on the political function of education to his discussions with Iqbal during their meeting in Lahore in October 1937; see Abu Tariq, *Mawlana Mawdudi ki taqarir,* 1:182–186.

67. *SAAM,* 1:291, and Naqi 'Ali, *Sayyid Mawdudi ka 'ahd* (Lahore, 1980), pp. 368–369.

68. Mawdudi, *Process of Islamic Revolution,* p. 17.

69. Ibid., pp. 16–17.

70. Mawdudi, *Tahrik-i Islami ka a'indah,* pp. 141–143.

71. *SAAM,* 2:70–72. Many of Mawdudi's proposals for education were first put to the test in the curriculum of the Medina University of Saudi Arabia, the establishment of which, in 1961 to 1962, Mawdudi played a part; see pp. 100–101.

72. See *TQ,* September 1934, pp. 2–9, and Binder, *Religion and Politics,* pp. 83–89. The Nadwah was the only traditional institution with which Mawdudi felt affinity, and which he sought to emulate. For more on the Nadwis, see Barbara D. Metcalf, *Islamic Revival in British India: Deoband, 1860–1900* (Princeton, N.J., 1982), pp. 335–347. Mawdudi had also been fond of Shibli Nu'mani, an eminent scholar and a founder of the Nadwatu'l-'Ulama; see Sayyid Abu'l-Khayr Mawdudi, "Abu'l-A'la ka uslub-i tahrir," in *SSMN,* pp. 365–366. On the possible influence of Nu'mani's attempts to augment the power of the ulama on Mawdudi's thinking, see S. M. Ikram, *Modern Muslim India and the Birth of Pakistan,* 2nd ed. (Lahore, 1965), p. 137.

73. Interview with Israr Ahmad.

74. Interview with Muhammad Tahiru'l-Qadri.

Chapter 5

1. Michael Walzer, *The Revolution of Saints: A Study in the Origins of Radical Politics* (Cambridge, Mass., 1965), p. 51.

2. Sayyid Abu'l-A'la Mawdudi, *Shahadat-i haqq* (Lahore, 1970), pp. 11–13; *TQ,* April 1941, pp. 90–101.

3. *TUTQ,* 1:25. Also see Charles J. Adams, "Mawdudi and the Islamic State," in John L. Esposito, ed., *Voices of Resurgent Islam* (New York, 1983), pp. 111–112.

4. Sayyid Abu'l-A'la Mawdudi, *The Islamic Way of Life* (Leicester, 1986), p. 9.

5. See Khurram Murad's preface to Mawdudi, *Islamic Way,* p. 22. Ayatollah Khomeini reacted in the same fashion to suggestions that Islam and politics were separate; he derided such suggestions as "imperialist plots against Islam"; see Hamid Algar, trans., *Islam and Revolution: Writings and Declarations of Imam Khomeini* (Berkeley, Calif., 1981), pp. 139–141.

6. *Report of the Court of Inquiry Constituted under Punjab Act 11 of 1954 to Enquire into the Punjab Disturbances of 1953* (Lahore, 1954), p. 228; see also Muhammad Munir, *From Jinnah to Zia* (Lahore, 1979), p. 65.

7. Sayyid Abu'l-A'la Mawdudi, *Islami tahzib awr uske usul'u mabadi* (Lahore, 1966).

8. Sayyid Abu'l-A'la Mawdudi, *The Ethical View-Point of Islam* (Lahore, 1953), p. 33.

9. Sayyid Abu'l-A'la Mawdudi, *Jama'at-i Islami; tarikh, maqsad awr la'ihah-i 'amal,* reprint (Lahore, 1963), pp. 8–9, 17–19; and Mawdudi, *Tahrik-i Islami ki akhlaqi buniadin* (Lahore, 1968), pp. 38–39.

10. Translation by Mohammed Marmaduke Pickthall, *The Meaning of the Glorious Koran,* reprint (New York, n.d.), p. 345.

11. Interview with Javid Ahmadu'l-Ghamidi, who studied the Qur'an with Mawdudi for a number of years.

12. Regarding the sovereignty of God, see Sayyid Abu'l-A'la Mawdudi, "Economic

and Political Teachings of the Qur'an," in M. M. Sharif, ed., *A History of Muslim Philosophy* (Wiesbaden, 1963), 1:178–198. For the thoughts on divine leadership and government, see Mawdudi, *Tahrik-i Islami ki akhlaqi*, pp. 9ff.; and *RJI*, 3:212–215.

13. Sayyid Abu'l-A'la Mawdudi, *Tahrik-i Islami ka a'indah la'ihah-i 'amal* (Lahore, 1986), pp. 30ff, and Mawdudi, *Islamic Law and Constitution* (Karachi, 1955), pp. 127–128.

14. Sayyid Abu'l-A'la Mawdudi, *The Process of Islamic Revolution*, 8th ed. (Lahore, 1980), p. 14; Mawdudi, *Tahrik-i Islami ki akhlaqi*, pp. 25–26; and Mawdudi, *Jama'at-i Islami; tarikh*, pp. 7–11.

15. Mawdudi, *Shahadat-i haqq*, pp. 17–18.

16. Mawdudi, *Tahrik-i Islami ka a'indah*, pp. 66ff.; Mawdudi, *Ethical View-Point*, pp. 13–14; Mawdudi, *Shahadat-i haqq*, pp. 5–8; and Mawdudi, *Islami riyasat* (Lahore, 1969), p. 131.

17. Sayyid Abu'l A'la Mawdudi, *Islamic Economic System: Principles and Objectives* (Delhi, 1980), p. 21.

18. Sayyid Abu'l-A'la Mawdudi, *Tanqihat*, 22nd ed. (Lahore, 1989), p. 123ff.

19. Maryam Jameelah, *Who Is Maudoodi?* (Lahore, 1973), p. 56.

20. Ibid., p. 57.

21. Mawdudi, *Process of Islamic Revolution*, p. 46, and Mawdudi, *Islamic Law*, p. 31. "Coercion" was not, however, fully explained, and Mawdudi's reasons for using this term remain open to interpretation.

22. *TUTQ*, 1:10, 17, and Mawdudi, *Shahadat-i haqq*, p. 6.

23. Sayyid Abu'l-A'la Mawdudi, *Let Us Be Muslims*, (Leicester, 1985), pp. 295–296.

24. Mawdudi, *Islamic Economic System*, pp. 20, 21.

25. For the traditional view on jihad, see Seyyed Hossein Nasr, "The Spiritual Significance of Jihad," *Parabola* 7.4 (fall 1982): 14–19. Regarding Mawdudi's views, see Mawdudi, *Let Us Be Muslims*, pp. 299–300; Mawdudi, *Tafhimat* (Lahore, 1965), 1:74–97; and Mawdudi, *Come Let Us Change the World* (Washington, D.C., 1972), pp. 142–445. See also S. Abdullah Schleifer, "Jihad: Sacred Struggle in Islam IV," *Islamic Quarterly* 28.2 (1984): 96.

26. Translation from Mawdudi's *Al-Jihad fi'l-Islam*, cited in Schleifer, "Jihad," pp. 97–98.

27. The term *hizbu'llah* was first used by Azad in reference to an organization that he had envisioned for the realization of Muslim political aspirations; see Ian Henderson Douglas, *Abul Kalam Azad: An Intellectual and Religious Biography* (Delhi, 1988), pp. 114–126. On Mawdudi's use of the term, see Mawdudi, *Tafhimat*, 1:86, and Mawdudi, *Mas'alah-i qaumiyat*, reprint (Lahore, 1982), p. 103. See also Israr Ahmad, *Islam awr Pakistan: tarikhi, siyasi, 'ilmi awr thiqafati pasmanzar* (Lahore, 1983), pp. 84–85.

28. *TQ*, May 1939, p. 9.

29. Mawdudi, *Ethical View-Point*; Mawdudi, *'Asr-i hazir main ummat-i muslimah ke masa'il awr unka hall* (Lahore, 1988), pp. 13–94; Mawdudi, *Let Us Be Muslims*, pp. 298–299; and Mawdudi, *Tahrik-i Islami ki akhlaqi*, pp. 27–56.

30. Mawdudi, *Tahrik-i Islami ki akhlaqi*, p. 3.

31. For a discussion of this question, see Adams, "Mawdudi"; Ishtiaq Ahmed, *The Concept of an Islamic State: An Analysis of the Ideological Controversy in Pakistan* (New York, 1987), pp. 93–111; Zafaryab Ahmed, "Maudoodi's Islamic State," in Asghar Khan, ed., *Islam, Politics and the State: The Pakistan Experience* (London, 1985), pp. 95–113; Hamid Enayat, *Modern Islamic Political Thought* (Austin, Tex., 1982), pp. 101–110; John L. Esposito, *Islam and Politics*, 3rd ed. (Syracuse, N.Y.: 1991), p. 147; and Eran

Lerman, "Mawdudi's Concept of Islam," *Middle Eastern Studies* 17.4 (October 1981): 492–509.

32. H. A. R. Gibb, *Modern Trends in Islam* (Chicago, 1947), p. 64; this tendency was previously associated with Islamic modernism.

33. On the emancipatory nature of nationalism, see Liah Greenfeld, *Nationalism: Five Roads to Modernity* (Cambridge, Mass., 1992), p. 10.

34. Stanley Wolpert, *Jinnah of Pakistan* (New York, 1984). For 'Ali's ideas, see Choudhary Rahmat Ali, *India: The Continent of Dinia or the Country of Doom?* (n.p., 1945).

35. For a general discussion of the role of elites in forming such identities, see Paul Brass, *Ethnicity and Nationalism: Theory and Comparison* (London, 1991), pp. 1–108.

36. For more on Mawdudi's contribution to Muslim communalism and his debates with Muslim supporters of the Congress party and Jinnah, see Seyyed Vali Reza Nasr, "Communalism and Fundamentalism: A Re-examination of the Origins of Islamic Fundamentalism," *Contention* 4.2 (winter 1995): 121–139.

37. Mumtaz Ahmad, "Parliament, Parties, Polls, and Islam: Issues in the Current Debate on Religion and Politics in Pakistan," *American Journal of the Islamic Social Sciences* 2.1 (spring 1985): 15–28.

38. See Seyyed Vali Reza Nasr, *The Vanguard of Islamic Revolution: The Jama'at-i Islami of Pakistan* (Berkeley, Calif.: 1994), pp. 28–44, for the reasons for this change in strategy.

39. Mawdudi, *Process of Islamic Revolution*, pp. 5–7.

40. For objections, see, for instance, Mawlana Muhammad Taqi 'Uthmani, "Hakimu'l-ummat ki siyasi afkar," *Al-Balagh*, March 1990, p. 33. For Mawdudi's views, see Sayyid Abu'l-A'la Mawdudi, *System of Government under the Holy Prophet* (Lahore, 1978), pp. 21–22.

41. Sayyid Abu'l-A'la Mawdudi, *The Message of Jama'at-i-Islami* (Lahore, 1955), p. 46.

42. Talmon made similar observations regarding Protestant messianism in nineteenth-century Europe. See Jacob Talmon, *Political Messianism: The Romantic Phase* (New York, 1960), p. 24. See also Arendt: "The thread of historical continuity was the first substitute for tradition; by means of it, the overwhelming mass of the most divergent values . . . were reduced to a unilinear, diametrically consistent development actually designed to repudiate not tradition as such but authority of all traditions." Hannah Arendt, "Tradition and the Modern Age," in Hannah Arendt, ed., *Between Past and Future* (New York, 1985), p. 28.

43. Sayyid Abu'l-A'la Mawdudi, *Khilafat'u mulukiyat* (Lahore, 1966), chap. 1, and *Islami riyasat*, p. 129. Mawdudi's claim for the superiority of Islam over secular democracy was often supported by what Esposito identified as one-sided polemics that compared Islam at its best with selective evils witnessed in the West, which Mawdudi took to represent the Western civilization as a whole. See John L. Esposito, *Islam the Straight Path* (New York, 1988), p. 189. A case in point in this regard is Mawdudi's continuous reference to the issue of slavery and minority rights in the West; see, for instance, Sayyid Abu'l-A'la Mawdudi, *Human Rights in Islam* (Leicester, 1976), p. 19, and *Islamic Law*, p. 173.

44. Khurshid Ahmad's talk at the University of South Florida and the World and Islamic Studies Enterprise conference, Tampa, Florida, May 15, 1993.

45. See Mumtaz Ahmad's discussion of this issue in Timothy D. Sisk, *Islam and Democracy: Religion, Politics, and Power in the Middle East* (Washington, D.C., 1992), pp. 25–26.

46. Said Amir Arjomand, "Religion and Constitutionalism in Western History and

in Modern Iran and Pakistan," in Said Amir Arjomand, ed., *The Political Dimensions of Religion* (Albany, N.Y., 1993), p. 93.

47. See *TQ,* January 1937, pp. 322–333, and Mawdudi, *System of Government,* pp. 6–7.

48. Mawdudi, *Islamic Law,* p. 81; Mawdudi, *Islamic Way,* p. 29; Mawdudi, *Khilafat'u,* (Lahore, 1966), chap. 1; and Mawdudi, *Human Rights,* pp. 10ff.

49. Cragg wrote that for Mawdudi, the dictum "there is no god but God" was understood as "there is no law-giver but God," see Kenneth Cragg, *Counsels in Contemporary Islam* (Edinburgh, 1965), p. 121. Regarding God's role as head of the sociopolitical order, see Mawdudi, *Process of Islamic Revolution,* pp. 13–17.

50. Mawdudi, *Khilafat'u,,* chap. 1. In the classical sources, it is man who is seen as God's vicegerent. Mawdudi, however, dissolved man's vicegerency into a collective vicegerency, which was vested in the Islamic state and its executive branch; see Mawdudi, *Islamic Law,* pp. 81–82.

51. Mawdudi, *Process of Islamic Revolution,* pp. 31–33.

52. Mawdudi, *Islamic Law,* p. 114.

53. Mawdudi, *Islami riyasat,* p. 127.

54. E. I. J. Rosenthal, *Islam in the Modern Nation State* (Cambridge, 1965), p. 138.

55. For instance, Mawdudi argued that the legislature was to have only an advisory role in the Islamic state; see Leonard Binder, *Religion and Politics in Pakistan* (Berkeley, Calif., 1961), p. 175.

56. Mawdudi, Islamic Law, pp. 115, 81–82.

57. Translation from Pickthall, *Meaning of the Glorious Koran,* p. 85.

58. Mawdudi, *Islami riyasat,* pp. 185–186, and Mawdudi, *Islamic Law,* pp. 119–120. For Khomeini's reference to and use of the same Qur'anic passage, see Said Amir Arjomand, *The Turban for the Crown: The Islamic Revolution in Iran* (New York, 1988), pp. 177–178.

59. *TQ,* January 1937, pp. 322–333, and December 1937, pp. 243–268; Mawdudi, *Islamic Law,* p. 122.

60. Mawdudi, *Islamic Law,* p. 124.

61. Mawdudi, *System of Government,* pp. 8–9.

62. The practice of *ijtihad* has, by and large, been suspended by Sunni Muslims and permitted on points not already decided by the recognized authorities. Modernist and revivalist thinkers since the nineteenth century have favored the reinstitution of *ijtihad* as a means of reforming the faith and reinterpreting its teachings in light of the modern world's requirements. For more on *ijtihad,* see D. B. Macdonald and J. Schacht, "Idjtihad," in *EI.* For a contemporary discussion of it, see N. J. Coulson, *A History of Islamic Law,* reprint (Edinburgh, 1978), pp. 202–217. For Mawdudi's views on *ijtihad,* see Sayyid Abu'l-A'la Mawdudi and Sh. Mohammad Abu Zahra, "The Role of 'Ijtihad' and the Scope of Legislation in Islam," *Muslim Digest* 9.6 (January 1959): pp. 15–20.

63. Cited in *Jasarat,* October 28, 1978, pp. 1, 9. Mujeeb characterized Mawdudi's program as naive; see Muhammad Mujeeb, *The Indian Muslims* (London, 1967), p. 403.

64. Mawdudi, *Islamic Law,* p. 81.

65. Ibid., p. 116.

66. For more on this theme, see M. Bernard, "Idjma'," in *EI.*

67. Mawdudi, *Islamic Law,* pp. 81–93.

68. For a discussion of this issue in Islamic revivalism in general, see Binder, *Islamic Liberalism: A Critique of Development Ideologies* (Chicago, 1988), pp. 243–44.

69. *TQ,* January–February 1936, pp. 388–400, and Mawdudi, "Economic and Political Teachings," p. 197.

70. Mawdudi, *Khilafat'u*, chap. 1.

71. Mawdudi, *Tafhimat*, 1: 98–113, and Mawdudi, *Human Rights* (Leicester, 1976), pp. 10–11. Mawdudi provided the example of slavery, which was abrogated in the West after a struggle but was banned in the *shari'ah*; see ibid., p. 19, and *SAAM*, 2:68–69.

72. Mawdudi argued that the Prophet's unwavering adherence to the *shari'ah* had preserved the Medina community and protected its democratic character; see Mawdudi, *System of Government*, pp. 6–7; see also Charles J. Adams, "The Ideology of Mawlana Mawdudi," in Donald E. Smith, ed., *South Asian Politics and Religion* (Princeton, N.J., 1966), p. 390.

73. Mawdudi, *Islamic Law*, p. 31.

74. *Ibid.*, pp. 128–129. Mawdudi argued that the caliphate, before it was corrupted, was also based on elections, and that democracy and Islamicity were already assimilated into its structure; see also Mawdudi, *Khilafat'u*.

75. Sayyid Abu'l-A'la Mawdudi, *Islam ka nazriyah siyasi* (Delhi, 1967), p. 86.

76. Mawdudi, *Islamic Law*, pp. 129–131, and Mawdudi, *System of Government*, pp. 9–13.

77. See *TQ*, February 1936, pp. 388–400, and January 1937, pp. 322–333.

78. Mawdudi was always emphatically opposed to primogeniture and often stated that rebellions were the result of fights against dynastic rule; he interpreted the uprising and martyrdom of Husain ibn 'Ali in the same light; see *TQ*, July 1960, pp. 194–206.

79. Mawdudi, *Islamic Law*, p. 151; see also Ahmed, *Concept of an Islamic State*, p. 113.

80. Sayyid As'ad Gilani, "Jama'at-i Islami, 1941–1947" (Ph.D. diss., University of Punjab, 1989–1990), pp. 299–347. For delegating more power to the judiciary and the legislature, see Mawdudi, *Islamic Law*, p. 131.

81. Schleifer, "Jihad," p. 97.

82. Mawdudi, *Tafhimat*, 3:129–152, and Mawdudi, *Islamic Law*, p. 131.

83. For more on these institutions, see Fazlur Rahman, "The Principle of Shura and the Role of the Ummah in Islam," in Mumtaz Ahmad, ed., *State, Politics, and Islam* (Indianapolis, 1986), pp. 87–96, and Editor, "Ahl al-Hall wa'l-'Akd," in *EI*.

84. Mawdudi, *Islamic Law*, pp. 136–137; and Mawdudi, *Islami riyasat*, p. 325.

85. Sayyid Abu'l-A'la Mawdudi, *First Principles of the Islamic State*, 6th ed. (Lahore, 1983), p. 6.

86. *TQ*, October–December 1938, pp. 315–316.

87. Mawdudi, *Islamic Law*, pp. 137–138, 151.

88. Ibid., p. 138.

89. Ibid., pp. 138–139, and Mawdudi, "Economic and Political Teachings, " p. 197.

90. Nasr, *Vanguard of Islamic Revolution*, pp. 28–43.

91. From the original draft of Mawdudi's speech before the extraordinary session of the Jama'at-i Islami in February of 1957; cited in *Mithaq* 38.12 (February 1990): 24.

92. Mawdudi, *First Principles*, p. 1.

93. See Mawdudi, *Islamic Law*, pp. 52–57.

94. Ibid., p. 51.

95. Ibid., pp. 3–6.

96. Mawdudi, *Islami riyasat*, p. 325.

97. Mawdudi, *Islamic Law*, pp. 32–35.

98. Ibid., p. 43. As *ijma'* is the only mechanism that includes the citizenry of the Islamic state in the constitution-making process, its importance as a source for new laws is discounted by Mawdudi. See Binder, *Religion and Politics*, pp. 320–327.

99. Mawdudi, *Islamic Law*, pp. 36–38.

100. Ibid., p. 57.

101. Ibid., pp. 67–73.

102. Ibid., pp. 6–7.

103. Ibid., pp. 158–159.

104. See his *System of Government*, p. 8.

105. Mawdudi, *Islamic Law*, pp. 146–147, 154–155; Mawdudi, "Economic and Political Teachings," p. 195; Mawdudi, *Human Rights*, pp. 11–30; and Mawdudi, "Three Virtues and Three Vices," *Muslim Digest* 9.12 (July 1959): 14.

106. Mawdudi, *Human Rights*, pp. 31–32, and Mawdudi, *Islamic Law*, p. 67.

107. Mawdudi, *Islamic Law*, p. 56.

108. Ibid., p. 24.

109. Mawdudi, *Human Rights*, pp. 24–26, 28. This pamphlet is the text of a lecture delivered in 1975.

110. Mawdudi, *Islamic Law*, p. 150.

111. Ibid., pp. 139, 161.

112. Cited in *Jasarat*, October 25, 1978, pp. 1, 9.

113. Schleifer, "Jihad," p. 95.

114. Khurshid Ahmad, *Studies in the Family Law of Islam* (Karachi, 1961), pp. 23–25. Women are excluded from the leadership of society and are generally entrusted to the care of men lest the Islamic state suffer the consequence of their greater freedom; see Mawdudi's *Purdah and the Status of Women in Islam*, reprint (Lahore, 1972), pp. 17–37, and Mawdudi, *Islamic Law*, pp. 86–87. Mawdudi cited the Qur'anic verse, "Men are in charge of women" (4:34) and the prophetic saying: "Verily, that nation would not prosper which hands over the reins of its government to a woman" to bolster his conclusions; see *Islamic Law*, pp. 139–140.

115. See Ann Elizabeth Mayer, *Islam and Human Rights: Tradition and Politics* (Boulder, Colo., 1991), pp. 93–108, 143–161.

116. *TQ*, August 1948, pp. 211–235.

117. Mawdudi, *Islamic Law*, pp. 171–172, and Mawdudi, *Islami riyasat main zimmiun ke huquq* (Lahore, 1954).

118. Mawdudi, *Islamic Law*, pp. 172–173.

119. *Report of the Court of Inquiry*, p. 228, and Munir, *From Jinnah to Zia*, p. 65.

120. Wolpert, *Jinnah*, p. 27.

121. For more on the *millet* system, see M. O. H. Ursinus, "Millet," in *EI*. On Mawdudi's reference to the *millet* system, see *White Paper on Electorate Issue* (Karachi, 1957).

122. Mawdudi, *Islamic Law*, p. 143.

123. Mawdudi, *Islami riyasat main zimmiun*; Mawdudi, *Islamic Law*, p. 45; and Mawdudi, *Al-Jihad*, chap. 1.

124. Cited in *RJI*, 5:178.

125. *SAAM*, 2:1–3.

126. Khurshid Ahmad, "The Nature of Islamic Resurgence," in John L. Esposito, ed., *Voices of Resurgent Islam* (New York, 1983), pp. 225–226.

127. Nasr, *Vanguard of the Islamic Revolution*, pp. 28–44, 81–100, 188–205.

128. For a general discussion of Islamic economics, see Farhad Nomani and Ali Rahnema, *Islamic Economic Systems* (London, 1994); Seyyed Vali Reza Nasr, "Towards a Philosophy of Islamic Economics," *Muslim World*, 77.3–4 (July–October 1987): 175–196; Nasr, "Islamic Economics: Novel Perspectives on Change," *Middle Eastern Studies* 25.4 (October 1989): 516–530; and Timur Kuran, "The Economic Impact of

Islamic Fundamentalism," in Martin Marty and R. Scott Appelby, eds., *Fundamentalisms and the State* (Chicago, 1993), pp. 302–341.

129. Sayyid Abu'l-A'la Mawdudi, *Economic System of Islam*, reprint (Lahore, 1984), pp. 17–18.

130. Mawdudi, *Islamic Economic System,* p. 26.

131. Mawdudi, *Economic System*, pp. 18–19.

132. Mawdudi, "Economic and Political Teachings," pp. 178–179; Mawdudi, *Economic System*, pp. 298–301; and Mawdudi, *Islamic Economic System*, p. 20.

133. Mawdudi, *Economic System*, pp. 10–11, 84.

134. Ibid., pp. 9–10.

135. Ishtiaq Ahmed, *Concept of an Islamic State*, p. 106.

136. Sayyid Abu'l-A'la Mawdudi, *Capitalism, Socialism and Islam* (Lahore, 1977), p. 65.

137. Ibid., pp. 66, 123–134.

138. Mawdudi, *Economic System*, pp. 90–92.

139. Ibid., pp. 87–88, 132ff.

140. Mawdudi, "Economic and Political Teachings," p. 179, and Mawdudi, *Mas'alah-i malikiyat-i zamin* (Lahore, 1982).

141. Mawdudi, *Economic System*, pp. 3–5; on the discussion of this issue in Islamic economics, see Nasr, "Towards a Philosophy of Islamic Economics," pp. 186–187.

142. Mawdudi, *Economic System*, pp. 3–5. See also Enayat, *Modern Islamic Political Thought*, p. 108. Some among Jama'at's senior leaders differed with Mawdudi on this issue. Amin Ahsan Islahi, one of Mawdudi's senior lieutenants in the 1950s, was far more anticapitalist and populist than Mawdudi. In fact, the American consul concluded that Islahi had Communist leanings; see U.S. Embassy, Karachi, Dispatch no. 660, December 11, 1951, 790D.00/11-2851, United States National Archives.

143. Mawdudi's attitude in this regard had interesting parallels to the Christian world. For instance, the origins of the Communion and Liberation movement of Father Luigi Giussani, established in northern Italy in the 1950s to spearhead Catholic revival in Italy, can be traced directly to competition with communism. The movement was also greatly influenced by the efficacy of Communist methods, especially in forming unified organizational structures. See Gilles Kepel, *The Revenge of God* (University Park, Pa., 1994), pp. 61–66. Mawdudi's association of socialism with challenge to the nizam's rule led to opposition to the Congress party and its socialist platform; see the text of Mawdudi's speech at the Madras gathering of the Jama'at in 1947, cited in *RJI*, 5:191–193.

144. Mawdudi's speech, *RJI*, 5:25–26, and Mawdudi, *Capitalism*.

145. Interview with Na'im Siddiqi in *Takbir,* September 26, 1991, p. 28.

146. Hamid Dabashi, "'Islamic Ideology': The Perils and Promises of a Neologism," in Hooshang Amirahmadi and Manoucher Parvin, eds., *Post-Revolutionary Iran* (Boulder, Colo., 1988), and Ervand Abrahamian, *Khomeinism* (Berkeley, Calif., 1993).

147. Mawdudi, *'Asr-i hazir*, pp. 114–115.

148. Mawdudi, *Economic System*, pp. 278–281.

149. Ibid., p. 103. When in 1990 the Soviet empire crumbled, Jama'at leaders viewed the events as a vindication of Mawdudi's views and a sign of his prescience, a message that was especially useful in their campaign to find a base of support in Central Asia.

150. From the text of lecture at a Labour Committee convention in 1957; reprinted in Mawdudi, *Economic System*, p. 284.

Chapter 6

1. For more on traditional Islam, see William A. Graham, "Traditionalism in Islam: An Essay in Interpretation," *Journal of Interdisciplinary History* 23.3 (winter 1993): 495–522, and Seyyed Hossein Nasr, *Traditional Islam in the Modern World* (London, 1987).

2. See, in this regard, Ernst Troeltsch, *The Social Teachings of the Christian Churches* (New York, 1949), and H. R. Niebuhr, *Social Sources of Denominationism* (New York, 1954).

3. For Mawdudi, learnedness was measured in terms of knowledge of the religious sciences and Arabic—a traditional qualification—as well as in terms of knowledge of modern subjects; see Sayyid Abu'l-A'la Mawdudi, *Economic System of Islam* (Lahore, 1984), pp. 298–299, 304. See also Sayyid Abu'l-A'la Mawdudi and Sh. Mohammad Abu Zahra, "The Role of 'Ijtihad' and the Scope of Legislation in Islam," *Muslim Digest* 9.6 (January 1959): 15–20; Sayyid Abu'l-A'la Mawdudi, *Tafhimat* (Lahore, 1965), 3:5–68; Hamid Enayat, *Modern Islamic Political Thought* (Austin, Tex., 1982), p. 101; and Sheila McDonough, *Muslim Ethics and Modernity: A Comparative Study of the Ethical Thought of Sayyid Ahmad Khan and Mawlana Mawdudi* (Waterloo, Ontario, 1984), p. 57. Mawdudi limited the scope of *ijtihad*, at least in part, to prevent its use in further corruption of the Islamic faith; see Mawdudi, *Tafhimat*, 3:11–13.

4. Hamid Dabashi, *Authority in Islam: From the Rise of Muhammad to the Establishment of the Umayyads* (New Brunswick, N.J., 1989), p. 71.

5. Robert Wuthnow, *Communities of Discourse: Ideology and Social Structure in the Reformation, the Enlightenment, and European Socialism* (Cambridge, Mass., 1989), p. 583.

6. Parallels here can be drawn with the recent history of the Muslim Brotherhood in Egypt. Sivan discussed debates within the ranks of the Muslim Brotherhood and other Egyptian revivalist groups as to whether they should leave Muslim society or remain attached to it. Central to this ideological debate, as can be discerned in the case of Mawdudi, was the issue of the prize at stake: Muslim society as a whole and the best strategy for winning it; see Emmanuel Sivan, *Radical Islam: Medieval Theology and Modern Politics* (New Haven, Conn., 1985), pp. 83–130. Mawdudi, for instance, was keen to win over the whole of Muslim society, rather than to give it up and start completely afresh.

7. For Jama'at's views on Islamic modernists, see Sayyid Abu'l-A'la Mawdudi, *Sunnat'u bid'at ki kashmakash* (Lahore, 1950); on Parwez, see Jalil Ahmad Rana and Salim Mansur Khalid, eds., *Tazkirah-i Sayyid Mawdudi* (Lahore, 1986), pp. 58–70; on the Khaksar, see Na'im Siddiqi, *Al-Mawdudi* (Lahore, 1963), pp. 38–39; on the Ahrar, see *Statement of Syed Abul Ala Maudoodi before the Punjab Disturbances Court of Inquiry* (Karachi, n.d.), p. 17; on Asad, see *Correspondences between Maulana Maudoodi and Maryam Jameelah*, 4th ed. (Lahore, 1986), p. 15; on Hakim, see Syed Riaz Ahmad, *Maulana Maududi and the Islamic State* (Lahore, 1976), pp. 91–93.

8. Leonard Binder, *Religion and Politics in Pakistan* (Berkeley, 1961), pp. 72–73, 225–227, and Charles J. Adams, "The Ideology of Mawlana Mawdudi," in Donald E. Smith, ed., *South Asian Politics and Religion* (Princeton, N.J., 1966), pp. 385–387. This article presents an excellent account of Mawdudi's debate with Islamic modernists. Mawdudi's ideas, method of argumentation, and style closely approximated the sort of modernist thought and style presented in H. E. Chehabi, *Iranian Politics and Religious Modernism: The Liberation Movement of Iran under the Shah and Khomeini* (Ithaca, N.Y., 1990), pp. 52–85. The need for distinction from modernism became more pronounced

for revivalism the more the two competed for the same classes or as the classes they represented began to contend for power; Leonard Binder, *Islamic Liberalism: A Critique of Development Ideologies* (Chicago, 1988), p. 357.

9. Parwez and his school of thought denied the authenticity of the hadith and hence rejected it as a source of Islamic law and practice. For more on Parwez, see Freeland Abbott, *Islam and Pakistan* (Ithaca, N.Y., 1968). Parwez had been a contributor to *TQ* during the journal's early years; see *TQ*, June 1938, pp. 279–284. Mawdudi also saw the "deniers of hadith" as leftists. He believed the Nizam-i Rububiyat (Divine Order) leftist movement to have been based on the works of Parwez, and, therefore, between 1960 and 1963, Mawdudi dedicated much effort to rejecting the ideas of Parwez; *SAAM*, 2:146–150. See also Rana and Khalid, *Tazkirah-i*, pp. 59–70; *TQ*, October–November 1960, pp. 97–120; and Sayyid Abu'l-A'la Mawdudi, *Sunnat ki a'ini haithiyat* (Lahore, 1963). For a thorough treatment of this subject, see Charles J. Adams, "The Authority of the Prophetic Hadith in the Eyes of some Modern Muslims," in Donald P. Little, ed., *Essays in Islamic Civilization Presented to Niyazi Berkes* (Leiden, 1976), pp. 25–47.

10. *SAAM*, 1:146, and 2:145, *TQ*, March 1934, pp. 57–64, and December 1958, pp. 29–43.

11. Mawdudi, *Tafhimat*, 1:202. Similarly, Mawdudi had criticized the Ahl-i Hadith, who recognized only the Qur'an and the hadith to the exclusion of the teachings of the schools of law. His criticism was essentially from the vantage point of the traditional perspective, enjoining adherence to the writ of the legal traditions (when he himself was attempting to break with them); *TQ*, July–October 1944, pp. 83–96.

12. Interview with Mian Tufayl Muhammad.

13. Clifford Geertz, "'Internal Conversion' in Contemporary Bali," in Clifford Geertz, ed., *The Interpretation of Cultures* (New York, 1973), pp. 170–189. For a general discussion of Islamic revivalism's break with traditional Islam, see Olivier Roy, *The Failure of Political Islam* (Cambridge, Mass., 1994), pp. 35–37.

14. See the introduction by Abu'l-Hasan 'Ali Nadwi to Mawlana Muhammad Manzur Nu'mani, *Mawlana Mawdudi mere sath rifaqat ki sarguzasht awr ab mera ma'uqaf* (Lahore, 1980), pp. 5–11, interview with Muhammad Tahiru'l-Qadri, in *Nida*, January 16, 1990, pp. 22–27; and Sayyid Abu'l-Hasan 'Ali Nadwi, *'Asr-i hazir main din ki tafhim'u tashrih* (Karachi, n.d.), pp. 31–42.

15. Israr Ahmad, "Naghz-i ghazal," *Mithaq* 39.1 (January 1990): p. 59.

16. *SAAM*, 1:315. See also Sayyid Abu'l-A'la Mawdudi, *Shahadat-i haqq* (Lahore, 1970), pp. 25–26.

17. Mawdudi, *Shahadat-i haqq*, pp. 25–26.

18. See, for instance, Abu Tahir Afaqi, *Fitnah-i mawdudiyat* (Jawharabad, n.d.). This appellation was later used by leftist intellectuals as a derogatory word for Mawdudi's reading of Islam; see Muhammad Safdar Mir, *Mawdudiyat Awr mawjudah siyasi kashmakash* (Lahore, 1970).

19. On the Ahmadis and the ulama's reaction to them, see Yohanan Friedmann, *Prophecy Continuous: Aspects of Ahmadi Religious Thought and Its Medieval Background* (Berkeley, 1989).

20. Interviews in Lahore.

21. For more on the idea of cumulative tradition, see Wilfred Cantwell Smith, *The Meaning and End of Religion* (New York, 1963). See also Nadwi, *'Asr-i hazir*. Schleifer argued that it was in the nature of his reliance on the fundamental sources of Islam rather than the cumulative tradition of Islam in India that distinguished Mawdudi from the ulama and placed him outside the pale of traditional Islam; see S. Abdullah Schleifer, "Jihad: Sacred Struggle in Islam IV," *Islamic Quarterly* 28.2 (1984): 93.

22. Enayat, *Modern Islamic Political Thought*, p. 102.

23. Maryam Jameelah, "An Appraisal of Some Aspects of Maulana Sayyid Ala Maudoodi's Life and Thought," *Islamic Quarterly* 31.2 (1987): 117.

24. See, Nadwi, *'Asr-i hazir*, p. 55. Here the author emphasized the sanctity of Islamic history and derided Orientalists and revivalists alike for misunderstanding that history and its place in the religion's spirituality. See also in this regard, Nadwi, *Islam and the World* (Beirut, 1983). For a discussion of this issue, see Seyyed Hossein Nasr, "Islam in the World Today: An Overview," in Cyriac Pullapilly, ed., *Islam in the Contemporary World* (Notre Dame, Ind., 1980), pp. 1–10.

25. Nasr, "Islam," pp. 6–7.

26. Mawlana Muhammad Manzur Nu'mani, *Tablighi Jama'at, Jama'at-i Islami, awr Brelwi hazrat* (Lucknow, 1980), p. 37.

27. Nasr, "Islam," pp. 6–7.

28. Shah Waliu'llah was a known Naqshbandi Sufi. He was also influenced by the transcendental theosophy of Mulla Sadra; see Hafiz A. Ghaffar Khan, "Shah Wali Allah: An Analysis of His Metaphysical Thought" (Ph.D. diss., Temple University, 1986). See also Sayyid Athar Abbas Rizvi, *Shah Wali-Allah and His Times* (Canberra, 1980).

29. For more on Sadra's philosophy, see Seyyed Hossein Nasr, *Sadr al-Din Shirazi and His Transcendent Theosophy* (Tehran, 1978), and Fazlur Rahman, *The Philosophy of Mulla Sadra* (Albany, N.Y., 1975). Regarding Mulla Sadra's dominance in India, see Seyyed Hossein Nasr, *Ma'rif-i Islami dar jahan-i mu'athir* (Tehran, 1969), pp. 123–132, and Ghaffar Khan, "Shah Wali Allah." In regard to the influence on the direction of Islamic theology, see Seyyed Hossein Nasr, "God," in Seyyed Hossein Nasr, ed., *Islamic Spirituality* (New York, 1987), 1:311–323.

30. For more on Sufism, see Martin Lings, *What Is Sufism?* (Berkeley, 1975); Annemarie Schimmel, *Mystical Dimensions of Islam* (Chapel Hill, N.C., 1975); and Seyyed Hossein Nasr, *Sufi Essays* (London, 1972).

31. Nu'mani, *Tablighi Jama'at*, p. 37.

32. Francis Robinson, "Scholarship and Mysticism in 18th Century Awadh," in A. L. Dallpiccola and S. Z. Lallemant, eds., *Islam and Indian Religions*, vol. 1: *Texts* (Stuttgart, 1993), pp. 377–398.

33. Nadwi, *'Asr-i hazir*, pp. 91–97.

34. See, for instance, his *Khilafat'u mulukiyat* (Lahore, 1966). For a general discussion of Islamic revivalism's attitude toward Islamic history, see Roy, *Failure of Political Islam*, pp. 73–74.

35. Nu'mani, *Mawlana Mawdudi mere Sath*, pp. 83–84.

36. For more on the Kharijis, see E. A. Salem, *Political Theory and Institutions of the Khawarij* (Baltimore, 1956); Dabashi, *Authority in Islam*, pp. 121–145; and W. Montgomery Watt, *Islamic Political Thought* (Edinburgh, 1968), pp. 54–57. Daryabadi cited in Mawlana Wahidu'ddin Khan, *Din ki siyasi ta'bir* (Lahore, n.d.), p. 5.

37. Cited in Wilfred Madelung, *Religious Trends in Early Islamic Iran* (New York, 1988), p. 54.

38. Nu'mani, *Mawlana Mawdudi*, pp. 84–85, and Khan, *Din ki siyasi ta'bir*, pp. 20–21.

39. Nu'mani, *Tablighi Jama'at*, pp. 54–55.

40. Regarding Mawdudi's claim of fidelity, see Sayyid Abu'l-A'la Mawdudi, "Abu Hanifah and Abu Yusuf," in M. M. Sharif, *A History of Muslim Philosophy* (Wiesbaden, 1963), 1:674–703. Mawdudi greatly extolled the efforts of Abu Yusuf, a Hanafi jurist, in reforming Islamic Law. For Mawdudi's approach, see *TQ*, July–October 1944,

pp. 86–93. See also *TQ*, November 1950, pp. 9–30, and February 1951, pp. 185–192.
Mawdudi encouraged others to choose one school of law after careful consideration
and remain bound by it. Otherwise, he gave equal weight to all schools, expressing no
preference among them; see Sayyid Asad Gilani, *Maududi: Thought and Movement*
(Lahore, 1984), p. 56.

41. Cited in *TUTQ*, 1:xvi–xvii.

42. Sayyid Abu'l-A'la Mawdudi, *Watha'iq-i Mawdudi* (Lahore, 1984), p. 83.

43. *TQ*, October 1980, p. 26, and Abad Shahpuri, *Tarikh-i Jama'at-i Islami* (Lahore,
1989), 1:525. During the same period, Mawdudi also made more direct overtures to
the Nadwi ulama. He traveled to Lucknow in 1940, staying at Nadwatu'l-'Ulama, where
he solicited advice and assistance from that institution for the Jama'at; interview with
Mawlana Sayyid Abu'l-Hasan 'Ali Nadwi.

44. Interviews with Islahi and Nadwi. 'Abdu'l-Ghaffar Hasan related a similar experience with his seniors when he joined the Jama'at; interview.

45. Sayyid Abu'l-A'la Mawdudi, *Islamic Law and Constitution* (Karachi, 1955),
pp. 105–106, and Mawdudi, *Tafhimat*, 1:202. The impact of this approach was clearly
evident in the favor shown for an "ulama-less" Islam by Islami Jam'iat Tulabah members, who were educated according to Mawdudi's prescriptions. This attitude was evident in the various interviews published in Sayyid Mutaqqinu'l-Rahman and Salim
Mansur Khalid, eds., *Jab vuh nazim-i a'la the* (Lahore, 1981).

46. See Abbott, *Islam and Pakistan*, p. 219, and Mawdudi, *Economic System*, p. 304.

47. See, for instance, Sayyid Abu'l-A'la Mawdudi, *A Short History of the Revivalist
Movement in Islam* (Lahore, 1963), pp. 44–87.

48. Cited in Maryam Jameelah, " Appraisal of Some Aspects," p. 121.

49. Israr Ahmad, *Islam awr Pakistan: tahriki, siyasi, 'ilmi awr thiqafati pasmanzar*
(Lahore, 1983), pp. 38–39.

50. Mas'ud 'Alam Nadwi, cited in *RJI*, 6:182–186.

51. Mawdudi viewed his campaign against the Jam'iat-i 'Ulama-i Hind's leaders
as ending *akabir-parasti* (worshipping the elders), a clear attack against the persons of
senior ulama and their institutional basis of authority; see Shahpuri, *Tarikh-i*, 1:348.
See also *TQ*, July–October 1935, pp. 82–88, and Sayyid Abu'l-A'la Mawdudi, *Musalman
awr mawjudah siyasi kashmakash*, vols. 1 and 2 (Lahore, 1939). Mawdudi equated the
alliance between Islam and nationalism, Hindu as well as Muslim, with Emperor Akbar's
din-i ilahi, as a syncretic pollution of the faith; see *RJI*, 5:182–183. On this issue see
also Ishtiaq Husain Qureshi, *Ulema in Politics: A Study Relating to the Political Activities
of the Ulema in South Asian Subcontinent from 1566–1947* (Karachi, 1972), pp. 330–339,
367–369, and Seyyed Vali Reza Nasr, *The Vanguard of the Islamic Revolution: The Jama'at-i
Islami of Pakistan* (Berkeley, 1994), pp. 103–115.

52. Nasr, *Vanguard of the Islamic Revolution*, pp. 116–146.

53. *RJI*, 5:97–98.

54. Cited in *SAAM*, 1:352.

55. Interview with Mawlana 'Abdu'l-Ghaffar Hasan. Regarding 'Uthmani's role in
Mawdudi's release, see *Chiragh-i Rah*, Qiyadat Number (September–November 1949),
pp. 123–125, and Sarwat Saulat, *Maulana Maududi* (Karachi, 1979), pp. 36–37. 'Abdu'l-
Ghaffar Hasan recalled that Mawdudi maintained contact with Mawlana 'Uthmani while
in prison through 'Abdu'l-Jabbar Ghazi and advised the eminent *'alim*, who was then in
the assembly, on various issues.

56. Binder, *Religion and Politics*, pp. 210–211.

57. Interview with Kawthar Niyazi.

58. Binder pointed out that Mawdudi was careful not to accede too much ground to the ulama. Hence, he did not approve naming the ulama as protectors of the *shari'ah* in the Board of Islamic Education and managed to remove a proposal to that effect from the twenty-two-points; see Binder, *Religion and Politics*, p. 217. Regarding Mawdudi's endorsement of Nadwi, see ibid., p. 214. For Mas'ud 'Alam Nadwi's role, see Akhtar Rahi, *Mas'ud 'Alam Nadwi: sawanih'u makatib* (Gujrat, Pakistan, 1975), pp. 38–39. For Sayyid Sulaiman's visit, see Rana and Khalid, *Tazkirah-i*, p. 149.

59. Binder, *Religion and Politics*, pp. 213–214.

60. I am grateful to Mumtaz Ahmad for pointing this out to me.

61. *RJI*, 6:93–94.

62. For the criticism of Mawdudi's views, see Shaikh Muhammad Iqbal, *Jama'at-i Islami par ik nazar* (Karachi, 1952), pp. 88–98. Gilani and Daryabadi had both known Mawdudi in Hyderabad at the 'Uthmaniyah University and had contributed to the *Tarjumanu'l-Qur'an* in its early years. For the *fatwas*, see *SAAM*, 1:394–406. For the campaign by Hasan and 'Ali, see Iqbal, *Jama'at-i Islami*, pp. 89–98.

63. In Saharanpur the *fatwa* was issued by Mufti Sa'id Ahmad of the Daru'l-Fatwa; in Malabar the campaign was headed by Mawlana Zafar Ahmad Thanwi; and in Lucknow the leader was 'Abdu'l-Bari Nadwi; see Iqbal, *Jama'at-i Islami*, pp. 98–101. For the accusations, see Mawlana Sayyid Ahmad Sa'id Kazmi, *Mukalamah-i Kazmi'u Mawdudi* (Lahore, n.d.), pp. 3–4; Mawlana Sayyid 'Abu'l-Haq, *Iza'-i fatawa: Mawlana Abu'l-A'la Mawdudi awr unki jama'at ke ara' par ik tabsarah* (Peshawar, n.d.), pp. 66–78; 'Allamah Mushtaq Ahmad Nizami, *Jama'at-i Islami ka shish mahall* (Lahore, n.d.), pp. 149–193; 'Allamah 'Amir 'Uthmani Fazil Deobandi, *Haqiqat* (Multan, n.d.); Afaqi, *Fitnah-i mawdudiyat*; Ahqar Mazhar Husain Ghafarlahu, *Mawdudi Jama'at ke 'aqa'id wa nazriyat par ik tanqidi nazar* (Jhelum, n.d.); Mawlana Ahmad 'Ali, *Haqq-parast 'ulama ki mawdudiyat se narazgi ke asbab* (Lahore, n.d.); Mawlana Sayyid Husain Ahmad Madani, *Mawdudi: Dastur Awr 'Aqa'id ki Haqiqat* (Delhi, n.d.); Qari 'Abdu'l-'Aziz, *Muhasabah-i Mawdudi* (Lahore, n.d.); and Iqbal, *Jama'at-i Islami*, pp. 98–101.

64. The Deobandi *'alim* and rector of a Deobandi seminary in Sind, Zafar Ahmad 'Uthmani, was incensed at Mawdudi's declaration and denounced him in the strongest terms; see Kawthar Niyazi, *Jama'at-i Islami 'awami 'adalat main* (Lahore, 1973), pp. 126–128.

65. Anonymous, *Khatre ki ghanti* (Lahore, n.d.).

66. For instance, among those who attacked Mawdudi through *fatwas* and books were Brelwi ulama Sayyid Ahmad Sa'id Kazmi of Jam'iat-i 'Ulama-i Pakistan; the Deobandi ulama, Sayyid 'Abdu'l-Haqq Zafar Ahmad 'Uthmani of Jam'iat-i 'Ulama-i Islam; Mufti Rashid Ahmad of the Ahl-i Hadith; and Abu Tahir Afaqi of the Tablighi Jama'at. Mawlana Ahmad 'Ali cited fifty-four ulama who supported the *fatwa* campaign against Mawdudi in Pakistan; Mawlana Ahmad 'Ali, *Haq-parast 'ulama*, pp. 15–50.

67. *TQ*, August and September 1936.

68. Sayyid Abu'l-A'la Mawdudi, *Tajdid'u ihya'-i din* (Lahore, 1952), p. 186.

69. Regarding Yusuf's defense of Mawdudi, see Mufti Muhammad Yusuf, *Mawlana Mawdudi par i'tirazat ka 'ilmi ja'izah*, reprint (Lahore, 1967); for a response, see Hazrat Mawlana Qazi Mazhar Husain, *Mufti Muhammad Yusuf sahab ke 'ilmi ja'izah ka 'ilmi muhasabah* (Jhelum, 1976). For the role of the ulama in Pakistan, see 'Abdu'l-Rahim Ashraf, *Kiya Jama'at-i Islami haqq par hey?*, reprint (Deoband, 1965). For other responses from the Jama'at, see *RJI*, 6:142–144; *TQ*, September 1951, pp. 74–91; Jamil Rana, *'Adilanah difa' awr 'ulama-i ahl-i sunnat* (Lahore, 1968); Abu Khalid, *Mawlana Mawdudi awr Jama'at-i Islami ke khalaf fatwa bazi ka ja'izah* (Gujranwalah, n.d.); Sajjad Jan,

Mawlana Mawdudi hi mujrim kiyun? (Lahore, n.d.); 'Asim Nu'mani, *Mawlana Mawdudi par jhute ilzamat awr unke mudallil jawabat* (Lahore, n.d.); Mawlana Abu Manzur Shaikh Ahmad, *Mawlana Mawdudi awr ghaltiyan* (Multan, 1958); and Sayyid Anwar 'Ali, *Radd-i sarguzasht* (Delhi, n.d.).

70. Sayyid Abu'l-A'la Mawdudi, *Witness unto Mankind: The Purpose and Duty of the Muslim Ummah* (Leicester, 1986), p. 72.

71. *SAAM,* 2:178–179.

72. For disputes surrounding Hanafi law, see ibid., pp. 365–366. For the uncharitable view of Caliph 'Uthman, see Mawdudi, *Khilafat'u,* chaps.1 and 2. For criticisms of Mawdudi regarding this book, see Khan, *Din ki siyasi ta'bir.* For a Jama'at response to Khan, see Malik Ghulam 'Ali, *Khilafat'u mulukiyat par i'tirazat ka tajziyah* (Lahore: Islamic Publications, 1972), and 'Asim Nu'mani, ed., *Makatib-i Sayyid Abu'l-A'la Mawdudi* (Lahore, 1977), 1:158–163. Although many ulama are aware of the shortcomings of Caliph 'Uthman's rule, criticisms of him are always guarded, to avoid lending support to the Shi'ite position. In this case, some may have overreacted, owing to their opposition to Mawdudi.

73. See Abu Yazid Muhammadu'ddin Butt, *Mujaddid-i tarikh jinab Mahmud Ahmad Sahab 'Abbasi ke khilaf Mawdudi sahab ki ghalat bayaniyun ka jawab* (Lahore, n.d.), pp. 18–19. For the damage to the Jama'at see the interview with Sayyid As'ad Gilani, in *Nida,* April 17, 1990, p. 12, and Ahmad Munir, *Mawlana Abu'l-A'la Mawdudi* (Lahore, 1986), pp. 110–111.

74. These were all produced in India; see Sayyid Ahmad Qadr, *'Asr-i hazir main din ki tafhim'u tashrih par ik nazar* (Lahore, 1979).

75. See, for instance, Hazrat Mawlana Qazi Mazhar Husain, *Tahaffuz-i Islam party ka intikhabi mauqaf* (Chakwal, 1977). Khurshid Ahmad argued that the ulama were particularly perturbed by the Jama'at's Yaum-i Shaukat-i Islam (Day of Islamic glory) rally in 1970, which was relatively successful; interview.

76. Imtiaz 'Alam, "Taraqqi-pasand talabah: lazzat-i shawq," in Salim Mansur Khalid, ed., *Talabah tahrikain* (Lahore, 1989), 2:36.

77. Interview with Khurshid Ahmad.

78. *Herald,* November 1992, p. 54.

79. Salim Mansur, "Islami university ka mutalabah," in Khalid, *Talabah,* 1:192.

80. On the Jam'iat's impact, see Rahat Gul, *Jama'at-i Islami ka tanha musafar* (Peshawar, 1992).

81. This section is based on interviews with Jan Muhammad 'Abbasi and Farid Ahmad Parachah; as well as with a number of ulama in the Jam'iat-i 'Ulama-i Pakistan and the Jam'iat-i 'Ulama-i Islam.

82. *Ijtima' se ijtima' tak (1963–1974): rudad-i Jama'at-i Islami, Pakistan* (Lahore, 1989), pp. 44–45. The *daru'l-'ulum* was later directed by Mawlana Fatih Muhammad, Mawlana Muhammad Chiragh, and Mawlana Gawhar Rahman, all educated as Deobandis, and, at the time of this writing, it is administratively under the supervision of Farid Ahmad Parachah.

83. Interview with Farid Ahmad Parachah. The first reference to a Jama'at *daru'l-'ulum* came in 1963; see Chaudhry Ghulam Muhammad, *Jamaat-e-Islami and Foreign Policy* (Karachi, 1963), p. 11.

84. Interview with Jan Muhammad 'Abbasi. See also Jan Muhammad 'Abbasi, *Khutbah-i istiqbaliyah, kull Pakistan 'ulama convention* (Lahore, 1989), and *'Ulama convention ki rudad* (Lahore, 1989), proceedings of the ulama convention held at Jama'at headquarters in Lahore, September 13 and 14, 1989.

85. The Jama'at also sought to change Mawdudi's image by arguing that his proc-

lamations were not personal, but official, reflecting the view of the party's *shura*'; interview with Farid Ahmad Parachah.

86. Interview with Qazi Husain Ahmad. See also Khurram Badr, *Qazi Husain Ahmad* (Karachi, 1988), pp. 21–28. It is probably with the same objective in mind that Mawlana Mawdudi's Deobandi *ijazahs* have been published and emphasized in recent years.

87. *RJI*, 3:160–161; see also Mawlana Shaikh Ahmad, *Mawlana Mawdudi awr tasawwuf* (Deoband, 1966).

88. Cited in *SAAM*, 1:175.

89. See Mawdudi, *Short History*, pp. 104–105, and Khurshid Ahmad, ed., *Adabiyat-i Mawdudi* (Lahore, 1972), pp. 216–293.

90. For more on this book, see Daryush Shayegan, *Hindouisme et Soufisme* (Paris, 1979).

91. For the important role of the *pirs* and *sajjadah-nishins* (hereditary community and religious leaders associated with Sufi shrines) in the Pakistan movement, see David Gilmartin, *Empire and Islam: Punjab and the Making of Pakistan* (Berkeley, 1988). For the role of the *pirs* in Punjabi society, see Katherine Ewing, "The Pir or Sufi Saint in Pakistan" (Ph.D. diss., University of Chicago, 1980). See also Sayyid Athar Abbas Rizvi, "Sufism in the Indian Subcontinent," in Seyyed Hossein Nasr, ed., *Islamic Spirituality* (New York, 1991), 2:239–258.

92. Ahmad, *Mawlana Mawdudi awr tasawwuf*. The author documented the negative responses that Mawdudi's attacks on Sufism generated.

93. *TQ*, September 1951, pp. 55–56, and November 1951, pp. 34–36. These denials happened just before the *fatwa* campaign against Mawdudi.

94. Interviews with disciples of 'Alau'ddin Shah. The correspondences were conducted over a number of years. They began as a debate between Mawdudi and the *pir* but ended with Mawdudi's acknowledgement of Sufism in the following terms: "I accept Sufism as you practice it."

95. 'Asim Nu'mani, *Tasawwuf awr ta'mir-i sirat* (Lahore, 1972). Mawdudi was by no means alone in trying to redefine Sufism. Since 1959 the Pakistan state, under Ayub Khan, Z. A. Bhutto, and Zia ul-Haq has also sought to reinterpret Sufism; see Katherine Ewing, "The Politics of Sufism: Redefining the Saints of Pakistan," *Journal of Asian Studies* 42.2 (February 1983): 251–268.

96. Sayyid Abu'l A'la Mawdudi, *Towards Understanding Islam* (Indianapolis, 1977), p. 111. Elsewhere he equated the Sufi *zikr* (mystical recitations) with remembering God and doing his work; cited in Philip Lewis, *Islamic Britain: Religion, Politics and Identity among British Muslims* (London, 1994), p. 107.

97. Sayyid As'ad Gilani, *Sayyid Mawdudi: bachpan, jawani, barhapa* (Lahore, 1978), p. 176. Gilani also argued that Mawdudi universalized Sufism, bringing it out of the *khaniqahs* (Sufi cloisters) into society.

98. A similar approach typified Mawdudi's treatment of such Sufi figures as Sirhindi and Sayyid Isma'il Shahid; see Mawdudi, *Shakhsiyat* (Lahore, n.d.), pp. 154–158, and Khurshid Ahmad, *Adabiyat*, pp. 225–229.

99. Khurshid Ahmad's talk at the University of South Florida, and World and Islamic Studies Enterprise conference, Tampa, Florida, May 15, 1993.

100. For use of Sufi terms by Mawdudi, see *JIKUS*, pp. 38–39, and Sayyid Abu'l-A'la Mawdudi, *Hidayat* (Lahore, 1967), pp. 14–15. For Mawdudi and the Sufi path, see Gilani, *Maududi*, pp. 242–257. For the Sufi influence on Mawdudi's organizational thinking, see Nasr, *Vanguard of the Islamic Revolution*, pp. 11–13.

101. For a general discussion of Sufism's role in transforming Islamic revivalism

from a radical force into a mainstream political actor, see John O. Voll, "Conservative and Traditional Brotherhoods," in Charles E. Butterworth and I. William Zartman, eds., *Annals of the American Academy of Political and Social Science* 524 (November 1992): 66–78.

102. Mawdudi's correspondences with 'Alau'ddin Shah dated from the time of this project. The Jama'at's overtures were received by some Qadri and Naqshbandi leaders; interview with Jan Muhammad 'Abbasi.

Chapter 7

1. The term is used here as it was used by Max Weber to distinguish charismatic authority from one rooted in bureaucratic structures, see his "Politics as Vocation" in H. H. Gerth and C. Wright Mills, eds. and trans., *From Max Weber: Essays in Sociology* (Oxford, 1946), pp. 77–128.

2. Interview with Josh Malihabadi, who had been a friend of the Mawdudi family since they lived in Hyderabad; cited in Ahmad Munir, *Mawlana Abu'l-A'la Mawdudi* (Lahore, 1986), p. 97. Mawdudi began writing poetry when he was nine; see Mujibu'l-Rahman Shami, "Kiran se aftab tak," in *HRZ*, p. 22; see also *SAAM*, 1:27, and Sayyid Abu'l-A'la Mawdudi, *Shakhsiyat* (Lahore, n.d.), pp. 209–211. Ghalib was an advocate of communal coexistence in India.

3. For more on Sirhindi's life and thought, see Yohanan Friedmann, *Shaikh Ahmad Sirhindi: An Outline of His Thought and a Study of His Image in the Eyes of Posterity* (Montreal, 1971).

4. Ja'far Qasmi in "Mujhe yad hey, sab zara zara," *Nida,* April 17, 1990, p. 32.

5. The depiction was made by Begum Mahmudah Mawdudi, cited in *SAAM,* 1:137–138.

6. Ibid., pp. 137–139.

7. Cited in Munir, *Mawlana Abu'l-A'la Mawdudi,* p. 125.

8. Interview with Begum Mahmudah Mawdudi.

9. Muhammad Yahya, "Sikandarpur se Lahore tak," in *QDMN*, p. 181.

10. Interview with Khwajah Amanu'llah.

11. *RJI*, vols. 3 and 4.

12. Letter from Mawdudi to Maryam Jameelah dated August 26, 1972, examined during an interview with Maryam Jameelah; see also Sarwat Saulat, *Maulana Maududi* (Karachi, 1979), pp. 89, 104–105.

13. *SAAM*, 1:203–206, and Sayyid Abu'l-A'la Mawdudi, "Pathankot se Lahore tak," in *QDMN*, pp. 225–226.

14. Mawdudi, "Pathankot se Lahore tak," p. 225.

15. Fazlur Rahman was convinced that in his own mind Mawdudi had resolved the conflict between scholarship and political activism. Rahman argued that Mawdudi coveted the title of scholar but cared little for scholarship. He recollected that, upon telling Mawdudi that he wished to pursue his doctoral studies, Mawdudi responded: "The more you study, the more your practical faculties will be numbed. Why don't you come and join the Jama'at." Cited in Fazlur Rahman, *Islam and Modernity: Transformation of an Intellectual Tradition* (Chicago, 1982), p. 117.

16. Sayyid Asad Gilani, *Maududi: Thought and Movement* (Lahore, 1984), p. 80. For a bibliography of Mawdudi's works, see Qazi Zulqadar Siddiq, S. M. Aslam, and M. M. Ahsan, "A Bibliography of Writings by and about Sayyid Abul A'la Mawdudi," in Khurshid Ahmad and Zafar Ishaq Ansari, eds., *Islamic Perspectives: Studies in Honour of Sayyid Abul A'la Mawdudi* (Leicester, 1979), pp. 3–14.

17. Interview with Hafizu'l-Rahman Ihsan.

18. Ibid.

19. *SAAM*, 2:478; and *SDMN*, p. 74.

20. Interview with Hafizu'l-Rahman Ihsan.

21. For Jama'at use of *unani* medicine, see Freeland K. Abbott, "The Jama'at-i-Islami of Pakistan," *Middle East Journal* 11.1 (winter 1957): 46. Regarding its use by the Deobandi ulama, see Barbara D. Metcalf, *Islamic Revival in British India: Deoband, 1860–1900* (Princeton, N.J., 1982), pp. 183–184.

22. Interview with Hafizu'l-Rahman Ihsan.

23. Ibid. Ihsan recalled that Mawdudi ordered Hakim Ni'mat's book to be reviewed and edited by a number of Jama'at figures, among whom were Ihsan and Sayyid As'ad Gilani, with a view to publishing it. The final manuscript remained with Mawdudi and was never published.

24. These are the words of 'Atiyah 'Inayatu'llah, a Western-educated politician and demographer who often visited the Mawdudis in the 1970s. Mawdudi never asked her to observe purdah when they were in his house. Interview.

25. Amin Ahsan Islahi, in *Mahnamah-i Chiragh,* October 1953, p. 10.

26. Ibid.; see also Khurram Murad's comments in Sayyid Abu'l-A'la Mawdudi, *The Islamic Movement; Dynamics of Values, Power and Change* (Leicester, 1984), pp. 11–13.

27. Malik Ghulam 'Ali, "Professor Mawdudi ke sath sath Islamiyah College se Zaildar Park tak," in *HRZ*, p. 125.

28. Interview with Chaudhri Aslam Salimi. In a similar fashion, many of Mawdudi's religious views were formed in discussions carried on in the pages of the *Tarjuman*.

29. Muhammad Saeed, *Lahore: A Memoir* (Lahore, 1989), p. 224.

30. Interviews.

31. Malik Ghulam 'Ali, "Professor Mawdudi," p. 122; he referred particularly to the years 1939 to 1940; and Yahya, "Sikandarpur se," p. 174. Yahya's observations pertain to the period when they lived in Pathankot, from 1941 to 1947. I am indebted to Mumtaz Ahmad for pointing out Mawdudi's debates with these Jama'at leaders.

32. Yahya, "Sikandarpur se," p. 176.

33. Interview with Javid Ahmadu'l-Ghamidi.

34. Regarding the schism in the Jama'at, see Mawlana Wahidu'ddin Khan, *Din ki siyasi ta'bir* (Lahore, n.d.), pp. 7–8, and Seyyed Vali Reza Nasr, *The Vanguard of the Islamic Revolution: The Jama'at-i Islami of Pakistan* (Berkeley, 1994), pp. 28–44. Islahi's complaint is in a letter from him to Mawdudi, in *Nida*, March 7, 1989, p. 28.

35. Interviews with Ghamidi, as well as with a number of current and former members of the Jama'at.

36. 'Aql-i-kull is a technical term in Sufism, meaning the Supreme Intellect. In common parlance, it has the meaning of "know-it-all." As used by Abu'l-Khayr Mawdudi to refer to his younger brother, it therefore had sarcastic connotations. Interview with Ja'far Qasmi.

37. Interview with Ja'far Qasmi.

38. Allahbukhsh K. Brohi, "Mawdudi, Pakistan ka sab se bara wakil," in *HRZ*, pp. 33–36. Jameelah made the point that Mawdudi's arguments in *Islamic Law and Constitution* were so compelling that even the Christian justice, A. R. Cornelieus, publicly advocated Mawdudi's position; see Jameelah, *Who Is Maudoodi?* (Lahore, 1973), p. 17.

39. Charles J. Adams, "The Authority of the Prophetic *Hadith* in the Eyes of Some Modern Muslims," in Donald P. Little, ed., *Essays in Islamic Civilization Presented to Niyazi Berkes* (Leiden, 1976), pp. 26–29.

40. See, for instance, Sayyid Abu'l-A'la Mawdudi, *The Islamic Way of Life* (Leicester, 1986); see also Mawdudi's introduction to *TUTQ*, 1:25.

41. At times, he elaborated on this dichotomy in terms of a comparative study of Islamic teachings with Western notions such as capitalism and socialism. In these cases, Mawdudi would outline fully the Western idea then systematically take it apart. See, for instance, Sayyid Abu'l-A'la Mawdudi, *Economic System of Islam* (Lahore, 1984).

42. Robert Wuthnow, *Communities of Discourse: Ideology and Social Structure in the Reformation, the Enlightenment, and European Socialism* (Cambridge, Mass., 1989), p. 13.

43. Martin Riesebrodt, *Pious Passion: The Emergence of Modern Fundamentalism in the United States and Iran* (Berkeley, 1993), p. 24.

44. Cited in Charles J. Adams, "The Ideology of Mawlana Mawdudi," in Donald E. Smith, ed., *South Asian Politics and Religion* (Princeton, N.J., 1966), p. 388.

45. H. A. R. Gibb, *Modern Trends in Islam* (Chicago, 1947), p. 64.

46. Sayyid Abu'l-A'la Mawdudi, *Purdah and the Status of Women in Islam*, reprint (Lahore, 1972), pp. 17–37. See also *TQ*, September 1936, pp. 53–80, and October 1936, pp. 126–50, where Mawdudi posited his arguments in a debate on Western thought and practice.

47. Gibb, *Modern Trends in Islam*, p. 64.

48. H. E. Chehabi, *Iranian Politics and Religious Modernism: The Liberation Movement of Iran under the Shah and Khomeini* (Ithaca, N.Y., 1990), p. 74.

49. A good example of Mawdudi's style of argumentation can be found in Sayyid Abu'l-A'la Mawdudi, *Khutbat*, 4th ed. (Lahore, 1989), chaps.1–3. The book has been published in English as *Fundamentals of Islam*, reprint (Delhi, 1978) and *Let Us Be Muslims* (Leicester, 1985).

50. On Mawdudi's Urdu style, see Na'im Siddiqi, "Mawlana Mawdudi rahmatu'llah alaihu ki lisani'u adabi khidmat," in *SSMN*, pp. 5–12. In a lecture at the Muslim Anglo-Oriental College of Amritsar in September 1939, Mawdudi presented twenty-five Urdu terms as equivalents for commonly used English political terms; see Abad Shahpuri, *Tarikh-i Jama'at-i Islami* (Lahore, 1989), 1:109–111.

51. For Mawdudi's style of debate, see Qasmi, "Mujhe yad hey," p. 32. For the discussion of his literary style, see Sayyid Abu'l-Khayr Mawdudi, "Abu'l-A'la ka uslub-i tahrir," in *SSMN*, pp. 365–366. Regarding his analytical approach, see Muhammad Yahya, "Sikandarpur se Lahore tak," in *QDMN*, p. 177.

52. On the importance of texts in defining new patterns of authority in a Muslim society, see Timothy Mitchell, *Colonising Egypt* (Cambridge, 1988), pp. 153–154.

53. Manzuru'l-Haq Siddiqi, "Tahrik-i Pakistan: talib-i 'ilm ki yadain," in Salim Mansur Khalid, ed., *Talabah tahrikain* (Lahore, 1989), 1:94.

54. Sayyid Abu'l-A'la Mawdudi, *Salamati ka rastah* (Pathankot, n.d.), p. 96.

55. Mawdudi, *Economic System*, pp. 87–112. Islam's teachings on economics do not advocate absolute equality but accept variations in wealth to the extent that they reflect differences in effort and skill. Moreover, Islam protects the right to private property and does not sanction expropriation of property or its nationalization. For more on Islam's views on economics, see Seyyed Vali Reza Nasr, "Towards a Philosophy of Islamic Economics," *Muslim World* 77.3–4 (July–October 1987): 175–196. For Mawdudi's writings on this issue, see Sayyid Abu'l-A'la Mawdudi, *Islamic Economic System: Principles and Objectives*, reprint (Delhi, 1980), pp. 6–7.

56. Sayyid Abu'l-A'la Mawdudi, *Al-Jihad fi'l-Islam*, reprint (Lahore, 1986), p. 25.

57. Maryam Jameelah, *Islam in Theory and Practice* (Lahore, 1973), pp. 318–319.

58. Sayyid Abu'l-A'la Mawdudi, *Islamic Law and Constitution* (Karachi, 1955), p. 204.

59. See, for instance, Islahi's letter to Mawdudi regarding the latter's leadership style. Islahi accused Mawdudi of Machiavellian tactics that sacrificed Islamic values. The letter is reprinted in *Nida*, March 7, 1989, p. 28.

60. Kawthar Niyazi, *Jama'at-i Islami 'awami 'adalat main* (Lahore: Qaumi Kutub-khanih, 1973), pp. 23–24, and Kalim Bahadur, *The Jama'at-i Islami of Pakistan* (New Delhi, 1977), p. 168.

61. For more on these issues, see Nasr, *Vanguard of the Islamic Revolution*, pp. 28–44.

62. See Zafar Ishaq Ansari's comments in *TUTQ*, 1: xx, 1–2.

63. See Francis Robinson, "Technology and Religious Change: Islam and the Impact of Print," *Modern Asian Studies* 27.1 (February 1993): 229–251. For a general discussion of the role of the oral tradition in Islam, see Seyyed Hossein Nasr, "Oral Transmission and the Book in Islamic Education: The Spoken and Written Word," *Journal of Islamic Studies* 3.1 (January 1992): 1–14.

64. Mawdudi was by no means unique in this regard. Mardin wrote that Badi'u'l-Zaman Sa'id Nursi of Turkey also relied on texts to establish the authority of his movement. He consciously sought to transfer charisma from personages to texts; Şerif Mardin, *Religion and Social Change in Modern Turkey: The Case of Bediüzzaman Said Nursi* (Albany, N.Y., 1989), pp. 181–182.

65. Regarding reliance on text as sign of Western influence, see Robinson, "Technology and Religious Change." For relevance of western influence to the failure of use of *tajdid*, see Abdelwahab El-Effendi, "The Long March from Lahore to Khartoum: Beyond the 'Muslim Reformation,'" *British Society for Middle Eastern Studies Bulletin* 17.2 (1990): 137–151.

66. Khurshid Ahmad's lecture at the University of South Florida and World and Islamic Studies Enterprise conference, Tampa, Florida, May 15, 1993.

67. Olivier Roy, *Islam and Resistance in Afghanistan*, 2nd ed. (New York, 1990), pp. 54–68.

68. Mawdudi's biographers have viewed Mawdudi as an heir to the widely popular Muhammad 'Ali and, to that end, have underscored his affiliation with him. Muhammad 'Ali is often depicted in Muslim accounts as a hero. The biographers state that Mawdudi rose to defend Islam after Muhammad 'Ali called on Muslims to do so before charges of "violence-mongering" were made against the religion in 1928, after the assassination of Swami Shradhanand. Although Mawdudi did not say he ever worked with Muhammad 'Ali on his journal, *Hamdard*, his biographies now claim that he did work at *Hamdard* before *Al-Jam'iat* in order to associate the two; see, for instance, Gilani, *Maududi*, p. 41. Mian Tufayl Muhammad stated that Mawdudi was deeply influenced by Azad's romantic notions of Muslim glory and his desire to restore Muslim political power; interview.

69. S. M. Ikram, *Modern Muslim India and the Birth of Pakistan* (Lahore, 1965), pp. 152–153.

70. Mawdudi's idea that the opening chapter of the Qur'an is a prayer to which the rest of the Qur'an is a response built on Azad's treatment of that chapter in his commentary. Mawdudi's understanding of the Qur'anic concept of *rabb* (lord) was close to Azad's understanding of *rububiyat* (lordship).

71. For more on Azad and the discussion of these themes in his life and works, see Ian Henderson Douglas, *Abul Kalam Azad: An Intellectual and Religious Biography* (Delhi, 1988).

72. Gail Minault, *The Khilafat Movement: Religious Symbolisms and Political Mobilization in India* (New York, 1982), p. 45.

73. Qazi Hasan Moizuddin, "Syed Abul A'la Maududi," in *The Muslim Luminaries; Leaders of Religious, Intellectual and Political Revival in South Asia* (Islamabad, 1988), p. 380.

74. Mawdudi's denial is cited in Abu'l-Afaq, *Sayyid Abu'l-A'la Mawdudi: sawanih, afkar, tahrik* (Lahore, 1971), p. 73. The statements by Mawdudi can be found in Moizuddin, "Syed Abul A'la Maududi," p. 385.

75. Sayyid Abu'l-A'la Mawdudi, *Musalman awr mawjudah siyasi kashmakash* (Lahore, 1940), 3:100, 123; see also Mawdudi's views on hadith commentary in Adams, " Authority of the Prophetic *Hadith*," pp. 25–47.

76. Cited in *SAAM*, 1:110–111.

77. Muhammad Yusuf Buhtah, ed., *Mawlana Mawdudi, apni awr dusrun ki nazar main* (Lahore, 1980), pp. 61–62; elsewhere, Chaudhri 'Abdu'l-Rahman 'Abd, *Mufakkir-i Islam: Sayyid Abu'l-A'la Mawdudi* (Lahore, 1971), pp. 158–164 outlined Mawdudi's exposition of this idea. 'Abd wrote that Mawdudi was highly aware of the history of *tajdid* movements, and especially about the reasons for their failure. He pondered much about applications of the doctrine to modern circumstances. In "Sikandarpur se Lahore tak," p. 132, Yahya wrote of Mawdudi's great awareness of the history of *tajdid* in Islam. For his discussion of the modernization of the doctrine of *tajdid*, see Sayyid Abu'l-A'la Mawdudi, "Ihya'-i Nizam-i Islami," *Al-Furqan*, Shah Waliu'llah Number (1940), p. 18.

78. See, for instance, Sayyid Abu'l-A'la Mawdudi, *Islam: An Historical Perspective* (Leicester, 1974), pp. 4–5.

79. Sayyid Abu'l-A'la Mawdudi, *A Short History of the Revivalist Movement in Islam* (Lahore, 1963), pp. 25–28. See also Sayyid Abu'l-A'la Mawdudi, *Khilafat'u mulukiyat* (Lahore, 1966).

80. Sayyid Abu'l-A'la Mawdudi, *Qur'an ki char buniadi istilahain: ilah, rabb, 'ibadat, din* (Lahore, 1988), p. 8. On the meaning and significance of *tajdid* and *islah*, see John O. Voll, "Renewal and Reform in Islamic History: *Tajdid* and *Islah*," in John L. Esposito, ed., *Voices of Resurgent Islam* (New York, 1983), pp. 32–47; see also Seyyed Hossein Nasr, "Decadence, Deviation and Renaissance in the Context of Contemporary Islam," in Khurshid Ahmad and Zafar Ishaq Ansari, eds., *Islamic Perspectives: Studies in Honour of Sayyid Abul A'la Mawdudi* (Leicester, 1979), pp. 35–42.

81. Mawdudi, *Short History*, pp. 44–78.

82. Ibid., p. 35.

83. Ibid., p. 36.

84. Sayyid Abu'l-A'la Mawdudi, *Towards Understanding Islam* (Indianapolis, 1977), pp. 36–38.

85. Regarding the roles of the mujaddid and the Mahdi, see Mawdudi, *Short History*, pp. 40–43. For the association of Mahdiism with *tajdid*, see Mawdudi, *Tajdid'u ihya'-i din* (Lahore, 1952), p. 55.

86. Mawdudi, *Short History*, pp. 36–38.

87. Ibid., p. 43.

88. Ibid., pp. 41–42.

89. See, for instance, Sayyid Abu'l-A'la Mawdudi, *Tahrik-i Islami ka a'indah la'ihah-i 'amal* (Lahore, 1986), pp. 87–110; Mawdudi, *Islam Today* (Beirut, 1985), pp. 15–17; and Yusuf, "While Green in Age," pp. 5–6. Significant in this regard is the Jama'at's efforts to vest Mawdudi's image with a millenarian aura. References to the premonitions of a clairvoyant who visited with Ahmad Hasan Mawdudi, and Mawdudi's own narration of his close escape from death in a car accident in Hyderabad, are cited in *SAAM*, 1:108, and are often utilized for that purpose.

90. *Tajdid* was important for the Jama'at's training of its members; see interview with Shaikh Mahbub 'Ali in *Jab vuh nazim-i a'la the* (Lahore, 1981), 2:25–27.

91. Saulat in *Maulana Maududi*, pp. 2–3, said that Mawdudi sought to establish his legitimacy independently, arguing that it mattered not with whom he studied, for such questions should concern those who have no literary or academic work of their own to present. Because he had publications, Mawdudi argued, his tutors mattered little for establishing his authority.

92. Sayyid Abu'l-A'la Mawdudi, *Tafhimat* (Lahore, 1965), 1:202

93. *TUTQ*, p. 4.

94. Sayyid Abu'l-A'la Mawdudi, *Islami hukumat kis tarah qa'im huti hey* (Lahore, n.d.), p. 28.

95. Mawdudi, in fact, referred to himself as a missionary in *TQ*, May 1935, p. 52.

96. See *JIKUS*, pp. 38–39, and Mawdudi, *Short History*, p. 109.

97. For a general discussion of Islamic biographies, see Marcia K. Hermansen, "Interdisciplinary Approaches to Islamic Biographical Materials," *Religion* 18 (1988): 163–82. *Karamat* (sing. *karamah*) translates into special grace bestowed by God on chosen men, usually Sufi saints. *Karamat* is manifested in the form of prescience, or as ability to perform miracles or display extraordinary powers as signs of divine blessings. *Haybah* can be translated as awe-inspiring. Both terms, especially the former, have been utilized as an Islamic equivalent for the Weberian notion of charisma. On the debate over this issue, see Hamid Dabashi, *Authority in Islam: From the Rise of Muhammad to the Establishment of the Umayyads* (New Brunswick, N.J., 1987), pp. 35–45.

98. Marcia K. Hermansen, "Biography and Hagiography," in John L. Esposito, ed., *The Oxford Encyclopedia of the Modern Islamic World* (New York, 1995).

99. Saulat, *Maulana Maududi*, p. x.

100. The statement about Mawdudi's demeanor, accent, and attire is from Gilani, *Maududi*, pp. 5–12. In a similar fashion, Maryam Jameelah emphasized Mawdudi's abilities as a statesman and a diplomat, citing his travels in Muslim countries and his meetings with political and religious leaders as proof of his exceptional leadership abilities in this regard; see Jameelah, *Who Is Maudoodi?* pp. 18–20. M. A. Malik commented in "Mawlana Abu'l-A'la Mawdudi: apne hath ki nuqush main" in Buhtah, *Mawlana Mawdudi*, pp. 299–319, that the lines of Mawdudi's hand, more than any other factor, indicated leadership abilities. The foretelling of Mawdudi's birth is in 'Abd, *Mufakkir-i Islam*, p. 49. The stories about Mawdudi's escapes from death are in Syed As'ad Gilani, *Sayyid Mawdudi: bachpan, jawani, barhapa* (Lahore, 1978), p. 91, and Jameelah, *Who Is Maudoodi?*, p. 61. God's response to his prayers is cited in Gilani, *Maududi*, p. 60: in jail, Mawdudi was disturbed by pain from his kidney stone; the pain was relieved soon after he requested it from God in prayer. The statements about his protection and the Jama'at's enemies is in *SAAM*, 2:444–445, 479. Mawdudi referred to the death of the Nawab of Kala Bagh—the governor of Punjab during the Ayub Khan era—at the hands of his son as proof of God's favor for the Jama'at's cause and disfavor toward those who opposed it.

101. Muhammad Salahu'ddin, "Qa'idin-i Jama'at ki khidmat main chand ma'ruzat," *Takbir*, November 16, 1989, p. 9.

102. For the quote about Mawdudi as founder of a school see Abul Afaq's preface to Abduh Rahman Abd, *Sayyed Mawdudi Faces the Death Sentence*, reprint (Lahore, 1978), p. iv, and 'Abd, *Mufakkir-i Islam*, pp. 29–30. For the statement about the *da'i-i 'awwal*, see Sayyid As'ad Gilani in *Jasarat*, Ijtima'-i 'Amm Number (November 11, 1989), p. 7. Israr Ahmad, a one-time Jama'at votary, cited Mawdudi as the bearer of the mantle of Sirhindi, Sayyid Ahmad Brelwi, Shah Wali'ullah, Shah Isma'il Shahid, and Muhammad Iqbal during a lecture commemorating the Khilafat movement; see *Takbir*, September 26, 1991, p. 40. See also 'Abd, *Mufakkir-i Islam*, pp. 81–82. For Mawdudi as a successor to Ahmad Khan, see Agha Shurish Kashmiri in *Thalith* 1.34 (November 9–15, 1989): 22.

103. 'Abdu'l-Ghani Faruqi, "Hayat-i javidan," in *HRZ*, pp. 23–31.

104. Throughout accounts given by Jama'at members and those who followed Mawdudi's teachings outside of the party—whether in interviews or in compilation of accounts of his life by those who knew him, such as Buhtah, *Mawlana Mawdudi*; Jalil Ahmad Rana and Salim Mansur Khalid, *Tazkirah-i Sayyid Mawdudi* (Lahore, 1986); or *HRZ*; *QDMN*; *SDMN*; and *SSMN*—it is Mawdudi's display of power and strong leadership that stands out, both in the emphasis placed on it and in the consistent appearance of references to it. Abd, *Sayyed Maududi*, pp. 18–19, stressed that Mawdudi was a sayyid. Regarding his stand in the face of opposition see, for instance, Amin Ahsan Islahi in *Mahnamah-i Chiragh,* October 1953, p. 10.

105. Interview with Mian Tufayl Muhammad.

106. Cited in Jameelah, *Who Is Maudoodi?*, p. 14. Khurshid Ahmad cited Mawdudi on this occasion in a more daring translation: "If it [time of death] has not come, they cannot send me to the gallows if they hang themselves upside down in trying to do so." See Khurshid Ahmad, *The Movement of Jama'at-e-Islami, Pakistan* (Lahore, 1989), pp. 3–4.

107. The refusal to request clemency is noted in *SAAM*, 1:447, 461. The impact on Mawdudi's followers is noted in Jameelah, *Who Is Maudoodi?* pp. 14–15, and Allahbukhsh K. Brohi, "Mawlana Abul A'la Mawdudi: The Man, the Scholar, the Reformer," in Ansari and Ahmad, eds., *Islamic Perspectives*, pp. 294–297.

108. Cited in 'Abd, *Sayyed Maududi*, pp. 22, 37.

109. *Ibid.*, p. 44. The author argued that Ghulam Muhammad, the governor general and the putative architect of the trial, died "shamefully" and was buried in "the grave of non-Muslims"; see p. 17.

110. The 1963 incident is noted in Jameelah, *Who Is Maudoodi?*, p. 21, and in *JIKUS*, p. 50. The 1964 imprisoning is discussed in Sayyid Abu'l A'la Mawdudi, *The Political Situation in Pakistan* (Karachi, 1965), pp. 21–41.

111. Gilani, *Maududi*, pp. 106–114.

112. For a discussion of Jameelah's life and works, see this author's entry on her in Esposito, *The Oxford Encyclopedia of the Modern Islamic World*.

113. Jameelah, *Who Is Maudoodi?*, p. 68.

114. Khalil Ahmadu'l Hamidi, "Taqdiru'l-rijal la taqdisu'l-rijal," in Rana and Khalid, *Tazkirah.*

115. Mawdudi, *Tajdid'u ihya'i*, pp. 56–57.

116. See *TQ,* September 1955, p. 210.

Glossary

'abd: slave

adab, pl. adabiyat: Literary work; in South Asia, it also refers to manners and proper mode of behavior.

'adl: Justice

ahl al-hall wa'l-'aqd: Those who unbind and bind; reference is to those who engage in consultation to manage the affairs of the community, that is, the ulama.

ahlu'l-bayt (ahl al-bayt): Literally, people of the house; refers to the descendants of the Prophet Muhammad. It is a term associated with the Shi'is.

akabir-parasti: Literally worshipping of the elders or forefathers.

Allah ke qurb'u raza: Closeness to and pleasure of God.

Allah'u akbar: "God is Great," popular Muslim invocation.

'allamah: Literally, the most learned; a title given to religious sages and widely respected men of letters.

'alim: Singular of ulama; see below.

'amali shahadat: Bearing witness in practice; here it refers to acting out the teachings of the faith.

amir: Military commander or leader; in the context of this study, it means director or president.

'Amr-i bi ma'ruf was nahy 'an'l-munkar: "Enjoining the good and forbidding the reprehensible," a tenet of the Islamic faith.

'aql-i kull: Literally, know-it-all; in Sufism and Islamic philosophy, it refers to the omnicompetent intellect.

ashraf: Plural of sharif; see below.

ayah: A verse of the Qur'an.

bai'ah: Oath of allegiance traditionally given to caliphs and, in Sufism, to Sufi masters.

balaghat: rhetoric.

barq: Modern word for electricity. (See also Kahruba.)

187

bid'at: Innovation.

da'i-i 'awwal: The foremost missionary.

dars-i nizami: A syllabus of religious education that was popular in South Asia in the eighteenth century and that continues to be taught to this day.

daru'l-harb: Abode of war, defined in contradistinction to daru'l-Islam.

daru'l-Islam: Abode of Islam.

daru'l-Kufr: Abode of blasphemy.

daru'l-'ulum: A seminary, a place of advance religious learning.

da'wah: Literally, invitation or call; refers to revivalist movements' call to observance of Islamic norms. It suggests a proselytical posture that seeks to reinforce Islamicity.

din: Religion.

din-i ilahi: Literally, divine religion; the name of the ecclectic faith introduced by Emperor Akbar that meshed the teachings of Islam and Hinduism.

diwanah: Madman.

fahsha': Immorality.

falsafah: Philosophy.

fara'iz: Obligatory religious duties.

farzanah: A sage, wise man.

fatwa: A religious decree issued by an 'alim.

fiqh: Islamic jurisprudence.

fuqaha: jurisprudents.

fussaq'u fujjar: The corrupt.

hadith: Saying(s) attributed to the Prophet Muhammad.

hajj: Pilgrimage to Mecca.

hakim: A wise man, well versed in the esoteric sciences and/or medicine.

harakah-i jawhariyah: Change in the essence of being; the term is used in Sadru'ddin Shirzai's philosophy.

haybah: Great presence.

hijrah: Literally, migration; usually refers to the Prophet's migration from Mecca to Medina in 622 A.D., which marked the beginning of the Muslim calender.

hikmat-i 'amali: Practical wisdom.

hikmat-i muta'aliyah: Transcendant theosophy; refers to the school of Sadru'ddin Shirazi.

hizbu'llah: Party of God.

huddud laws: Plural of *hadd*, which literally means limit. These are punishments for crimes clearly defined in the Qur'an and the *sunnah* (see below).

hukumat-i ilahiyah: Divine government.

'ibadah: Worship.

ihsan: Benevolence or benediction.

ihya': Revival.

ihya'-i rabaniyah: Divine revival.

ijazat or *ijazah*: The recognition that a student has completed his requirements and may now teach other students in those subjects.

ijma': Consensus; stipulates that legal and juridical reforms and changes become established and binding once they enjoy the approval of the majority of the lawmakers.

ijtihad: Independent judgment, adaptation, in the interpretation of Islamic law.

ilah: God, divinity.

'ilm-i ma'ani: Hermeneutic sciences, esoteric knowledge.

imam: Leader; commonly refers to a religious leader, especially a leader of Friday prayers at a mosque. (Capitalized when used with a person's name.)

imamat-i salihah: Virtuous leadership.

iman: Faith.

inqilab-i imamat: Literally, revolution in leadership.

iqamat-i din: Literally, establishing the rule of the religion.

iqbaliyat: Iqbal studies.

iqbal-shinasi: Iqbal studies.

'irfan: Mysticism.

islah: Reform.

islam: Literally, peace and submission to God.

islami hukumat: Islamic government.

istihsan: The practice of invoking the spirit of the *shari'ah* in contending with new circumstances.

istinbat-i ahkam: One's understanding of religious orders.

jagirdar: The hereditary right to the revenue from a piece of land given by the government in return for services; a patronage system based on heredity and centered in control of rural land.

jahiliyah: Pre-Islamic era; also refers to ignorance and paganism.

jama'at: Party, social organization, congregation.

jihad: Holy war; *jihad-i kubra*: Striving in the path of God; *Jihad-i sughra*: defense of Islam against physical enemies.

jiziyah: Poll tax levied on religious minorities in accordance with Islamic law.

jur'at-i rindanah: Manly courage.

kafir: Unbeliever.

kahruba: Electricity.

kalam: Theology.

kalimah-i khatibah: Literal profession of the Muslim testimony of faith.

kalimah-i tayibbah: Pure profession of the Muslim testimony of faith.

karamat: Special gifts, charisma.

khalifatu'llah: God's vicegerent.

khaniqah: Sufi cloister.

Kharijis or *Khawarij*: A revolutionary and puritanical sect that broke away from Sunni Islam in the seventh century A.D. Condemned by the orthodox for their reading of Islam and their violent excesses, they were defeated militarily by the armies of the caliphs.

khilafat: Caliphate.

khilafatu'llah fi'l-arz: God's vicegerency on earth.

khudi: Literally, self; the term was used by Muhammad Iqbal in his *Asrar-i Khudi*.

kufr: blasphemy.

la ilahah illa'llah: "There is no god but God," the Muslim testimony of faith.

lisenu'l-'asr: Tongue of the age.

madarij-i sama': States of ecstasy; refers to stations of spiritual ascension attained by Sufis.

madrasah: Traditional religious seminary.

Mahdi: The messiah, whose era will usher in the reign of justice. For Shi'is, he is the twelfth imam.

malishe (mleccha): Hindu term for barbaric outsider, outcast.

mantiq: Logic.

marizanah zihniyat: Sick mind.

ma'rufat: Those actions that have been enjoined by Islam.

mashayikh: Plural of *shaikh*, Sufi master.

masiha: Healer.

masih-i Dajjal: False Messiah, refers to the Beast as described in the biblical book of Revelation in relation to the end of time.

mawlana: Title reserved for those learned in Islamic sciences and the ulama. (Capitalized when used with a person's name.)

mawlvi: One who is learned in Islamic sciences. (Capitalized when used with a person's name.)

mazahir: Literally, appearances. In Islamic esoteric sciences, it means epiphanies.

millet: This system in the Ottoman Empire was a case of implementation of Islamic injunctions on *zimmis*, wherein each non-Muslim community in the Empire practiced its own laws within its community, paid the ascribed poll tax (*jiziyah*) to the state, and was, in turn, limited in its political influence in the affairs of the state.

mufassir: Commentator on the Qur'an or the hadith.

mufsid: Corrupt.

muhaddithin: Relaters of the hadith.

mujaddid: Renewer of the faith.

mulla: A low-ranking cleric. (Capitalized when used with a person's name.)

munkarat: The reprehensibles; what has been outlawed by Islamic law.

munkirin-i hadith: Those denying the authenticity of the hadith.

mushahadat: Realizations.

na'ib amir: Vice-president.

naqd: Cash.

na't: Devotional poetry for the Prophet Muhammad, popular with Brelwis in particular.

nawafil: Nonobligatory religious practices.

nawab: An honorific title of Muslim rulers, princes, and noblemen in India. (Capitalized when used with a person's name.)

nazim: Overseer, organizer.

nechari: Naturalist; the term has been used with negative connotations to refer to Sayyid Ahmad Khan's school of thought.

nifaq: Seditious discord.

nizam: Title of hereditary rules of the princely state of Hyderabad.

nubuwwah: Prophecy.

pir: Sufi master.

purdah: The social and sartorial system of segragation of the sexes practiced by South Asian Muslims based on interpretation of the Islamic law.

qadi: Judge.

qat'i: Definitive.

qiyas: Logical reasoning; a source of Islamic law.

rabb: Lord; God.

Rashidun caliphs: Abu Bakr, 'Umar, 'Uthman, and 'Ali, the first four elected caliphs, whose reigns (A.D. 632–661) are viewed by revivalist thinkers as the only period of true Islamic rule following the death of the Prophet Muhammad.

riba': Usury; forbidden by Islamic law.

risalat: Prophecy.

ru'asa, sing. *ra'is*: Leaders.

rububiyat: Literally, lordship; divinity.

rukn: Member.

ruku': Bowing during prayer.

sadr: Leader, president.

Sadra-khandih: One who is educated in Sadru'ddin Shirazi's philosophy.

safar: Journey.

sajjadah-nishini: Hereditary leadership centered on Sufi shrines in South Asia.

sarparast: Overseer.

satyagraha: Mahatma Gandhi's term for nonviolent action in pursuit of justice and the attainment of national independence.

sawm: Fasting.

sayyids: Descendants of the Prophet of Islam through the progeny of his daughter, Fatimah. (Capitalized when used with a person's name.)

shahadah: Literally, bearing testimony: *la ilahah illa'llah*. It is by this declaration that one becomes a Muslim.

shaikh: Sufi master.

shaikhu'l-shuyukh: Master of all Sufi masters.

shari'ah: The body of laws that governs Muslim personal and social life.

sharif: Muslim nobleman in South Asia.

shirk: Polytheism.

shudra: Outcast.

shura': A consultative body.

silsilah: Literally, dynasty; in Sufism, it refers to the chain of authority that in each Sufi order extends back to the Prophet Muhammad.

sudkhar: Usurer.

sujud: Prostration during prayer.

sukun: Stability.

suluk: Sufi path.

sunnah: The tradition of the Prophet's practice; also refers to acceptance of the legitimacy of the rightly guided caliphs.

ta'alluq bi'llah: Dedication to God.

tabligh: Propagation, missionary work.

tafsir: Commentary on the Qur'an or hadith.

tahajjud: Nonobligatory prayers offered at late hours of the night in the tradition of the Prophet Muhammad.

tahrif: Deliberate misreading.

tahrik: Social, political, or religious movement.

tajalli: Reflection.

tajdid: Renewal, revival.

taqlid: Literally, emulation. The process of following the practices and pronouncements of a religious authority in matters relating to religious law without independent investigation.

taqwa: Faith in religious truth and consciousness of God.

taraqqi-pasand: Literally, one who favors progress, but used to refer to modernists.

tasawwuf: Sufism.

tashkik: Gradation.

tawhid: Unity of God.

ta'wil: Hermeneutics.

tazkiyah-i nafs: Cleansing the soul.

tise: Credit.

'ulama: Those educated in Islamic law and capable of issuing opinion on religious matters.

ulau'l-amr: Those in authority.

ummah: The Islamic community.

unani tibb: Medicine; literally, Greek medicine—referring to the classical medical practices in vogue among Muslims for several centuries.

ustad: Master.

wahy: Revelation.

wajibat: Obligatory practices sanctioned by Islamic law.

waqf: A religious endowment.

zakat: An annual flat tax of 2.5 percent levied on accumulated savings, to be paid voluntarily by Muslims to charitable projects of their own choice. It is one of the articles of Islam.

zikr: Religious phrases uttered and chanted by Sufis in sessions of meditation.

zimmi: Non-Muslims whose religions are tolerated by Islam; they are protected under Islamic law and must give a poll tax to Muslims.

Bibliography

Abbreviations

EI   *The Encyclopaedia of Islam*, 2nd ed. H. A. R. Gibb et al., eds. (Leiden: E. J. Brill, 1960 – present)

HRZ   *Haftroza Zindagi* (Lahore), Mawdudi Number (September 29–October 5, 1989)

JIKUS   *Jama'at-i Islami ke untis sal* (Lahore: Shu'bah-i Nashr'u Isha'at-i Jama'at-i Islami, 1970)

KN   Sayyid Abu'l-A'la Mawdudi, "Khud niwisht," in Muhammad Yusuf Buhtah, ed., *Mawlana Mawdudi: apni awr dusrun ki nazar main* (Lahore: Idarah-i Ma'arif-i Islami, 1984), pp. 23 – 39. This article is an autobiography, written by Mawdudi in 1932 at the request of a friend, Sayyid Manzar 'Ali Sahab, who was then preparing a book on the literati of Hyderabad.

QDMN   *Qaumi Digest*, Mawdudi Number (1980).

RJI   *Rudad-i Jama'at-i Islami*, 7 vols. (Lahore, 1938 – 1991). These volumes contain the proceedings of the various Jama'at congresses between 1941 and 1955.

SAAM   Masudul Hasan, *Sayyid Abul A'ala Maududi and His Thought*, 2 vols. (Lahore: Islamic Publications, 1984).

SDMN   *Sayyarah Digest*, Mawdudi Number (December 1979).

SSMN   *Sayyarah*, Sayyid Mawdudi Number (April–May 1980).

TQ   *Tarjumanu'l-Qur'an* (1932–present). *TQ* has been the main forum for the exposition of Mawlana Mawdudi's theological views since 1932 and has also been the Jama'at's official ideological journal since 1941. It was edited by Mawdudi from 1932 to 1979 and is currently edited by Na'im Siddiqi.

TUTQ   Sayyid Abu'l-A'la Mawdudi, *Towards Understanding the Qur'an*, translated by Zafar Ishaq Ansari, (Leicester: Islamic Foundation, 1988–present). This book is the English translation of Mawdudi's *Tafhimu'l-Qur'an*. The *Tafhim* is Mawdudi's famous Urdu translation of and commentary on the Qur'an. It was begun in 1942 and completed in 1972.

Interviews

'Abbasi, Jan Muhammad, deputy amir and amir of Sind, Karachi, May 8, 1990

Ahmad, 'Abdu'l-Ghafur, deputy amir, Karachi, May 3, 1990

Ahmad, Israr, former Jama'at member and leader of Tanzim-i Islami, Lahore, November 12, 1989

Ahmad, Khurshid, deputy amir, Islamabad, November 19, 1989

Ahmad, Qazi Husain, amir, Lahore, January 22, 1990

'Ali, Malik Ghulam, former justice of the Shari'at Court, Lahore, January 31 and March 11, 1990

Amanu'llah, Khwajah, confidant of Mawlana Mawdudi, Lahore, April 8, 1990

Ansari, Zafar Ishaq, director of Islamic Research Institute, Islamabad, October 21, 1989, and May 5, 1990

Ghamidi, Javid Ahmadu'l-, former Jamacat member, Lahore, September 19, 1989

Gilani, Sayyid As'ad, amir of Lahore, Lahore, December 4, 1989, and March 11, 1990

Gurmani, Begum 'Abidah, confidant of Mawlana Mawdudi, Lahore, April 8, 1990

Hamidi, Khalil Ahmadu'l, director of Daru'l-'Urubiyah, Lahore, February 4, 1990

Hasan, Mawlana 'Abdu'l-Ghaffar, former Jama'at leader, Faisalabad, November 17 and 18, 1989

Hasan, Sayyid Munawwar, secretary-general, Karachi, May 19, 1990

Ihsan, Hafizu'l-Rahman, member of the Jama'at and a close companion of Mawdudi, Lahore, April 16, 1990

'Inayatu'llah, 'Atiyah, politician and friend of the Mawdudi family, Lahore, March 9, 1990

Iqbal, Javid, former justice of the Supreme Court, Lahore, November 7, 1989

Islahi, Mawlana Amin Ahsan, former Jama'at leader, Lahore, October 7, 1989

Jameelah, Maryam, Jama'at thinker and associate of Mawdudi, Lahore, October 6, 1989

Mawdudi, Begum Mahmudah, Mawlana Mawdudi's wife, Lahore, April 1, 1990

Muhammad, Mian Tufayl, former amir, Lahore, September 21 and 23, 1989

Murad, Khurram Jah, deputy amir, Lahore, September 14, 1989, and January 22, 1990.

Nadwi, Mawlana Sayyid Abu'l-Hasan 'Ali, Nadwi leader and one of the Jama'at's founders, Lucknow, December 27, 1989

Niyazi, Kawthar, former amir of Punjab and former minister of religious affairs, Islamabad, October 3, 1989, and May 6, 1990

Parachah, Farid Ahmad, director of 'Ulama Academy, Lahore, December 4, 1989

Qadri, Muhammad Tahiru'l-, leader of Minhaju'l-Qur'an, Lahore, March 7, 1990

Qasmi, Ja'far, former Jama'at follower, Faisalabad and Lahore, November 18, 1989, and January 23 and 25, 1990

Salimi, Chaudhri Aslam, former secretary-general, Lahore, October 8, 1989, and March 24, 1990

Shafi', Mian Muhammad, Muhammad Iqbal's secretary, Lahore, December 21, 1989

Primary Source Collections

Archives of Idarah-i Ma'arif-i Islami of Jama'at-i Islami, Lahore

Archives of Institute of Islamic Culture, Lahore

National Archives of United States of America, Washington, D.C., and Suitland, Maryland

Public Records Office, London

Magazines, Newspapers, and Urdu Journals

Asia, Lahore
Al-Balagh, Karachi
Chatan, Lahore
Chiragh-i Rah, Karachi
Criterion, Karachi
Al-Furqan, Lucknow
Haftrozah Zindagi, Lahore
Herald, Karachi
Al-Jam'iat, Delhi
Jang, Lahore
Jasarat, Karachi
Kawthar, Lahore
Khudabakhsh Library Journal, Patna
Al-Ma'arif, Lahore
Mahnamah-i Chiragh, Lahore
Mahnamah-i Zikri, Lahore

Mithaq, Lahore
Muslim Digest, Durban (South Africa)
Al-Nadwah, A'zamgarh
Nawa'-i Waqt, Lahore
New Trend (Indianapolis)
Nida, Lahore
Nigar, Delhi
Qaumi Digest, Lahore
Sayyarah, Lahore
Sayyarah Digest, Lahore
Takbir, Karachi
Tasnim, Lahore
Thalith, Lahore
Tarjumanu'l-Qur'an, Hyderabad,
    Pathankot, Lahore
Zindagi-i Naw, Rampur

Urdu and Persian Sources

'Abbasi, Jan Muhammad. Khutbah-i istiqbaliyah, kull Pakistan 'ulama convention (Welcoming speech to the all-Pakistan ulama convention). Lahore: Jama'at-i Islami, 1989.

'Abd, Chaudhri 'Abdu'l-Rahman. Mufakkir-i Islam: Sayyid Abu'l-A'la Mawdudi (Thinker of Islam: Mawlana Sayyid Abu'l-A'la Mawdudi). Lahore: Islamic Publications, 1971.

'Abdu'l-'Aziz, Qari. Muhasabah-i Mawdudi (Critical examination of Mawdudi). Lahore: Hizbu'l-Islam, n.d.

Abu Khalid. Mawlana Mawdudi awr Jama'at-i Islami ke khalaf fatwa bazi ka ja'izah (Review of the fatwa campaign against Mawlana Mawdudi and Jama'at-i Islami). Gujranwala; Pakistan: Maktabah-i Falah, n.d.

Abu'l-Afaq. Sayyid Abu'l-A'la Mawdudi: sawanih, afkar, tahrik (Sayyid Abu'l-A'la Mawdudi: Biography, thought, and movement). Lahore: Islamic Publications, 1971.

Abu'l-Haqq, Mawlana Sayyid. Iza'-i fatawah: Mawlana Abu'l-A'la Mawdudi awr unki Jama'at ke ara' par ik tabsarah (Clarification of fatwas: A commentary on the ideas and practices of Mawlana Mawdudi and his Jama'at). Peshawar, n.d.

Abu Tariq, ed. Mawlana Mawdudi ki taqarir (Mawlana Mawdudi's speeches). 2 vols. Lahore: Islamic Publications, 1976.

Afaqi, Abu Tahir. Fitnah-i Mawdudiyat (Discord of Mawdudiism). Jawharabad: Idarah-i Adabistan-i Jawharabad, n.d.

Ahmad, 'Abdu'l-Ghafur. Pher Martial law a-giya (Then came the martial law). Lahore: Jang Publications, 1988.

Ahmad, Israr. Islam awr Pakistan: tarikhi, siyasi, 'ilmi awr thiqafati pasmanzar (Islam and Pakistan: Historical, political and cultural background). Lahore: Maktabah-i Markazi-i Anjuman-i Khuddamu'l-Qur'an, 1983.

———. Minhaj-i inqilab-i nabawi (Path of the Prophetic revolution). Lahore: Matbu'at-i Tanzim-i Islami, 1987.

———. Tahrik-i Jama'at-i Islami: ik tahqiqi mutala'ah (The movement of Jama'at-i Islami: A critical study). Lahore: Daru'l-Isha'ah-i Islami, 1966.

———. "Naghz-i ghazal" (Felicity of the ode). Mithaq 39.1 (January 1990).

Ahmad, Khurshid. "Jama'at-i Islami Kiya Hey, Uski Zarurat Kiya Thi?" (What is the Jama'at, and what was its necessity?), *Haftrozah Zindagi* (November 10 – 16, 1989): 13–15.

———. ed., *Adabiyat-i Mawdudi* (Mawdudi's literature). Lahore: Islamic Publications, 1972.

Ahmad, Mawlana Abu Manzur. *Mawlana Mawdudi awr ghaltiyan* (Mawlana Mawdudi and the falsehood). Multan, Pakistan: Friends Publications, 1958.

Ahmad, Mawlana Shaikh. *Mawlana Mawdudi awr tasawwuf* (Mawlana Mawdudi and Sufism). Deoband: Maktabah-i Tajalli, 1966.

Akhtar, Safir. "Mawlana Mawdudi awr ma'arif" (Mawlana Mawdudi and knowledge), in Jalil Ahmad Rana and Salim Mansur Khalid, eds., *Tazkirah-i Sayyid Mawdudi* (Biography of Sayyid Mawdudi). Lahore: Idarah-i Ma'arif-i Islami, 1986, 141–142.

'Alam, Imtiaz. "Taraqqi-pasand talabah: lazzat-i shawq" (The progressive students: Pleasure of the longing), in Salim Mansur Khalid, ed., *Talabah tahrikain* (Student movements). Lahore: Al-Badr Publications, 1989, 2:29–46.

'Ali, Malik Ghulam. *Khilafat'u mulukiyat par i'tirazat ka tajziyah* (An analysis of criticisms made of *Khilafat'u mulukiyat*). Lahore: Islamic Publications, 1972.

———. "Ik rafiq ke ta'athurat" (Impressions of a friend), in Muhammad Yusuf Buhtah, ed., *Mawlana Mawdudi: apni awr dusrun ki nazar main* (Mawlana Mawdudi: In his own and others' view). Lahore: Idarah-i Ma'arif-i Islami, 1984, 247–260.

———. "Professor Mawdudi ke sath sath Islamiyah College se Zaildar Park tak" (With Professor Mawdudi from Islamiyah College to Zaildar Park). *Haftrozah Zindagi*, Mawdudi Number (September 29–October 5, 1989): 118–127.

'Ali, Mawlana Ahmad. *Haqq-parast 'ulama ki mawdudiyat se narazgi ke asbab* (Reasons for the disenchantment of truth-loving ulama with Mawdudism). Lahore: Anjuman-i Khuddam-i Din, n.d.

'Ali, Sayyid Anwar, *Radd-i sarguzasht* (Refutation of legacy) (Delhi, n.d.).

'Ali, Naqi. *Sayyid Mawdudi ka 'ahd* (Sayyid Mawdudi's covenant). Lahore, 1980.

Allahwala, Mahmud Ahmad. "Mard-i haqq agah" (The man who was aware of the truth). *Takbir* (September 28, 1989): 41–43.

Ashraf, 'Abdu'l-Rahim. *Kiya Jama'at-i Islami haqq par hey?* (Is the Jama'at-i Islami on the right path?). Deoband: Maktabah-i Tajalli, 1965.

Badr, Khurram. *Qazi Husain Ahmad.* Karachi: Saba Publications, 1988.

Brohi, Allahbukhsh K. "Mawdudi: Pakistan ka sab se bara wakil" (Mawdudi: Pakistan's greatest advocate). *Haftrozah Zindagi,* Mawdudi Number (September 29–October 5, 1989): 33–36.

Buhtah, Muhammad Yusuf, ed. *Mawlana Mawdudi: apni awr dusrun ki nazar main* (Mawlana Mawdudi: In his own and others' views). Lahore: Idarah-i Ma'arif-i Islami, 1984.

Butt, Abu Yazid Muhammadu'ddin. *Mujaddid-i tarikh jinab Mahmud Ahmad Sahab 'Abbasi ke khilaf Mawdudi sahab ki ghalat bayaniyun ka jawab* (A response to the wrongful assertions of Mawlana Mawdudi against the renewer of history, Mahmud Ahmad 'Abbasi). Lahore: Anjuman-i Muhibbin-i Sahabah, n.d.

Dabashi, Hamid. "Didgahi bar afkar-i ijtima'i-i Mulla Sadra: nizami ijtima'i dar jahan-i sarmadi" (An outlook on Mullah Sadra's social thought: A social order in an eternal world). *Iran Nameh* 3.3 (spring 1985): 407–428.

Deobandi, 'Allamah 'Amir 'Uthmani Fazil. *Haqiqat* (Truth). Multan: Maktabah-i Ta'mir-i Millat, n.d.

Faruqi, 'Abdu'l-Ghani. "Hayat-i javidan" (Eternal life). *Haftrozah Zindagi*, Mawdudi Number (September 29–October 5, 1989): 23–31.

Faruqi, Abu Rashid. *Iqbal awr Mawdudi* (Iqbal and Mawdudi). Lahore: Maktabah-i Ta'mir-i Insaniyat, 1977.

Gauhar, Altaf. "Pakistan, Ayub Khan, awr Mawlana Mawdudi, *Tafhimu'l-Qur'an* awr main" (Pakistan, Ayub Khan, Mawlana Mawdudi, *Tafhimu'l-Qur'an* and Me). *Haftrozah Zindagi*, Mawdudi Number (September 29–October 5, 1989): 41–45.

Ghafarlahu, Ahqar Mazhar Husain. *Mawdudi Jama'at ke 'aqa'id wa narzriyat par ik tanqidi nazar* (A critical review of the ideas of Mawdudi and the Jama'at). Jhelum, India: n.p., n.d.

Gilani, Sayyid As'ad. *Iqbal, Daru'l-Islam awr Mawdudi* (Iqbal, Daru'l-Islam, and Mawdudi). Lahore: Islami Academy, 1978.

———. *Sayyid Mawdudi: bachpan, jawani, barhapa* (Sayyid Mawdudi: Childhood, youth, and old age). Lahore: Islamic Academy, 1978.

———. "Jama'at-i Islami, 1941–1947." Ph.D. dissertation, Department of Political Science, University of Punjab, 1989–1990.

———. "Ta'limi nazariyat-i 'Allamah Iqbal awr Daru'l-Islam ki ta'limi iskim" (Iqbal's views on education and the educational scheme of Daru'l-Islam), in Ja'far Baluch, ed., *Iqbal-shinasi awr Sayyarah* (Iqbal studies and Sayyarah). Lahore: Bazm-i Iqbal, 1989, 74–86.

Gul, Rahat. *Jama'at-i Islami ka tanha musafar* (Jama'at-i Islami's lone traveler). Peshawar, 1992.

Haftrozah Zindagi, Mawdudi Number (September 29–October 5, 1989).

Hamidi, Khalil Ahmadu'l. "Taqdiru'l-rijal la taqdisu'l-rijal" (Praise of men, not worship of men), in Jalil Ahmad Rana and Salim Mansur Khalid, eds., *Tazkirah-i Sayyid Mawdudi* (Biography of Sayyid Mawdudi). Lahore: Idarah-i Ma'arif-i Islami, 1986, i–iii.

Husain, Hazrat Mawlana Qazi Mazhar. *Mufti Muhammad Yusuf sahab ke 'ilmi ja'izah ka 'ilmi muhasabah* (A scholarly examination of Mufti Muhammad Yusuf's rational review), reprint. Jhelum, India: Tahrik-i Ahl-i Sunnat'u Jama'at, 1976.

———. *Tahaffuz-i Islam party ka intikhabi mauqaf* (The electoral platform of the Tahaffuz-i Islam party) n.p., n.d.

Ijtima'se ijtima'tak (1963–1974); rudad-i Jama'at-i Islami, Pakistan (From convention to convention (1963–1974): Proceedings of Jama'at-i Islami of Pakistan). Lahore: Jama'at-i Islami, 1989.

Ikram, Shaikh Muhammad. *Rud-i kawthar* (River of paradise), 12th ed. Lahore: Idarah-i Thaqafat-i Islam, 1988.

Iqbal, Javid. *Zindarud* (Eternal river), 3rd ed. Lahore: Shaikh Ghulam 'Ali & Sons, 1989.

Iqbal, Shaikh Muhammad. *Jama'at-i Islami par ik nazar* (A look at Jama'at-i Islami). Karachi, 1952.

Ja'fari, Ra'is Ahmad. *'Ali baradaran* ('Ali brothers). Lahore: Muhammad 'Ali Academy, 1963.

———. "Mawlana Sayyid Abu'l-A'la Mawdudi," *Sayyarah*, Sayyid Mawdudi Number (April–May 1980): 213–215.

Kazmi, Mawlana Sayyid Ahmad Sa'id. *Mukalamah-i Kazmi'u Mawdudi* (The debate between Kazmi and Mawdudi). Lahore: Markazi Jam'iatu'l-Mashayikh-i Pakistan, n.d.

Khatre ki ghanti (Bell of alarm). Lahore: Jam'iat-i 'Ulama-i Pakistan, n.d.

Khalhwari, Sabir. "Sayyid Mawdudi Awr Iqbal" (Sayyid Mawdudi and Iqbal). *Sayyarah Digest*, Mawdudi Number (December 1979): 100–104.

Khan, Mawlana Wahidu'ddin. *Din ki siyasi ta'bir* (Political interpretation of religion). Lahore: Al-Maktabah Al-Ashrafiyah, n.d.

———. *Din kiya hey?* (What is religion?) Delhi: Maktabah-i Risalah, 1978.

————. *Ta'bir ki ghalti* (Mistaken interpretation). Delhi: Maktabah-i Risalah, 1975.

Kirmani, Muhammad Riyaz. *Basa'ir-i Mawdudi: Tafhimu'l-Qur'an main jadid 'ulum se istifadah* (Mawdudi's insights: The use of modern sciences in the *Tafhimu'l-Qur'an*). Lahore: Maktabah-i Ta'mir-i Insaniyat, 1988.

Madani, Mawlana Sayyid Husain Ahmad. *Mawdudi: dastur awr 'aqa'id ki haqiqat* (The truth about Mawdudi's beliefs and program). Delhi: Al-Jami'at Book Depot, n.d.

Malik, M. A. "Mawlana Abu'l-A'la Mawdudi: apne hath ki nuqush main" (Mawlana Abu'l-A'la Mawdudi: The lines on his hands), in Muhammad Yusuf Buhtah, ed., *Mawlana Mawdudi: apni awr dusrun ki nazar main* (Mawlana Mawdudi: In his own and others' views). Lahore: Idarah-i Ma'arif-i Islami, 1984, 299–319.

Mansur, Salim. "Islami university ka mutalabah" (Demand for the Islamic university), in Salim Mansur Khalid, ed., *Talabah tahrikain* (Student movements). Lahore: Al-Badr Publications, 1989, 1:191–196.

Mawdudi, Abu Mahmud. "Hamara khandan" (Our family), in Ahmad Munir, *Mawlana Abu'l-A'la Mawdudi.* Lahore: Atashfishan Publications, 1986, 11–14.

Mawdudi, Begum Mahmudah. "Mawlana Mawdudi apne ghar main" (Mawlana Mawdudi in his own house), in Muhammad Yusuf Buhtah, ed., *Mawlana Mawdudi: apni awr dusrun ki nazar main* (Mawlana Mawdudi: In his own and others' views). Lahore: Idarah-i Ma'arif-i Islami, 1984, 261–264.

Mawdudi, Sayyid Abu'l-A'la. *'Asr-i hazir main ummat-i muslimah ke masa'il awr unka hall* (The problems of Muslims in contemporary times and their solution), 2nd ed., edited by Khalil Ahmadu'l-Hamidi. Lahore: Idarah-i Ma'arif-i Islami, 1988.

————. *Dakter ka nishtar ya daku ka khanjar* (Doctor's lancet or the dacoit's dagger). Lahore: Daru'l-Fikr, n.d.

————. *Da'wah awr 'amal* (Calling and action). Lahore, n.d.

————. *Dawlat-i asifiyah wa hukumat-i Britaniyah* (Asifiyah government and Britain). n.p., 1924.

————. *Hidayat* (Directions). Lahore: Islamic Publications, 1967.

————. *Hikmat-i tabligh* (Logic of missionary work). Lahore: Islami Academy, 1987.

————. *Islam ka nazriyah-i siyasi* (Islam's political theory). Delhi: n.p., 1967.

————. *Islami hukumat kis tarah qa'im huti hey?* (How is the Islamic state established?). Lahore, n.p., n.d.

————. *Islami riyasat* (The Islamic state). Lahore: Islamic Publications, 1969.

————. *Islami riyasat main zimmiun ke huquq* (The rights of minorities in the Islamic state). Lahore: n.p., 1954.

————. *Islami tahzib awr uske usul'u mabadi* (Islamic civilization and its principles and foundations). Lahore: Islamic Publications, 1966.

————. *Istifsarat.* (Questions), 2 vols. Lahore: Idarah-i Tarjumanu'l-Qur'an, n.d.

————. *Jama'at-i Islami ke untis sal* (Twenty-nine years of Jama'ar-i Islami). Lahore: Shu'bah-i Nashr'u Isha'at-i Jama'at-i Islami, Pakistan, 1970.

————. *Jama'at-i Islami: tarikh, maqsad, awr la'ihah-i 'amal* (Jama'at-i Islami: History, aims, and plan of action), reprint. Lahore: Islamic Publications, 1963.

————. *Al-Jihad fi'l-Islam* (Jihad in Islam), reprint. Lahore: Idarah-i Tarjumanu'l-Qur'an, 1986.

————. *Jihad fi sabil Allah* (Jihad in the path of God), reprint. Lahore: Islamic Publications, 1989.

————. *Khilafat'u mulukiyat* (Caliphate and monarchy). Lahore: Islamic Publications, 1966.

————. *Khutbat* (Sermons), 40th ed. Lahore: Islamic Publications, 1989.

————. *Mas'alah-i malikiyat-i zamin* (Question of land ownership). Lahore: Islamic Publications, 1982.

———. *Mas'alah-i qaumiyat* (Question of nationality), reprint. Lahore: Islamic Publications, 1982.

———. *Murtad ki saza* (Apostate's punishment), reprint. Lahore: Islamic Publications, 1981.

———. *Musalman awr mawjudah siyasi kashmakash* (Muslims and the current political struggle), 3 vols. Lahore: n.p., 1938–1940.

———. *Musalman ka mazi, hal awr mustaqbal* (Muslims' past, present, and future). Lahore: Islamic Publications, 1963.

———. *Qadiyani mas'alah* (Ahmadi issue). Lahore: n.p., 1951.

———. *Qur'an ki char buniadi istilahain: ilah, rabb, 'ibadat, din* (Qur'an's Four Basic Terms: Divinity, Lord, Worship, Religion), reprint. Lahore: Islamic Publications, 1988.

———. *Rasa'il'u masa'il* (Queries and responses), 4 vols. Lahore: n.p., 1951–1965).

———. *Risalah-i diniyat* (Treatise on religion). Hyderabad: n.p., 1932.

———. *Salamati ka rastah* (The healthy path). Pathankot: Daru'l-Islam, n.d.

———. *Shahadat-i haqq* (Testimony of truth). Lahore: Islamic Publications, 1970.

———. *Shakhsiyat* (Personalities), edited by Sami'u'llah and Khalid Humayun. Lahore: Al-Badr Publications, n.d.

———. *Sunnat ki a'ini haithiyat* (Constitutional status of the Prophetic traditions). Lahore: Islamic Publications, 1963.

———. *Sunnat'u bid'at ki kashmakash* (The struggle between tradition and innovation). Lahore: Idarah-i Tarjumanu'l-Qur'an, 1950.

———. *Tafhimat* (Explanations), 3 vols. Lahore: Islamic Publications, 1965.

———. *Tahrik awr karkun* (Movement and the workers), edited by Khalil Hamidi. Lahore: Al-Manar, 1979.

———. *Tahrik-i azadi hind awr Musalman* (India's independence movement and the Muslims), 2 vols. Lahore: Islamic Publications, 1973.

———. *Tahrik-i Islami ka a'indah la'ihah-i 'amal* (Islamic movement's future course of action). Lahore: Islamic Publications, 1986.

———. *Tahrik-i Islami ki akhlaqi buniadin* (The ethical foundations of the Islamic movement). Lahore: Islamic Publications, 1968.

———. *Tahrik-i Pakistan awr Jama'at-i Islami* (Pakistan movement and Jama'at-i Islami). Multan, Pakistan: Ikhwan Publications, n.d.

———. *Tajdid'u ihya'-i din* (Renewal and revival of religion). Lahore: n.p., 1952.

———. *Ta'limat* (On education). Lahore: Islamic Publications, n.d.

———. *Tanqihat* (Inquiries), 22nd ed. Lahore: Islamic Publications, 1989.

———. *Tawhid'u risalat awr zindagi ba'd mawt ka 'aqli subut* (A rational proof of the unity of God, prophecy, and life after death). Lahore: Islamic Publications, n.d.

———. *Watha'iq-i Mawdudi* (Mawdudi's documents). Lahore: Idarah-i Ma'arif-i Islami, 1984.

———. "Ham ne tahrik-i Pakistan ka sath nehin diya tha" (We were not with the Pakistan movement). *Nawa'-i Waqt.* (August 15, 1975): 3.

———. "Ihya'-i nizam-i Islami" (Revival of Islamic order). *Al-Furqan*, Shah Waliu'llah Number (1940): 16–20.

———. "Khud niwisht" (Autobiography), in Muhammad Yusuf Buhtah, ed., *Mawlana Mawdudi: apni awr dusrun ki nazar main* (Mawlana Mawdudi: In his own and others' views). Lahore: Idarah-i Ma'arif-i Islami, 1984.

———. "Mera bachpan" (My childhood), in Muhammad Yusuf Buhtah, ed., *Mawlana Mawdudi: apni awr dusrun ki nazar main* (Mawlana Mawdudi: In his own and others' views). Lahore: Idarah-i Ma'arif-i Islami, 1984.

———. "Mera mutala'ah" (My readings). *Sayyarah*, Sayyid Mawdudi Number (April–May 1980): 390–392.

————. "Pathankot se Lahore tak" (From Pathankot to Lahore), *Qaumi Digest*, Mawdudi Number (1980): 225–226.

————. "Saw baras pahle ka Hindustan" (India of one hundred years ago), in Muhammad Yusuf Buhtah, ed., *Mawlana Mawdudi: apni awr dusrun ki nazar main* (Mawlana Mawdudi: in his own and others' views). Lahore: Idarah-i Ma'arif-i Islami, 1984, 149–261.

Mawdudi sahab awr unki tahrirat ke muta'aliq chand ahamm mazamin (A few important points about Mawlana Mawdudi and his writings). Karachi: Daru'l-Isha'at, n.d.

Mawdudi, Sayyid Abu'l-Khayr, "Abu'l-A'la ka uslub-i tahrir" (Abu'l-A'la's literary style). *Sayyarah*, Sayyid Mawdudi Number (April–May 1980): 364–366.

Munir, Ahmad, *Mawlana Abu'l-A'la Mawdudi*. Lahore: Atashfishan Publications, 1986.

Mutaqqiu'l-Rahman and Salim Mansur Khalid, eds. *Jab vuh nazim-i a'la the* (When they were nazim-i a'la), 2 vols. Lahore: Idarah-i Matbu'at-i Talabah, 1981.

Nadwi, Sayyid Abu'l-Hasan 'Ali. *'Asr-i hazir main din ki tafhim'u tashrih* (Explanation and understanding of religion in contemporary times). Karachi: Majlis-i Nashriyat-i Islam, n.d.

Nasr, Seyyed Hossein. *Ma'arif-i Islami dar jahan-i mu'athir* (Islamic learning in the contemporary world). Tehran: Jibi, 1969.

Niyazi, Kawthar. *Awr line kat ga'i* (And the line was cut). Lahore: Jang Publications, 1987.

————. *Jama'at-i Islami 'awami 'adalat main* (Jama'at-i Islami in the court of the people). Lahore: Qaumi Kutubkhanih, 1973.

Nizami, 'Allamah Mushtaq Ahmad, *Jama'at-i Islami ka shish mahall* (Jama'at-i Islami's palace of mirrors). Lahore: Maktabah-i Hamidiyah, n.d.

Nu'mani, 'Asim. *Mawlana Mawdudi par jhute ilzamat awr unke mudallil jawabat* (False accusations against Mawlana Mawdudi, and the responses to them). Lahore: Maktabah-i Faisal, n.d.

————. *Tasawwuf awr ta'mir-i sirat* (Sufism and the building of character). Lahore: Islamic Publications, 1972.

———— ed., *Makatib-i Sayyid Abu'l-A'la Mawdudi* (Correspondences of Sayyid Abu'l-A'la Mawdudi), 2 vols. Lahore: Islamic Publications, 1977.

Nu'mani, Mawlana Muhammad Manzur. *Mawlana Mawdudi mere sath rifaqat ki sarguzasht awr ab mera mau'qaf* (The story of my friendship with Mawlana Mawdudi, and my position now). Lahore: Quraishi Book Agency, 1980.

————. *Tablighi Jama'at, Jama'at-i Islami, awr Brelwi hazrat* (Tablighi Jama'at, Jama'at-i Islami, and Brelwis). Lucknow: Al-Furqan Book Depot, 1980.

Qadr, Sayyid Ahmad. *'Asr-i hazir main din ki tafhim'u tashrih par ik nazar* (A glance at 'Asr-i hazar main din ki tafhim'u tashrih). Lahore: Maktabah-i Ta'mir-i Insaniyat, 1979.

Qadri, Mahiru'l-. "Chand nuqush-i zindagi" (Few sketches of life), in Muhammad Yusuf Buhtah, ed., *Mawlana Mawdudi: apni awr dusrun ki nazar main* (Mawlana Mawdudi: In his own and others' views). Lahore: Idarah-i Ma'arif Islami, 1984, 234–246.

————. "Tarikhsaz shakhsiyat" (The history-making personality). *Sayyarah*, Sayyid Mawdudi Number (April–May 1980): 216–220.

Qadri, Muhammad Tahiru'l. *Minhaju'l-afkar* (Path of thought), 10 vols. Lahore: Idarah-i Minhaju'l-Qur'an, 1990.

Qasmi, Ja'far. "Mujhe yad hey, sab zara zara" (My recollections, little by little). *Nida*, April 17, 1990, 28–34.

Qaumi Digest, Mawdudi Number (1980).

Rahat Gul, Mawlana. *Jama'at-i Islami ka tanha musafir* (Jama'at-i Islami's sole traveler). Peshawar: Markaz-i 'Ulum-i Islamiyyah-i Pakistan, n.d.

Rahi, Akhtar. *Mas'ud 'Alam Nadwi: sawanih'u makatib* (Mas'ud 'Alam Nadwi: Biography and correspondences). Gujrat, Pakistan: Maktabah-i Zafar, 1975.

Rana, Jamil. *'Adilanah difa' awr 'ulama-i ahl-i sunnat* (Equitable defense and the Brailwi ulama). Lahore: Daru'l-Fikr, 1968.

Rana, Jalil Ahmad and Salim Mansur Khalid, eds. *Tazkirah-i Sayyid Mawdudi* (Biography of Sayyid Mawdudi). Lahore: Idarah-i Ma'arif-i Islami, 1986.

Rudad-i Jama'at-i Islami (Proceedings of Jama'at-i Islami), 7 vols. Lahore: Islamic Publications, 1938–1991.

Safdar Mir, Muhammad. *Mawdudiyat awr mawjudah siyasi kashmakash* (Mawdudiism and the current political crisis), 2nd ed. Lahore: Al-Bayan, 1970.

Sajjad Jan. *Mawlana Mawdudi hi mujrim kiyun?* (How can Mawlana Mawdudi alone be guilty?). Lahore: Maktabah-i Tafsir, n.d.

Salahu'ddin, Muhammad. "Qa'idin-i Jama'at ki khidmat main chand ma'ruzat" (A few considerations of the leadership of the Jama'at). *Takbir* (November 16, 1989): 8–11.

———. "Tajziah" (Analysis). *Takbir* (September 28, 1989): 31.

Sayyarah, Sayyid Mawdudi Number (April–May 1980).

Sayyarah Digest, Mawdudi Number (December 1979).

Shahpuri, Abad. *Tarikh-i Jama'at-i Islami* (History of Jama'at-i Islami). Lahore: Idarah-i Ma'arif-i Islami, 1989.

Shami, Mujibu'l-Rahman. "Kiran se aftab tak" (From rays to the sun). *Haftrozah Zindagi*, Mawdudi Number (September 29–October 5, 1989): 31–33.

Siddiqi, 'Abdu'l-Hamid. *Iman awr akhlaq* (Faith and ethics), reprint. Lahore: Al-Badr Publications, n.d..

Siddiqi, Manzuru'l-Haq. "Tahrik-i Pakistan: talib-i 'ilm ki yadain" (A student's recollections of the Pakistan movement), in Salim Mansur Khalid, ed., *Talabah tahrikain* (Student movements). Lahore: Al-Badr Publications, 1989, 1:91–104.

Siddiqi, Na'im. *Al-Mawdudi*. Lahore: Idarah-i Ma'arif-i Islami, 1963.

———. "Mawlana Mawdudi rahmatu'llah alaihu ki lisani'u adabi khidmat" (The late Mawlana Mawdudi's linguistic and literary contributions). *Sayyarah*, Sayyid Mawdudi Number (April–May 1980): 5–12.

Siddiqi, Rahman. "Mawlana Azad awr Mawlana Mawdudi ke mabain ik gumshudah kari" (A lost link in the relations between Mawlana Azad and Mawlana Mawdudi). *Nida* (February 7–13, 1990): 20–22.

Ulama convention ki rudad (Proceedings of the ulama convention). Lahore: Jami'at-i Ittihad-i 'Ulama, 1989.

'Uthmani, Mawlana Muhammad Taqi. "Hakimu'l-ummat ke siyasi afkar" (The political views of the sage of the ummah). *Al-Balagh* (March 1990): 23–53.

Yahya, Muhammad. "Sikandarpur se Lahore tak" (From Sikandapur to Lahore). *Qaumi Digest*, Mawdudi Number (1980): 169–189.

Yusuf, Mufti Muhammad. *Mawlana Mawdudi par i'tirazat ka 'ilmi ja'izah* (A rational response to criticisms of Mawlana Mawdudi), 2 vols., reprint. Lahore: Islamic Publications, 1967.

Yusuf, Muhammad. "Mawlana Mawdudi bihaithiyat-i ik adib" (Mawlana Mawdudi as a literary figure). *Sayyarah*, Sayyid Mawdudi Number (April–May 1980): 115–117.

English and French Sources

Abbott, Freeland. *Islam and Pakistan*. Ithaca, N.Y.: Cornell University Press, 1968.

———. "The Jama'at-i-Islami of Pakistan." *Middle East Journal* 11.1 (winter 1957): 37–51.

————. "Mawlana Mawdudi on Qur'anic Interpretation." *Muslim World* 48 (1958): 6–19.

Abd, Abdur Rahman. *Sayyed Maududi Faces the Death Sentence*, reprint. Lahore: Islamic Publications, 1978.

Abrahamian, Ervand. *Khomeinism*. Berkeley: University of California Press, 1993.

Adams, Charles J. "The Authority of the Prophetic *Hadith* in the Eyes of Some Modern Muslims," in Donald P. Little, ed., *Essays in Islamic Civilization Presented to Niyazi Berkes*. Leiden: E. J. Brill, 1976, 25–47.

————. "The Ideology of Mawlana Mawdudi," in Donald E. Smith, ed., *South Asian Politics and Religion*. Princeton, N.J.: Princeton University Press, 1966, 371–397.

————. "Mawdudi and the Islamic State," in John L. Esposito, ed., *Voices of Resurgent Islam*. New York: Oxford University Press, 1983, 99–133.

Ahmad, Aziz, *Iqbal and the Recent Exposition of Islamic Political Thought*. Lahore: Muhammad Ashraf, 1950.

————. *Islamic Modernism in India and Pakistan, 1857–1964*. London: Oxford University Press, 1967.

————. "Mawdudi and Orthodox Fundamentalism of Pakistan." *Middle East Journal* 21.3 (summer 1967): 369–380.

Ahmad, Eqbal. "Islam and Politics," in Yvonne Y. Haddad et al., eds., *The Islamic Impact*. Syracuse, N.Y.: Syracuse University Press, 1984, 7–26.

Ahmad, Hazrat Mirza Bashir-ud-Din Mahmud. *Invitation to Ahmadiyyat*. London: Routledge & Kegan Paul, 1980.

Ahmad, Imtiaz. *Modernization and Social Change among Muslims in India*. Delhi: Manohar, 1983.

————. ed. *Caste and Social Stratification among the Muslims*. Delhi: Manohar, 1973.

Ahmad, Khurshid. *The Movement of Jama'at-e-Islami, Pakistan*. Lahore: Jama'at-e-Islami, Pakistan, 1989.

————. *Studies in the Family Law of Islam*. Karachi: Chiragh-i Rah Publications, 1961.

————. "The Nature of Islamic Resurgence," in John L. Esposito, ed., *Voices of Resurgent Islam*. New York: Oxford University Press, 1983, 218–229.

Ahmad, Khurshid and Zafar Ishaq Ansari. "Mawlana Sayyid Abul A'la Mawdudi: An Introduction to His Vision of Islam and Islamic Revival," in Khurshid Ahmad and Zafar Ishaq Ansari, eds., *Islamic Perspectives: Studies In Honour of Mawlana Sayyid Abul A'la Mawdudi*. Leicester: Islamic Foundation, 1979, 359–384.

Ahmad, Mumtaz. "Islamic Fundamentalism in South Asia: The Jamaat-i-Islami and the Tablighi Jamaat," in Martin E. Marty and R. Scott Appleby, eds., *Fundamentalisms Observed*. Chicago: University of Chicago Press, 1991, 457–530.

————. "Parliament, Parties, Polls, and Islam: Issues in the Current Debate on Religion and Politics in Pakistan." *American Journal of the Islamic Social Sciences* 2.1 (spring 1985): 15–28.

Ahmad, Syed Riaz. *Maulana Maududi and the Islamic State*. Lahore: People's Publishing House, 1976.

Ahmed, Akbar S. *Discovering Islam: Making Sense of Muslim History and Society*. London: Routledge & Kegan Paul, 1988.

Ahmed, Ishtiaq. *The Concept of an Islamic State: An Analysis of the Ideological Controversy in Pakistan*. New York: St. Martin's Press, 1987.

Ahmed, Rafiuddin. "Redefining Muslim Identity in South Asia: The Transformation of the Jama'at-i Islami," in Martin E. Marty and R. Scott Appleby, eds., *Accounting for Fundamentalisms: The Dynamic Character of Movements*. Chicago: University of Chicago Press, 1994, 669–705.

Ahmed, Zafaryab. "Maudoodi's Islamic State," in Asghar Khan, ed., *Islam, Politics and the State: The Pakistan Experience*. London: Zed Press, 1985, 95–113.

Aijaz, S. Zakir. *Selected Speeches and Writings of Mawlana Mawdudi*. Karachi: International Islamic Publishers, 1981.

Algar, Hamid, trans. *Islam and Revolution: Writings and Declarations of Imam Khomeini*, annotated. Berkeley, Mizan Press, 1981.

Ali, Choudhary Rahmat. *India: The Continent of Dinia or the Country of Doom?* N.p., 1945.

Anderson, Benedict. *Imagined Communities: Reflections on the Origin and Spread of Nationalism*, 2nd ed. New York: Verso, 1991.

Anwar, Zainah. *Islamic Fundamentalism in Malaysia*, 2nd ed. Kuala Lumpur: Pelanduk Publications, 1989.

Arendt, Hannah. *On Revolution*. New York: Viking Press, 1965.

———. "Tradition and the Modern Age," in Hannah Arendt, ed., *Between Past and Future*. New York: Penguin, 1985, 17–40.

Arjomand, Said Amir. *The Shadow of God and the Hidden Imam: Religion, Political Order, and Societal Change in Shi'ite Iran from the Beginning to 1890*. Chicago: University of Chicago Press, 1984.

———. *The Turban for the Crown: The Islamic Revolution in Iran*. New York: Oxford University Press, 1988.

———. "The Emergence of Islamic Political Ideologies," in James A. Beckford and Thomas Luckmann, eds., *The Changing Face of Religion*. London: Sage Publications, 1989, 109–123.

———. "History, Structure, and Revolution in the Shi'ite Tradition in Contemporary Iran." *International Political Science Review* 10.2 (1989): 111–119.

———. "Religion and Constitutionalism in Western History and in Modern Iran and Pakistan," in Said Amir Arjomand, ed., *The Political Dimensions of Religion*. Albany, N.Y.: SUNY Press, 1993, 69–99.

———. "Shi'ite Islam and the Revolution in Iran." *Government and Opposition* 16.3 (summer 1981): 293–316.

Ayubi, Nazih. *Political Islam: Religion and Politics in the Arab World*. New York: Routledge, 1991.

Aziz, K. K. *A History of the Idea of Pakistan*, 4 vols. Lahore: Vanguard Books, 1987.

Bahadur, Kalim. *The Jama'at-i Islami of Pakistan*. New Delhi: Chetana Publications, 1977.

Bayat, Mangol. "The Iranian Revolution of 1978–79: Fundamentalist or Modern?" *Middle East Journal* 37.1 (winter 1983): 30–42.

Binder, Leonard. *Islamic Liberalism: A Critique of Development Ideologies*. Chicago: University of Chicago Press, 1988.

———. *Religion and Politics in Pakistan*. Berkeley: University of California Press, 1961.

Brass, Paul. *Ethnicity and Nationalism: Theory and Comparison*. London: Sage, 1991.

———. "Elite Groups, Symbol Manipulation and Ethnic Identity among the Muslims of South Asia," in David Taylor and Malcolm Yapp, eds., *Political Identity in South Asia*. London: Curzon Press, 1979, 35–77.

Briggs, F. S. "The Indian Hijrat of 1920," *Muslim World* 20.2 (April 1930): 167–186.

Brohi, Allahbukhsh K. "Mawlana Abul A'la Mawdudi: The Man, the Scholar, the Reformer," in Khurshid Ahmad and Zafar Ishaq Ansari, eds., *Islamic Perspectives: Studies in Honour of Sayyid Abul A'la Mawdudi*. Leicester: Islamic Foundation, 1979, 289–312.

Chaterjee, Partha. *Nationalist Thought and the Colonial World: A Derivative Discourse*. Tokyo: United Nations University, 1986.

Chehabi, H. E. *Iranian Politics and Religious Modernism: The Liberation Movement of Iran under the Shah and Khomeini*. Ithaca, N.Y.: Cornell University Press, 1990.

Correspondences between Maulana Maudoodi and Maryam Jameelah, 4th ed. Lahore: Muhammad Yusuf Khan, 1986.

Coulson, N. J. *A History of Islamic Law*, reprint. Edinburgh: Edinburgh University Press, 1978.

Cragg, Kenneth. *Counsels in Contemporary Islam*. Edinburgh: Edinburgh University Press, 1965.

Dabashi, Hamid. *Authority in Islam: From the Rise of Muhammad to the Establishment of the Umayyads*. New Brunswick, N.J.: Transaction Publishers, 1989.

———. "'Islamic Ideology': The Perils and Promises of A Neologism," in Hooshang Amirahmadi and Manoucher Parvin, eds., *Post-Revolutionary Iran*. Boulder, Colo.: Westview Press, 1988, 11–21.

———. "Symbiosis of Religious and Political Authorities in Islam," in Thomas Robbins and Ronald Robertson, eds. *Church-State Relations: Tensions and Transitions*. New Brunswick, N.J.: Transaction Books, 1987, 183–203.

Desai, Niranjan, ed. *Contemporary Relevance of Sufism*. New Delhi: Council for Cultural Relations, 1993.

Douglas, Ian Henderson. *Abul Kalam Azad: An Intellectual and Religious Biography*, edited by Gail Minault and Christian W. Troll. Delhi: Oxford University Press, 1988.

Edwards, David B. "Summoning Muslims: Print, Politics, and Religious Ideology in Afghanistan." *Journal of Asian Studies* 53.3 (August 1993): 609–628

El-Effendi, Abdelwahab, "The Long March from Lahore to Khartoum: Beyond the 'Muslim Reformation,'" *British Society for Middle Eastern Studies Bulletin* 17.2 (1990): 137–151.

Enayat, Hamid. *Modern Islamic Political Thought*. Austin, Tex.: The University of Texas Press, 1982.

Esposito, John L. *Islam and Politics*, 3rd ed. Syracuse, N.Y.: Syracuse University Press, 1991.

———. *The Islamic Threat: Myth or Reality?* New York: Oxford University Press, 1992.

———. *Islam the Straight Path*. New York: Oxford University Press, 1988.

Ewing, Katherine. "The Pir or Sufi Saint in Pakistan." Ph.D. dissertation, Department of Anthropology, University of Chicago, 1980.

———. "The Politics of Sufism: Redefining the Saints of Pakistan." *Journal of Asian Studies* 42.2 (February 1983): 251–268.

Freitag, Sandria. *Collective Action and Community: Public Arenas and the Emergence of Communalism in India*. Berkeley: University of California Press, 1989.

Friedmann, Yohanan. *Prophecy Continuous: Aspects of Ahmadi Religious Thought and Its Medieval Background*. Berkeley: University of California Press, 1989.

———. *Shaikh Ahmad Sirhindi: An Outline of His Thought and a Study of His Image in the Eyes of Posterity*. Montreal: McGill University Press, 1971.

Geertz, Clifford. *Islam Observed: Religious Development in Morocco and Indonesia*. Chicago: University of Chicago Press, 1971.

———. "'Internal Conversion' in Contemporary Bali," in Clifford Geertz, ed., *Interpretation of Cultures*. New York: Basic Books, 1973.

Gellner, Ernest. *Postmodernism, Reason and Religion*. New York: Routledge, 1992.

Gerth, H. H. and C. Wright Mills, eds. and trans. *From Max Weber: Essays in Sociology*. Oxford: Oxford University Press, 1946.

Ghaffar Khan, Hafiz A. "Shah Wali Allah: An Analysis of His Metaphysical Thought." Ph.D. dissertation, Department of Religion, Temple University, 1986.

Gibb, Hamilton A. R. *Modern Trends in Islam*. Chicago: University of Chicago Press, 1947.

————. *Studies on the Civilization of Islam,* 2nd ed., edited by Stanford Shaw and William Polk. (Princeton, N.J.: Princeton University Press, 1982).

Gibb, Hamilton A. R. et al., eds. *Encyclopaedia of Islam,* 2nd ed. Leiden: E. J. Brill, 1960–Present.

Gilani, Sayyid Asad. *Maududi; Thought and Movement.* Lahore: Islamic Publications, 1984.

Gilmartin, David. *Empire and Islam: Punjab and the Making of Pakistan.* Berkeley: University of California Press, 1988.

————. "Democracy, Nationalism and the Public: A Speculation on Colonial Muslim Politics." *South Asia* 14.1 (June 1991): 123–140.

Graham, William A. "Traditionalism in Islam: An Essay in Interpretation." *Journal of Interdisciplinary History* 23.3 (winter 1993): 495–522.

Gran, Peter. *Islamic Roots of Capitalism: Egypt, 1760–1840.* Austin, Tex.: University of Texas Press, 1979.

Greenfeld, Liah. *Nationalism: Five Roads to Modernity.* Cambridge: Harvard University Press, 1992.

Haddad, Yvonne Y. and Jane I. Smith. *Mission to America: Five Islamic Sectarian Communities in North America.* Gainesville: University Press of Florida, 1993.

Hardy, Peter. "The Ulama in British India," unpublished paper.

Hasan, Masudul. *Sayyid Abul A'ala Maududi and His Thought,* 2 vols. Lahore: Islamic Publications, 1984.

Hermansen, Marcia K. "Biography and Hagiography," in John L. Esposito, ed., *The Oxford Encyclopedia of the Modern Islamic World.* New York: Oxford University Press, 1995.

————. "Interdisciplinary Approaches to Islamic Biographical Materials." *Religion* 18 (1988): 163–182.

Hourani, Albert. *Arabic Thought in the Liberal Age, 1798–1931.* Cambridge: Cambridge University Press, 1962.

Huntington, Samuel P. *Political Order in Changing Societies.* New Haven, Conn.: Yale University Press, 1968.

Ikram, S. M. *Modern Muslim India and the Birth of Pakistan,* 2nd ed. Lahore: Institute of Islamic Culture, 1965.

Jalal, Ayesha *The State of Martial Rule: The Origins of Pakistan's Political Economy of Defence.* Cambridge: Cambridge University Press, 1990.

Jameelah, Maryam. *Islam and Modernism,* reprint. Lahore: Mohammad Yusuf Khan, 1988.

————. *Islam and Orientalism,* reprint. Lahore: Mohammad Yusuf Khan, 1987.

————. *Islam in Theory and Practice.* Lahore: Mohammad Yusuf Khan, 1973.

————. *Islam versus the West,* reprint. Lahore: Mohammad Yusuf Khan, 1988.

————. *Is Western Civilization Universal?* Lahore: Mohammad Yusuf Khan, 1969.

————. *Manifesto of the Islamic Movement.* Lahore: Mohammad Yusuf Khan, 1969.

————. *Who Is Maudoodi?* Lahore: Mohammad Yusuf Khan, 1973.

————. "An Appraisal of Some Aspects of Maulana Sayyid Ala Maudoodi's Life and Thought," *Islamic Quarterly* 31.2 (1987): 116–130.

Jones, Kenneth W. *Arya Dharm.* Berkeley: University of California Press, 1976.

————. *Socio-Religious Reform Movements in British India.* Cambridge: Cambridge University Press, 1992.

Jurgensmeyer, Mark. *The New Cold War? Religious Nationalism Confronts the Secular State.* Berkeley: University of California Press, 1993.

Keddie, Nikki. *Roots of Revolution.* New Haven, Conn.: Yale University Press, 1981.

Kepel, Gilles. *The Revenge of God,* translated by Alan Braley. University Park, Pa: Pennsylvania State University Press, 1994.

Kerr, Malcolm. *Islamic Reform.* Oxford: Oxford University Press, 1966.

Khan, M. R. *The Delusion of Grandeur: Maulana Maudoodi and His Jamaat.* Karachi: Lahore Book House, 1964.

Khan, Mawlana Wahidu'ddin. *Tabligh Movement.* N.p., 1986.

Knysh, Alexander. "*Irfan* Revisited: Khomeini and the Legacy of Islamic Mysticism." *Middle East Journal* 46.4 (autumn 1992): 631–653.

Kuran, Timur. "The Economic Impact of Islamic Fundamentalism," in Martin Marty and R. Scott Appelby, eds., *Fundamentalisms and the State.* Chicago: University of Chicago Press, 1993, 302–341.

Lambton, Ann K. S. *State and Government in Medieval Islam: An Introduction to the Study of Islamic Political Theory: The Jurists.* London: Oxford University Press, 1981.

Lapidus, Ira M. "Islamic Political Movements: Patterns of Historical Change," in Edmund Burke III and Ira M. Lapidus, eds., *Islam, Politics, and Social Movements.* Berkeley: University of California Press, 1988, 3–16.

———. "The Separation of State and Religion in the Development of Early Islamic Society." *International Journal of Middle East Studies* 6 (1975): 363–385.

Lawrence, Bruce. *Defenders of God: The Fundamentalist Revolt against the Modern Age.* San Francisco: Harper and Row, 1989.

Lelyveld, David. *Aligarh's First Generation: Muslim Solidarity in British India.* Princeton, N.J.: Princeton University Press, 1978.

Leonard, Karen. "Banking Firms in Nineteenth-Century Hyderabad Politics." *Modern Asian Studies* 15.2 (April 1981): 177–201.

———. "The Deccani Synthesis in Old Hyderabad: A Historiographic Essay." *Journal of Pakistan Historical Society* 21.4 (October 1973): 205–218.

———. "The Hyderabad Political System and Its Participants." *Journal of Asian Studies* 30.3 (May 1971): 569–582.

Lerman, Eran. "Mawdudi's Concept of Islam." *Middle Eastern Studies* 17.4 (October 1981): 492–509.

Lewis, Philip. *Islamic Britain: Religion, Politics and Identity among British Muslims.* London: I. B. Tauris, 1994.

Lings, Martin. *What Is Sufism?* Berkeley: University of California Press, 1975.

Madelung, Wilfred. *Religious Trends in Early Islamic Iran.* New York: Columbia Lectures on Iranian Studies, 1988.

Malik, Hafeez, ed. *Iqbal: Poet-Philosopher of Pakistan.* New York: Columbia University Press, 1971.

Manifesto of Jamaat-e-Islami, Pakistan. Karachi: Jamaat-e-Islami, 1958.

Manifesto of Jama'at-i Islami of Pakistan. Lahore: Jama'at-i Islami, 1970.

Mardin, Şerif. *Religion and Social Change in Modern Turkey: The Case of Bediüzzaman Said Nursi.* Albany, N.Y.: SUNY Press, 1989.

Marwa, I. S., "Tabligh Movement among the Meos of Mewat," in M. S. A. Rao, ed., *Social Movement in India.* New Delhi: Manohar, 1979, 2:79–100.

Mawdudi, Sayyid Abu'l A'la. *Capitalism, Socialism and Islam,* translated by Sharif Ahmad Khan, Lahore: Islamic Book Publishers, 1977.

———. *Come Let Us Change the World,* edited and translated by Kaukab Siddiq. Washington, D.C.: Islamic Party of North America, 1972.

———. *Economic System of Islam,* edited by Khurshid Ahmad, translated by Riaz Husain, reprint Lahore: Islamic Publications, 1984.

———. *The Ethical View-Point of Islam,* translated by Maahur al-Din Siddiqi. Lahore: Markazi Maktaba Jama'at-e-Islami Pakistan, 1953.

———. *First Principles of the Islamic State,* 6th ed. Lahore: Islamic Publications, 1983.

———. *Fundamentals of Islam,* reprint. Delhi: Markazi Maktabah-i Islami, 1978.

————. *Human Rights in Islam*, translated by Khurshid Ahmad and Ahmad Said Khan. Leicester: Islamic Foundation, 1976.

————. *Introduction to the Study of the Qur'an*. Delhi: Maktaba Jamaat-e-Islami Hind, 1971.

————. *Islam: An Historical Perspective*, translated by Ashraf Abu Turab. Leicester: Islamic Foundation, 1974.

————. *Islamic Economic System: Principles and Objectives*, reprint. Delhi: Markazi Maktabah Islami, 1980.

————. *Islamic Law and Constitution*, edited by Khurshid Ahmad. Karachi: Jamaat-e-Islami Publications, 1955.

————. *The Islamic Movement; Dynamics of Values, Power and Change*, edited and translated by Khurram Murad. Leicester: Islamic Foundation, 1984.

————. *Islam Today*. Beirut: International Islamic Federation of Student Organizations, 1985.

————. *The Islamic Way of Life*, edited and translated by Khurram Murad and Khurshid Ahmad. Leicester: Islamic Foundation, 1986.

————. *Kashmir: A Call to the Conscience of Humanity*. Lahore: Jama'at-e-Islami, 1966.

————. *Let Us Be Muslims*, translated and edited by Khurram Jah Murad. Leicester: Islamic Foundation, 1985.

————. *The Message of Jama'at-i-Islami*. Lahore: n.p., 1955.

————. *The Message of the Prophet's Seerat*. Kuwait: Islamic Books Publishers, 1982.

————. *Nationalism in India*. Pathankot: Maktab-e-Jama'at-e-Islami, 1947.

————. *The Political Situation in Pakistan*. Karachi: Jamaat-e-Islami, 1965.

————. *The Process of Islamic Revolution*, 8th ed. Lahore: Islamic Publications, 1980.

————. *Purdah and the Status of Women in Islam*, reprint Lahore: Islamic Publications, 1972.

————. *The Religion of Truth*, edited and translated by Misbahu'l-Islam Faruqi. Delhi: Markazi Maktaba Jamaat-e-Islami Hind, 1972.

————. *A Short History of the Revivalist Movement in Islam*, translated by Al-Ash'ari, reprint. Lahore: Islamic Publications, 1963.

————. *System of Government under the Holy Prophet*. Lahore: Islamic Publications, 1978.

————. *Towards Understanding Islam*, translated and edited by Khurshid Ahmad, reprint. Indianapolis: Islamic Teaching Center, 1977.

————. *Towards Understanding the Qur'an*, translated by Zafar Ishaq Ansari. Leicester: Islamic Foundation, 1988–present.

————. *Witness unto Mankind: The Purpose and Duty of the Muslim Ummah*, edited and translated by Khurram Murad. Leicester: Islamic Foundation, 1986.

————. "Abu Hanifa and Abu Yusuf," in M. M. Sharif, ed., *A History of Muslim Philosophy*, 2 vols. Wiesbaden: Otto Harrasowitz, 1963, 1:674–703.

————. "Economic and Political Teachings of the Qur'an," in M. M. Sharif, ed., *A History of Muslim Philosophy*. Wiesbaden: Otto Harrasowitz, 1963, 1:178–198.

————. "Foundations of Culture," *Criterion* 6.4 (July–August 1971): 9–11.

————. "Political Thought in Early Islam," in M. M. Sharif, ed., *A History of Muslim Philosophy*. Wiesbaden: Otto Harrasowitz, 1963, 1:656–672.

————. "Three Virtues and Three Vices." *Muslim Digest* 9.12 (July 1959): 14–17.

————. and Sh. Mohammad Abu Zahra. "The Role of 'Ijtihad' and the Scope of Legislation in Islam." *Muslim Digest* 9.6 (January 1959): 15–20.

Mayer, Ann Elizabeth. *Islam and Human Rights: Tradition and Politics*. Boulder, Colo.: Westview Press, 1991.

McDonough, Sheila. *Muslim Ethics and Modernity: A Comparative Study of the Ethical*

Thought of Sayyid Ahmad Khan and Mawlana Mawdudi. Waterloo, Ontario: Wilfred
   Laurier University Press, 1984.

Metcalf, Barbara D. *Islamic Revival in British India: Deoband, 1860–1900.* Princeton, N.J.:
   Princeton University Press, 1982.

———. "Living Hadith in the Tablighi Jama'at." *Journal of Asian Studies* 53.3 (August
   1993): 584–608.

Minault, Gail. *The Khilafat Movement: Religious Symbolisms and Political Mobilization in
   India.* New York: Columbia University Press, 1982.

Mir, Mustansir. *Coherence in the Qur'an.* Indianapolis: American Trust Publications, 1986.

Mitchell, Richard P. *The Society of the Muslim Brothers,* 2nd ed. New York: Oxford University Press, 1993.

Mitchell, Timothy. *Colonising Egypt.* Cambridge: Cambridge University Press, 1988.

Moizuddin, Qazi Hasan. "Syed Abul A'la Maududi," in *The Muslim Luminaries: Leaders
   of Religious, Intellectual and Political Revival in South Asia.* Islamabad: National Hijra
   Council, 1988.

Morris, James. *The Wisdom of the Throne: An Introduction to the Philosophy of Mulla Sadra.*
   Princeton, N.J.: Princeton University Press, 1981.

Moten, A. Rashid. "Pure and Practical Ideology: The Thought of Mawlana Mawdudi
   (1903–1979)." *Islamic Quarterly.* 28.4 (1984): 217–240.

Mottahedeh, Roy. *Mantle of the Prophet: Religion and Politics in Iran.* New York: Simon
   and Shuster, 1985.

Moussalli, Ahmad S. *Radical Islamic Fundamentalism: The Ideological and Political Discourse of Sayyid Qutb.* Beirut: American University of Beirut, 1992.

Muhammad, Chaudhri Ghulam. *Jamaat-e-Islami and Foreign Policy.* Karachi: Rajab Ali,
   1963/1964.

Mujeeb, Muhammad. *The Indian Muslims.* London: Allen & Unwin, 1967.

Munir, Muhammad. *From Jinnah to Zia.* Lahore: Vanguard Books, 1979.

Nadwi, Sayyid Abu'l-Hasan 'Ali. *Islam and the World,* translated by Muhammad Arif Kidwai,
   repring. Beirut: International Islamic Federation of Student Organizations, 1983.

———. *Life and Mission of Maulana Mohammad Ilyas,* reprint. Lucknow: Academy of
   Islamic Research and Publications, 1983.

Nasr, Seyyed Hossein. *Ideals and Realities of Islam,* 3rd ed. London: Allen & Unwin,
   1975.

———. *Sadr al-Din Shirazi and His Transcendent Theosophy.* Tehran: Imperial Iranian
   Academy of Philosophy, 1978.

———. *Sufi Essays.* London: Allen & Unwin, 1972.

———. *Traditional Islam in the Modern World.* London: Routledge & Kegan Paul, 1987.

———. ed. *Islamic Spirituality,* 2 vols. New York: Crossroads, 1987.

———. "Decadence, Deviation and Renaissance in the Context of Contemporary Islam,"
   in Khurshid Ahmad and Zafar Ishaq Ansari, eds., *Islamic Perspectives: Studies in
   Honour of Sayyid Abul A'la Mawdudi.* Leicester: Islamic Foundation, 1979, 35–42.

———. "God," in Seyyed Hossein Nasr, ed., *Islamic Spirituality.* New York: Crossroads,
   1987, 1:311–323.

———. "Islam in the World Today: An Overview," in Cyriac Pullapilly, ed., *Islam in
   the Contemporary World.* Notre Dame, Ind.: Cross Roads Books, 1980, 1–10.

———. "Oral Transmission and the Book in Islamic Education: The Spoken and Written Word." *Journal of Islamic Studies* 3.1 (January 1992): 1–14.

———. "The Spiritual Significance of Jihad," *Parabola* 7.4 (fall 1982): 14–19.

Nasr, Seyyed Vali Reza. *The Vanguard of the Islamic Revolution: The Jama'at-i Islami of
   Pakistan.* Berkeley: University of California Press, 1994.

———. "Communalism and Fundamentalism: A Re-examination of the Origins of Islamic Fundamentalism," *Contention* 4.2 (winter 1995): 121–139.

———. "Islamic Economics: Novel Perspectives on Change." *Middle Eastern Studies* 25.4 (October 1989): 516–530.

———. "Religious Modernism in the Arab World, India and Iran: The Perils and Prospects of a Discourse." *Muslim World.* 83.1 (January 1993): 20–47.

———. "Towards a Philosophy of Islamic Economics." *Muslim World*, 77.3–4 (July–October 1987): 175–196.

———. "Maryam Jameelah," in John L. Esposito, ed., *The Oxford Encyclopedia of the Modern Islamic World*. New York: Oxford University Press, 1995.

Niazi, Kausar. *Zulfiqar Ali Bhutto of Pakistan: The Last Days*. New Delhi: Vikas Publishing House, 1992.

Niebuhr, H. R., *Social Sources of Denominationalism*. New York: Shoe String Press, 1954.

Nomani, Farhad and Ali Rahnema. *Islamic Economic Systems*. London: Zed Press, 1994.

Pickthall, Mohammed Marmaduke. *The Meaning of the Glorious Koran*, reprint. New York: Mentor Books, n.d.

Poston, Larry. *Islamic Da'wah in the West: Muslim Missionary Activity and the Dynamics of Conversion to Islam*. New York: Oxford University Press, 1992.

Qureshi, Ishtiaq Husain. *Ulema in Politics; A Study Relating to the Political Activities of the Ulema in South Asian Subcontinent from 1566 to 1947*. Karachi: Ma'aref, 1972.

Rahman, Fazlur. *Islam and Modernity: The Transformation of an Intellectual Tradition*. Chicago: University of Chicago Press, 1982.

———. *The Philosophy of Mulla Sadra*. Albany, N.Y.: SUNY Press, 1975.

———. "The Principle of Shura and the Role of the Ummah in Islam," in Mumtaz Ahmad, ed., *State, Politics, and Islam*. Indianapolis: American Trust Publications, 1986, 87–96.

Ramadan, Abdel Azim. "Fundamentalist Influence in Egypt: The Strategies of the Muslim Brotherhood and the Takfir Groups," in Martin E. Marty and R. Scott Appelby, eds., *Fundamentalisms and the State: Remaking Polities, Economies, and Militance*. Chicago: University of Chicago Press, 1993, 152–183.

Report of the Court of Inquiry Constituted under Punjab Act 11 of 1954 to Enquire into the Punjab Disturbances of 1953. Lahore: Government of Punjab, 1954.

Riesebrodt, Martin. *Pious Passion: The Emergence of Modern Fundamentalism in the United States and Iran*. Berkeley: University of California Press, 1993.

Rizvi, Sayyid Athar Abbas. *Shah Wali-Allah and His Times*. Canberra: Ma'rifat, 1980.

———. "Chishtiyyah," in Seyyed Hossein Nasr, ed., *Islamic Spirituality*. New York: Crossroads, 1991, 2:127–143.

———. "Sufism in the Indian Subcontinent," in Seyyed Hossein Nasr, ed., *Islamic Spirituality*. New York: Crossroad, 1991, 2:239–258.

Robinson, Francis. *Separatism among Indian Muslims: The Politics of the United Provinces' Muslims, 1860–1923*. Cambridge: Cambridge University Press, 1974.

———. "Islam and Muslim Separatism," in David Taylor and Malcolm Yapp, eds., *Political Identity in South Asia*. London: Curzon Press, 1979, 78–112.

———. "Scholarship and Mysticism in 18th Century Awadh," in A. L. Dallapiccola and S. Z. Lallemant, eds. *Islam and Indian Religions*, Vol. 1: Texts. Stuttgart: Steiner, 1993: 377–398.

———. "Technology and Religious Change: Islam and the Impact of Print." *Modern Asian Studies* 27.1 (February 1993): 229–251.

Rosenthal, Erwin I. J, *Islam in the Modern Nation State*. Cambridge: Cambridge University Press, 1965.

Roy, Olivier. *The Failure of Political Islam*, translated by Carol Volk. Cambridge: Harvard University Press, 1994.

──────. *Islam and Resistance in Afghanistan*, 2nd ed. New York: Cambridge University Press, 1990.

Saeed, Muhammad. *Lahore: A Memoir.* Lahore: Vanguard Books, 1989.

Salem, E. A., *Political Theory and Institutions of the Khawarij.* Baltimore: Johns Hopkins University Press, 1956.

Saulat, Sarwat. *Maulana Maududi.* Karachi: International Islamic Publishers, 1979.

Sayeed, Khalid bin. *Pakistan: The Formative Phase, 1857–1948.* London: Oxford University Press, 1968.

Schimmel, Annemarie. *Gabriel's Wing.* Leiden: E. J. Brill, 1963.

──────. *Mystical Dimensions of Islam.* Chapel Hill: University of North Carolina Press, 1975.

Schleifer, S. Abdullah "Jihad: Sacred Struggle in Islam IV." *Islamic Quarterly* 28.2 (1984): 87–102.

Shaikh, Farzana. *Community and Consensus in Islam: Mulism Representation in Colonial India, 1860–1947.* Cambridge: Cambridge University Press, 1989.

Shayegan, Daryush. *Hindouisme et Soufisme* (Hinduism and Sufism). Paris: Editions de la Difference, 1979.

──────. *Qu'est-ce qu'une revolution religieuse?* (What is a religious revolution?). Paris: Les Presses D'Aujourdhui, 1982.

──────. *Le regard mutile, schizophrenie culturelle: Pays traditionnels face a la modernite.* (The Distorted Vision: Cultural schizophrania: traditional countries face modernity). Paris: Albin Michel, 1989.

Short Proceedings of the 2nd Annual Conference, Jamaat-e-Islami, East Pakistan. Dacca: Jamaat-e-Islami, Pakistan, 1958.

Siddiq, Qazi Zulqadr, S. M. Aslam, and M. M. Ahsan. "A Bibliography of Writings by and about Sayyid Abul A'la Mawdudi," in Khurshid Ahmad and Zafar Ishaq Ansari, eds., *Islamic Perspectives: Studies in Honour of Sayyid Abul A'la Mawdudi.* Leicester: Islamic Foundation, 1979, 3–14.

Siddique, Kaukab. "Islam and Social Change." *New Trend* (July 1977): 4–12.

Sisk, Timothy D. *Islam and Democracy: Religion, Politics, and Power in the Middle East.* Washington, D.C.: United States Institute of Peace, 1992.

Sivan, Emmanuel. *Radical Islam: Medieval Theology and Modern Politics.* New Haven, Conn.: Yale University Press, 1985.

Smith, Wilfred Cantwell. *Islam in Modern History*, 2nd ed. Princeton, N.J.: Princeton University Press, 1977.

──────. *The Meaning and End of Religion.* New York: Macmillan, 1963.

Talmon, Jacob. *Political Messianism; The Romantic Phase.* New York: Praeger, 1960.

Statement of Syed Abul Ala Maudoodi before the Punjab Disturbances Court of Inquiry. Karachi: n.p., n.d.

Tilly, Charles. *From Mobilization to Revolution.* Reading, Mass.: Addison-Wesley, 1978.

Troeltsch, Ernst. *The Social Teachings of Christian Churches*, translated by Olive Wyon, 2 vols. New York: Macmillan, 1949.

Troll, Christian W. "The Meaning of Din: Recent Views of Three Eminent Indian Ulama," in Christian W. Troll, ed., *Islam in India: Studies and Commentaries.* Delhi: Vikas Publishing House, 1982, 1:168–177.

van der Veer, Peter. *Religious Nationalism: Hindus and Muslims in India.* Berkeley: University of California Press, 1994.

Voll, John O. "Conservative and Traditional Brotherhoods," in Charles E. Butterworth and I. William Zartman, eds., *Annals of the American Academy of Political and Social Science* 524 (November 1992): 66–78.

———. "Religion and Politics in Islamic Africa," in Matthew Moen and Lowell S. Gustafson, eds., *The Religious Challenge to the State.* Philadelphia: Temple University Press, 1992, 209–235.

———. "Renewal and Reform in Islamic History: *Tajdid* and *Islah*," in John L. Esposito, ed., *Voices of Resurgent Islam.* New York: Oxford University Press, 1983, 32–47.

Walzer, Michael. *The Revolution of Saints: A Study in the Origins of Radical Politics.* Cambridge: Harvard University Press, 1965.

Watt, W. Montgomery. *Islamic Political Thought.* Edinburgh: Edinburgh University Press, 1968.

Weber, Max. *Economy and Society: An Outline of Interpretive Sociology*, edited by G. Roth and C. Wittich, 2 vols. Berkeley: University of California Press, 1978.

———. *The Sociology of Religion*, translated by Ephraim Frischoff. Boston: Beacon Press, 1963.

Weismann, Itzchak. "Sa'id Hawwa: The Making of a Radical Muslim Thinker in Modern Syria." *Middle Eastern Studies* 29.4 (October 1993): 601–623.

White Paper on Electorate Issue. Karachi: Jama'at-i-Islami of Pakistan, 1957.

Wolpert, Stanley. *Jinnah of Pakistan.* New York: Oxford University Press, 1984.

Wright, Jr., Theodore P. "Inadvertant Modernization of Indian Muslims by Revivalists." *Journal of the Institute of Muslim Minority Affairs* 1.1 (1979): 80–89.

Wuthnow, Robert. *Communities of Discourse: Ideology and Social Structure in the Reformation, the Enlightenment, and European Socialism.* Cambridge: Harvard University Press, 1989.

———. and Matthew P. Lawson. "Sources of Christian Fundamentalism in the United States," in Martin E. Marty and R. Scott Appleby, eds., *Accounting for Fundamentalisms.* Chicago: University of Chicago Press, 1994, 18–56.

Yarshater, Ehsan, ed. *Encyclopaedia Iranica.* London and Boston: Routledge & Kegan Paul, 1982–present.

Yusuf, Muhammad. *Maududi: The Formative Phase.* Karachi: Universal Message, 1979.

———. "While Green in Age: Maulana Maudoodi's Childhood," in *The Universal Message.* Karachi: Islamic Research Academy, 1980, 4–20.

Index

Farangi Mahal, 18, 149n118
Fatih Muhammad, Mawlana, 178n82
Fatihpuri, Mawlana Niyaz, 14
Fatihpuri mosque, 18, 29
Fatimid dynasty, 23
Fazlu'l-Rahman, Mawlana, 120
Fichte, Johann, 15
Al-Furqan, 38

Gandhi, Mahatma, 5, 16, 20, 22, 101, 149n102
Gawhar Rahman, Mawlana, 178n82
Geertz, Clifford, 110
Ghalib, Mirza Asadu'llah, 11, 15, 126, 180n2
Ghazi, 'Abdu'l-Jabbar, 117, 176n55
Al-Ghazzali, 93, 136, 163n11
Ghulam Muhammad. *See* Chaudhri Ghulam Muhammad
Gibb, H. A. R., 131
Gilani, Sayyid As'ad, 75, 115–16, 129, 139, 179n97, 181n23
Gilani, Sayyid Manazir Ahsan, 23–24, 27–28, 30, 36, 38, 115, 117, 177n62
Gilani, Shaikh 'Abdu'l-Qadir, 113
Giussani, Father Luigi, 172n143
Goethe, Johann W. von, 15
Government of India Act of 1935, 31
Gran, Peter, 157n7
Great Mutiny of 1857, 10, 32, 54, 127

Hakim Ajmal Khan, 155n116
Hali, Altaf Husain, 139
Hanafi school of law, 99, 113–14, 115, 118, 119, 121, 135
Hanbali school of law, 114
Hamdard, 17, 183n68
Hanif, Pirzadah Ibrahim, 109
Hardy, Peter, 18
Hasafiyah Sufi order, 150n122
Hasan, 'Abdu'l-Ghaffar, 117, 176n55
Hasan al-Basri, 113
Hasan, Masudul, 28
Hasan, Mawlana Sayyid Mahdi, 118
Hawwa, Sa'id, 150n122
Hayat-i javid, 139
Hayat-i javidan, 139
Hegel, Georg F., 15
Al-Hilal, 12, 132, 134–35

Hinduism, 21–22, 49–51, 53–54, 63–64, 69, 80–81, 84–85, 99, 100–2, 104, 105, 116, 122, 144n14, 150n125, 150n2, 161n104, 162n127
Hindu revivalism, 4, 21–22, 148n101
Hizarwi, Mawlana, 120
Hobson, J.A., 49
Hudud laws, 98
Hudud Ordinances, 98
Hujwiri, Sayyid 'Ali, 124
Huntington, Samuel, 163n4
Husain ibn 'Ali, 139, 170n78

Ibn Hanbal, 135, 136
Ibn Khaldun, 163n4
Ibn Khallikan, 23, 24
Ibn Saud, King 'Abdu'l-'Aziz, 31
Ibn Taimiyah, 114, 115, 136, 138
Idarah-i Ma'arif-i Islami, 128
Ihsan, Hafizu'l-Rahman, 181n23
Ikram, S.M., 134
Iliyas, Mawlana Muhammad, 39, 113, 144n14
'Inayatu'llah, 'Atiyah, 181n24
Indian National Congress Party. *See* Congress party
Interim Constitutional Report, 116
Iqbal, Muhammad, 15, 18, 23, 34–35, 134, 154n86, 156n3, 158n27, 185n102
    status in Pakistan, 36–37, 153n76
Iranian Revolution of 1979, 3–4, 25, 69, 70, 75, 76, 79
Irfan, 112–13
Iskandar Mirza, General, 44, 155n132
Al-Islah, 38
Islahi, Mawlana Amin Ahsan, 38, 110, 115, 116, 123, 129–30, 172n142, 183n59
Islam. *See also* Islamic economics, Islamic modernism, Islamic philosophy, Islamic revivalism, Sufism, Traditional Islam
    and politics, 80–81
"Islam ka qanun-i jang", 23
"Islam ka sarchashmih-i qudrat", 20
Islami Jam'iat-i Tulabah, 45, 73, 78, 88, 124, 132, 176n45
Islami Jumhuri Ittihad, 72, 164n25

222

Index